THE
BRAVEST
BATTLE

BOOKS BY DAN KURZMAN

Kishi and Japan

Subversion of the Innocents

Santo Domingo: Revolt of the Damned

Genesis 1948: The First Arab-Israeli War

The Race for Rome

The Bravest Battle

Miracle of November: Madrid's Epic Stand 1936

Ben-Gurion: Prophet of Fire

Day of the Bomb: Countdown to Hiroshima

A Killing Wind: Inside Union Carbide and the
Bhopal Catastrophe

Fatal Voyage: The Sinking of the U.S.S. Indianapolis

DAN KURZMAN

THE BRAVEST BATTLE

The Twenty-eight Days of the
Warsaw Ghetto Uprising

DA CAPO PRESS

Library of Congress Cataloging-in-Publication Data

Kurzman, Dan.
    The bravest battle : the twenty-eight days of the Warsaw ghetto
uprising / Dan Kurzman. -- "1st Da Capo Press ed."
        p.   cm.
    Originally published: New York : Putman, 1976.
    Includes bibliographical references.
    ISBN 0-306-80533-2
    1. Warsaw (Poland)--History--Uprising of 1943.   I. Title.
D765.2.W3K87   1993
940.53'18'094384--dc20   93-20702
                                                                        CIP

First Da Capo Press edition 1993

This Da Capo Press paperback edition of *The Bravest Battle* is an
unabridged republication of the edition published in New York
in 1976. It is reprinted by arrangement with Dan Kurzman.

Published by Da Capo Press, Inc.
A Member of the Perseus Book Group
Visit us on the World Wide Web at www.perseuspublishing.com
10 9 8

Manufactured in the United States of America

To Stephen and Joel

whose generation, hopefully, will not forget

WARSAW GHETTO

- ━━━━ Boundaries of ghetto • Nov. 15, 1940
- ▬ ▬ ▬ Boundaries of ghetto • July 22, 1942
- ─ ─ ─ Area of ghetto at beginning of uprising • Apr. 19, 1943
- ▲ Openings to sewer system
- A Judenrat Building
- B Jewish Police Hq.
- C Pawiak Prison
- D Czyste-Benson-Bauman Hospital
- E Umschlagplatz
- F Rettungskommando hq.
- G Church of the Virgin Mary

ACKNOWLEDGMENTS

I am deeply indebted to Florence Knopf for lending her exceptional talent to the refinement of this work. Miss Knopf is an editor with an eye for the smallest literary defect, and her suggestions invariably proved sound and wise. Confronted with a mountain of information that had to be compressed into a book of reasonable length, I might never have completed this task without her help.

Yehiel Kirshbaum skillfully translated sections of scores of books published in Polish, Hebrew, Yiddish, Spanish, and German, and also conducted research for me. Each translation came with enlightening comments and observations, since Yehiel, who was himself trapped in a Warsaw Ghetto bunker when the uprising broke out, saw at first hand what was happening. During the revolt he managed to escape with his parents, who bribed their way to safety.

I am also especially grateful to Miriam Rimer, who interpreted Hebrew for hours at a time during many exhausting interviews; to William Targ, my editor at Putnam's, for his sensitive editorial advice; and to Berenice Hoffman for her valuable counsel.

I wish to express my appreciation as well to Maty Grünberg for her fine translations from Hebrew; to Ulrike Bürger, who interpreted for me in Germany; and to Alfred Chlapowski, who interpreted in Poland; to Dr. Joseph Kermish and Shmuel Krakowski, of Yad Vashem, and Yitzhak Zuckerman, Zivia Lubetkin, and

Simcha Rotem (Rathajzer), for checking the final manuscript for inaccuracies; to Miriam Novitch, of Beit Lohamei Haghetaot, for helping me to understand; to Ruth Aley, my agent, for her boundless work on my behalf; to Frank Kurtz, for copy editing the manuscript with dedication and skill; and to Denise Philip, for typing the manuscript swiftly and virtually without error.

Among those who furnished me background information or in other ways facilitated my research were:

Ora Alcalay—head librarian, Yad Vashem, Jerusalem

Yitzhak Arad—board chairman, Yad Vashem, Jerusalem

Shaul Bar-Schlomo—interpreter, Hebrew

Wladyslaw Bartoszewski—Polish writer

David Bass—librarian, Yad Vashem, Jerusalem

Perla Bauman—librarian, Yad Vashem, Jerusalem

Wieslaw A. Bednarozuk—press secretary, Polish Embassy, Washington, D.C.

Petra Borrock—interpreter, German

Gerhard Buck—archivist, Bibliothek für Zeitgeschichte, Stuttgart

Erni Deicher—archivist, Bibliothek für Zeitgeschichte, Stuttgart

Reinhard Dietrich—judge, Hamburg

Gabriele Franz—archivist, Bibliothek für Zeitgeschichte, Stuttgart

Elmar Frischeisen—state prosecutor, Ludwigsburg

Marian Fuks—deputy director, Jewish Historical Institute, Warsaw

Helge Grabitz—state prosecutor, Hamburg

Erwin Grosse—state prosecutor, Hamburg

Clara Guini—librarian, Yad Vashem, Jerusalem

Werner Haupt—vice-director, Bibliothek für Zeitgeschichte, Stuttgart

Anton Hock—vice-director, Institut für Zeitgeschichte, Munich

Zymunt Hoffman—deputy director, Jewish Historical Institute, Warsaw

Maurycy Horn—director, Jewish Historical Institute, Warsaw

Kazimierz Iranek-Osmecki—Polish writer

Bronya Klibanski—archivist, Yad Vashem, Jerusalem

André Klos—press attaché, Polish Embassy, Cologne

Christopher Komornicki—executive editor, Interpress, Warsaw

Ándrzej Konopacki—deputy director, Polish Foreign Ministry, Warsaw

M. Kuhlmann—state prosecutor, Hamburg
Tadeusz Kur—Polish journalist
Chaim Lazar—Israeli writer
Yitzhak Len—librarian, Yad Vashem, Jerusalem
M. Liczmanski—official, Polish Foreign Ministry, Warsaw
Czeslaw Lisowski—official, Interpress, Warsaw
Eugene Lubomirski—official, Sikorski Museum, London
Ludwik Lubomirski—official, Radio Free Europe, Munich
Czeslaw Madajczyp—professor, Institut d'Histoire de l'Academie Polonaise des Sciences, Warsaw
James J. Mandros—press attaché, U.S. Embassy, Warsaw
Irene Marchewicz—executive editor, Interpress, Warsaw
Leon Penner—lawyer who prosecuted General Jürgen Stroop
Czeslaw Pilichowski—director, Main Commission for the Investigation of Nazi Crimes in Poland, Warsaw
Dr. Ruckerl—chief prosecutor, Central Agency for Prosecution of Crimes Stemming from Nazi Times, Ludwigsburg
Iosi Rufeisen—interpreter, Hebrew
Ruta Sakowska—researcher, Jewish Historical Institute, Warsaw
Karl-Heinz Schaper—librarian, *Der Spiegel,* Hamburg
Rolf Sichting—state prosecutor, Stuttgart
Franz Stroop—brother of General Jürgen Stroop
Janusz Tazbir—professor, Institut d'Histoire de l'Academie Polonaise des Sciences, Warsaw
Ludwig Többens—nephew of Walther Caspar Többens
Vered Wahllen—librarian, Yad Vashem, Jerusalem
Henryk Walenda—editor in chief, Dziennik Lodzki, Lodz
Helena Walewski—wife of Richard Walewski, ZZW fighter
Wolfram Weber—state prosecutor, Ludwigsburg
Simon Wiesenthal—Nazi hunter
Hermann Weiss—archivist, Institut für Zeitgeschichte, Munich
Christa Wichman—librarian, Wiener Library, London
Eli Zborowski—president, American Federation of Jewish Fighters, Camp Inmates, and Nazi Victims
Anton Zirngibl—official, Institut für Zeitgeschichte, Munich
Kazimierz Zygulski—Polish professor of sociology

Characters in the drama of the Warsaw Ghetto uprising who kindly agreed to let me interview them include the following (identified by the positions they held at the time):

Gustaw Alef-Balkowiak—People's Guard officer
Marek Arczynski—Polish official of Zegota
Rachel Auerbach—Jewish writer on the Aryan side of Warsaw
Josef Barski—director of CENTOS, Jewish children's institute
Adolf Berman—Jewish leader on the Aryan side of Warsaw
Meir Bieliscki—ghetto resident
Adolf Josef Cedro—ghetto resident
Aharon Chmielnicki (Karmi)—ZOB fighter
Adam Ciolkosz—Polish Socialist Party official
Alphons Czapp—German policeman
Antoni Czarnecki—vicar of All-Saints Church in the ghetto
Anna Czuperska-Sliwicka—Polish Home Army officer
Marek Edelman—commander in the ZOB
Felicja Frenkel—ghetto resident
Kalman Friedman—ghetto resident
Yitzhak Gitler (Ben-Moshe)—ghetto resident
Masha Glytman (Putermilch)—ZOB fighter
Stefan Grajek—ZOB fighter
Israel Guttman—ZOB fighter
Adam Halperin (Harten)—ZZW fighter
Ruth Helman—ghetto resident
Simcha Holzberg—ghetto resident
Henryk Iwanski—captain in the Polish Home Army
Tadeusz Jaegermann—Polish Home Army officer
Noemi Judkowski—ghetto resident
Feliks Kanabus—Polish doctor
Maria Kann—Polish writer who helped the Jews
Tadeusz Kern-Jedrychowski—Polish Home Army officer
Franz Korner—General Stroop's driver
Emilka Kosower (Rosenzwieg)—Jewish partisan in the Home Army
Henryk Kotlicki—Polish PPR officer
Henryk Kroszczor—hospital superintendent in the ghetto
Leopold Kummant—Polish Home Army officer
Maria L.—ghetto resident
Michael L.—ghetto resident
Heinrich Lauts—director of brush factory
Zivia Lubetkin—commander in the ZOB
Miriam Medrzycki—ghetto resident
Zbigniew Mlynarski—Polish Home Army partisan

Kazimierz Moczarski—Polish Home Army officer and journalist
Leon Najberg—ghetto fighter
Matis Nasberg—ghetto resident
Ze'ev Pachter—ghetto resident
Pnina Papier (Frimer)—ZOB fighter
Jurek Plonski—ZZW fighter
Yehoshua Prechner—ZZW fighter
Jacob Putermilch—ZOB fighter
Simcha Rathajzer (Rotem)—ZOB fighter
Moshe Ring—ghetto resident
Anna Rochman—ghetto resident
Irena Rojek—ghetto resident
Henryk Rolirad—Polish Home Army officer under Iwanski
Yaacov Rosen—ghetto resident
Israel Rotbalsam (Rom)—doctor in the ghetto
Wanda Rothenberg—ZOB fighter and sister of Pola Elster
Zymunt Rytel—Socialist partisan
Hela Schipper—ZOB fighter
Hella Schmetkort—wife of German Sergeant Major Bernard Schmetkort
Fela Shapsik (Finkelstein)—ZZW fighter
Zymunt Sliwicki—Polish Home Army officer
Antoni Slupik—colonel in the Polish Army
Sewek Toporek—ghetto resident
Jonas Turkow—Yiddish actor in the ghetto
Leon Wanat—Polish teacher
Henryk Wasser—ZOB fighter and Emmanuel Ringelblum's secretary
Stanislas Weber—major in the Polish Home Army
Lewi Zlocisty—ghetto resident
Yitzhak Zuckerman—deputy commander in the ZOB

CONTENTS

PREFACE

The daily sufferings of the Warsaw Ghetto during World War II have been the subject of a number of fictional and nonfictional works. But this is the first attempt at a full-scale account of the twenty-eight-day armed uprising that grew out of such conditions.

The uprising, when dealt with at all in other books, has usually been telescoped into a few climactic pages. And many of these brief accounts are based more on legend than on firsthand testimony and original documentation. Those few works that do concentrate on the uprising itself are either short, skeletal summaries or records of individual experiences.

Yet the military encounter was one of the most stirring, impossible, and important battles in history. Seldom, if ever, before has a single armed conflict produced greater heroism or more explosive political consequences. Indeed, this conflict, an enduring symbol of resistance to man's inhumanity to man, reverbrated far beyond the pale that enclosed it.

Although groups of Jews have at various times revolted against their persecutors, the Warsaw Ghetto uprising, more than any other event, symbolically ended two thousand years of Jewish submission to discrimination, oppression, and finally, genocide. It signaled the beginning of an iron militancy rooted in the will to survive, a militancy that was to be given form and direction by the creation of the state of Israel.

17

To understand fully that nation's mood and mentality, its pride and policies, and thus the tensions shaking the Middle East and the world today, it is necessary to know the story of the uprising, to glimpse the anguish, the euphoria, the eternal hope of the ghetto defenders, young men and women in love with life yet determined to fight to the death.

For twenty-eight days (according to official German calculation, but actually longer) some fifteen hundred fighters, armed with little more than pistols and homemade bombs and supported by about sixty thousand civilians passively resisting in hidden bunkers, fought off several thousand Nazi soldiers equipped with rifles, artillery, tanks, armored cars, flamethrowers, and aircraft. Whole nations fell under the German yoke in a far shorter period.

This battle lasted as long as it did because, essentially, there was no room for bargaining on either side. The Germans, led by SS Major General Jürgen Stroop, were bound by Nazi ideology to murder all captured Jews, either on the spot or in death camps. The Jews, most of them led by Mordechai Anielewicz, were bound by a pact of honor to die by their own hands rather than surrender. This was truly a battle to the death. And it took time to root out and kill tens of thousands of people.

But not every Jew was a hero as he faced death. One of the great tragedies of the ghetto, as in the concentration camp, was not simply that so many died but that the pressures exerted on the condemned were so overwhelming that some turned into beasts in the insane struggle for survival. Thus from the ghetto cauldron emerged not only the bravest and most altruistic but the greediest and most cowardly, the best and worst in the most exaggerated degrees. The wonder of the Warsaw Ghetto was that under genocidal circumstances the worst represented such a small part of the total. General Stroop attributed many of his difficulties to the willingness of so few Jews to betray their people, even when offered the chance to survive.

The ghetto tested not only the Jewish soul but the Polish heart. A relatively small number of Poles risked their lives to save the Jews, and some, indeed, died in the effort. Another small group of Poles betrayed the Jews and even killed them. The great mass of Poles, traditionally anti-Semitic, were indifferent, and watched the extermination of the Jews with greater curiosity than sympathy. Thus the Poles played no small role in strengthening the argument for Zionism.

18

In this book, which took more than two years to research and write, I have tried to tell the story of the Warsaw Ghetto uprising through the participants, focusing in particular on General Stroop and Mordechai Anielewicz. The research task was difficult, not because sources of information were lacking but because they were so scattered, with each witness or document able to throw light on only limited aspects of the revolt.

To get as much of the full story as possible I interviewed approximately five hundred people, including most of the surviving fighters, more than one hundred civilians who lived through the uprising, and scores of Germans and Poles who were involved. I tracked these people down in Israel, the United States, Poland, West Germany, and Austria.

I also studied several thousand documents in these countries, dealing with every facet of the subject, and consulted about three hundred books and countless periodicals, many in Hebrew, Yiddish, Polish, German, French, and Spanish, as well as in English.

From this sea of information I fashioned a daily account of the fighting. Since even many of the participants could not recall dates, places, and similar details, I compared verbal accounts with those given in various diaries, memoirs, and other documents in order to reconstruct events accurately. Sometimes I could determine the date of a particular incident only through a long and tedious process of cross-matching and elimination.

Nothing has been fictionalized. All quotations and descriptions, as well as thoughts attributed to characters in this book, come from the writings of the persons involved, from personal interviews with them, or from the records of individuals to whom these persons told their stories. Sources for each section of each chapter, specifically including those of all dialogue and other quotations, are indicated in the Notes.

I first became interested in writing the story of the Warsaw Ghetto uprising while researching another book, *Genesis 1948: The First Arab-Israeli War.* Some of the people I interviewed for that work had lived in the Warsaw Ghetto and reminisced about the uprising there. My interest grew while I was working on my next book, *The Race for Rome,* which included material on the destruction of the Roman Jews. After conducting some preliminary research on the uprising, I decided to undertake this project.

I was convinced that the facts were so dramatic, so moving in themselves, they did not need embellishment. My problem was how to bring these facts together, how to impose order on so much raw reality, how to write a humanized history, intended for the general public as well as for scholars, while keeping the details from submerging the central importance of the story—the ways people in desperate conditions acted individually and in concert to express their common humanity and their personal and communal dignity.

It was a melancholy experience visiting the site of the Warsaw Ghetto thirty years after the uprising. The area has been rebuilt, and no hint of the destruction remains. Only a statue commemorating the battle and a large stone at the spot where Mordechai Anielewicz died bear witness to the disappearance of the largest Jewish community in Europe. A small section of the wall that enclosed the ghetto remained as a further reminder until 1975, when the Polish government, which wants the Jewish uprising to be known as a Polish revolt, removed it to make room for a sports arena.

I asked a passerby where the wall had stood. He did not know there had been one. And the synagogue had been locked because too few Jews had been attending services. But the Yiddish theater was giving a performance. If only ten people were in the audience, the show would go on.

The Jewish community was dead, forgotten by those who most need to remember. But the supreme heroism of the ghetto fighters left a mark on every person, and would forever. Their stubborn defiance of the negation of life, in an uprising as timeless and inspirational as those of Masada and Spartacus, reaffirmed the capacity of the human spirit to survive in any circumstances.

D.K.

20

PROLOGUE

The day burst forth in a flood of sunlight that illuminated every corner of the dark, dismal Warsaw Ghetto. It was April 19, 1943, the morning before Passover, which celebrates the liberation of the children of Israel from the Pharaoh's brutal grip. The fighters, fondling their pistols, crouched behind windows and on balconies, waiting to greet the troops of a new and even more terrible Pharaoh. At any moment these troops would storm through the ghetto gates to carry out Adolf Hitler's order to deport all the Jews remaining in Warsaw.

But this time the Jews were ready for them. As ready as they could be. While they waited restlessly, eagerly, they inhaled the perfumes of spring and roamed the forests and green fields of their imaginations, bathing in crystal streams, listening to the laughter of children at play amid flowers gaily ablaze and trees damp with dew. How good to be alive on this beautiful April day. Suddenly reverie dissolved in the mocking cruelty of nature.

"Had the city been dark, if a storm had been raging, if gusts of rain had been pouring down, perhaps it would have been easier to accept death," wrote one fighter later. "Yet, it seemed that nature had allied itself with the enemy, and had provoked us the more on the threshold of oblivion."

Lending a grotesque glitter to nature's trick was the "snow" that covered the streets like a thick white rug. The snow of the ghetto: down and feathers from Jewish bedding left behind by the doomed and thrown out of windows by discriminating Nazi scavengers, together with unusable clothing, kitchenware, furnishings, and other personal articles. The pathetic relics of a community dying after more than a thousand years of vigorous life.

It was in the year 893, according to legend, that the first Jews settled in Poland (earlier, some historical accounts indicate). A group, fleeing persecution in the land of the Francs, were wandering in search of a safe refuge when, one day, as they stopped to pray for guidance, a tablet fell from heaven with the words "Go to Poland!" inscribed on it. The Jews obeyed, and the ruling prince of Poland, an idol worshiper, warmly greeted them: "My land is open to you. You may settle wherever you desire. . . . But you must bring down the rain by praying to your God whenever needed."

The Jews agreed and settled in Poland, and God brought down the rain. The settlers multiplied, especially after the fourteenth century, when Casimir the Great welcomed victims of persecution from Spain and Germany. By 1939 Jews represented ten percent of Poland's population, a vital, hardworking—and unhappy—community.

Not only did most Jews remain poor, but their Polish overlords despised and oppressed them, especially with the growth of Polish nationalism in the nineteenth century. Though the Jews played a role in a number of Polish uprisings against foreign rulers, most clung to their Yiddish language and separate traditions.* They were no longer welcome. Finally, in September 1939, the Germans stormed into Poland and promised to settle the "Jewish problem." They were as good as their word.

In October 1940 they locked all the Jews of Warsaw into a deadly ghetto pressure cooker surrounded by a brick wall ten feet high

*When the Cossacks launched a revolt against their Polish rulers in 1648, the Jews, the chief target of Cossack atrocities, joined the Poles in defending their regime. In Nemirov, the Jewish defenders were overjoyed to see an army with Polish banners approach the city. But when they opened the gates, they found themselves under attack by a Cossack horde in Polish uniforms. The Cossacks thus massacred 6000 Jews—in connivance with the Poles. The Poles also betrayed the Jews in Tulchin. Only in Lvov did the Poles refuse to surrender the Jews, and with their help they successfully defended the city. In 1668, the Poles betrayed the Jews of Uman to the terrible Gonta and his savage hordes. The Jews withdrew to the synagogue and fought to the last drop of blood, either taking their lives or dying in battle.

and eleven miles long with fourteen tightly guarded entrances. Atop the wall were glass splinters embedded in plaster to discourage escape. Shaped like a hammerhead, the ghetto covered 840 acres of slumland in the northern section of the city. Impoverished Poles who had shared with the Jews the solid blocks of nineteenth-century slope-roofed tenements, two to six stories high, now were transferred to the "Aryan side of town," where they were given the homes forcibly abandoned by Jews.

Simultaneously, into the festering ghetto jungle pressed almost a half-million Jews, about a third of Warsaw's population, including many thousands of refugees from other towns. They squeezed into every corner of every brick-and-stucco building and even overflowed into the stairways leading to courtyards from which high arched gateways opened to the street or to courtyards of neighboring buildings. They averaged thirteen to a room, people with hardly any food, with no medicine or hope who would die of starvation and disease at the rate of fifty thousand a year.

Indeed, the Nazi design was not simply to segregate the Jews but to deliberately create conditions that would destroy them. Each ghetto resident was thus condemned to die with an official daily food ration of under three hundred calories, many times less than a human being needed: twenty grams of bread; a spoonful of kasha, or groats; a thimbleful of condensed milk; and sometimes a few ounces of sugar.

Soon, skeletal figures with yellow swollen faces sat propped against the walls of buildings, their puffy slitlike eyes vacant, their gnarled hands reaching out to indifferent pedestrians for bread.* Others, already dead, lay covered with old newspapers along the curbs, awaiting the gravediggers who would haul them off in handcarts to mass graves. Children crawled on all fours, resem-

*When Emmanuel Ringelblum, the Warsaw Ghetto historian, asked one ghetto cultural figure, Shmuel Stupnitski, the reason for the "heartless indifference" with which people walked past corpses in the street, Stupnitski replied, "It is little short of a miracle that people are not depressed and broken by these macabre street scenes, that they do not lose their equilibrium at the sight of large hosts of naked, barefoot, emaciated children in the streets. Were it not for this heartless indifference these encounters in the streets would paralyze all existence, would induce a mood of melancholy and despair causing resignation and decline. For this reason I regard the callousness which the Jews of the ghetto have developed as a positive manifestation. They walk past the dead bodies and continue the battle for existence."

bling monkeys. They snatched packages of food from people on the street, swallowing as much as possible before they could be caught. When one "snatcher," or *khapper* as he was called in Yiddish, dropped a jar of soup, he lapped up the contents, mud and all, hardly aware that the screaming owner was kicking him in the head. One woman even cannibalized her dead baby. And with starvation came typhus, which filled the understaffed hospitals with people fated to die on filthy lice-ridden straw mattresses—often three or four to a mattress—without medical care.

But to the Nazis' rage and frustration, the Jews found ways to survive. House committees were set up in each building to help the poorest. Soup kitchens were opened. Gardens were cultivated on balconies and roofs. And, most important of all, clandestine trade links were established with the Aryan side. Risking instant execution, daredevil amateur smugglers, often children, crawled through sewer pipes and small breaches in the wall to exchange precious family possessions for a pocketful of food. Professional smugglers, Jews and Poles, engaged in more sophisticated operations with key ghetto guards on their payroll. They ruthlessly exploited their starving customers while living lavishly among them. Often they stepped over corpses to enter glittering ghetto cabarets, where they caroused with other underworld profiteers and Nazi collaborators. Yet their services were indispensable.

"Garbage collectors" left the ghetto with refuse in their wagons and returned with food. "Milkmen" funneled milk into a pipe that ran from a rooftop on the Aryan side to another in the ghetto. "Undertakers" hid goods in their hearses. "Butchers" herded live cows and oxen over specially constructed mobile ramps on both sides of the wall. Raw materials were smuggled in to nourish a thriving improvised industrial system that produced goods for sale on the Aryan side. These materials supplemented the tons of waste products collected inside the ghetto for recycling. Dresses, sweaters, and coats were fashioned from rags. Suitcases were made from the fiber of old ledgers. Brushes were created from hair, feathers, and broom bristles. House slippers were manufactured from woven paper and wood.

Thus, most people managed to eat more than they were supposed to, thwarting the Nazi effort to destroy ghetto morale, the will to survive. The Jews even persisted in enriching their minds and souls in the midst of all the horror. The Yiddish theater and other cultural institutions thrived, and schools, though forbidden, secretly served child and adult alike in attics, cellars, and public kitchens, courtesy of the youth and welfare organizations.

The Germans decided they must use a more reliable method of extermination. At first, in spring 1942, they depended on SS men like Heinrich Klaustermeyer and Josef Blösche—the latter known to the Jews as Frankenstein—to sap morale and thereby clear the way. This dreaded pair would fire at strollers or people standing in windows, rape and then slay young women, and force some victims to drink poison. This was only the beginning.

By early summer, swarms of people began gathering in little groups behind the housegates, and with frightened eyes and hushed voices they exchanged the latest rumors. The whole ghetto was to be deported! No, that was impossible! Not a half-million people! And besides, many of the Jews worked in ghetto factories, or "shops," which turned out goods for the Wehrmacht, the German Army. The Nazis needed them. The tension grew, and finally, on July 22, the posters appeared. "Resettlement!" The rumors were true. But where would they be sent?

That day a long line of boxcars pulled into Umschlagplatz, a great square at the northern edge of the ghetto that would be the railhead for resettlement. Amid scenes of chaos and hysteria, thousands of men, women, and children were jammed into the boxcars. Day after day the grisly caravans departed for the gas chambers with their loads of human flesh. But even as reports of their destination spread, the people did not, would not, believe.

And those few who did still would not resist or, in most cases, even try to hide, either fearing discovery and execution or feeling they could not let their loved ones leave alone.

Janusz Korczak, a gentle bearded man who ran an orphanage, knew. But when the Germans came for his two hundred children, he insisted on going with them even though he himself was not yet marked for deportation. He brushed and polished them and dressed them in their best clothes, buttoning the coat of one child, straightening the cap of another, wiping away the tears of a third. No crying! And they must take their schoolbooks so they could study when they weren't "working in the forest." Then, holding one child by the hand, he calmly signaled to the others, silently lined up behind him in neat rows, and began marching toward the boxcars.

Finally, on September 13, the cars ground to a halt. The *Aktion,* as the Germans called their roundups, was over. And the ghetto shrank within the encircling wall, with survivors herded mainly into three areas.

The largest was the Central Ghetto in the north, which had been whittled down to about a dozen square blocks. Here lived the "nonproductive" Jews, the most expendable since only one large factory here was producing goods for the Wehrmacht. Separated from this area by a wall to the east was the Brushmakers' District, about a single square block where several factories turned out brushes of every kind for military consumption. The third enclave, the Productive Ghetto, was concentrated mainly on three isolated streets to the south and embraced most of the factories. Stone walls stretched around each plant and its workers' quarters, and Jews had to remain within the walls.

Between the Central and Productive ghettos was the Wild Ghetto, a no-man's-land uninhabited since the first deportations of summer 1942. Providing shelter for Jews, Poles, smugglers, thieves—almost anyone hiding from Nazi terror—it was a mecca of desperate men. Even the police feared to challenge the ghosts peering from behind the fluttering curtains in the shattered windows.

At the southern corner of the ghetto, separated from the Productive Ghetto by many blocks of deserted dwellings, was nestled the Small Ghetto, where a few thousand Jews worked in a German factory on Prosta Street.

The surviving ghetto population numbered about sixty thousand, a little more than half of them legally registered workers, the rest "wild" Jews who had hidden and failed to report for "selection." These survivors had been segregated into little knots of humanity, all the easier to scoop up in the next *Aktion.*

It came on January 18, 1943—a total surprise. But by now the people knew that the boxcars dumped their loads in the gas chambers of Treblinka. The fighters among them greeted the Nazis with gunfire, knives, stones, fists, and the Germans slunk away in shock after four days.

The ghetto had fought—and won! But the Nazis would be back. And so the fighters prepared in earnest for the final showdown. They would redeem the honor of their people, who had gone to Treblinka without a fight. The survivors would depart as their forefathers had arrived—with a gift of rain. Not water this time, but bullets. They would not give themselves up alive. They would emulate Masada, where two thousand years earlier another group of besieged Jews had slain themselves rather than bow to the conquering Romans.

And so, on this glorious spring morning of the last *Aktion,* in the frivolous glare of sun and "snow," the fighters awaited their hour of sublime triumph, their moment of death.[1]

The Eve

April 18

The young man's thin, usually pale face was oddly alight as he savored with his comrades the sanctity of their final moments together before the storm.

"The time we've been waiting for has come," he said in a calm, deliberate manner that could not mask his excitement.

Mordechai Anielewicz, the twenty-four-year-old commander in chief of the Jewish Fighting Organization (Zydowska Organizacja Bojowa), or ZOB, was briefing his commanders late in the afternoon in a shabby apartment at Zamenhof 32, in the Central Ghetto, amid the melancholy mementos of a family that had already been resettled. Mordechai flashed no brass buttons, no medals on his chest. He was in his customary battle dress: threadworn gray jacket, knickers, and golf socks. But though he and his fighters were by no means polished soldiers, they were ready, Mordechai knew, for the next—and final—*Aktion*.

They had first suspected Nazi intentions two days earlier, when First Lieutenant Karl Brandt, chief of the Gestapo's Jewish department in Warsaw, visited the ghetto and addressed the Judenrat, the Jewish community council that "ruled" the ghetto under German orders.* With his Roman nose, dark hair, and swarthy

*The Judenrat was composed of twenty-four Jews, all chosen by the Germans. It created a Jewish police force, levied taxes, furnished work battalions for the Nazis, operated hospitals and a sanitation system, and ran a workshop for the

complexion, Brandt looked more Semitic than Germanic. And he was as deceptive as his appearance. His deeply circled eyes, protruding under bushy brows, mirrored false anger as he ranted about the neglect of the ghetto children: They were not getting enough fresh air. Why could not the courtyard of the Judenrat building be turned into a playground where they could laugh and play? Nor were they eating enough vegetables. As for Passover, well, he would supply the ghetto with matzos.

On this note of good cheer Brandt departed with a smile on his fleshy face; and the Jews, only too familiar with Nazi perfidy, surmised that disaster would soon strike.

Nevertheless the ghetto bristled with the coming of Passover. Bakers plopped slabs of dough into the oven to bake matzos while housewives lugged long-hoarded bottles of wine from dank cellars and scrubbed concealed rooms and subterranean bunkers, where most Jews were hiding. Seders—festive ceremonial dinners served on the first two nights of Passover—would be conducted mainly underground, and ZOB women would meticulously prepare one of the biggest dinners on the first night for the ghetto's ZOB, political, and cultural leaders. The Jews would celebrate the salvation of their ancestors in the midst of their own destruction.

But then, on April 18, a Jewish policeman secretly working with the ZOB rushed to Mordechai with the news that "something would happen" by the next morning, apparently confirming the suspicions aroused by Brandt's visit. Word later filtered through that SS troops and Polish police had begun mobilizing at 2 P.M. and had thrown a heavy cordon around the ghetto at about 6 P.M. The Seder for the ghetto leaders was abruptly canceled, and all underground fighters dashed to their posts.

Now, at his final briefing, Mordechai assured his commanders: "We shall wear out the enemy by constantly attacking from behind the gates, windows, ruins, day and night. The basis of our plan is the ghetto labyrinth. The Germans will have to fight for months on end. If we can get all the arms, ammunition, and explosives we need, the enemy will pay with a sea of blood."

Months on end? A Nazi sea of blood? Mordechai spoke as if this were to be a battle between two genuine armies. The commanders, who proudly wore pistols in their belts—about the only weap-

---

Wehrmacht. Many members willingly collaborated with the Germans, hoping thereby to save themselves and their families, but some cooperated to the minimum possible degree in the hope of limiting each Nazi blow.

ons they had—knew differently. But they reveled in the imagery of revenge and redemption. How sweet to die with a gun in hand, watching their murderers drown in their own blood.

The Warsaw Ghetto uprising would be one of the first of its kind in history. An uprising doomed in advance to fail, to be crushed, with surrender equivalent to death—even if, as Mordechai wishfully hoped, the revolt spread to the rest of Warsaw. An uprising that would flare in complete isolation, that would begin when and where the enemy wished and could not be fueled by surprise.

About fifteen hundred largely untrained Jewish fighters, most of them organized but some not, would face the fury of German tanks, artillery, and machine guns, armed with only a few automatic weapons and rifles, some mines, several thousand grenades and Molotov cocktails, and a pistol per man. The Germans would have about a hundred times their firepower in what might be the most uneven battle ever fought. Furthermore, since the fighters had only limited space for maneuvering in the ghetto and few possibilities for withdrawal to another battlefield, their strategic position could hardly be worse.

But the Jews would enjoy two advantages, as reflected in Mordechai's words: the will to fight to the death—they could choose only the *method* of dying; and paradoxically, the "ghetto labyrinth," which, though a strategic curse, was a tactical blessing. Defenders manning key posts throughout this labyrinth, especially at intersections, could take a big enemy toll. At the same time, by knocking down attic walls in all defensible areas, the fighters had created an ingenious system of interconnected attics which would allow them to shift positions, retreat, or bring up supplies through the maze while being completely hidden from view.

Fighting would take place mainly in the Central Ghetto, since most of the Jews in that sector, unlike in the others, were "unproductive" and therefore at the head of the Nazi death list. But the Brushmakers' District and the Productive Ghetto, where smaller fighting units were based, would certainly share the limelight.

The ZOB fighters, who numbered about eight hundred, often called Mordechai "Angel." Not only because the name Anielewicz was derived from the Polish word for angel *(aniol)*, but because he embodied to them the tortured yet ultimately triumphant Jewish spirit, the spirit that had kept his people alive through two thousand years of darkness and dispersion. He was as gentle as a

31

wailed psalm yet as hard as the rock of Zion. He was the man to lead the remnants of his people to a glorious death so that their feat would live forever. He had earned his credentials in battle.

Mordechai had started fighting as a child, when he lived in the impoverished Warsaw district of Powisle, where his father eked out a bare existence from his grocery store. The few Jews daring enough to live in this crime-ridden slum stayed together in a few buildings on Solec Street to protect themselves more easily from attacks by hoodlums, even though every Jew paid protection money to local gang leaders.

Mordechai's family was crammed into a one-room flat full of iron beds and was so poor that his mother would often tell him to streak the leftover fish with a red dye so it could be sold as fresh. A slim, sickly child, he was always hungry. His parents could not even afford to give him breakfast; but he was nevertheless buoyant and played every day with the neighborhood children in the bacon-and-sauerkraut-smelling courtyard of his run-down apartment building, which the Jews shared with the gentiles. Even the gentile children liked Mordechai until they made the mistake of telling him he was not at all like a *zhid,* the Polish equivalent of "kike." His temper would flare, and after a heated exchange of blows he would emerge, usually victorious, with bleeding nose and blackened eyes.

As Mordechai grew older the remarks became more offensive and the fighting more brutal. Seldom did he arrive home from school unbruised or with his clothes unripped. To avoid being pummeled by gangs, he developed the tactic of coaxing one member to follow him; then, when they were alone, he would beat his tormentor ruthlessly. Sometimes he would have the help of his younger brother, Pinchas, a short flat-nosed boy who would become a wrestler. Eventually Mordechai formed a band of his own that greeted Polish gangs with sticks, stones, and brass knuckles whenever they closed in on a Jewish residence.

Mordechai excelled in history and literature and learned Hebrew on his own. His mother sent him to high school, although his father felt education was a waste of time and money. To help earn his way Mordechai tutored students who lagged behind, finally earning enough to replace his faded, shabby jacket with a new one that became the school conversation piece.

From the age of fifteen Mordechai spent most of his time teaching the Hebrew language and culture as a member of the Marxist-

Zionist youth group, Hashomer Hatzair, which shared his own dual yearnings for social justice and a homeland. He rose swiftly to leadership and moved into an urban kibbutz that his group set up in an apartment building. To the despair of his parents, he seldom came home.

"Make something of yourself," his mother pleaded. His father urged him to go to work like a decent Jewish boy. They could not understand his strange new communal world, a world of foolish idealists who thought they had the magic answer to misery, suffering, and bigotry. But it was a world, too, that demanded many personal sacrifices. Members of Hashomer Hatzair were forbidden to smoke, drink, or even indulge in sexual activity. Only in the Holy Land would they be free to experience all the joys of life.

But Mordechai, in his ideological zeal, did not greatly miss such joys. Women found him attractive with his dark hair, firm jaw, and greenish eyes that seemed to smile even in moments of stress. But he showed little interest in them—until Mira Fuchrer joined his group. Mira, twenty-three, came from a family even more impoverished than Mordechai's. Her mother, a seamstress, supported her as a child after her Communist father had apparently fled to Russia to avoid arrest by the Polish police.

Mira's gay temperament was a tonic for the overburdened Mordechai. She was a whirlwind of activity, and seldom did a day pass when she wasn't seen darting from place to place on errands for Mordechai, her small, straight-backed figure wrapped in a sheepskin coat.

Mordechai wasn't the only one touched by her spirit. With a steely glint in her slightly oriental eyes and a quiet passion in her voice, she could hold an audience of her comrades spellbound while instilling them with strength and hope.

"The critical moments of our lives will soon be before us," she told them one day. "But up to the last moment our aim must be to be human beings. . . . We must hold our flag high. . . . Your great test will come when each one of you remains completely alone, face to face, with the enemy. . . ."

But Mordechai would never be completely alone, even when he faced the enemy. Mira would always be with him. After the Germans occupied bleeding Warsaw in 1939, Mordechai and Mira fled with their comrades to the Soviet-occupied zone of Poland and finally settled in Vilna. But Mordechai knew his place was with his people in Warsaw. He would help to organize an underground to protect them. When Mira insisted on going back with him, he strolled with her through the narrow streets of old Vilna one frosty night and painted a black picture of his future life in Warsaw. But he couldn't discourage her; nor did he really wish to. A year later she wrote from Warsaw to a friend in Vilna: "Mordechai is very busy. . . . I am also working. . . . But do not think that I am complaining. I have never been so happy . . . and I have never loved him so with body and soul. . . ."

But shortly, personal happiness lost all importance and even meaning. Mordechai, operating clandestinely from a rented room while trying to organize a resistance, watched in horror while the Nazis locked the Jews of Warsaw into a walled-off ghetto. No one yet dreamed that the Germans had the ultimate crime in mind—systematic mass murder. Not even Mordechai. But on moving his headquarters into the ghetto, he bitterly reproached himself. Why had he stressed for so many precious years the study of culture and ideology instead of military tactics?

Mordechai was still convinced that constant constructive work absorbing all the senses could help to preserve human beings, even in the Nazi era. In the evenings he continued to devour books on history, sociology, and economics. He was proud that he and Mira had taught other young Jews to live idealistically, to hold their flag high. Nevertheless, dead men could not hold flags.

Now, as the Nazi danger grew, so did Mordechai's problems. Not only was he unable to contact the Polish underground for help, but few Jews would cooperate with him. Even many in the youth organizations, including his own, felt that resistance, especially with arms, was not possible. As for the older Jewish leaders, most had already fled from Warsaw. Paradoxically, these leaders, though having lived more than half their lives, dreamed of survival, of life, while Mordechai and some other young people like him thought only of death with honor. Most inhabitants felt that the ghetto should simply concentrate on feeding those who were starving.

Mordechai persisted in meeting after meeting with influential Jews. Couldn't they at least resist passively? No one should wear hats or caps, he urged, even in the icy cold. Let the hair grow long instead. That way the Jews wouldn't have to humiliate themselves by removing their headpieces every time they passed a German, as the Nazis required.

Mordechai set the example, personally resisting every regulation. In the spring of 1941, Jewish policemen on Nazi orders began snatching people for work in German labor camps, and two of them broke into Mordechai's room and commanded him to go with them. Instead Mordechai leaped at them, beat up both of them, threw them out of the room, and fled with Mira to another hideout. He spread the word that all Jews should do the same.

Once, at a meeting of his organization in the Jewish cemetery on Okopowa Street, he told members, as they sat on marble slabs amid the only flowers and greenery in the ghetto:

> The most difficult struggle of all is the one within ourselves. Let us not get accustomed and adjusted to these conditions. The one who adjusts ceases to discriminate between good and evil. He becomes a slave in body and soul. Whatever may happen to you, remember always: Don't adjust! Revolt against the reality!

And on June 22, 1941, the day Germany invaded Russia, Mordechai and other Zionist leaders set up a fighting organization. Though lacking arms, training, and popular support, they would lead a "revolt against reality" until the Red Army arrived.

The reality, when it seeped out, shook even Mordechai. In late 1941 some of his comrades in Vilna who had been trapped there by the conquering Nazis escaped and made their way to Warsaw. The Jews of Vilna, they breathlessly reported, had been resettled. Then came news of the first gassings—at Chelmno. Jews had been sealed into vans to be killed by exhaust fumes.

Mordechai's appeal for resistance suddenly rang with reason to the youth, though still not to the fearful Jewish masses, who rationalized that the reports were exaggerated. It was absurd, they insisted, to think that the entire Jewish population of Warsaw could be exterminated wholesale, whatever happened elsewhere. And the Nazis encouraged such skepticism by arranging for letters from deportees to appear in Warsaw, letters either forged or dictated by the Germans. They had been sent to work, said the writers. There was no need to fear resettlement.

Among those who echoed Mordechai's demand for resistance were the leaders of the Communist Polish Workers' Party (PPR), which Stalin had purged and virtually destroyed during his honeymoon with Hitler but was trying to revive now that the Führer had betrayed him. Pinkus Kartin, alias Andrzej Schmidt, was the principal leader. He had fled to Russia after fighting with the Polish International Brigade in the Spanish civil war, and in January

35

1942 he parachuted into Nazi-occupied Poland. His orders were to organize a resistance movement in the Warsaw Ghetto, though the main purpose was to fight in the forests as partisans in support of the Red Army, not to defend the ghetto itself.

Kartin and the veteran Communist leader already in the ghetto, Josef Lewartowski, known as Finkelstein, secretly met with Mordechai and other leaders of the Zionist "fighting organization" in February, and an Anti-Fascist Bloc crystallized. Its name reflected the Communists' reluctance to distinguish between the immediate objective of rescuing the Jews and the more distant aim of aiding the Red Army. The bloc would organize underground cells, train fighting groups, and stir the ghetto to resistance. At Zionist insistence, at least some groups would remain in the ghetto to defend it.

But when the Bloc set up an underground press to arouse the people, the Gestapo responded on the night of April 17, 1942, by massacring fifty-two prominent Jews. After that there were killings almost daily. The people were petrified, but they still did not rally round the resistance. And when the Germans bagged Pinkus Kartin and many other Warsaw Communist leaders in May 1942, the Anti-Fascist Bloc crumbled.

Even the deportations that began on July 22 could not put it together again. Nor did they change the attitude of most Jews toward resistance. The Nazis were deporting them, they now had to concede, but only to labor camps; and if some, even most, *were* killed, others, perhaps they, would survive. To the Orthodox, resistance would, in fact, be a sin, since the Nazi doctrine of collective responsibility and punishment would doom a greater number of Jews that might otherwise die. Indeed, to most Jews, Mordechai and other activists who wanted to rebel against deportation were provocateurs who would only assure the deaths of all. The ghetto was counting on a miracle, not on suicidal heroics.

Within a week after the first packed boxcars pulled out, Jewish leaders sat around a table and carried on their debate in stormy desperation. Only Mordechai was absent, since he was in the provinces at the time helping to form fighting groups there.

A conservative Zionist declared, "It may be assumed with certainty that in Warsaw, in the heart of Europe, the Germans will not dare to [exterminate the Jews]."

A leader of the Hebrew Social Democratic Party, known as the Bund, was less optimistic but also warned against undue alarm.

The Bund, which embraced many of Poland's Jewish workers and artisans, supported Jewish cultural autonomy but was closely tied to the Polish Social Democratic Party and opposed any "corrupting" bond with "bourgeois," Zionist, or Communist movements, even at this moment of common crisis.

"Not only Jews are perishing," the Bundist argued. "Thousands of Poles are deported to death. . . . An uprising is doomed to failure in advance. Jewish masses will be called to common struggle by the Polish working class when the time ripens."

Only members of the Communist PPR and Zionist youth organizations—Hashomir Hatzair, Dror, and Akiva—smashed their fists on the table and demanded that a resistance movement be formed immediately. Shortly afterward, these groups founded the ZOB. In October the Bund joined the organization, finally persuaded that the Poles would not help in a common struggle to save the Jews; and Mordechai, who had since returned from the provinces, was chosen its commander in chief.* Simultaneously a Jewish coordinating committee was set up as a political body to deal primarily with the Polish underground and maintain contact with the outside world.†

It was on January 18, 1943, that Mordechai finally *made* the people listen. The Germans, without warning, swooped down once again on the Jews. Mordechai and nine comrades, each armed with a pistol or a grenade, joined a terrified procession of Jews being led to Umschlagplatz. Suddenly one fighter hurled a grenade at the German guards, and a firefight broke out. Mordechai emptied his pistol at the Nazis, then snatched one from a German and continued firing until a comrade pulled him into a courtyard. Mordechai emerged from the battle as the only survivor.**

*Other members of the ZOB command were: Yitzhak Zuckerman (Dror), second in command; Abraham Shneidmil (Bund), later replaced by Marek Edelman; Yochanan Morgenstern (Poalei Zion Z.S.); Hersh Berlinski (Poalei Zion Left); and Michal Rosenfeld (PPR).

†A Jewish National Committee was originally set up as a political counterpart of the ZOB to convince the Polish underground that the ZOB represented the Jewish community as a whole. However, when the Bund joined the ZOB it refused to become part of this political grouping. As a result, the Coordinating Committee was formed to facilitate relations between the Bund and the other ZOB groups in their dealings with the Poles.

**Mordechai led another heroic action on January 17, hours before the surprise *Aktion* began. A group of his men raided Halman's clothing factory and

But this show of resistance, together with other spontaneous actions and the threat of a simultaneous Polish uprising, forced the Germans to end the *Aktion* after four days. And the surviving Jews, euphoric over the revolt, realized at last that if they had to die, it was best to fall proudly in battle. Besides, many thought now, why give up so easily when German defeats at Stalingrad and in the Middle East signaled an early end to the war?

Mordechai personally sensed this new attitude when he went out on the street and talked with people.

"What is the latest news?" he asked one stranger.

"Shit, my friend," the man answered. "In Cracow there is another *Aktion*, in the Lublin region an *Aktion*. Soon our turn will come, and that will be the end. . . ."

"What end, mister?"

"What has happened will not be repeated. They will not take us like sheep to slaughter."

Mordechai silently rejoiced. "Today," he said, "you're a hero. But tell me, what would you do if they came to take you?"

"What do you mean what would I do? I would assemble all my friends, seize axes, iron bars, and hammers, and go down to the cellars or fortify ourselves in our flats. Let them come! Let them shoot to the right and to the left with their machine gun. What will they do to me if I hide behind a door? And if one of them sticks his head into the room, he'll be mine. He will fall under my ax. Maybe I would be next. But at least it would be worthwhile dying like that."

The man showed Mordechai a long shiny knife. "God help anyone who starts with me!" he exclaimed.

Mordechai was astonished. He felt that his work had not been in vain. It was still possible to kindle a spark in his people. A new Jew was rising, proud and strong, who would fight for his life. True, most ghetto residents were not fit for combat; and some who were could not be trusted, for the ghetto was seething with Gestapo agents; and there were only enough guns for a fraction of the youth. But the whole Warsaw Ghetto would now resist, if not actively then passively, by hiding in bunkers.

"I don't know if we shall meet again," Mordechai told his com-

poured acid over a Jewish traitor working there. During the operation a guard captured one of the fighters, but Mordechai and several others broke into the factory again and freed their comrade.

manders as his final briefing ended. "If we don't, at least we will die knowing we have done all we could."[1]

Late in the afternoon, shortly before Mordechai Anielewicz briefed his commanders, a German military automobile escorted by two civilian vehicles sped toward the Productive Ghetto, where Jewish slave laborers were turning out clothes and other supplies for the German Army. A man wearing an officer's coat without insignia sat stiffly in the back seat of the chauffeur-driven car. Major General Jürgen Stroop of the SS was taking no chances as he inspected this area; a Jewish sharpshooter might not be able to resist firing at a German general.*

A lower-ranked officer, Colonel Ferdinand von Sammern-Frankenegg, the SS and police commander in Warsaw, would head the force that would sweep through the ghetto the following day, April 19, in honor of the Führer's birthday on the twentieth. But Stroop would play a role. On April 16, Reichsführer Heinrich Himmler had personally telephoned him in Eastern Galicia and, in his quiet monotone, ordered him to proceed at once to Cracow—the seat of the General Government, as the Germans called Nazi-occupied Poland. From there, General Friedrich Wilhelm Krüger, chief SS and police commander of the General Government, hurried him off to Warsaw to aid von Sammern-Frankenegg in the planned *Aktion.*

Himmler did not quite trust von Sammern-Frankenegg's ability to crush a likely uprising, especially after his setback in the January revolt, in which Mordechai Anielewicz had played so heroic a role. Stroop, on the other hand, had proved himself a master of suppression. In 1939 he had crushed the Czech partisan movement in the Sudetenland and massacred two thousand Poles in Poznan; and in 1941, after the invasion of Russia, he had led a

---

*The Schutzstaffel, or SS, was originally a select group of bodyguards chosen to protect Hitler and other Nazi leaders, but Himmler, on taking it over in 1929, transformed it into a racial elite formation. He set up the Sicherheitsdienst, or SD, as the exclusive intelligence service of the SS under Reinhard Heydrich. In 1939 the SD and the Secret State Police, or Gestapo, were united under the SS in a Security Office of the Reich. By the time Ernst Kaltenbrunner replaced Heydrich, who was assassinated in Prague on May 28, 1942, the SD and the Gestapo could hardly be distinguished from each other.

39

bloody struggle against Soviet partisans. So impressed were his superiors that they sent him to Berlin for a special course on terrorism conducted by Himmler himself. Assigned to Eastern Galicia in 1943, Stroop used his new knowledge to organize the slaughter of Jews there.

Stroop learned a good deal from that experience. First of all, phase one of the roundup was always easy. One simply stuffed the Jews into the bag like chickens. The passive masses did not resist and thus paralyzed even the activists, who found themselves trapped in the bag. But phase two was an extremely difficult task. For those who survived phase one were courageous, strong, and crafty. They had good equipment and offered skillful resistance. No, this small residue of Jews—the Zionist elite, the intelligentsia—could not be underestimated.

From his car Stroop carefully studied the ghetto borders and checked the vigilance of the security forces just outside the ghetto area. They were mostly Ukrainian, Latvian, and Lithuanian Fascists serving under the SS command, and they had received orders to mobilize at 2 p.m. The Germans had "liberated" these men from Soviet control and taken full advantage of their virulent anti-Semitism, training them in the persecution and destruction of Jews. Stroop, however, was not overly impressed with these soldiers—*Askaris,* as the Germans called them. They were uneducated and uncultured and were always lying and cheating. Nothing more than savages, thought Stroop. Nevertheless, they were obedient and brutal and would be useful.

As his car crossed the checkpost from the Polish, or Aryan, part of the city into the ghetto, Stroop breathed in the "Jewish stench" with disgust. The streets, strewn with debris, garbage, and filth, were deserted, and an eerie silence prevailed. Although Jews normally feared to be seen in the streets, Stroop sensed that they had learned of the upcoming *Aktion* and were quietly preparing to resist.

As he stopped to inspect one factory, he questioned a Wehrmacht lieutenant: Were the Jewish workers acting strangely, as if expecting something to happen?

"No," replied the lieutenant. "I haven't noticed anything unusual."

Stroop seethed with contempt. This lieutenant, he thought, was living so well from Jewish bribes that he was sabotaging Himmler's plan, which would eliminate his source of income. He was typical of the men working for von Sammern-Frankenegg. Soon, Stroop was sure, things would change—when *he* took over the operation.

Von Sammern-Frankenegg, he felt, was chaotic and inefficient. A soft Austrian intellectual, a doctor of law who liked comfort, women, and alcohol. It was a disgrace for a man in his position, thought the straightlaced Stroop, to be seen carousing in the nightclubs. Von Sammern-Frankenegg did not even know the strength of the Jews; nor did he intend to deport all of them anyway. After all, he was doing business with some of them in league with the German industrialists and Wehrmacht officers. He was filling his coffers, Stroop was sure, with valuables, furs, and foreign currency. But Stroop would not interfere with his plans. Instead he would give him enough rope with which to hang himself.

That morning Stroop walked into a meeting in von Sammern-Frankenegg's office as the SS leaders were discussing final plans for the *Aktion*. When he had shut the door behind him, he glanced at his fellow commander. How uneasy he looked. Did he think Stroop's presence in Warsaw was a bad omen? Stroop did not utter a word throughout the meeting. Why should he improve the colonel's ill-conceived plan? The more mistakes he made, the faster he would be thrown out of his job.

After the conference Stroop rushed to his suite at Hotel Bristol and telephoned the other SS commanders in Warsaw.

"What is the true situation?" he asked.

"The attack will last longer than three days," predicted Lieutenant Colonel Ludwig Hahn, the Gestapo and SD chief. Hahn was a shrewd, arrogant, thirty-five-year-old lawyer skilled at ingratiating himself with his superiors and covering up evidence of his personal involvement in the savage crimes he ordered. After all, the Nazis might lose the war. He had hard, sly eyes and thin lips turned down at the ends that lent to a perpetual scowl. The situation was complicated, he said. The Jews left in the ghetto were the cleverest of the bunch, and they had a politico-military organization that would offer strong resistance. Stroop agreed.

But the Poles were the greatest danger, Hahn insisted. The Polish underground was not well armed, but it might attack. Then the Germans would be faced not simply with a ghetto uprising but a full-scale Warsaw revolt, and the road to the Russian front ran through Warsaw. The Germans, he worriedly suggested, might have to destroy the whole city of Warsaw in such an event.

Stroop was also concerned. To provoke the Poles now would be a political and strategic error. But would the Germans, by deporting and killing the Jews, really be provoking the anti-Semitic Poles? The Germans had to take that risk. Not a single Jew in Warsaw must remain alive—except, temporarily, the most essential workers.

Stroop, now forty-eight, had learned to obey orders slavishly since he was a child. His father had been a proud policeman who ruled his children with a fierce hand, and his mother had been a strict taskmaster who severely punished her children for the slightest disobedience. Stroop would never forget his first beating—for using his mother's best cushion to sit on while he slid down a board in the yard. Nor would he forget his mother's slap after he had beaten up his elder brother for "borrowing" his Christmas gift. But on that occasion his father had intervened.

"Beat up the enemy, my little son," his father had said, "as brutally as you can, mercilessly, just as I fought our fatherland's enemies and just as I beat up that miserable Knopf for trying to steal the hen of Director Muller's wife."

Stroop also remembered the day his father pointed to the passing carriage of the local prince. As they both bowed deeply, his father had whispered, "Look and remember. This is our prince, our ruler. Obey him and be faithful to him as I am. Always."

His parents had reflected the spirit of the tightly disciplined society of Detmold, which historically resounded with the martial blare of the military band, the booted cadence of the holiday parade, the measured fervor of the patriotic song, the rhythmic hoofbeat of the prancing horse. Detmold, capital of the former duchy of Lippe-Detmold, which before World War I had been an independent territory within the Imperial Reich, was dominated by a huge statue in the wooded hills outside the town: Arminius, or Hermann, a German tribal prince who in A.D. 9 had crushed a powerful Roman army, glared down imperiously upon his subjects.

Stroop was a mediocre student who quit his studies after elementary school, though he resumed them later, finally earning a high school diploma at the age of twenty-seven. He had only the most superficial knowledge of German history and culture; yet he was captivated by what little he knew of Hermann, by the power and pride embodied in his statue.

In the shadow of this monument to military invincibility, the young Stroop played soldier with his brothers and dreamed of resurrecting the glory of Hermann. Here he often lingered long after dark, immersed in a world of fantasy, a euphoric mix of past and future only fleetingly flavored with the prosaic present, as on the night when he kissed a girl for the first time—Marta, with the "golden hair" and "rosy lips."

Here he came to soothe his wrath after suffering wounds in World War I and to nourish his ego after being shunned by the town's aristocracy, which was uninterested in petty, low-paid bureaucrats like surveyor Stroop. And here, at a political rally in 1931, he listened enraptured as Adolf Hitler thunderously promised to imbue all of Germany with the spirit of Hermann. He had met Himmler at the rally. Himmler liked him, and soon Stroop was beating up the Jews in town.

He harbored no particular enmity for the Jews; in fact, he rather admired the attractive Jewish girls in town. But Hitler awakened him to the "evilness" of the Jewish influence on German culture. And soon, as he worked his way up the SS hierarchy, he learned to feel the same pitiless disgust toward Jews as one feels toward roaches.

Why not please his superiors, then, by exterminating as many "roaches" as possible. One day, he was confident, they would present him with the gift he most coveted: an estate of his own in the conquered Ukraine. He would be the prince riding down the street in splendor, accepting tribute from his subjects. And to think that he had once been a lowly surveyor scorned by the elite!

Stroop looked every bit the perfect Nazi brute. No officer wore boots shinier than his, carried a whip with more arrogant aplomb, or tried harder to accentuate his Nordic appearance. Though tall, blond, and blue-eyed, as prescribed by Nazi racial doctrine, Stroop could seldom pass a mirror or even a well-washed window without stopping to analyze his hard, immobile face. With saliva he would stick his hair to his forehead to narrow it in accordance with his concept of the ideal Nordic look.

Yet Stroop was too primitive to understand more than the surface and symbolic aspects of the Nazi philosophy. An SS inspector, after visiting him in Warsaw, wrote for the files, "He is a pure soldier who acts according to orders. As a political leader he lacks wider horizons and the capacity to enter into the spirit of others. . . . Stroop seems to be more than he is. But a good man."

The right man for the ghetto, anyway, if von Sammern-Frankenegg blundered.

Like Mordechai Anielewicz, Stroop could not conceive of compromise in the coming battle. For contrary to most battles, this one would be waged not simply to gain or retain territory and power but to refine the quality of man. Mordechai would fight to the death to purify man's spirit. Stroop would kill to purify man's blood. And since purity was absolute, so must be the ghetto's destruction; though Stroop could not perceive, as could Mordechai, that the victims would shape the soul of a new generation, a new nation, of Jews.

How happy were those days and dreams in Hermann's shadow. . . .

As Stroop was leaving the ghetto, he heard a rifle shot. He looked around, and finding that a young Latvian soldier had fired, he vigorously scolded him. After all, the bullet might have hit Stroop. But the Latvian, standing at attention, smiled foolishly and said in pidgin German, thinking that the general was just another officer, "It is so boring, Lieutenant. When shall we finally start shooting at those animals behind the wall of the Jewish zoo?"

Stroop slapped the soldier's blond head with his glove, lightly, almost affectionately, and shoved a mark into his hand. Stroop liked the young man. Not only was he a Nordic type racially, but he was a tough soldier with the right spirit. Yes, Stroop thought, he could count on the *Askaris* to take care of the Jews.[2]

"Can you hear us? Can you hear us?"

Arie Wilner still trembled from the cries of the Gestapo men trying to revive him. He was hanging by his hands, and the soles of his feet were bleeding from savage blows inflicted with a club. A splash of cold water. Then more torture. . . .

The pain wracking his body was intense now, even several weeks after his escape, which his ZOB and Polish comrades had miraculously engineered. But the pain in his heart was even greater on this night of April 18. For twenty-six-year-old Arie, code name Yurek, had been one of the organizers of the ZOB and one of its most dedicated and inspiring leaders. Now, as the uprising was about to start, he was a helpless invalid who had to hide in a bunker.

The bunker, one of the most magnificently camouflaged hideouts in the Central Ghetto, was an enlarged cellar under a building at Franciszkanska 30, a huge apartment compound with three courtyards. It was called the "honeymakers' bunker" because it had been built mainly by people in the building who worked in an artificial-honey plant, one of the many shops in the ghetto run by Germans with Jewish slave labor. Only those helping to build or finance this bunker for their own use were supposed to know its location, a rule that applied to every hiding place. Nobody trusted anybody else. Too many Gestapo agents were lurking in the shadows, and who could tell what information even a trustworthy Jew might reveal to the Gestapo under torture.

Thus, virtually the whole Warsaw Ghetto now lived underground, though few knew the whereabouts of anybody not in their own bunker.

However, Franciszkanska 30 was an exception. The ZOB had never built bunkers of its own because Mordechai Anielewicz feared they would dampen the fight-to-the-death spirit of his fighters. Mordechai thus arranged to use this hiding place in an emergency. And he based here one of his auxiliary ZOB units, whose five members were to protect the bunker with pistols purchased on the black market with their own private funds.

The bunker residents had dug deeply into the cellar and converted its mossy cells into a single great room honeycombed with bunkers. The ventilation openings were well masked, and stacked up high in one corner were sacks of sugar, groats, and flour that could feed the seventy-odd occupants for months. Electricity was diverted in from the municipal grid passing through the ghetto; dozens of books were brought down to ward off boredom; and even a radio set had been scrounged up, a magic box that would keep the bunker entertained and in touch with the outside world.

During the night of April 18, with the ghetto on the alert, Israel Guttman, the bunker security guard, rushed from door to door, instructing people in the building to rush down to the bunker, each with one valise or bag. They filed in by the light of hand torches; and many brought their Passover meals, which they hoped to enjoy uninterrupted.

Arie Wilner was not on the list of occupants, but Mordechai had brought him here. Even in pain, Arie retained his calm, dignified bearing. Before the war many people had thought he lacked drive and aggressiveness, that he was too soft; and his timid manner and baby face reinforced this impression. But since the German occupation of Warsaw, where he was born, his manner and appearance had proved to be only a deceptive shield for an iron will and unshatterable courage. As one of Mordechai's deputies in Hashomer Hatzair, he had helped to found a Jewish underground in Vilna and then the ZOB in Warsaw. He was, even by Nazi racial standards, a man.

During the January uprising—after Arie had returned to the ghetto from the Aryan side, where he was based—a German soldier suddenly burst into his room. Arie coolly removed his pistol from his pocket and aimed it at the intruder, who stood paralyzed in fear and shock.

"Mensch, was machst du!" ("Man, what are you doing!") the German gasped.

A Jew with a gun in his hand was a man.

Arie replied with a bullet. . . .

Now, as he helplessly lay on his cot in Franciszkanska 30, he agonized over the thought that he would have to die without fighting. His deep depression was only relieved, it appeared, when he thought about Tosia Altman. Like Arie, Tosia was one of Mordechai's top deputies in the Hashomer Hatzair and the ZOB. Because of her blond curly hair and Aryan features, she could pass for a Pole; and from the beginning of the German occupation of Poland, she had traveled throughout the country disguised as either a sophisticated, elegantly dressed lady of breeding or a fresh-faced peasant girl with leather boots, colorful apron, and kerchief around her head.

In each town, she visited members of her Zionist organization, bringing into the ghetto a ray of love and light. She relayed orders, injected hope, consoled the bereaved. She had been the first to bring back news of the Vilna deportations, the signal that the Warsaw Ghetto was also doomed. Tosia, like Arie Wilner, showed an interest in everyone. Both, therefore, suffered more than most of their fellow fighters.

Arie was always worried about Tosia, and she would confide in him when she returned from one of her harrowing trips. So distressed was she each time—especially after she learned her whole family had been killed—that she would go into seclusion for days, shutting herself off in a room on the Aryan side to nurse her deep wounds. Yet she, like Arie, never abandoned hope.

"Listen carefully, brother," she had told one group in 1940, "you who are presently draining sewers and are stricken with dysentery, you who are facing death by starvation within the locked ghetto . . . we shall make a stand; we shall rise again and begin all over again."

Now, as they were about to make a stand, Tosia was with Mordechai's command, and Arie could not share this moment with her. He lay instead in a comfortable bunker. But he did not want comfort, books, or sweet radio music to help him escape the horrors of reality. He wanted to fight, to die fighting. . . .

"How can you think of fighting when the Germans are so strong? And the Home Army can't significantly help you. We are not ready for a citywide uprising."

Arie regarded the speaker, Major Stanislaw Weber, code name Chirurg, with a rather sad tolerance tinged with contempt. As the chief ZOB agent on the Aryan side, Arie was meeting in a secret apartment with Home Army leaders in November 1942. The Home Army (Armia Krajowa), or AK, was the underground military arm of the Polish government-in-exile based in London. Arie hoped to obtain arms from them.

"We wish to sell our lives dearly," he said.

"And after the fighting, how will you escape?"

"I, for one, shall not escape. I shall fight until I die."

Major Weber was impressed, as was his superior, Warsaw Commander Colonel Antoni Chrusciel, known as Monter. They saw in Arie a man who would fight, and one to whom they felt strangely akin. With his small features, blue eyes, and fair hair, he could not be distinguished from a Pole. No wonder the ZOB had selected this "Jewish knight," as the Polish officers often referred to Arie, to represent them on the Aryan side. The Home Army could deal with him without too much concern that he might be picked up on the street and forced to talk.

"What do you need?" Chrusciel asked. "Money?"

"No, we can get money by squeezing the rich in the ghetto. We need arms and ammunition, grenades, explosives, combat training, specialists to build bunkers."

Chrusciel smiled. He promised to do all he could.

Arie doubted that this would be much. He had first met Home Army officers in August, three months earlier, and had pleaded for help. Couldn't they disrupt the deportations that had just started? Only small guard details were assigned to each death train. The answer was no. The risk was too great. Arie then contacted another officer, Henryk Wolinski, or Waclaw, head of the Home Army's Jewish affairs department, whose task was to find out what the Nazis were doing against the Jews.

Wolinski, who had a Jewish wife, eagerly wished to aid the Jews and so arranged this new meeting with Chrusciel and Weber. They also wanted to help, but many other officers, especially in the national command, did not share this desire. Either because they feared being dragged into battle prematurely or simply because they were anti-Semitic, they opposed taking any direct action to hinder the extermination program.

This reluctance was reflected at a secret conference of the Home Army's national command that took place more than a month before Arie's meeting with Chrusciel and Weber. General Stefan Rowecki, the Home Army commander, said he wished to help the ghetto because, he predicted, the Germans intended to murder all the Poles after they had wiped out the Jews. But most of his officers nodded disapproval. After all, they argued, if the United States and Great Britain, with all their resources and military power, could not prevent Nazi crimes in the other occupied countries, how could the weak Polish underground do any better? And the Jewish leaders themselves, they added, expected no more than sixty thousand Jews to be killed and wanted only a loud Allied protest. (This was actually a position held by many Jews but not by any fighting group.) Besides, the officers stressed, a ghetto uprising might spread to the rest of Warsaw, and the Home Army was not equipped to fight the Germans. The whole Polish population would be slaughtered, together with the Jews. Then, too, a full-scale uprising at this time would help the Red Army. And wasn't it the Home Army's aim to let the Germans and Russians pulverize each other in the interests of Poland? What's more, an uprising would strengthen the Communists on both sides of the wall and perhaps lead to civil war.

Rowecki was impressed. Anyway, as a practical man, he could not ignore the sentiments of several strongly anti-Semitic groups that belonged to the Home Army.* He was, in fact, trying to lure

*From 1941 to 1943 the Home Army was responsible to a Government Delegate appointed by the Polish Council of Ministers (government-in-exile) in London after consultations with the Home Political Representation, a sort of parliament. Groups represented in this body were the Polish Socialist Party, the conservative Peasant Party, the liberal Labor Party, and the right-wing National

into his army the fascist National Armed Forces (NSZ), which was openly grateful to the Nazis for cleansing Poland of Jews.

The general pondered what to do. The Communist issue was especially disturbing. Many of the Jewish activists, he was sure, were Communists, even though they were trying to hide this fact. So to help the Jews might be to help the Communists. Could he risk giving guns to people who might, if they survived, turn them against their benefactors? On September 30 he cabled General Wladyslaw Sikorski, prime minister of the Polish government-in-exile and commander in chief of the Polish forces, that the Communists were calling for "partisan warfare, in support of Soviet diversion. This threatens the unleashing, against our will, of fighting directed by the Communists."

Rowecki also decided to remind the Allies that it was *their* responsibility to help the Jews, though he knew the Poles alone were in a position to take direct action on the ground. He met with Sikorski's delegate in Warsaw and they called in Jan Kozielewski, code name Karski, a Home Army lieutenant. They threw the fate of the Jews into his lap.

Kozielewski was a tall, dark young man with burning eyes that reflected both keen intelligence and innocent candor. He had his bags packed, ready to leave for London, where he was going on a special mission. He would now report to both his own government and the Allied leaders on the extermination of Polish Jewry.* To learn the facts, his superiors informed him, he would meet with two ZOB agents.

Party. A number of smaller groups not represented in this body also supported the Government Delegate. They included the openly fascistic National Radical Group, which was formed, soon after Hitler's rise to power, from the extremists of the National Party. All the parties in the Home Political Representation placed their military formations under the Home Army command, though some military units of the National Party broke away and formed the National Armed Forces, or NSZ, which became the armed force of the most extreme elements of the National Radical Group. Both the political and military arms of the London-directed Polish underground had an anti-Semitic majority, while the Fascists approved of Hitler's Jewish policy.

*When the British government received reports of mass gassings in death camps, shortly after the first deportations from the Warsaw Ghetto on July 22, 1942, it would not broadcast them, regarding them as exaggerated. On August 27, the foreign office cabled Washington about a planned public declaration concerning German atrocities in Poland: "On further reflection we are not convinced that evidence regarding use of gas chambers is substantial enough to justify inclusion in a public declaration. . . ."

Shortly, in early October 1942, Kozielewski and the two Jews gathered at twilight in a deserted, partially ruined mansion outside Warsaw. While Kozielewski sat rigidly at a table in a shabby old armchair, as if pinned there by the tension, a Zionist representative and a Bundist, Leon Feiner, "paced the floor violently." According to Kozielewski, "their shadows danced weirdly in the dim light cast by the single candle we could allow ourselves. It was as though they were unable even to think of their dying people and remain seated."

"You other Poles are fortunate," the Zionist said. "You are suffering, too. Many of you will die, but at least your nation goes on living. . . . The Polish Jews will no longer exist. We will be dead. Hitler will lose this war against the human, the just, and the good, but he will win his war against the Polish Jew."

The Zionist then held his head between his hands and sobbed like a child, though the moaning wind almost drowned out the sound.

"What's the good of talking? he continued. "What reason do I have to go on living? . . . If all the Jews are killed they won't need any leaders. . . . But it's no use telling you all this. No one in the outside world can possibly understand. You don't understand. Even I don't understand, for my people are dying and I am alive."

Feiner, an older man with silvery hair, an upturned mustache, and a beard, had been a well-known lawyer before the war and was now posing as the prosperous Polish owner of a large store. He put one hand on his comrade's shoulder while nervously clenching and unclenching his other hand at his side.

"We have work to do," he said, resting his hands on the table, "and very little time to do it. We have to talk to the point. . . ."

"Germany can be impressed only by power and violence," the Zionist then went on. "The cities of Germany ought to be bombed mercilessly, and with every bombing, leaflets should be dropped informing the Germans fully of the fate of the Polish Jews. And we ought to threaten the entire German nation with a similar fate both during and after the war."

Feiner interrupted, "We know that . . . this plan cannot be carried out, that it cannot fit into Allied military strategy, but we can't help that. The Jews and those who wish to help them cannot afford to approach this war from a purely military standpoint."

"It is an unprecedented situation in history," the Zionist said, "and can be dealt with only by unprecedented methods. Let the Allied governments, wherever their hand can reach, in America, England, and Africa, begin public executions of Germans, any they can get hold of. That is what we demand."

"But that is utterly fantastic," Kozielewski replied. "A demand like that will only confuse and horrify all those who are sympathetic with you."

"Of course," the Zionist answered. "Do you think I don't know it? We ask it because it is the only rebuttal to what is being done to us. We do not dream of its being fulfilled, but nevertheless we demand it. We demand it so people will know how we feel about what is being done to us, how helpless we are, how desperate our plight is, how little we stand to gain from an Allied victory as things are now."

Kozielewski felt tired and feverish. "More and more," he wrote, "these two frantic figures pacing the floor in the shadowy room, their steps echoing in the hollow silence, seemed like apparitions, their glances filled with a burden of despair, pain, and hopelessness they could never completely express. Their voices were pitched very low, they hissed, they whispered, and yet I constantly had the illusion that they were roaring. It seemed to me that I was listening to an earthquake, that I was hearing cracking, tearing sounds of the earth opening to swallow a portion of humanity. One could hear the cries and shouts of the frantic people falling into the chasm."

Feiner violently gripped Kozielewski's arm, and the Pole "looked into his wild, staring eyes with awe, moved by the deep, unbearable pain in them."

"Tell the Jewish leaders," Feiner hammered, "that this is no case for politics or tactics. Tell them that the earth must be shaken to its foundations, the world must be aroused. . . . Tell them to go to all the important English and American offices and agencies. Tell them not to leave until they have obtained guarantees that a way has been decided upon to save the Jews. Let them accept no food or drink, let them die a slow death while the world is looking on. Let them die. This may shake the conscience of the world."

As Kozielewski sank into his armchair, his whole body chilled and sore, the Zionist said, "This we did not intend to tell you, but I want you to know it. We do not demand such sacrifices from our

leaders abroad out of cruelty. We expect to make them here ourselves. The ghetto is going to go up in flames. We are not going to
die in slow torment, but fighting. We will declare war on Germany—the most hopeless declaration of war that has ever been
made."

According to Kozielewski, Feiner then "whispered delicately, as
if afraid that someone was lurking behind the wall or that the
wind might take up his words and scatter them so that the plan
would come prematurely to the ears of the Gestapo":

"We are organizing a defense of the ghetto, not because we
think it can be defended, but to let the world see the hopelessness
of our battle—as a demonstration and a reproach. We are even
now negotiating with your commander for the arms we need. If
we get them, then one of these days the deportation squad is going to get a bloody surprise."

But the Jewish version of what Feiner said in regard to arms, as
indicated in a message from Feiner to a colleague in London, dif-
fered considerably from that recorded in Kozielewski's memoirs:
"There is one crime we will never forgive—we asked for arms in
order to die like human beings in an organized resistance against
the murderers. We didn't get them. They refused. . . ."

Whatever was said, Kozielewski promised to carry the message
to London. It was a message he could not forget.

Meanwhile, Prime Minister Sikorski pressed General Rowecki
to give at least some help to the Jews. Not only was this a matter of
principle, he indicated, but Poland had to show its best face to the
Allies, on which its whole future depended.

Pressure also came from another source—a large and influential group of Poles who, at the risk of their lives, had formed the
Council for Aid to Jews known as Zegota. Representing most
political and social groups, Zegota helped Jews escape from the
ghetto and found hiding places for them on the Aryan side. It also
supported them financially, with funds contributed mainly by
Jews throughout the world. (The government-in-exile was to con-
tribute only about $250,000, less than one percent of the money
transferred to the Home Army.) The Zegota, though embodying
only an idealistic minority of Poles, helped to counter the influence of those who were urging Rowecki not to help the Jews in
armed struggle against their murderers.

Thus, Rowecki arranged for Colonel Chrusciel and Major Web-

52

er to meet with Arie Wilner to determine what the ZOB needed. Following this meeting, Rowecki discussed Arie's requests with Chrusciel and agreed to give limited aid—if the ZOB would demonstrate that it was anti-Communist. It would have to commit itself to join the Poles in fighting the Russians if such a battle erupted.

Mordechai Anielewicz and the other ZOB leaders found themselves in a dilemma. Many were leftist-inclined and did not want to fight the Russians, even though some, including Mordechai, had been somewhat disillusioned by Soviet communism while in Russian-controlled territory. The Soviet system, calling for the suppression of Zionism and the basic freedoms, had less in common with their voluntary kibbutz philosophy than they had realized. Still, however misguided its brand of socialism, Russia *was* the first socialist state. And it *was* fighting the Nazis.

Furthermore, one ZOB faction, the People's Guard, military arm of the PPR, was itself communist; though during the spring uprising it was to form only four of the ZOB's twenty-two groups, with the Zionists making up fourteen and the Bundists four.* And the mother branch of the PPR on the Aryan side was supplying the ZOB with what weapons it could and planned to attack the Germans in support of an uprising.

Mordechai finally authorized Arie to tell the Home Army, with diplomatic ambivalence, "Since we are citizens of Poland, the decisions of the Polish government are binding upon us."

Rowecki then agreed, on November 11, to recognize the ZOB as a "partly Polish organization," and he vaguely promised arms and training. A few weeks later the first weapons were turned over to Arie: ten pistols! With cold anger Arie complained to Wolinski that this niggling shipment was a "scandal." Especially since four of the pistols did not even work. Wolinski embarrassingly agreed and protested to his superiors. But they simply replied, referring to prospects for threat and robbery, "The Jews should learn that every pistol can produce an additional one. That is what we have learned."

General Rowecki was more direct in a cable he sent to Sikorski on January 2, 1943: "Jews from all kinds of Communist groups are . . . asking us for arms as if we had full arms de-

---

*The fourteen Zionist groups were divided among seven organizations: Dror (5 groups), Hashomer Hatzair (4), Akiva (1), Gordonia (1), Hanoar Hazioni (1), Paolei Zion, Z.S. (1), and Paolei Zion Left (1).

pots. . . . As an experiment, I sent out several pistols. I am not convinced that they will even utilize these arms. I will give them no further arms, since you know that we ourselves have none. . . ."*

The Poles later claimed that the cable actually began, "Jews from all kinds of groups, including Communists. . . ." But as some historians have pointed out, even if the originally reported version was wrong, the tone of the cable as a whole hardly reflected overwhelming sympathy for the doomed Jews.

Meanwhile, the Home Army launched a program to train insurgents. However, the training officer failed to appear at the first session, and when he showed up for a new appointment, he staggered into the room completely intoxicated. Thus ended the training program.

Finally, under ZOB pressure and on orders from the Sikorski government, the Home Army handed over ten more pisols as well as written instructions on sabotage and the manufacture of Molotov cocktails. Just in time to permit the Jews to smash the *Aktion* that began on January 18 and ended prematurely because of the exploits of Mordechai Anielewicz and his comrades.

Rowecki was as impressed as he was surprised by these Jewish heroics, and he finally agreed to be more helpful. He even permitted his commanders to draw up a plan for a Home Army attack in any new uprising. Units would breach the wall blocking off the Productive Ghetto on Leszno Street and streak northward to join Jewish forces while, unknown to Rowecki, PPR fighters on the Aryan side would strike southward from Umschlagplatz under a secret arrangement with the ZOB. The general also turned over

*In July 1943, Leon Mitkiewicz, the Polish military attaché in Washington, submitted to the Allied High Command a memorandum outlining the military potential of the Home Army. According to this document, in spring 1943, at the time of the ghetto uprising, the Home Army possessed the following weapons: 600 heavy machine guns, 1000 light machine guns, 25,000 rifles, 6000 pistols, and 30,000 grenades. On April 1, 1941, the following arms were held in Warsaw alone: 135 heavy machine guns, 190 light machine guns, 6,045 rifles, 1,070 pistols, and 7,561 grenades. Moreover, from April 1941 to April 1943 the Home Army acquired additional arms as a result of British air drops, its own production, and purchases from German and Italian soldiers. The Poles claim that many of the weapons hidden in 1939 had become useless by 1943 because of poor storage conditions, but the report to the Allied High Command in July 1943 did not reflect this damage.

to the Jews some more pistols, ammunition, grenades, and material for manufacturing Molotov cocktails.*

But Arie Wilner pressed for still more. What were a few tens of pistols in a battle against the Nazi hordes? he asked. On March 5 Wolinski walked into Arie's one-room apartment, which contained only a bed, a cupboard, and a single chair. Noting some weapons under the bed, Wolinski demanded, "What is that under your bed? In God's name, are you buying weapons on the black market? Don't you know this is forbidden for members of the underground? You cannot afford the risk of such connections."

"What am I to do?" Arie replied, unperturbed. "Are you giving us enough? Do I have any choice?"

Wolinski said that as long as Arie had connections with Home Army headquarters, such dealings were forbidden.

Later that day disaster struck. The Gestapo smashed into the apartment and arrested Arie Wilner, but not because they thought he was a Jew. They thought he was a Home Army officer. At Gestapo headquarters, the Germans slapped him and shouted, "You will sing about everything. Birds of your kind have already visited us."

This is what the Home Army feared, and not without reason; for Arie knew where many officers lived and much of what they were planning. In panic, the Home Army cut off all relations with the Jews, and officers scampered to new hideouts. But Arie stood up under torture, and even volunteered with pride that he was a Jew. How had he left the ghetto? demanded his inquisitioner. Where had he obtained the weapons found in his apartment?

"I have no connection with any organization," he stubbornly replied, "because I don't recognize any. I want to avenge my parents' deaths. This is why I have guns."

Neither whip not electric torture could change his story. In his cell, Arie wanted to hang himself for fear of breaking down, but his cellmates stopped him. Finally, because of an administrative error, he was shipped off to Pawiak prison at the edge in the Wild

*According to official Home Army figures, the complete list of arms delivered to the Jewish fighters was as follows: 1 light machine gun, 90 pistols, 600 grenades, and some explosives. It is not clear whether these figures, which are somewhat higher than those of the ZOB, include material sent also to the ZZW. In any event, Captain Iwanski supplied the ZZW with many more arms without the top Home Army commanders' knowledge.

Ghetto and then put to work on the railroad, though normally he would have been executed.

Tosia Altman made superhuman efforts to rescue Arie, spending great sums to bribe top police officials, but to no avail. When at last she learned of his whereabouts, the ZOB dispatched a friendly Pole, Henryk Grabowski, to the work camp where Arie was being kept. Grabowski entered the guardhouse and asked whether there was a Pole or Jew in the camp named Jerzy Borucki, Arie's false Polish name. Borucki had lived at his house for a month, Grabowski said, and had not paid his rent. He was in desperate financial straits. Could he please see the culprit in order to get the money?

The guard, nodding his sympathy, departed and soon returned with an emaciated limping figure. Arie threw his arms around Grabowski, his friend, but the Pole winked at him and gruffly demanded, "Why did you live with me and then leave without paying for the room?"

"What money?" Arie asked, failing to understand.

"Don't pretend to be a fool. Let me have the money you owe me. Otherwise I'll have to notify the Gestapo. . . . I came here today especially to get the money, and I must get it."

Finally Arie understood. Grabowski then left, "warning" that in the evening he would come back for the money.

In the evening he was back. He managed to reach Arie's barracks and drag out his Jewish friend, who could barely walk on his almost raw soles. By five the next morning they reached Grabowski's home, where the Pole treated Arie with homemade medicine.

Several days later Arie was back in the ghetto. Mordechai and his other comrades welcomed him with a gay party at which everybody exchanged stories and told jokes, forgetting the future, while Mira Fuchrer prepared the finest meal tasted by any of them in a long time. Arie looked around and saw weapons everywhere. No, he was no longer able to fight. But at least he could die beside those who were. . . .

"Listen carefully, brother. . . . We shall make a stand, we shall rise again and begin all over again . . ."[3]

Yitzhak Zuckerman was homesick for the ghetto. True, he had bribed his way to the Aryan side and set up his headquarters in a secret apartment there only a few days earlier, on April 13. But

56

why, he wondered, should he not return to attend the Seder being planned for the ghetto leaders on April 19, the first night of Passover? Yitzhak, code name Antek, was the ZOB's second-in-command. He had left the ghetto reluctantly in the first place, after the ZOB command decided he should replace Arie Wilner as the chief ZOB representative on the Aryan side.

Since everything seemed to depend on the ZOB's success in getting arms from the Home Army, the choice for this position was crucial. Thus it had to be one of the organization's two top leaders, Mordechai or Yitzhak.

No one had despaired more than Mordechai after Arie's capture, especially when the other ZOB agents on the Aryan side were unable to renew contact with the Home Army leaders. Although Mordechai could understand the Home Army's initial fear that Arie might talk and endanger the whole underground, Arie had since escaped without revealing any secrets. And had not his pleas for arms gone largely unanswered, even before his capture? The real reason why the Home Army was ignoring the ZOB, and its needs, Mordechai felt, lay simply in anti-Semitism.

And his bitterness grew when, on March 18, he led an attack on two Baltic soldiers who had been robbing and shooting Jewish workers. The ZOB fighters killed both soldiers and wounded a German who tried to interfere; but now Mordechai feared that the Nazis might strike back, and his fighters did not have enough arms to resist. He sat down and scribbled a note to his agents on the Aryan side:

In the next few days, an end may come for Warsaw Jewry. Are we prepared? . . . Out of 49 weapons, only 39 can function, because of lack of ammunition. . . . I would ask that you inform the authorities in our name that unless a great deal of help arrives, we shall regard them as indifferent to the fate of Warsaw Jewry. Our remaining without weapons makes it look as if there were a cynical lack of concern as to our fate, and supports the assumption that anti-Semitic feeling continues to be active among those in authority in Poland in spite of the cruel and tragic experiences of the last three years.

We do not have to convince anyone of our fighting ability and readiness to take up arms. As of January 18 the Jewish community in Warsaw has been in a state of continuous war against the invader and his servants. Whoever denies or doubts this is a vicious anti-Semite. . . .

57

I ask that you read [the Polish authorities] this letter and demand persistently that they supply us with at least 100 hand grenades, 50 pistols, 10 rifles, and several thousand rounds of various calibers.

Mordechai ended the note with a postscript describing the ZOB attack that day.

"We are tensely awaiting developments," he concluded.

He did not have to wait long. A few hours later the Nazis sealed off several houses in the Central Ghetto, dragged out 150 men, women, and children, and shot them.

The ZOB could no longer remain paralyzed in the face of such atrocities. They *had* to get arms! And some of the ZOB commanders thought Mordechai himself was the man to do it, especially since his Warsaw accent would presumably arouse less suspicion than Yitzhak's eastern Polish accent. But others pointed out that because Mordechai did come from Warsaw, many Poles could identify him. Also, twenty-eight-year-old Yitzhak, with his light blue eyes, bushy blond hair, scraggly mustache, and tall, wiry physique, looked more like a Pole. Thus, to his great disappointment, Yitzhak was selected to be reborn as Witold Kimsztacz, a Polish businessman.

His job would not be easy. It might not even be possible. Still, there was hope. For on April 12, after more than a month of silence, the ZOB leaders learned that the Home Army was at least ready to talk again.

The following day, Yitzhak met with Mordechai and Zivia Lubetkin, another top ZOB leader, to exchange farewells before he departed for the Aryan side. There were few words. For what could people say to each other when it seemed certain they would never meet again? Especially when two were man and wife and the other a close friend of both.

Yitzhak and Zivia had married in 1940. Zivia was an attractive girl of twenty-nine with short black hair, firm, stubborn lips, and dark, brooding eyes afire with zeal. Together the couple had led the Zionist Hehalutz, or pioneer movement, and its youth affiliate, Dror, in Warsaw. Unlike Hashomer Hatzair, which was also a Hehalutz affiliate but was largely recruited from the Warsaw middle classes, Dror was mainly of provincial and working-class origin. Now, separately, the couple would help to lead the ghetto uprising, with Zivia substituting for her husband in the ZOB command inside the ghetto.

At this moment of parting they were strangely devoid of personal feelings. They had seen so many die that death had become, in a sense, a way of life. They had learned to accept the death of a loved one as a person living under normal conditions might accept a month's absence. Nothing was important anymore—except to take revenge and uphold the honor of their ravished people.

When three Jewish policemen, actually ZOB agents, arrived to guide Yitzhak out of the ghetto, he kissed his wife, shook hands with Mordechai, and draped several shirts over his arm so he could claim to be a Pole smuggling them out of the ghetto. He followed the policeman to the ghetto exit, where guards were bribed to let him pass. His heart sank. Now he would die not by fighting the Nazis but by trying to escape their detection. He would die in fine clothes, with a desperately carefree glow in his eyes hiding the hunted look that gave away most Jews trying to pass as Poles.

Yitzhak saw Frania Beatus, his chief courier, waiting for him near the gate. He smiled to himself as he noted her high heels and large handbag. Frania was trying to look older than her sixteen years. Actually, with her innocent round face, pug nose, and thick blond ponytail, she seemed about fourteen. Yet she was one of the most courageous of the ghetto fighters and crossed without hesitation into the ghetto and back again with messages, arms, and money for bribes.

Frania's smile was too bright for the enemy to guess that she was Jewish but too sad for her fellow Jews to doubt that her every breath of life was agony. Her whole family had perished, and she herself had left Ostrowiec for Warsaw just one day before most of the Jews in that town were deported. She carried the burden of every massacred Jew on her slim shoulders, and the crushing weight had all but snuffed out the last remnants of hope sustaining her. Only the thought of her beloved fiancé, a ZOB fighter in the ghetto, gave her the strength and will to survive.

Yitzhak took Frania gently by the arm, and they went to an apartment at Marszalkowsk 118, where Yitzhak immediately began work based on contacts that Frania had already rekindled.

Four days later, on April 17, Yitzhak dictated a letter to Frania, who would smuggle it into the ghetto. Addressed to Mordechai and Zivia, the letter stated that Yitzhak would return to the ghetto to attend the Seder two days later, on April 19. It also contained some discouraging news.

Yitzhak had met Henryk Wolinski on a street corner, and Wolinski sadly reported that the Home Army would not help the Jews prepare for an uprising or participate in one but would only aid them in leaving the ghetto and reaching the forests, where they could fight as partisans. Wolinski said that a man named Tannenbaum, who represented a member of the Judenrat, Abraham Stolzman, had asked Home Army officers not to give weapons to the fighters. A revolt, Tannenbaum had said, would only make matters worse.

Yitzhak was furious. "ZOB's job is to defend the ghetto," he roared. "If we survive a revolt, we can then go to the forests to fight as partisans. When the deportations started, you Poles blamed us for dying quietly like sheep. . . . And now you propose that we shouldn't fight. Well, no one will leave the ghetto until after the revolt." Then he added bitterly, "So that's why you didn't want to meet us for so many weeks."

In his letter to Mordechai and Zivia, Yitzhak advised them to arrest Stolzman immediately. It would be a sad Seder.

The following day, April 18, Yitzhak received two letters smuggled out of the ghetto. His wife Zivia wrote in a brusque manner, Mordechai in a friendly way, but both said the same thing: Don't come. He should remain on the Aryan side and seek other sources of weapons. But Yitzhak had made up his mind. He could not bear to be away from his wife and comrades when they were celebrating Passover only a few blocks away, on the other side of the wall.

He wrote another letter saying that, regardless, he would enter the ghetto at 4 P.M. on April 19, disguised as a worker returning with his group.

A sad Seder was better than none.[4]

Captain Henryk Iwanski, a Polish Home Army officer, stood impatiently by an open manhole in the courtyard of Zlota 49 on the Aryan side, waiting to leave for the ghetto. Next to him was a man in rubber boots—Tomasz, a city employee who knew the sewer system almost better than he did the streets above. Iwanski glanced across the street at the building where he lived, Zlota 56A. Just about now, 5 P.M., his deputy, Lieutenant Wladyslaw Zajdler, should be emerging from Iwanski's apartment with the last shipment of arms to be smuggled into the ghetto before the uprising: crates of machine guns, rifles, pistols, and grenades.

Iwanski would turn these weapons over to the Jewish Military Organization (Zydowski Zwiazek Wojskowy), or ZZW, which he and his group of Polish partisans supported at great risk to themselves. The ZZW was a separate Jewish fighting organization with no ties to Mordechai Anielewicz's ZOB. Though embracing fighters of all political colors, its nucleus was Betar, the youth arm of the Revisionist Zionist movement founded by Ze'ev Jabotinski, whose aim was to set up a Jewish state by force and terror if necessary.

Iwanski, though a gentile, had helped to form the ZZW. It all started one day in October 1939, a month after the Nazis had captured Warsaw. Lieutenant David Appelbojm, a Jewish comrade who had fought alongside Iwanski in the defense of the city, came with three other Jewish officers to St. Stanislaw Hospital at Wolska 37. Here Iwanski now secretly commanded a unit of the Underground Security Corps (Korpas Bezpieczenstaw), or KB, which was later to join the Home Army.

"Captain Iwanski," Appelbojm said, "you must help us to organize the Jewish youth. There are difficult days in store for us. The Germans have already started their campaign against us. They humiliate us. We cannot stand idle in the face of this degradation and oppression."

Iwanski, code name Bystry, was a vigorous man with blond wavy hair and intense blue eyes. He listened sympathetically.

"First of all," he replied, "you must forget the name Iwanski. The name is Bystry. Anybody who is ready to fight the Germans is a friend of ours. You Jews are in the first line of fire. You must lose no time in preparing to fight. We'll help you all we can."

Iwanski then got up, left the room for a while, and returned smiling with four 9mm Weiss pistols and reserve ammunition clips. The four visitors left the hospital euphorically, armed with the first weapons carried by Jewish partisans in Warsaw. Each one would now form an underground cell of trustworthy people known to him.

At the end of December 1939, after several more meetings, Iwanski and Appelbojm signed an agreement making Appelbojm's group a semi-independent unit in the Home Army. They took an oath of allegiance and formed a fighting organization called Swit. Soon it would expand into the ZZW under the command of Pawel Frenkel, a dark, lean, delicate-featured intellectual in his early twenties. Appelbojm would be his deputy, together

61

with Leon Rodal, a journalist who had inherited from his Hassidic father a messianic fervor which he brought to the Revisionist, and now the ZZW, cause.

Unlike many Poles, Iwanski was unprejudiced against the Jews and was eager to help them, especially fighters such as Appelbojm.

"Mietek," he told Appelbojm casually, calling him by his code name, "I must confess that I never expected to find such a brave soldier as you among the Jews."

"There were once many like me in Poland," Appelbojm replied. "I am sure that in the free world there are still tens of thousands like me, and even better than me."

Iwanski liked fighters because he was one himself. The Germans had taught him to be one. He had fought them in the Upper Silesian uprisings from 1919 to 1921, as well as in September 1939, defending Warsaw to the end. Now he was fighting them as a partisan. St. Stanislaw Hospital was an ideal base for his cell since it was supposed to deal with contagious diseases and, thus, was hardly a magnet for the epidemic-conscious Germans.

Soon Iwanski's group was buying and concealing arms, training fighters, operating a clandestine radio network, distributing leaflets and news bulletins, and rescuing, hiding and arming Jews. One of Iwanski's coups was the abduction of several young Jewish women who had been working as Gestapo agents, and their conversion into double agents on the Jews' behalf.

Iwanski reported to Colonel Andrzej Pietrykowski, commander of the Security Corps, who apparently was himself a Jew. Pietrykowski did not bother to consult with General Rowecki or other top Home Army leaders about the aid being given the ZZW, possibly because he knew they were reluctant to help the Jews defend themselves. So while the ZOB scrounged for stray pistols, Iwanski was feeding the ZZW with Sten guns and even machine guns.

The ZZW leaders, with their single, simplified Revisionist philosophy, had little in common with the mixed bag of idealists in the ZOB, many of whom, before the deportations started, had viewed resistance as more of an anti-Fascist struggle than one of sheer survival. Indeed, some ZOB members regarded the ZZW, whose hard core had stressed military training for years, as Fascist-inclined, though Mordechai Anielewicz himself had been a Betarist for a short period in his early teens.

Nevertheless, leaders of the two groups had met occasionally to discuss a merger in the face of the Nazi threat. After much arguing they reached a provisional agreement for the defense of the Central Ghetto: The ZZW would defend Muranowski Square and the areas adjacent to it, and the ZOB would defend the rest of the Central Ghetto. But there would be no merger. The ZOB insisted that Mordechai Anielewicz be the commander of any union since the ZOB, with about eight hundred fighters, was twice the size of the ZZW. But the ZZW wanted one of its own at the helm, contending that its leaders were generally older and had more military experience.

Nor did the ZZW approve of the Bund's close ties with Polish politicians, which they felt could endanger Jewish security since Polish anti-Semitic parties might learn of ghetto defense plans and report them to the Gestapo. No, replied the ZOB, it was the ZZW that might endanger security, demanding open membership to all Jews! Didn't they realize that the Gestapo could penetrate a mass organization? Furthermore, a large influx of recruits might wreck the network of close personal and ideological relationships that would be essential in a suicidal, last-ditch battle. This dispute led to another: Why didn't the ZZW leaders reveal their source of arms so that ZOB fighters could get some, too? No doubt the Fascists were supplying them, the ZOB cynically hinted.

Despite this mutual distrust, a few days before the final *Aktion* was to start, Mordechai Anielewicz and Zivia Lubetkin visited ZZW headquarters for new unity talks and departed with smiles and an understanding that they would shortly return to seal the union—at 1 A.M., April 19. If there was still time before the Germans struck.

Mordechai had apparently begun to appreciate the practical nature of the ZZW. It could be a useful partner. Unlike his own organization, it did not call on its members to die in the ghetto, weapons in hand. The ZZW fighters hoped to use their weapons long after the ghetto had gone up in smoke, fleeing to the forests to continue the battle. To make their escape possible—and also to smuggle in arms and supplies before and during the uprising—they built, as the ZOB did not, special bunkers and several subterranean tunnels to the Aryan side.

One tunnel, fifty yards long, stretched from the cellar of ZZW headquarters, at Muranowska 7, to the cellar of Muranowska 6, on the other side of the wall. A masterful engineering triumph, it was the creation of another Polish officer, Captian Cezarea Ketling-Harpad, who, on his own initiative, supervised its construction while also smuggling arms to the ZZW.* The fighters had to bolster the tunnel roof with a forest of props because the heavy traffic in Muranowski Square overhead might have caused the road to collapse. When the tunnel was finally completed, they dug passageways that branched off from it to the cellars of heavily fortified buildings all along the way.

Another tunnel led from the sewer system to a cellar at Karmelicka 5, ZZW headquarters in the Productive Ghetto. Now, in the late afternoon of April 18, Captain Iwanski and his men would tread this route into the ghetto, laden with arms—arms for greeting the Germans with a deadly surprise.

From his position by the manhole in the courtyard of Zlota 49, Iwanski could see the porter of his own building, standing with one of his men across the street by the gate. They were pretending to talk lightheartedly while glancing in all directions. Iwanski slowly pulled a handkerchief from his breast pocket, removed his cap, and wiped his forehead. That was the signal. In a moment his deputy, Lieutenant Zajdler, and a companion were rolling a tarpaulin-covered handcart piled with boxes across the street and into the courtyard of Zlota 49.

When the cart arrived at the manhole, Iwanski's men pulled off the tarpaulin and with ropes lowered the boxes into the sewer. Then each of them grabbed a box and started on the long trek through the sewer, following Tomasz, who carried an electric torch. For about half an hour they trudged through evil-smelling muck while water dripped on them maddeningly from the ceiling. . . . Finally, the signal came: "Attention—silence!"

They had reached their destination—the exit at Karmelicka 5.

*The following document from the Home Army archives deals with the effort of Ketling, whose code name was Arpad, to help the ZZW, and reflects the attitude of many Home Army officers toward the Jewish plight:

"Home Army 203/IX—12. Documents of the Special Military Tribunal in the case of 'Arpad.' Arpad established contact with the ghetto. . . . Allegedly there are 150 young Jews there who are fairly well armed and determined to take all risks. He conducts with this group business affairs and supplies arms. . . . The above mentioned Jewish group seeks through Arpad to establish contact with Teodor . . . in order to coordinate certain large sabotage actions which they want to carry out in the nearest future. [Signed] Mal. [Annotation by hand] Arpad, it seems, has found for himself a new field of activity. My opinion is that this man is heading for deep trouble. I prohibited Malakie . . . from giving [the Jews] any contacts whatsoever. [Signed] M."

In a few moments the men found themselves in a low basement without windows, where several Jews were waiting for them. They all shook hands, and someone asked, "How was it, tell us, how was it?"

"There was . . . shit," Zajdler replied succinctly.

"Well, don't you think I smell it?"

When Iwanski and the others had unloaded their burdens, they entered an adjoining cellar where, in the light of electric torches, they could discern the dim outlines of human figures. A child was crying, and people talked in whispers. They had gathered in the hope of returning to the Aryan side with Iwanski.

A woman with a kerchief around her head approached Zajdler. She was a weird skeletal figure with sunken cheeks and huge eyes that glittered in the light of the torches.

"Will you take us with you, gentlemen?" she pleaded. "I am with my little daughter. I beg you, please take us out of this hell."

Zajdler felt like choking. The only thing he could see were her big black eyes filled with wild fear, staring at him. He cleared his throat.

"Of course, ma'am."

She took his hand. "Oh, how wonderful, how good that is!"

Iwanski quietly instructed the departing civilians how to enter the manhole. Shadows played eerily upon the peeling walls and ceiling, lending to an atmosphere like that of a medieval torture chamber. A woman sobbed softly in a corner. A man quieted her: "Hush! Next time, maybe, I'll get out of here, and we'll be together again. Now then, calm down. . . ."

A final farewell. A kiss. A handshake. Then into the manhole again.

Dragging weapons through the sewer had been almost relaxing compared to the problems now burdening Iwanski and his men. They took turns carrying the children piggyback, but they could not walk very far like this since they had to move in a stooped position to avoid hitting their heads against the ceiling. Every dozen steps or so, the men felt a sharp pain in their backs and had to stop and rest.

Finally the party arrived at the sewer opening in the courtyard of Zlota 49, where their trek had begun. On emerging, all hurried to Iwanski's flat across the street. Some would be sent to other hiding places, while a few would stay and be cared for by the captain's wife, Wiktoria. Although Wiktoria didn't know it, she had already

65

contracted tuberculosis from treating a sickly Jewish girl with that disease.

Never mind the risks. What they had to do, they had to do.[5]

Shortly after Mordechai Anielewicz's final briefing, in the late afternoon of April 18, Lutek Rotblatt, one of the ZOB commanders present, glumly arrived home at Muranowska 44 and ordered his wife, Hela Schipper, to move up to their bunker in the attic. In the morning the SS would launch a new *Aktion*, he explained.

"But I want to go with you to fight them," Hela protested.

"Never mind. Just go up there with mother. She needs you."

Hela knew from the look in Lutek's intense dark eyes that nothing she could say would persuade him. How foolish he was. They were all doomed, anyway. Why should they not die together? And besides, like Lutek, she was a leader of the conservative Zionist youth group, Akiva, and was used to taking chances and risking her life.

Normally based in the ghetto of Cracow, Hela was a courier who dared to travel openly in trains around Poland. Weeks earlier she had come to the Warsaw Ghetto to get money to buy arms for the Cracow fighters; but as she was trying to sneak out, she was detained by the police, who claimed she had a "Jewish nose." She broke away, however, and escaped, though she was shot in the leg. She had to remain in the Warsaw Ghetto. But her leg was well enough now. She could fight; yet she did not insist. Perhaps it was her duty to remain with Maria, Lutek's mother.

Maria. What a saintly person, Hela felt. And Lutek and his mother were so close, so dear to each other. Some months earlier, Lutek had been reluctant to join the ZOB together with the other members of Akiva because he felt he could not leave his mother or his children. Lutek and Maria had run an orphanage. Now there was only his mother. . . .

"The eighty children, as you can see, have been protected by us from the first day, and we have pulled them through safely despite all the deportations, selections, and other accursed problems." Lutek was speaking with his friend Jonas Turkow, in September 1942, while both hid in Lutek's bunker during an intensive *Aktion*.

"Let us hope we will live to see the liberation together with the children," he continued. "But it will not come by itself. It has to be won with arms in hand."

Lutek, wearing swimming trunks, and Jonas, stripped to the waist, were sitting in a corner of the steaming, almost airless bunker. Jonas, a famous Yiddish actor, deeply admired his host. Resembling a bronzed god, Lutek was indefatigable as he directed life in the hideout, which sheltered about 120 persons, including the 80 orphans and their teachers.

If he wasn't caring for someone who had fainted, he was distributing medicine and food or quietly telling the children stories. Meanwhile, Maria darted from child to child to see that each was as comfortable as possible. Because she wanted to stay with the children, she had rejected an opportunity to escape from the ghetto and work for a Polish friend in a provincial town where she would be relatively safe. She had even adopted a teenaged girl, Dolcia.

Suddenly Lutek and Jonas heard someone running up the stairs. One of Lutek's friends burst in and cried, "They are coming!"

A group of Jewish policemen working for the Gestapo were searching the houses for people who had not reported for selection as ordered. They carried axes, pickaxes, and hammers to break down doors—those that they could find. The occupants of Lutek's attic bunker, which had a carefully camouflaged entrance, froze as they heard the policemen crash into room after room in the building.

They could distinctly hear the voice of the dreaded Major Jacob Lejkin, the new chief of the Jewish Order Service, whose predecessor, Colonel Josef Szerynski, had recently been shot and severely wounded by a ZOB fighter. Lejkin was a lawyer and, oddly enough, a professed Zionist. His motive for cooperating with the Gestapo was said to be more sophisticated than that of the two thousand policemen under his command.

Most of these policemen, sons from wealthy families who could buy this relatively safe job, served with fiendish dedication. They hoped to survive at the expense of other Jews while lining their pockets with bribes offered by their helpless prey in return for freedom. When the Gestapo required each to round up at least seven Jews daily, some even turned in their own parents to meet the quota, rationalizing that they were old and would soon die anyway. The Nazi extermination program had brought out the most savage as well as the most heroic instincts in some of its intended victims.

Lejkin's zeal in tracking down Jews more than matched the bestiality of his men. But he was motivated mainly, according to subordinates, by the theory of the "lesser evil": the brutal, rapid snatching of four thousand persons today and five thousand tomorrow would in the long run save two hundred thousand. The Germans would be content with exterminating a sizable minority.

Whatever his ultimate aim, Lejkin tried his best to round up as many Jews as possible. At one point he managed to overload the death trains with hungry "volunteers" whom he had offered three kilos of bread and one of jam if they reported to Umschlagplatz for transfer to "labor camps."

Lutek and his fellows now heard Lejkin approach the attic and stop just on the other side of their bunker wall. Then the police chief searched through rooms strewn with the belongings of the children and teachers.

"But there are people hiding here," he exclaimed. "And Lejkin does not give up."

After a while, however, he did give up; and the children survived—for some weeks. But eventually almost all were found and deported; and Lutek, almost crazed with grief and lust for vengeance, joined the ZOB and turned his home into a training ground for its members.

"I can now look into the sky and see the stars," he told Hela as they sat by the window one night.

And the stars were bright on the night of April 18, 1943.[6]

Earlier that day Chaim Frimer had been thankful that all was quiet in the ghetto. He could now go home to visit his father and his teenaged sister, who lived only several blocks from Mila 29 in the Central Ghetto, where his combat group was based. There he would clean up, wash his clothes, relax, and prove to his frantically worried father that he was still alive.

His father had been worried ever since he learned that Chaim had joined the ZOB, for his capture would mean torture and certain death. But Chaim might escape extermination if he just minded his own business and continued working for the Germans in Brauer's shop, a large clothing factory in the Central Ghetto.

68

He was young and strong, and the Germans needed such workers.

It was in November 1942 that Chaim had first made contact with the ZOB. He had gone to the post office one day to seek a letter when he saw a tall, dark, Semitic-looking man with glasses, a large mustache, and a beard. The man looked familiar. Could it be Israel Kanal in disguise? Israel, who had shared with him all the joys and sorrows of childhood and youth? Memories flooded Chaim's mind. He went outside to wait for the man, who came out and motioned with his eyes for Chaim to follow him. It was indeed Israel. They entered a courtyard and Israel whispered, "We'll meet tomorrow evening at the corner of Mila and Zamenhof. It is a matter of great importance."

Chaim had vaguely heard that a Jewish underground had been formed. He guessed that Israel Kanal was a member and was thrilled at the thought that he might get a chance to fight before he died. . . .

What Chaim did not know was that Israel had made his mark on Jewish history by having been the first Jew to shoot an enemy in the Warsaw Ghetto. Shortly after the first great *Aktion* started on July 22, the Communist PPR, which had hardly any weapons of its own, decided on a symbolic action against the Nazis. A PPR agent, Henryk Kotlicki, hiding a pistol in the sleeve of his stolen black leather SS jacket, managed to sneak into the ghetto. He casually walked through the streets until he came to CENTOS, a child-care institution.

As Kotlicki entered an outer office, Josef Barski, another PPR agent who was an official at the institution, stood up in alarm as he heard an employee cry, "The Germans are coming!"

Barski almost fainted. The intrusion, he thought, undoubtedly meant deportation, especially when he came out and saw a man wearing an SS jacket pull a pistol out of his sleeve.

"Here's the pistol you asked for," Kotlicki said.*

*The PPR managed to smuggle into the ghetto four more pistols shortly after the deportations started, but on September 3, 1942, the Gestapo captured a woman fighter while she was carrying this "arsenal" from one point to another, once more leaving members of the future ZOB without any arms at all. The same day, two of the top Jewish underground leaders, Josef Kaplan and Shmuel Breslaw, were also captured. An early uprising was thus out of the question.

Barski gasped in relief. Within two weeks Israel Kanal, with this pistol in hand, was ready to fire the first bullet of resistance. Israel seemed the logical man for the job. He was to assassinate the then chief of the Jewish police, Colonel Szerynski, a convert from Judaism who in a frenzy of fear and hatred for his former coreligionists, was cooperating so unreservedly in the deportations that he would not even permit the release or escape of certain Jews whom some decent German officers had tried to save. Since Israel was himself a policeman, serving as a spy for the ZOB, he would have an easier time than other underground fighters obtaining access to Szerynski.

Dressed in his policeman's attire, Israel managed to enter Szerynski's well-guarded house on the pretext that he had a letter for him. While the police chief was reading the letter, Israel shot and severely wounded him. Szerynski, though tortured by pain, continued to live for several months, then committed suicide. A few weeks later his replacement, Major Lejkin, also fell dead from a ZOB bullet. Israel had fired the symbolic shot that was to signal the beginning of the Jews' campaign to fight their torturers and slayers, a shot that would still be echoing more than thirty years later in the Middle East. . . .

The evening after their first encounter, Chaim Frimer met Israel Kanal again, and they walked into a courtyard to talk. As Chaim expected, his friend told him about a new resistance organization that had few weapons other than knives and sticks. Would Chaim like to join? Trying hard to conceal his excitement, Chaim replied that he would. Now he had to recruit five men in his factory who would eventually become full-fledged ZOB members.

A few days later Chaim and some of his recruits met with Israel, who briefed them on the workings of the ZOB. From that time on, the group gathered twice a week for weapons training in Lutek Rotblatt's house, at Muranowska 44, while Lutek's mother, Maria, with one of her orphans beside her, sat guard in the corridor by the door.

Finally the long-awaited moment came. The weapons instructor said that his pupils now knew enough about pistols, and he marked the occasion with a shot into the ceiling. The noise reverberated like a command from heaven, and Chaim and his fellow novices stood amazed and somehow enthralled by the miracle.

They were no longer sheep, but fighters.

70

Now, several weeks later, Chaim went home a "seasoned veteran." His sister Krysia greeted him joyfully. She worshiped her brother, regarding him as some kind of magic creature designated by God to take part in sublime actions. She had long pleaded with him to get his superiors to let her join the ZOB, too. But Chaim preferred that she stay with their father, who was worried enough about him. And the ZOB hardly had enough weapons for its present members, anyway. So Krysia had to be satisfied with listening to accounts of her brother's exploits. . . .

Chaim told her, for example, about his role in "tax-collecting" operations designed to squeeze cash for arms from rich ghetto residents, by force if necessary. On one occasion, a tax of fifty thousand zlotys was imposed on the Judenrat chief, Marek Lichtenbaum, who was despised as a zealously obedient German puppet. Lichtenbaum had replaced Adam Czerniakow, a weak, servile, but well-meaning man who had committed suicide in July 1942, when he learned that he was to facilitate the deportation of his people to death camps.* When Lichtenbaum refused to pay the tax, Chaim and his comrades decided to kidnap his son for ransom.

Lutek Rotblatt, who knew the son by sight, called at the Lichtenbaum home one day, posing as a doctor visiting a sick member of the family after arranging the hoax with the real doctor. As he left the house he kept his hat on, thereby signaling that the son was in. Other plotters then entered, kidnapped the boy, and took him to the ZOB "prison," a well-guarded hidden room where he was well cared for. The next day the father paid the tax, and his son was freed, dramatically demonstrating that the Jewish fighters, and not the Nazi-controlled Judenrat, now ruled the ghetto.

Krysia was enthralled by Chaim's stories about ZOB efforts to

*On July 23, 1942, the second day after the deportations from the Warsaw Ghetto started, Czerniakow wrote in his diary, "It is 3 o'clock. So far there are 4000 who have to go. By 4 o'clock—according to the orders—there have to be [another] 4000." He then wrote a note to the Judenrat executive committee saying that he could not hand over helpless children to the Nazis. "I am powerless," he went on. "My heart trembles in sorrow and compassion. I can no longer bear all this. My act will prove to everyone what is the right thing to do." He had cooperated with the Germans too long, he apparently felt, even though he did so in the hope of alleviating each blow. Czerniakow removed a potassium cyanide tablet from his desk drawer and swallowed it, dying before he could carry out any further orders.

assassinate Jewish traitors such as Szmerling, who headed the especially brutal Jewish police detachment that loaded fellow Jews into the boxcars at Umschlagplatz. Chaim and his group captured the compound where the Jewish police lived and, after lining up all the policemen, demanded that they reveal the secret apartment where Szmerling lived. When they refused, the families of the policemen were led into the courtyard as if they were about to be executed.

"Tell them everything!" one woman cried. "We don't have to die because of him."

The policemen finally cracked. The fighters rushed to Szmerling's apartment and broke in, but the traitor locked himself in a room. Chaim looked through the keyhole and saw him standing by an open window. Szmerling was waiting for the Jews to try the door; then he would call the German guards standing nearby at an entrance to the ghetto. Chaim and his fellows therefore decided to retreat, but Szmerling became so fearful that he apparently lost the confidence of his masters. He disappeared, and it was rumored that the Germans killed him. . . .

But the most heroic incident of all to Krysia took place only several days before her brother's visit home. Chaim was assigned the task of taking five pistols and twenty thousand zlotys from his group at Mila 29 to another at Nalewki 33, several blocks away. He asked his commander, Berl Broide, for an escort, but Berl replied, "It's very early. The streets are empty, and I'm sure you'll manage."

When Chaim reached the corner of Mila and Nalewki, however, hands suddenly grabbed him from behind. Two Polish policemen who had been guarding the Judenrat bank had captured him. Chaim identified himself as a member of the ZOB. After all, they were Poles, not Germans. If they harmed him, he said, his comrades would take revenge. He was carrying money and weapons for the resistance, and reaching his destination was a matter of life and death for the Jews.

The policemen took the money and pistols from Chaim and led him into the bank building. But he broke away and ran for help. A short time later, on orders from Mordechai Anielewicz, ZOB fighters surrounded the building and cut the telephone line. One of them then delivered a message to the besieged policemen, ordering them to give up the money and arms or be killed. But they agreed to surrender only the weapons. Chaim volunteered to go into the bank once more to try to convince them to give back the money. As soon as he stepped in the door, however, the policemen took him prisoner again. As they all sat down, Chaim said, "Fine, now we are all prisoners. I'm yours and you're ours."

While Chaim appealed to their Polish patriotism, the bank manager arrived and demanded to know what was going on. In the confusion Chaim again escaped. The policemen followed but found themselves facing a group of armed ZOB fighters at the door. The two Poles agreed to give up the money as well as the weapons.

When Chaim went home that evening and was putting his pistol under his pillow, his father, who had been told that his son was seen fleeing during a bank robbery, lamented with tears in his eyes, "These are wonderful days. My own son has become a bandit who robs banks."

But when Chaim explained to his father and sister what really happened, "my son, the bandit" suddenly became a messiah. . . .

Now Chaim was home again. He had just begun to relate new adventures to his adoring sister when the messenger of Israel Kanal, who had just been appointed the new commander of the Central Ghetto sector, burst in with a message. Chaim must return immediately to his group. Had anything happened? he asked. The messenger did not know.

Chaim guessed. He rushed out, sensing that his next adventure would be one he would never get to relate to Krysia.[7]

Feigele Peltel crouched atop the brick ghetto wall, clutching the package of dynamite wrapped in greasy paper. On the eve of the uprising she was going into the ghetto on a smuggling mission. The atmosphere was uneasy near the gate, but Polish smugglers, paid well to assist her, had placed a ladder against the wall, which she quickly climbed.

On reaching the top she had looked for her ghetto contacts, who were to help her descend on the ghetto side. But they were nowhere to be seen. That meant trouble inside the ghetto. Suddenly gunfire echoed in the distance, and while everyone ran for cover, including the Polish smugglers, the ladder was snatched away. . . .

"*Alle Juden herunter!*" ("All Jews come down!")

Feigele and her family pulled on their coats and moved on tiptoes. Perhaps the SS would not search their apartment. They heard shots and the crash of glass, then hoarse cries.

"Down! Lie down on the floor!"

Through the wall they could hear furniture being moved and a woman begging for mercy for her ailing father. Then a banging on the door. The soldiers, German-led Ukrainians, entered Feigele's flat.

"Downstairs all of you, and be quick about it!"

It was August 2, 1942, a little more than a week after the first *Aktion* had started. The turn of Feigele and her family had come. Treblinka beckoned. Hugging bundles they had previously prepared, they clambered down the stairs into the courtyard to join a trembling mass of Jews already assembled there. A man lay in a pool of blood, whimpering for help. Another was felled by a rifle butt when he pleaded that he had a work certificate giving him the right to live. Where was her mother? Her brother? Feigele, almost suffocating in the crush of jostling humanity, could barely move. Oh, God, where were they?

"Have your employment cards ready for inspection!"

Almost every hand clasped a scrap of paper. Some were legitimate work certificates, others fake. When the *Aktion* began, the Germans announced that registered workers would not be deported. Panic to find work swept through the ghetto, and Jews were ready to give up anything to the German industrialists—money, jewels, all that they owned—in return for a life-preserving employment card.

"Left! . . . Left! . . . Right! . . ."

Two Jewish policemen escorted each person. They directed their victims either to the right, a place on the sidewalk, meaning life; or to the left, the middle of the street, signifying death.

"Man to the right; wife and child to the left!"

The man pleaded. Then a cry of anguish, and all were shoved to the left.

A moon-faced German read the letter Feigele had placed in his hand. Not a genuine employment card but a scribbled note simply

74

authorizing her to register at a workshop run by Walter Caspar Többens, the German industrialist. He looked into her pleading blue eyes.

"Is this *your* employment card?"

"Yes, my employment card from Többens."

Feigele numbly waited for the verdict.

"To the right!"

"Feige—Feige—" Feigele, as she stood on the sidewalk dazed and nearly drained of consciousness, thought she heard her brother's voice calling from one of the trucks in which the Jews were being piled. . . .

"Vladka, Vladka! Hold on!"

It was Jurek Blones, one of Feigele's ghetto contacts, calling her by her code name. Within a minute, he had helped her climb down into the ghetto. They streaked into a building opposite and ran up the stairs to the attic, where they crawled under a heap of feathers and bedsheets. Footsteps and voices grew louder, then gradually faded in the distance. They were safe for the moment. They went down into the street again and stealthily made their way to Swientojerska 32 in the Brushmakers' District, the ZOB headquarters for this sector.

Fighters of the Bund were defending this area, and Feigele, who worked for the Bund on the Aryan side, brought the precious dynamite to add to the ZOB store of explosives. Things had changed since her last visit. There were new bunks, new people, and a new feeling of pride and confidence. During one light moment a fighter posed fiercely in a German uniform that had been stolen from a clothing factory. The uniform would be used to confuse the Nazis when the fighting began.

Feigele's friends showed her the new "munitions factory" they had set up in a dark room with tightly curtained windows. As she walked through the door, a pungent odor assaulted her nostrils. Gradually, in the blackness, she made out two young men sitting at a long table splotched with chemicals. One was slowly stirring the contents of a huge cask, the other carefully bottling the fluid.

A scrawny thirteen-year-old boy, Lusiek Blones, Yurek's brother and the youngest ZOB member, suddenly noticed Feigele and rushed to her. Could she send more bottles for Molotov cocktails from the Aryan side? When she had promised to try, he returned to his work, lining up bottle after bottle against the wall. Feigele stared at the determined faces around her. Each somehow reflected the sancitity of the room.

"Several nights ago we tested a grenade of our own making," someone remarked, breaking the silence. "You should have heard the bang and seen the flash! The German sentry must have been frightened out of his wits."

Then Abrasha Blum entered. The inspirational Bund political leader was as calm and unperturbed as ever. A lanky intellectual with glasses and thinning hair, he was the idol of the Bundist fighters, though he himself was too physically weak to fight. . . .

It had been Abrasha who recruited Feigele in October 1942, when she was working in a ghetto factory. She looked like a gentile, he said. She had fair hair and classic features, although her blue eyes were somewhat mournful, as Jewish eyes usually were at the time. She would serve as a ZOB agent, buying weapons, finding hideouts for Jews.

Feigele was thrilled. She could hardly believe the offer. To work full-time for the resistance. To leave behind the horrors of the factory. . . .

"They're already in the courtyard!"

The heart pounded in a moment of terrifying stillness. Then a crash, and the tramp of boots on creaky stairs. The supervisor called out, "They're here! Do not look at the door. Keep busy!"

Sewing machines chattered. "They" burst in.

"Are all the workers here? Is no one hiding?"

"No, *Herr Offizier.*"

They rummaged through stacks of cut cloth. Heads stayed down, eyes on the needles. A maddening orchestra of death. A child cried. A woman wailed. They had found the hidden youngster.

"Keep working, keep working!" hissed the supervisor.

The orchestra grew louder. Then: "They're gone!"

Bedlam. Who had been taken? How many? Several old people. The mother. The child.

Back to work. Suddenly the pain again. The terrible pain in her feet, which had swollen from hunger.

"Keep working! Keep working!"

They would be back. . . .

One night, shortly after her talk with Abrasha, Feigele heard a knock on the door, and a tall blond man entered.

"Michal, what a pleasant surprise. What brings you here?"

Michal Klepfisz, an engineer who had long been active in the Bund, replied, "I've come to take you away, Feigele. Get ready. You'll be leaving the ghetto within two days. I'll wait for you by the ghetto gate at eight in the morning. You'll have to walk out with a labor battalion; that's the best way."

Soon Feigele was at work on the Aryan side, buying arms from Polish merchants who had stolen or purchased them from German soldiers and Polish policemen. Then, with Arie Wilner and later Yitzhak Zuckerman cooperating, these arms were smuggled into the ghetto. But there were never enough. Yurek Blones came from the ghetto one day and reported on how the fighters were frantically preparing for the forthcoming battle. He had come to plead for more arms.

"But we hardly know anyone who will sell us arms," Feigele started to explain.

"That is your problem. I can't help you with that. All I want is to urge you to hurry—or it may be too late."

The next morning, with a sense of desperation, Michal Klepfisz came to visit Feigele in her cellar hideout on Gornoszlonska Street. He opened a chemistry book he was carrying and read aloud a passage explaining how to make a bomb from potash, hydrochloric acid, cyanide, sugar, and gasoline.

"It's worth a try," Michal said.

"But what about the equipment?"

"We'll try to mix the chemicals in ordinary bottles. Something just might come out of it."

"Do you really think these bottles will help the ghetto?"

"Do I think so! If we can only succeed!"

Michal studied the formula late into the night. . . .

Now, on her visit to the ghetto munitions factory on the eve of the uprising, Feigele observed with joy and wonder the fruit of that conversation.

The ZOB was anticipating an *Aktion* at any moment, said Abrasha Blum when he greeted her. The Germans would try to deport all the Warsaw Jews, but they would not succeed without a fight. ZOB observers, changed every two hours, were watching the Nazis' every move.

"On your next visit," Abrasha added, "I will show you a whole row of bunkers. If the struggle should continue for a considerable time, you will know where to find us."[8]

Walther Caspar Többens, a tall handsome man of thirty-four, stared with cold blue eyes at each of his Jewish managers as he stood imperiously before them in his long leather coat, booted legs apart and hands gripping a riding whip. Többens was the most important German industrialist in the ghetto. His workshops on Leszno and Prosta streets employed some twelve thousand workers—almost half of the surviving ghetto employees—who turned out military clothing and other products for the Wehrmacht.

Többens and the other industrialists were tightly bound to their Jewish workers by a cord of common interest. The Jews needed these Germans to give them jobs that might prolong their "right" to live, and these Germans needed the Jews to serve as slaves in their profitable enterprises.*

As dusk blended into night, Többens called in the Jewish managers of his factories and spoke to them in a foreboding tone. The SS, he said, would carry out an *Aktion* in the Central Ghetto the next day, but the Productive Ghetto would not be touched. All his workers and their families must "volunteer" for work in the labor camp at Poniatow, in the Lublin district to the east, where they would live out the war in comfort and security.

When he finished speaking, Többens walked out and ordered an aide to lock all the managers in the room until morning so that they could not spread news of the new *Aktion*.

Többens was in a surly mood. Millions of marks were at stake, but neither Himmler nor the Jews would cooperate with him. Perhaps now, with death the only alternative, the stubborn ghetto workers would agree to be transferred east. Since Himmler was determined to destroy the ghetto, Többens, as the newly appoint-

---

*In April 1942, Ringelblum noted in his diary: "The history of man knows no similar tragedy. A nation that hates the Germans with all its soul can ransom itself from death only at the price of its contribution to the enemy's victory, a victory which means its complete extermination in Europe and perhaps in the whole world."

ed commissioner for resettlement, had to move not only his own workers and equipment but those of other ghetto industrialists to the Lublin area—either to Poniatow, where his would go, or to a second labor camp at Trawniki. If the workers refused to volunteer, the SS might send all of them to the gas chambers and perhaps destroy all of his equipment.

Did he deserve such treatment? Hadn't he collaborated closely with the SS? How often, at Umschlagplatz, had he bent forward to glance at documents, numbers, faces, and indicated with a jerk of his whip those workers he could do without, those who must die? Now, if *all* of them were killed, he would be left without a labor force; or at best he would be forced to hire Poles, whom he would have to pay and treat like human beings. Why kill Jews who could do valuable work for the Germans, who would pay for this honor with everything they owned?

And if he had been magnanimous enough to hire them, thus saving them from death, should they not be grateful enough to volunteer for transfer? Typical Jewish arrogance. In the past few weeks, he had appealed to them, pleaded with them, promised them everything. But still, except for a handful, they would not budge.

The root of Többens' trouble was the Jewish underground. Ever since it had forced the Germans to call off the *Aktion* started on January 18, the Jews listened to the resistance. And through wall posters, clandestine literature, and agents in the shops the resistance was telling the workers not to leave voluntarily for the labor camps. The transfer was a new trick to feed the gas chambers. Even if they were sent to work, they would be killed within a few months. They should stay in the ghetto and resist if the Germans tried to take them by force. The underground would help them. Better to die resisting, whether actively or passively. And almost all the workers obeyed.

Többens demanded that the Judenrat order the workers to leave. But its usually pliant leader, Marek Lichtenbaum, threatened by the resistance with death and already forced to pay ransom to the ZOB for his kidnapped son, could only reply, "Another government rules here."

Többens then visited the shops personally, sometimes drunk, almost always with a riding whip, and warned the workers that the underground was simply irresponsible rabble that didn't care what happened to the people. He plastered posters alongside those of the resistance.*

"Only I can save you," he repeated again and again.

Though Többens never dared to admit openly that Jews sent "elsewhere" were exterminated, he made it clear that if they wanted to live they had better choose Poniatow and Trawniki over Treblinka. How could they refuse? Schools, hospitals, even a swimming pool and a concert orchestra would be theirs. They would be living in a worker's heaven.

Többens had sent a dozen Jewish collaborators to the two camps to verify the conditions, and they had returned with glowing reports. But the underground shot one and beat up some of the others, and the workers still would not bite. Többens persevered. He challenged the ZOB to meet with him for a debate, but the ZOB contemptuously ignored the challenge.

When persuasion had clearly failed, Többens considered transferring the workers by force. But the risks involved in a full-scale *Aktion* would be too great, he decided. The underground threatened to destroy all the shops, and all his precious workers might be killed—either in battle or in the death camps, where the SS wanted to send them anyway. Himmler was a shortsighted idealist, Többens silently raged. Killing Jews was more important to him than producing military goods—and making money. The Reichsführer had no sense of balance.

Többens thus arranged his own discreet *Aktionen.* On March 29

*Többens posted the following proclamation throughout the ghetto on March 20, 1943: "The headquarters of the Jewish Fighting Organization issued a proclamation on the night of March 14–15 which I want to answer. I can state categorically that: (1) there is no question of deportation; (2) neither Mr. Schultz nor myself has received orders, at gunpoint, to proceed with deportations; (3) the last transport has indeed reached its destination. . . . Jewish armament workers, don't believe those who are trying to mislead you! They want to force you into acts whose consequences would be incalculable. The bunkers offer no safety and life in them or in the Aryan quarter is not possible. Insecurity and inactivity will undermine the morale of men who are used to working. Let me ask you: Why are the rich Jews leaving the Aryan quarter and coming to me to ask for employment? They have enough money to live in the Aryan quarter, but they cannot put up with such a hunted existence. I advise you to go to Trawniki or Poniatow. You can live there and wait for the end of the war. The leaders of the Jewish Fighting Organization cannot help you; they can only make hollow promises. . . . You have enough experience to understand and see through their tricks. Have confidence in the German factory managers; they are always on your side. . . . Take your wives and children with you; we shall care for them."

he stood at a ghetto gate with his managers, and when workers from the Aryan side returned to the ghetto, he herded many of them directly to Umschlagplatz, where boxcars were waiting to take them to the labor camps. On April 5 he had the workers of one factory surrounded during working hours and hauled off to the cars.

Többens also tackled the problem of parents who were reluctant to transfer for fear that their children might be taken from them. He set up a kindergarten in the ghetto, telling the parents that the children would be "taken care of" there while they were at work. He kept his word.

One day a truck drove up to the kindergarten, and all the children were taken to Umschlagplatz. However, the parents learned of this and ran from the workshops in panic to plead with Többens to save their children. Többens, condemning this "scandalous" event, brought them back. According to eyewitnesses, Többens then called for another truck and personally helped to remove the children quickly and quietly, before the parents could find out. Now they had no offspring to worry about, and of course, the SS was pleased with the catch.

Finally Többens decided to test the strength of the resistance. He would evacuate the machinery of another, smaller industrialist's factory, Hallman's woodworking shop. After all, why should he experiment with his own equipment? But the workers at Hallman's refused to allow the machines to be dragged out, and that night a ZOB group set fire to the building, destroying everything in it.

Többens tried again. The machines from the Schultz and Schilling Brush Works were loaded onto trucks, but before the vehicles reached Umschlagplatz for unloading on freight cars, another ZOB unit set the trucks afire and wrecked their contents. Out of 1600 workers, 250 volunteers accompanied the trucks but changed their minds and managed to escape in the confusion. And though sixty were caught by the thirty soldiers guarding the convoy, they were freed by other ZOB partisans.

Többens was desperate, and even alcohol, which he imbibed in vast quantities, could not ease his misery. Nor could the parties at which he forced young Jewish girls to dance in the nude. Not only might he lose the chance to make more millions, but he might lose what he had. He might even end up on the Russian front or in a concentration camp. The whole painstakingly built industrial em-

81

pire of Walther Caspar Többens was teetering on the brink of disaster—after all the work, the dreams, the bribes. . . .

Többens had worked in a Bremen coffee roasting plant until he realized that he could amass enormous wealth from Hitler's Jewish policy. He joined the National Socialist Party in 1937, then bought out seven Jewish shops for almost nothing. Building his career on this cornerstone, he swiftly moved into the Polish economic vacuum after Poland's fall in 1939 and found the ghetto a vulture's paradise. By 1943, with the approval of well-bribed and lavishly entertained Nazi officials, he had confiscated the plants and machinery of countless Warsaw Jews, who offered to pay him to remain as his managers and thereby be under his protective wing.

Nor were Többens' workers an overhead drain. They, too, paid him for jobs, which they were led to believe meant life instead of death. They didn't complain either when, after the deportations began in July 1942, Többens saw no need to give them even the minimal wages he had paid previously or to require less than a twelve- or fourteen-hour working day. Let the Jews survive on a daily piece of bread and bowl of watery soup. They would soon be dead, anyway. And there would be others to replace the dead . . . if the SS was not too greedy for victims.

But Többens was not the only profiteer in the ghetto. Other ambitious industrialists, most notably Fritz Schultz, also bribed their way in, while some German officers grabbed a piece of the action for themselves.

First Lieutenant Franz Konrad, a food merchant in civilian life, could just visualize the marks rolling in when he was appointed manager of the Werterfassung, an SS department that collected abandoned Jewish property after an *Aktion* and shipped it off to Germany. After all, who would care if he kept a few odds and ends for himself: stamp collections, richly woven carpets, ancient objects of art. His appetite grew.

Finally, he and two Jewish businessmen, Kohn and Heller, who were well-known Nazi collaborators, opened several enterprises, some for the sale of Jewish property. In early 1943 these enterprises merged to form an SS-controlled company, Ostindustrie.

Other shareholders whose pockets were splitting from their gains included General Krüger, Colonel von Sammern-Frankenegg, and Major General Odilo Globocnik, SS and police commander in Lublin and head of Operation Reinhardt, the code word for the confiscation of Jewish property throughout the General Government. Not among them was General Stroop, whose ideological puritanism would not permit him to mix money with murder.

Despite the threat of civilian and SS competition, Többens could see nothing ahead but mounting profits—until Himmler visited the ghetto on January 9, 1943. The Reichsführer was enraged. Three months earlier he had ordered that all the Jews be deported by the end of the year. And here it was January and "forty thousand" were still infesting the ghetto. Disgraceful. The remaining Jews must be resettled immediately, he ordered.

It was Többens who was responsible for this, Himmler was sure, Többens and the other greedy businessmen. They wanted to keep the Jews to fatten themselves on war profits. They could learn patriotism better on the Russian front, he hinted. No more than sixteen thousand workers were needed for the factories, and they would be transferred with the machines and raw materials to the Lublin labor camps. Himmler then stormed off to Cracow and ordered General Krüger to audit Többens' profits, since "Többens had apparently become a millionaire thanks to the cheap Jewish labor force."

So Többens was in danger of losing everything, including his life. He needed time, time to worm his way back into Nazi favor. Mordechai Anielewicz and his comrades helped him when, on January 18, SS troops carrying out Himmler's order to round up the surviving Jews were greeted with gunfire and forced to leave the ghetto. Többens had a chance to exploit the shock and confusion.

On January 31 he signed an agreement with General Globocnik, who like Többens was consumed with two passions: whiskey and wealth. Globocnik, whose duties included running the whole concentration camp system in Poland, also enjoyed sending Jews to their death—if they could not be used to enrich him. He once stood watching the smoking chimney at Auschwitz while chatting enthusiastically with the camp commander about the "fantastic" extermination plans that he would soon put into effect. His superiors admired his ingenuity and shrewdness.

"Beginning with Lublin," Goebbels wrote in his diary on March 27, 1942, "the Jews in the General Government are now being evacuated eastwards. The procedure is a pretty barbaric one and not to be described here more definitely. Not much will remain of the Jews. . . . The Former Gauleiter of Vienna [Globocnik], who is to carry this measure through, is doing it with considerable circumspection and according to a method that does not attract too much attention. . . . "

Now, in his deal with Többens, Globocnik would also operate with considerable circumspection and without attracting too much attention. He appointed Többens technical manager of the SS workshops that would be set up in Poniatow to turn out textiles, clothing, and leather goods for the Wehrmacht. The two men would split the profits. After the agreement, Globocnik took the Warsaw Ghetto factories under his control until men, machines, and materials could be transferred, and he designated Többens his commissioner for resettlement.

Többens had bounced back. Everything was once again going his way—until he found that the Jews he was trying to save would not cooperate. Now the final *Aktion* was about to start, and many of his workers were armed and might choose to die fighting rather than risk moving.

On leaving his managers locked up in his factory, Többens possibly had an urge to snap his whip, a habit he had in moments of rage. Ungrateful Jews![9]

"We want you to tell us where the bunkers are, where your Jewish friends are hiding."

Sewek Toporek took a deep breath. He knew his life hung by a thread. He had to weigh his every word to the Gestapo officer who had come to Rettungskommando headquarters at Wolynska 5 in the Central Ghetto with orders to squeeze the secret out of Sewek and the other employees. Sewek was thankful that he didn't know where any of the bunkers were.

The Rettungskommando was a sanitary inspection group ostensibly set up to control epidemics and give emergency first aid. It had been no easy task for Sewek to get a job with this organization, which he joined shortly after the ghetto was formed in 1940. His father, a wealthy businessman from Lodz, had paid the Gestapo a fortune to enlist Sewek and another son in the outfit. The Rettungskommando was a privileged group run by Jewish Gestapo agents whose real duty was to report on ghetto conditions and underground activities. Its members were relatively well-fed and were likely to survive longer than most other Jews in the ghetto.

Sewek had been enjoying the benefits of his job while trying his best not to cooperate with the Gestapo. One had to be shrewd to manage such a feat, and now, with the last *Aktion* to start the following day, April 19, he would have to be shrewder than ever if he expected to live.

His superior, Leon Skosowski, known as Lolek, expected to live a long time, at least longer than almost all the other Jews. A wealthy playboy who had thrown in his lot with the Gestapo, he had told Sewek, "If only a thousand Jews remain alive in the ghetto, we will be among them."

Meanwhile, Lolek tried to wring everything he could from life by sending others to death. He drank the finest black-market whiskey in the night clubs and enjoyed the favors of the most beautiful Gestapo women. The Gestapo even gave him a new car every week so that the Jewish underground would have a harder time finding him.

On February 11, 1943, he threw one of his gay parties at the apartment of a friend who worked at the brush factory in the ghetto. Many members of the Rettungskommando were there, including Sewek Toporek. Suddenly, when the gaiety was at its peak, fifteen masked men burst in—ZZW fighters. Sewek and several others present were told to leave the room. Lolek, who remained with his top aides, offered to buy his release. The reply came in a burst of bullets that killed four collaborators and severely wounded Lolek, who somehow managed to escape.

Party time was over, and in the next days the ghetto population might in fact dwindle to the last thousand Jews. Nervously composing his answer under the hard stare of the Gestapo officer who wanted to know where the bunkers were, Sewek, his dark eyes feigning sincere regret, replied, "I don't know where they are. The people don't trust us, and they won't say anything. Everybody is hiding, but I don't know where."

The Gestapo man responded quietly, "Then you'll find them for us."[10]

Dr. Israel Rotbalsam was playing bridge in the Czyste-Bauman-Berson Hospital in the Central Ghetto while waiting to die. He sat with several of his colleagues in a concealed room on the second floor, pondering his next play. Silence pervaded the ghetto; not a sound could be heard. Most of the hospital personnel and patients were hiding in the building, though some stayed in the underground bunkers in the courtyard. The hospital administrators occupied the largest and most elaborate of them.

Rotbalsam especially missed the sound of children's voices. He was a pediatrician, but where were the children? Almost all had been piled into boxcars in previous *Aktionen* and taken to Treblinka. In fact, the Bauman-Berson Hospital, which had been exclusively for children, had merged with the Czyste Hospital because there were so few children left to treat.

Nor were there many adults in the combined hospital. The ill and the elderly, together with the children, had been among the first to be massacred, being the most dispensable and the least mobile. Only the fittest had survived until now.

Rotbalsam made his play. . . . He could still hear the sounds, the sounds from the January revolt. The Germans had entered the hospital and shot all the patients in their beds. He could hear the gunfire and the screams . . . and the silence of death. And now they would come again, and there were new patients in the lice-infested beds that had long since been stripped of pillows and linen, items which could be exchanged for food. Patients feeble from starvation, burning with typhus. There was no room for them in the hidden bunkers, and anyway, they were too ill to be moved. . . . Rotbalsam made another play.

After the January revolt, Rotbalsam had bribed his way to the Aryan side, where he found a Polish family who took him in for a large sum. When the family learned he had more money, two Polish policemen suddenly called at the house. He must either go with them or pay four thousand zlotys, apparently to be shared with the family. He paid. The family then sent him to another address. There, two other policemen came, and this time he paid two thousand zlotys while the second family looked on with barely suppressed satisfaction.*

*Ringelblum writes: "Polish Fascism and its ally, anti-Semitism, have conquered the majority of the Polish people. . . . The guilt is theirs for not having saved tens of thousands of Jewish children who could have been taken in by Polish families or institutions. The fault is entirely theirs that Poland has given asylum at the most to 1 percent of the Jewish victims of Hitler's persecutions."

Ringelblum himself was hidden by one Pole on the Aryan side and betrayed to the Nazis by another. He was shot after watching the Nazis kill his young son.

Rotbalsam decided that he had had enough of Polish hospitality. He gave his last funds to a smuggler, who helped him climb a ladder to the top of the wall, from which he lowered himself into the ghetto once more. Strangely, he felt safer. He had returned to a dying people, but they were his people. Until he died with them, he could at least get some sleep.

A guard tapped a signal on the door. The underground had passed the word. The Nazis were surrounding the ghetto. Rotbalsam made his last play. . . . Damn, he never was very good at bridge. . . . He and his colleagues then entered a second room, hidden by a false wall. Here Rotbalsam lay down on a mattress in the dark silence that was broken only by the unrelenting echoes of the January massacre.[11]

"I address you again, brothers and sisters, on the eve of Passover. It is a feast of liberty, celebrated in captivity. . . . We know that you often accuse us of not making all possible efforts to help you. I wish you to know that your accusations, born of pain and sufferings, are not justified. I want you to know that we are endeavoring to move the world and its conscience. . . . "

The voice of Dr. Isaac Ignacy Schwarzbart, the Zionist representative in the Polish government-in-exile in London, reached the Warsaw Ghetto over the British Broadcasting Corporation on April 17, two days before the last *Aktion*. Schwarzbart and his Bundist partner, Artur Zygielbojm, the other Jewish representative, knew only too well of the genocide ravishing the ghetto. They learned of it from Jan Kozielewski, who met with them on December 2, 1942, a few weeks after two ZOB agents in Warsaw gave Kozielewski their dramatic message.

From that day, Schwarzbart and Zygielbojm trudged from office to office in London, begging their Polish colleagues to order the Home Army to supply more arms to the ghetto fighters, pleading with Allied officials to retaliate against the Germans with air attacks and to broadcast reports of the genocide. But all they got was sympathy.

The proposals for Allied support were not technically feasible, it was argued, nor did they fit into overall Allied military strategy. Besides, Kozielewski's account seemed exaggerated. Who could believe that even the Germans were capable of committing such inhuman crimes?

And while Prime Minister Sikorski joined in the pleas for Allied retaliation—to help the Poles as well as the Jews—he apparently feared the power of Polish anti-Semitism. For he did nothing more than encourage the Home Army to hand over to the Jews a few dozen more pistols to keep them quiet. On one of Zygielbojm's written appeals the harassed Sikorski reportedly wrote in the margin: "He insulted us again."

But Zygielbojm would not give up, no matter how insulting his drumbeat demands might appear. He had to save his people.

Born into an impoverished working-class family, Zygielbojm was active in politics and labor ever since his days as a glove worker. Eventually he became secretary of the Polish Trade Union Federation and a member of the Bund central committee. When the Germans goosestepped into Warsaw in September 1939, they took him hostage. But they soon freed him, and he joined the Judenrat, hoping to soften the Nazi terror.

Some days later, in October, the SS demanded that the Judenrat set up a ghetto, and the majority of members were too frightened to disagree. But Zygielbojm vigorously protested and threatened to resign, forcing the Judenrat to compromise. They would not take part in setting up a ghetto but would simply inform the Jews of the plan so that they could prepare to move out of what was to be the Aryan section of Warsaw.

The following morning, as a crowd of ten thousand panic-stricken Jews gathered before the Judenrat building, Zygielbojm, supported on the shoulders of two comrades, urged them to refuse to enter a ghetto and to resist if they were forced to do so. Flung in the face of the Gestapo, his courageous words exhilarated the people; and the Wehrmacht, which had not yet turned over control of Warsaw to the SS, nullified the plan, at least temporarily, to avert a possible revolt.

Zygielbojm, however, had to go into hiding immediately. Eventually he reached London, where he joined the Polish government-in-exile. But his heart and soul remained in Warsaw with his wife and child, his comrades, his people. And so Zygielbojm, a man possessed, fought from London.

In late December 1942 he asked to see Jan Kozielewski again. He wanted to know more, more, more. . . .

"What do you want to hear about?"

"About Jews, my dear man. I am a Jew. Tell me what you know about the Jews in Poland."

Zygielbojm sat stiffly, legs apart and a hand on each knee, his dark eyes staring at a point on the ceiling behind Kozielewski, his cheek contorting slightly in a tic as he listened, transfixed.

"Conditions are horrible. The people in the ghetto live in constant agony, a lingering, tormenting death. The instructions their leaders gave me cannot be carried out for political and tactical reasons. I spoke to the British authorities. The answer was the one your leaders in Poland told me to expect: 'No, it is impossible, it can't be done.' "

Zygielbojm rose suddenly and lurched toward Kozielewski, his eyes angry and contemptuous. Waving his hand in a slapping motion, he almost shouted, "Listen, I didn't come here to talk to you about what is happening here. Don't tell me what is said and done here. I know that myself. I came to you to hear about what is happening *there*, what *they* want *there*, what *they* say *there!*"

"Very well, then. This is what *they* want from their leaders in the free countries of the world; this is what *they* told me to say: 'Let them go to all the important English and American offices and agencies. Tell them not to leave until they have obtained guarantees that a way has been decided upon to save the Jews. Let them accept no food or drink; let them die a slow death while the world looks on. Let them die. This may shake the conscience of the world.' "

Zygielbojm began to pace the room, his thin body trembling, and with a look of agony he held one hand to his head. "It is impossible, utterly impossible. You know what would happen. They would simply bring in two policemen and have me dragged away to an institution. Do you think they would let me die a slow, lingering death? Never. They would never let me."

Zygielbojm then bombarded Kozielewski with questions. What did the houses look like, the children, the corpses sprawled on the ghetto streets? Did he remember the words of the dying child?

"Ah, I forget. You can't talk Yiddish; you are not a Jew," Zygielbojm said.

Finally the meeting ended.

"Mr. Karski [Kozielewski's code name], I'll do everything I can to help them. Everything! I'll do everything they demand. If only I am given a chance. . . . You believe me, don't you?"

Kozielewski felt tired and frustrated. He had attended so many meetings. Did he believe him? What difference did it make whether he did or not? He no longer knew what he believed.

"Of course I believe you," he said. . . . "I feel certain you will do all you can, all they demand. My God, every single one of us tries to do his best."

Zygielbojm had no right to harass or perplex him any further. And why should this unhappy Jew promise to do more than he was willing to do? Had not the ghetto delegates demanded that the Jewish leaders abroad die if necessary to awaken the world? A rather thoughtless character. Still, a tragic one. They were dying. His people, his own wife, Manya, his child. . . .

"Manya, we could take care of your Artek on the other side. Unfortunately, we cannot yet provide shelter for both of you."

Manya Zygielbojm reflected for a moment before answering Feigele Peltel during one of Feigele's visits to the ghetto from the Aryan side.

"I can't do it, believe me. I can't part with him. My son has no one but me now. I guard him as the apple of my eye. Together we have endured the misery and the misfortune brought on by the Germans. No, he would perish without me."

Feigele tried to persuade her. Her son would live with a trustworthy Polish railroad worker who had been recommended to her by the wife of a member of the Bund central committee.

"No, I can't do it!" Manya said. "Whatever is fated for me will also be the fate of my son. We've been through so much together."

Perhaps they would survive. After all, on April 19, the first day of Passover, Allied representatives would meet in Bermuda to discuss a solution to the war refugee problem. And the radio message from London had come through loud and clear: "We are endeavoring to move the world and its conscience."[12]

General Stroop was in a good mood when he strutted into his suite after dark from his inspection trip into the ghetto. He felt in his bones that things would not go well with General von Sammern-Frankenegg when he launched his *Aktion* the next morning. Then he, Stroop, would take over and demonstrate how to crush a gang of rebellious Jews.

He took a bath, massaged his body with eau de cologne, put on his pajamas and robe, and sat down at the table to enjoy the dinner that Colonel Hahn, the Gestapo chief, had sent up to him. What a delicious meal. His favorite dish: dumplings. Also, roast beef with French fried potatoes and a bottle of fine Burgundy. After eating, Stroop sat back and smoked an Egyptian cigarette, then telephoned Hahn to thank him for the excellent meal. How, he asked, did Hahn know that he liked dumplings? The two men laughed and joked.

Stroop then telephoned an aide to awaken him at 4 A.M. and went to bed.[13]

In the pale moonlight, Chaim Frimer stood on the veranda of Mila 29 at the corner of Mila and Zamenhof streets and eagerly awaited the enemy. He understood now why Israel Kanal, the new ZOB Central Ghetto commander, had sent a messenger to bring him back from his home shortly after he had arrived there for a visit with his father and his sister Krysia. The Germans were apparently planning an *Aktion* the next morning, April 19, and the fighters had been put on the alert.

Chaim was now standing guard with orders to inform Mordechai Anielewicz, Israel Kanal, and Berl Broide, his group commander, who were all based in Mila 29, of any suspicious enemy movements. As soon as the Germans stepped into the ghetto, he was to signal the ZOB fighters by throwing a grenade. He considered himself well-armed. He had a Mauser pistol with forty cartridges and a few grenades.

The moonlight somehow accentuated the darkness of the ghetto night. All windows were blacked out, hiding the feverish activity of people packing bundles of food, linen, and other necessary items to be taken into the bunkers. On the street and in the courtyards, Chaim could see shadowy figures moving stealthily: civilians heading for the bunkers, or underground fighters, some disguised in German uniforms snatched from clothing factories, knocking on house gates and warning stragglers to hurry.

They didn't have to prod too hard. Ghetto residents had been aware for hours that the time was at hand. Rumors had spread like wildfire. Someone had heard from a relative who worked in a Többens shop that many SS troops had gathered near the wall. A Polish policeman had informed another Jew that a new *Aktion* was imminent. And Jews who had gone to work outside the ghetto had noticed on returning that the guard at the gates was heavier than usual. Tension gripped the ghetto, but the people did not panic. They had read the last appeal posted on the ghetto walls: TO FIGHT, TO DIE, FOR THE HONOR OF OUR PEOPLE!

In the few hours since returning from home, Chaim never stopped moving. He went to the storehouse in the building and removed Wehrmacht helmets and shoes that had recently been confiscated from German stores in daring night raids for distribution to the various groups. He checked the weapons in his group and issued ammunition. He filled baskets with Molotov cocktails and gave food—sugar and corn—to people who came from other groups. He piled sandbags at the windows and helped to block the courtyard gate with a wagon turned upside down and heavy cupboards from the flats.[14]

Mordechai Anielewicz and Israel Kanal moved from room to room in every apartment to make sure that fighters were stationed at all strategic positions. Mordechai was excited but, as usual, outwardly calm. He had felt the same tension many times in the past. Perhaps never more acutely than in 1937, after he volunteered to go to a summer camp run by the Polish Army where high school boys received paramilitary training.

Mordechai and the other Jewish youths, segregated in their own tent, only clenched their fists in silence when the gentile boys cried that they would "never be any good for fighting and war." But when some hooligans stole their rifles to get them into trouble, Mordechai's patience came to an end. He plotted a daring surprise move and, on the following night, led an attack on the hooligans' tent. The Jews beat up the culprits and forced them to run away half-naked. Mordechai was ousted from the camp as a "troublemaker," but he was satisfied. He had avenged the Jews, as now he would again in a great final clash.

Later in the evening, Mordechai, accompanied by Lutek Rotblatt, walked into the street and stopped a car marked with a blue Magen David, indicating it belonged to a Judenrat official. They spoke to the occupants and then let the vehicle pass. The Judenrat leaders, they learned, had been ordered to appear at their building nearby.

Shortly afterward, Pawel Frenkel, the ZZW commander, sent a

message to Mordechai: The Germans had barred the doors to the Judenrat building, arrested all members, and told them that a new *Aktion* would start the next morning. One member had managed to escape and had broken the news.

Ironically, Mordechai was scheduled to meet with Pawel at ZZW headquarters at 1 A.M. the same morning to complete plans for uniting the ZOB and the ZZW. Now, after months of conflict, they were a few hours too late. The two organizations would have to fight separate and uncoordinated battles in each of the three combat zones, which were themselves isolated from each other. Yet Mordechai and the other fighters did not think of such difficulties at this long-awaited hour.

Twenty-two ZOB groups—nine in the Central Ghetto, eight in the Productive Ghetto, and five in the Brushmakers' District—were poised to strike. So were three ZZW units, one in each of the sectors. In the Central Ghetto, the Jews had set up a triangular defense system designed to cover all gates. At the base of the triangle were two intersections: Zamenhof-Mila, where five ZOB groups were bunched, and Nalewki-Gensia-Franciszkanska, where four ZOB groups stood by. At the apex was Muranowski Square, the ZZW stronghold.

No, the difficulties were not really important. The idea was to fight, not to win; the Jews could not possibly win. Basing his strategy on this premise, Mordechai was ready to play what he was sure would be his last troublemaking role.[15]

The First Day

April 19

With the first glimmer of dawn, General Stroop was sitting in his suite, dressed in field uniform and eagerly awaiting word that Colonel von Sammern-Frankenegg had failed in his mission. Beside him was a table with three telephones that kept him informed of minute-to-minute preparations and progress. Drivers, messengers, communications men, and aides rushed in with further news and out with urgent orders.

Gazing from the window, Stroop observed with pleasure the trees with thin branches that were quivering against the rose-tinged clouds. The air was pure. The birds were singing. He imagined himself back in the woods near Detmold, where he had spent so many happy youthful hours in the company of Hermann. Today he would prove himself worthy of Hermann's company.[1]

At 6 A.M., Colonel von Sammern-Frankenegg, standing on a street corner with his aides, watched confidently as his men goose-stepped toward the ghetto, singing lustily. The 16 well-equipped officers and 850 men he was sending in—Waffen SS, police, Wehrmacht, and Askari units—would certainly be able to crush a disorganized band of Jews if they tried to resist the *Aktion.*

Just to make sure, a tank and two armored cars escorted the

troops. And if this force was not enough, about two thousand more men stood ready to help, not to mention seven thousand others who had been brought into Warsaw in case a ghetto revolt spread to the Aryan side. Furthermore, to minimize Nazi casualties, Jewish policemen were leading the way to draw fire. More than ten who had refused to go or had tried to escape had earlier been shot on the spot.

True, the Jews had forced him to call off the January *Aktion*, von Sammern-Frankenegg had to admit. And this withdrawal had damaged his reputation. But this time he would clean out the ghetto once and for all, within three days. He knew that Himmler had sent Stroop to Warsaw to take over his command if he faltered again. And Stroop was now waiting in the wings like a hungry vulture for the chance to destroy his whole career.

Von Sammern-Frankenegg's plan was simple. The ghetto was already sliced into three main sections, each sealed off from the other. He would now drag the Jews out of their homes and hiding places section by section, starting with the Central Ghetto, whose fall could frighten the workers in the factory areas to volunteer for transfer to Lublin.

A part of his force would march through the Nalewki Street gate, then north to Muranowski Square. The other part, including the armor, would move through the gate at the Gensia-Zamenhof intersection and up Zamenhof in a parallel advance. The Jews in the Central Ghetto would thus be trapped between the two forces and the ghetto wall to the north. And the Brush-makers' District would be isolated, making it easy pickings in the next swoop.

As von Sammern-Frankenegg listened to the proud, singing voices of his troops marching into the ghetto, he was sure they would not let him down.[2]

Zivia Lubetkin watched with alarm from the attic of Nalewki 33 as "hundreds" of Germans armed with submachine guns poured through the Nalewki Street gate and marched toward Gensia. Her post, commanded by Zachariah Artstein, was one of the three guarding the corner of Nalewki and Gensia. Lutek Rotblatt commanded one of the other two.

Zivia, who was substituting in the ZOB command for her husband, Yitzhak Zuckerman, had chosen to fight with Zachariah's group because it was made up mainly of members of Dror-Hehalutz, the Zionist movement that she and Yitzhak headed in Warsaw. Also because she was a close friend of Zachariah's, one of the bravest of the fighters and, at twenty, one of the youngest commanders. . . .

Like Mordechai Anielewicz, Zachariah had been a hero of the January revolt. When the Germans had entered Dror-Hehalutz headquarters to snare its occupants, they found Zachariah sitting in the front room, calmly reading. Ignoring him for the moment, they started toward the inside rooms, where Zivia and other fighters were hiding. Suddenly Zachariah leaped up and shot them in the back, killing two.

His comrades simultaneously rushed out and riddled Germans in the hall; then, with Zachariah, they fled to another building, only to be confronted by Germans there, too. This time Zachariah walked into the hall with his hands up, putting them off guard just long enough for other fighters to kill a few and chase the rest down the stairs. At the foot of the stairs the Germans were greeted by a new hail of bullets—fired by Zachariah, who had raced down in time to meet them. . . .

Now, exactly three months later, the Germans were coming for them again. As they emerged from the gate like ants out of a hole, Zivia, gripping a pistol, felt as if they were heading for the eastern front to fight the Russian hordes. Yet Zachariah's group numbered little more than twenty youngsters, each armed with only a pistol and a grenade, except for one big red-headed youth who proudly clung to a rifle he had captured from a German; he would not let his comrades even touch this wonder weapon. The group—posted at windows, on balconies, and in the courtyard—also had a few Molotov cocktails and crudely assembled home-made bombs that, like the grenades, had to be lit with matches. How strange, how enthralling, to see this score of boys and girls stand up against a great armed enemy, happy even though they were sure they would die.

Closer, closer came the troops; then, suddenly, an explosion. A fighter had hurled a grenade. Within seconds the intersection of Nalewki-Gensia-Franciszkanska simmered into a bubbling caldron of death and destruction. Missile after missile sent geysers of smoke and rubble mingled with bits of human flesh into the blue spring sky, while the sound of gunfire echoed like the merry crackle of firecrackers at a holiday celebration. Zivia and her fellows rejoiced at the sight of German blood staining the ghetto streets. Each spilt drop seemed somehow to ease the agony of remembering a loved one's being dragged off to death.

The attacking column crumbled into small groups, and the Nazis hid in doorways and hugged the walls of the buildings as they slowly began to retreat, too frightened even to collect their dead and wounded. An SS officer shouted, *"Verflucht!"* ("Damn!"), ordering his men to collect the casualties regardless of the fire while taking refuge himself under a balcony.

Finally, when the invaders recovered from their initial shock, they began to return fire; but they were easy targets because they were exposed while the Jews were concealed. Zachariah leaped from one position to another, encouraging his fighters. Liaison men ran around, delivering orders and reports on the fighting. Everyone was deafened by the explosions and the rattle of heavy machine guns, but they were ecstatic in the midst of bedlam.

Zivia Lubetkin explained afterward, "What would happen tomorrow did not worry us. Behold the wonder and the miracle! Those German heroes retreated, afraid and terrorized by homemade bombs and hand grenades."

When a lookout girl arrived with news that the enemy had vanished, Zachariah went to survey the battle scene and returned radiating joy. Zivia and her comrades, including Lutek Rotblatt, whose squad had been firing from another corner building, swarmed into the street and threw their arms around each other in an orgy of unrestrained emotion. They then removed the uniforms, helmets, and weapons from the enemy corpses for their own use.

The Jews had routed the Nazis without suffering a single casualty.[3]

While fighting at the corner of Nalewki and Gensia had raged, a German-Ukrainian force, some on foot, others mounted on motorcycles or transported in trucks, advanced along Zamenhof from Gensia after setting up headquarters in the little square facing the Judenrat building. The headquarters was complete with tables, chairs, telephones, and field kitchen. Leading this force were two single files of Jewish policemen sent ahead as decoys.

Mordechai Anielewicz and the other fighters based at Mila 29, at the corner of Zamenhof and Mila, awaited with fatalistic calm the magic moment of resistance. All the months of training, arming, and planning would now crystallize in one great bloody clash—if their expectations materialized. Some weeks earlier Mordechai had written in a note that was smuggled out of the ghetto and sent to a friend in Palestine: "We will give our death a historic meaning and full significance for future generations. But soon, very soon, I shall go to a place where no one wants to go, and from which no traveller returns."

The moment had finally come. The voyage was about to end. But it was comforting to know that the few survivors and their descendants could forever take pride in the knowledge that some Jews had fought back.

Mordechai darted from post to post, making sure that everybody was in place and clearly understood that each precious bullet must pierce the flesh of a Nazi. Their last voyage must be a happy one. They must drift into oblivion on a sea of enemy blood.

When Chaim Frimer saw the Jewish policemen edging toward his post overlooking Zamenhof, he quickly sent a messenger to Israel Kanal, the Central Ghetto commander. Should he open fire? Israel consulted with Mordechai. No, wait, came the reply, until the center of the enemy column following the Jewish policemen marched by Chaim's veranda. Chaim was then to throw a grenade, signaling an attack by all five groups posted in corner buildings.

Chaim anxiously waited, and in a few minutes the Nazis reached the veranda. He then tried to light the fuse of the primitive grenade with a match, but the gusty wind kept blowing out the flame. Finally, in disgust, he reported his failure to headquarters, and another fighter was given the mission—and honor—of throwing the first missile.

It exploded in the middle of the enemy ranks, and from all the corner buildings a hail of grenades, bombs, and bullets tore into the advancing force. Chaim fired from his balcony with his Mauser. The Germans and Ukrainians were stunned, confused, panicky. The air was filled with cries and shouts as they raced each other for cover behind gates and in devastated stores, the Germans pushing the Ukrainians out if there was no room for both. But the Jews opened up on these hiding places, and the enemy, trapped, fell like tenpins.

"*Juden haben Waffen!*" one German yelled as he managed to scramble into a doorway. "The Jews have weapons!"

Chaim felt a thrill of satisfaction. For hours that cry would ring in his consciousness: "The Jews have weapons!"

He watched with vengeful pleasure as one German, struck by a Molotov cocktail, ran down the street like a living torch, screaming in agony, a sight that spread further panic among the victim's comrades. Chaim felt as if he were witnessing the transfer of the pain wracking his own dying people to their murderers.

Yes, the Jews had weapons.

Across the street, at Zamenhof 32, Masha Glytman fired her pistol from a window, then ducked inside the room before the Germans could respond. But one of them had apparently seen her.

"Hans, eine Frau schiesst!" he shouted. "Hans, a woman is shooting!"

Masha felt a certain pride in adding to German humiliation. The Nazi superman was cringing before a Jewish woman.

On the balcony of another corner building, a fighter named Yehiel, almost completely exposing himself to enemy fire, hung over the balustrade to fire more accurately with his Schmeisser. After each hit, he had told his comrades inside the flat, he would make a motion with his foot to let them rejoice in his success. Yehiel moved his foot many times, then made no motion at all. An enemy bullet had severely wounded him.

Finally the Germans, wielding riding whips, emerged from their holes and forced the Ukrainians back into battle positions. But after about half an hour the attackers fled, leaving behind many dead and wounded in the street. They soon returned, however, this time led by von Sammern-Frankenegg's tank and two armored cars. Chaim watched calmly from his balcony, and when the tank reached his house, he joined in unleashing a barrage of grenades and Molotov cocktails. The monster was set afire and its crew burned alive. The two armored cars turned back, one of them also on fire.

German ambulances then came to gather the wounded, but the fighters greeted them with a new lethal storm. Mercy for the killers of their loved ones?

Among the fallen were two Jewish police collaborators. One of them, before dying, cried out, "How happy I am—struck by my brethren's bullet!"

Shortly, German artillery from outside the ghetto began hitting the Jewish defense positions. Mordechai, cool as always but flushed with jubilation, rushed to the veranda and ordered Chaim, "Get up! We're leaving!"

Chaim followed Mordechai through the dusty plaster-strewn apartment to the stairs, down to the courtyard, then through an entrance leading to the cellar. They crawled through an opening hidden behind a big stove and found themselves in the ZOB headquarters bunker, where all the groups at the intersection had gathered. Only one man had fallen—Yehiel, the overzealous fighter who had been shot on the balcony. He lay on a cot badly wounded.

The fighters embraced each other, excitedly exchanged stories of the battle, and later listened, enthralled, to BBC and Polish underground radio reports of their incredible feat, while Mordechai, Israel, and Berl Broide sat in a corner planning their next moves.

What a story he had to tell his dear sister Krysia, thought Chaim.

But one tragedy marred the joyous ending. Yehiel moaned and writhed in agony, and there was no way to help him—until Mordechai Growas, his group leader, aimed his pistol at him and ended his suffering.[4]

On the Aryan side Yitzhak Zuckerman was fast asleep when the Nazis entered the ghetto at 6 A.M. He had gone to bed with the expectation that he would be joining his wife, Zivia, and his comrades at the Seder to be held in the evening for ghetto leaders. Suddenly he began to dream that he was caught in the middle of an artillery barrage. And this nightmare persisted until he heard another noise. Someone was weeping.

Yitzhak opened his eyes and saw standing by the bed his young aide, Frania Beatus. He glanced at his watch and wondered what she was doing there. He had arranged for her to meet with certain bribed Polish policemen to organize his entry into the ghetto later that day with a group of returning Jewish workers. She was to meet the policemen at 6 A.M. Now, he noted, it was only 6:30. Had she finished negotiating already?

The puzzle was soon solved. There would be no Seder that night. The Nazis, Frania reported, had just entered the ghetto and were attacking. So Yitzhak's dream of a barrage had been no dream. He had observed a surge of military activity on the Aryan side the day before but had not expected this. Not even the Germans, he had wishfully believed, could keep him from celebrating Passover with his wife and comrades.

Frania sobbed. "There's no hope anymore. I'm going to kill myself."

Yitzhak, shocked by this remark, didn't know whether to comfort her or scold her. He wondered whether she was serious.

"What nonsense!" he finally said, almost shouting. "Your duty is to live and do what you are ordered to do."

Within minutes Yitzhak was dressed and in the street. So far, Frania had told him, the Germans had assaulted only the Central Ghetto. Thus, since that sector had no communication with the others, as Mordechai Anielewicz's deputy he would telephone a ZOB contact in the Productive Ghetto and order the fighters there to attack northward through the Wild Ghetto and join in the battle.

Yitzhak rushed into a nearby restaurant to phone and dialed the number of a factory in the Productive Ghetto. In a calm, quiet voice he said to the party at the other end, "A feast started just now at the angel's place. You should take part at once. I am ordering you to take part in this joyous event."

According to Yitzhak, the contact, familiar with the ZOB code, replied that he understood and would comply with the order. But for some reason he told the commander of the Productive Ghetto, Eliezer Geller, that Yitzhak had ordered him *not* to take part in the Central Ghetto battle. And so Eliezer and his men stayed where they were, waiting for the Germans to attack their sector.

Yitzhak then went looking frantically for arms to smuggle into the ghetto. It would not be easy. Money that was to come from the ghetto had not reached him, limiting his purchasing power. And the Home Army still refused to part with any more weapons.[5]

More hopeful of squeezing arms and even armed units from the Poles were the Bund agents on the Aryan side. After all, the Bund *was* Polish and had always considered itself so. Jews, yes, but Polish Jews. Members had never dreamed of emigrating to Palestine or anywhere else and were, in fact, strongly anti-Zionist. Therefore, the gentile counterpart of the Bund, the Polish Socialist Party (PPS), would certainly not let its Jewish brothers down at this critical moment.

That is what Leon Feiner, the chief Bund representative on the Aryan side, felt that morning as he briefed a small group of his comrades in his apartment at Zurawia 24. (Feiner had been one of the two ZOB agents who had asked Lieutenant Kozielewski of the Home Army to persuade the Allies to help the Jews.)

"All the Bundists on the Aryan side must be assembled and formed into a fighting group," he said. "Efforts must be made immediately to obtain arms. The group must hurl grenades at the units entering the ghetto."

Those present, including Feigele Peltel, nodded approval. Feigele would gladly crawl over the wall again with arms, battle or no battle, if only there were some to take.

Leon then chose Jacob Celemenski as commander of the fighting group to be formed on the Aryan side. Celemenski's first task was to contact the PPS. As this party was represented in Prime Minister Sikorski's Polish government-in-exile, it should be able to come up with weapons and armed fighters. It might even be able to spark a citywide uprising.

Celemenski was excited by the prospects. Earlier that morning, after hearing the ghetto explode, he had rushed out into the street and made his way through curious crowds that had suddenly gathered near the wall, until he was stopped by guards with fixed bayonets. He stood among the Poles, watching smoke spiral into the clear azure sky and listening to the incredulous reaction of the observers.

"The Jews are killing the *Shwabs!*" the Poles cried, calling the Germans a derogatory name derived from the German word for "cockroach."

Some Poles crossed themselves, and others expressed sorrow that they had stood by for months watching the Jews being systematically murdered. At this moment of shock and disbelief, few anti-Semitic remarks could be heard.

The ghetto was fighting!

Suddenly, Celemenski heard someone say, "Now we must attack on this side."

The words had burrowed into his mind. Yes, Jew and gentile must mobilize and attack the Germans from "this side." And now he had the go-ahead to organize such an assault.

Celemenski's heart pounded as he boarded a streetcar that would take him to some PPS contacts. He could not wait to form his diversionary army. Within half an hour he was sitting with two

PPS members, Wacek and Johanna Praga. Wacek, a tall, slim intellectual, looked disturbed. Actually he had already consulted some of his companions about extending active aid to the Jews. But "unfortunately" they had refused. No, the PPS units were not prepared for such a battle, and an attack on the Germans could end in a massacre of the entire Polish population.

Well, what about arms?

No, "unfortunately" the PPS could give no arms either.

Why? Did the PPS really have no arms? Or had they so few that they wanted to keep them all for themselves?

Celemenski got no reply.

He departed, shocked and exhausted. The remnants of his people were being exterminated, and his good friends, the best and least anti-Semitic of the Poles, were just sitting by until all had perished.[6]

Before 7 A.M., the telephones in General Stroop's quarters began jangling all at once, relaying reports of the disaster. As the details accumulated, Stroop felt a certain gloating satisfaction. What could one have expected from a blundering fool like von Sammern-Frankenegg? But at the same time, he was horrified: German SS men, even if under such stupid generalship, retreating before a mob of cowardly Jews!

Colonel Hahn, the Gestapo chief, then arrived, his youthful face gray with despair.

Hahn had tried with vigor and imagination to trick the Jews into emerging from their bunkers that morning so they could be rounded up and the underground isolated. His tool for this task had been a well-known Jewish collaborator, Abraham Ganzweich. Ganzweich, a journalist, had originally come from Lodz shortly after Warsaw was occupied and intimidated other journalists, as well as artists and philanthropists, into joining an organization ostensibly formed to give "relief" and to fight profiteering. The Gestapo sponsored him and hoped, through his organization, to keep its fingers on the ghetto pulse.

Ganzweich's men were gangsters and black marketeers known as "Thirteeners" because their headquarters was at Leszno 13. They conducted raids to gather subversive political material while supposedly hunting for gangsters and black marketeers. Ganzweich posed as a "realist." He warned the people, who feared him as much as they did the SS, not to heed "Communists," who urged sabotage and resistance. After all, Hitler would triumph in the end, Ganzweich hammered, so it was best to cooperate with the Germans.

With the final *Aktion* under way, Ganzweich was expected to lure the Jews into cooperating in their own murder. That morning his agents flooded the ghetto with leaflets signed by a Captain Lecki, "commander" of a "Polish fighting organization" calling on the Jews to come out of their bunkers and fight in the ghetto streets. But the ZOB and ZZW had warned the population not to accept the authority of any resistance organizations other than theirs, and Ganzweich's appeal floundered, to Hahn's bitter disappointment.

The Gestapo chief now broodingly warned Stroop about the political consequences of the rout. His job was to keep order in Warsaw. But how orderly would the Poles now be after seeing what Jewish resistance had achieved?

The phone rang again. General Krüger was calling from Cracow. When Stroop told him the bad news, Krüger was shocked. He cursed and ranted. It was a "shame," a "political defeat," a "military failure," a "dirty spot on the honor and reputation of the SS." Stroop, he bellowed, must immediately arrest von Sammern-Frankenegg, the "doctor of philosophy," the "cow," the "stupid fool." Stroop was to remove all troops from the ghetto, take over von Sammern-Frankenegg's, and within two hours throw all the SS soldiers in Warsaw into the battle.

The troops had already retreated on their own, Stroop replied, and he and Hahn were afraid of Polish reaction. Krüger screamed through the phone, "Throw all the SS forces against the ghetto! To keep the Poles in check, proclaim a state of alert for all German formations—the army, party, railroad, and guards!"

Two more frantic phone calls from Krüger. Then it was Himmler. He was calmer than Krüger but was also furious and did not speak with the delicacy and subtlety that had always appealed to Stroop. Von Sammern-Frankenegg could not be arrested, Himmler said, for he was an Austrian, and his arrest might unnecessarily strain German-Austrian relations within SS ranks.

"I do not know whether von Sammern will be punished for his clumsiness," Himmler said. "I think we shall transfer him to some post in southern Europe. But tell him, dear Stroop, that as of this moment he is removed from his post as SS and police commander of the Warsaw District. We are going to send a telex with appropriate orders. Remember, you must not hurt Sammern's self-esteem. The affair must be arranged delicately and without noise."

Himmler then embellished Krüger's order. All Germans in Warsaw, especially the army, must be put on a state of alert. But nothing should be done to provoke the Poles, he ordered. As for the Home Army, it could do nothing more than a little sabotage and hit-and-run fighting. Appease the Poles, he repeated, and *don't* provoke them. But "just in case," all the armed forces in the General Government should stand ready to act.

About 7:30 A.M., while Stroop was calmly shaving, von Sammern-Frankenegg burst into his suite.

"All is lost in the ghetto!" he cried almost hysterically. "We are not in the ghetto! We cannot get into the ghetto! We have wounded and dead!"

He suggested that bombers be flown in from Cracow, but Stroop rejected the idea. No, he said, Germany would be humiliated and shamed before the world.

"I'm taking command," Stroop declared. "I'm going into the ghetto."

His face smoothly shaven, his boots highly polished, his field uniform immaculate, Stroop went to clean up the mess left by his predecessor.

Half an hour later, about 8 A.M., Stroop led a group of officers through the Gensia-Zamenhof gate into the ghetto and sat down at one of the command tables in the square facing the Judenrat building. Here, within firing range of the Jews, he laid out plans for a new attack, displaying his personal courage in order to raise the morale of his badly shaken units, even though he later admitted that he feared assassination.

On this first day of battle he was more intent on restoring confidence among his men than in crushing the Jews. His immediate aim was to clear a small area of Jews and use it as a springboard the next day for penetrating the rest of the ghetto.

Whereas von Sammern-Frankenegg had planned to take the whole Central Ghetto in one fell swoop with troops strutting in parade formation, Stroop would concentrate his attack on a single point at a time with small scattered units. He would capture one Jewish post after another until the fighting area had shrunk into an undefendable trap.

He would also use much greater force than his predecessor did—twice as many officers and fifty percent more troops—though he saw no need to throw every last soldier in Warsaw into the fray as his superiors had ordered in a moment of shock and frenzy. His troops would be supported by a tank, two armored cars, and artillery—a howitzer and three antiaircraft guns.

Stroop would begin by demolishing the posts at the Gensia-Nalewki-Franciszkanska intersection, where Zivia Lubetkin, Lutek Rotblatt, and their comrades were victorious on the first day of the uprising. His troops, many of them nervous and battle-worn, were no longer singing as they prepared to move at noon.[7]

It was now the Jews who were in a musical mood. At about noon, the strains of Beethoven and Schubert, sounding like the wail of an angel at prayer, were wafting from the shattered windows of Nalewki 33 over the wreckage of burnt steel and cold flesh that littered the Gensia-Nalewki-Franciszkanska intersection. One of Zachariah Artstein's fighters sat playing these classics on his concertina while other men, exhausted from the morning's battle and the euphoric aftermath, slept on shredded mattresses with their guns in their hands.

Suddenly a messenger arrived and breathlessly reported to Zivia and Zachariah. Armor and troops had entered the Gensia-Zamenhof gate. They were nearing Nalewki, hugging the walls along Gensia. Hardly had the messenger completed his report when the house shook under heavy artillery, machine gun, and small arms fire from all sides. The Schubert symphony was never finished.

Almost before the fighters could leap to their posts, the Germans set up a barricade of sea-grass mattresses taken from a nearby Werterfassung warehouse across the entrance to Franciszkanska, the eastern extension of Gensia. Crouching behind this barricade, they fired furiously at the corner houses, though they were afraid to raise their heads to aim. The Jews, on the other hand, had few bullets to spare and so fired less but hit more. Soon, Molotov cocktails whizzed through the air, setting the barricade on fire. And the Nazis, suddenly exposed, were mowed down one by one.

106

Meanwhile, fire from Stroop's tank and two armored cars failed to hit their targets since the general was afraid to move them too close for fear that they, too, would be knocked out. They stood fairly far behind the front line, protected by a ring of SS grenadiers. Even so, the Jews barely missed hitting them with Molotov cocktails, astonishing Stroop, who surmised that the missiles were being hurled by highly trained athletes.

The Germans then began throwing incendiary bombs, setting fire to Nalewki 33. Zivia and Zachariah organized their fighters for retreat but awaited the return of several men sent to burn the Werterfassung warehouse. Plans for a possible withdrawal had been made long before. The fighters were to retreat through attics linked by holes knocked in the walls leading to Gensia 6.

Hardly had Zivia and Zachariah started leading the way to this new base, only a few attics away, when a messenger caught up with them: The Germans had occupied Gensia 6. The fighters stared at each other in despair. They could not advance, and they could not go back. Nalewki 33 was aflame. Scouts were sent out to look for an opening to safety.

Meanwhile the fighters stayed where they were, trapped in a dark attic that soon filled with smoke. They started to choke, and their eyes teared. Flames began to lick at them, pieces of burning wood fell from the roof, and the floor started to crumble.

To add to their troubles, the Jews, through the swirling smoke, sighted Germans in the next attic—Gensia 6. Though nearly blind, the hunted fired wildly at the hunters. The Germans lurched back in shock as a fighter killed one of them and took his weapon. The sight of the dead German made the Jews forget their catastrophic situation for a moment.

But no longer. Like trapped animals, engulfed by smoke and flame, the fighters stumbled from corner to corner, hole to hole, desperately trying to find a way out. All seemed lost. The end had finally come, and they began to lie down to die.

They were seconds from death when the scouts returned. They had discovered a route of retreat. All followed in a line, clinging to each other. But again all looked hopeless. They would have to squirm through passages that seemed too narrow to accommodate even the frailest fighter. Yet somehow they managed the feat, crawling inch by inch, barely daring to breathe.

Zivia and the other fighters thus left the burning house behind

them, and after crossing a labyrinth of attics and roofs, they finally arrived at Nalewki 37. Searching in the courtyard for traces of a
bunker to hide in, they stumbled on a hidden cellar that sheltered
many Jews. Drained of energy and still choking from the smoke,
the fighters collapsed on the floor like sacks of potatoes.

However, they drew no sympathy from the bunker inhabitants,
who were afraid that the presence of armed people would further
endanger them. The women became hysterical, and some ran out
into the street looking for another hiding place. The newcomers
could hardly believe that even during the uprising there were still
Jews who thought that noncombatants had a better chance of surviving than fighters.

But rather than create further panic, they left the bunker and
wandered for hours through the attics, trying in vain to find a
base. They met many fugitives from houses that were in flames,
frightened people who ran aimlessly back and forth, stopping
only to cower in corners during explosions.

After a long and exhausting walk, Zivia and her comrades finally staggered into a bunker at Kurza 3, a dark narrow cellar so
crowded that bodies were lying upon bodies with arms and legs
intertwined. One could hear the loud heartbeats and the gasps of
people nearly suffocating.

Death somehow seemed less frightening with every black, nearly airless minute that passed.[8]

By midafternoon General Stroop felt proud of his men's
achievements. They now controlled the Gensia-Nalewki-Franciszkanska intersection and surrounding areas from which they could
launch a new assault deep into the heart of the Central Ghetto. He
briefed his commanders amid the smoking wreckage, praising
them for the fighting skill of their units and singling out his assistant, Major Ewald Sternhagel. He had behaved magnificently,
calmly, and courageously, Stroop beamed, and on the following
day he would become the general's second-in-command.

Yes, the troops had made up nicely for the previous losses, and
from now on it would be easier to root out the "subhumans." But
why was there such a small bag of prisoners? Especially since the
main aim of the operation was not to capture territory, but Jews.
Only about four hundred were seized, and not a single fighter

among them. They had all escaped through the sewers and labyrinths of underground passages.

Well, the day wasn't over yet.[9]

At about 4 P.M., the German forces, divided into two units,
moved northward up Nalewki, and from a northern gate, southward toward Muranowski Square. Once his troops controlled the
square, Stroop calculated, the Jews in the whole northeastern corner of the ghetto, including the Brushmakers' District, would be
cut off. Once more his men moved in small groups, staying close
to the walls on either side of the street.

Sixteen-year-old David Plonski knelt at a second-story window
in the well-fortified Brauer's shop at the corner of Nalewki and
the square. Brauer's had produced uniforms for the Wehrmacht
before being abandoned to the Jews. David watched with pounding heart as the Germans cautiously approached. At last he would
avenge the murder of his family. From the age of thirteen, he had
managed to keep alive his family of eight by smuggling in food
from the Aryan side. He had crawled through holes in the wall,
climbed over the wall, wormed his way through stinking sixteen-
inch sewage pipes, attached himself to workers' groups leaving
and entering the ghetto. Often the Nazis shot smugglers on the
spot or machine-gunned them in groups. But this did not deter
David. It was better to die quickly from a bullet in the head than
slowly from starvation. And he had many mouths to
feed.

David had wanted to smuggle his family out of the ghetto when
the deportations began, but his parents refused to go. They
feared that Polish blackmailers on the Aryan side would force
them to give up everything they owned and then perhaps turn
them over to the Gestapo for further profit.

"What happens to the ghetto will happen to us," his mother had
told him.

David decided to stay with his family. What happened to his
family would happen to him. But then he met a ZZW officer, Richard Walewski, who talked him into serving as an underground
liaison with the Aryan side. David had the right experience and
the right appearance. With his blue eyes and blond unruly hair,
he resembled a typical Polish urchin. When he protested that he

109

wished to remain with his family, Walewski argued, "I have a higher mission for you. It is your duty to accept."

He did, and he was soon smuggling arms for the ZZW as well as food for his family, until they were deported.

"Why should they die and I live?" he sobbed.

"So that you may avenge their death," Walewski replied.

And now David would.

The ZZW forces defending Muranowski Square were far more powerfully entrenched than the ZOB fighters who had earlier battled the Germans, thanks to the arms smuggled to them by the Polish officers, Iwanski and Ketling, and to the military expertise of the ZZW leaders. And they were more mobile as well. Their tactic was to move constantly from one post to another to confuse the enemy.

Aside from Brauer's, the best-fortified building was Muranowska 7, off the square. The cellar, ZZW headquarters, buzzed with activity, especially when people entered or came out of the opening to a tunnel that led to Muranowska 6 on the Aryan side of the wall. On the roof, fighters crouched behind one of the two ZZW heavy machine guns, the only two in the ghetto. The whole square and the approaches to it lay within range.

David aimed his pistol at one of the advancing Germans and waited for the signal. When the enemy was about forty yards away, someone threw a grenade and David fired, one bullet in a fusillade that showered the enemy from all sides. The Germans smashed into some of the houses with submachine guns rattling but found no one inside. The fighters who had been there were now shooting at them from other positions.

Meanwhile the machine gun on the roof of Muranowska 7 swung into action, mowing down many Germans. Stroop's tank and two armored cars started to rumble into the fray from the north, only to be frightened back by exploding Molotov cocktails. Stroop, who had moved his headquarters just outside the ghetto after nearly being hit by snipers, was shocked at the firepower greeting his troops. How had the Jews gotten hold of machine guns?

Then came the worst humiliation of all. Atop Muranowska 7, next to the machine gun, the fighters hoisted the blue and white Zionist and the red and white Polish flags. Stroop was enraged— and fearful. The flags represented a direct challenge to German

110

power, authority, and honor, and since they were clearly visible on the Aryan side, they could, as was intended, excite the Poles to join in the uprising.

Stroop sent fresh troops into the battle, determined to take the square before nightfall. However, the flags fueled the passions not only of the Germans but of the Jews. David now felt invincible as he dashed from window to window, balcony to balcony, roof to roof, firing his pistol. This one was for his mother, his father. . . . He would kill at least one German for each member of his murdered family.

Finally, as darkness descended, the Germans fell back, leaving most of their casualties behind. The machine gun then halted its deadly chatter, and only occasional shots echoed in the night. The battle was over.

David ran down to the courtyard, where his joy was suddenly tempered by the sight of several wounded being treated by his commander, Richard Walewski, who was a physician. One youth was in a critical condition. When he had come under heavy fire while shooting from a roof, he tried to climb down a rope, but the rope snapped and he fell four stories and broke his back.

"Kill me! Please kill me!" he pleaded. And a comrade gave him a capsule of poison to swallow. But this only intensified his agony. Someone had to shoot him, but no one would volunteer. And so all the fighters in his group, including David, drew lots to choose the mercy killer. But the man who "lost" still refused to kill his comrade, until the victim's screams became unbearable. The "loser" then aimed his pistol and fired.

With tears in his eyes, David looked up and saw the flags still fluttering in the spring breeze. What a glorious victory.[10]

Stroop's troops, after retreating from the battle at Muranowski Square, reorganized and headed south toward the Productive Ghetto, which they would pass through en route to their base. They marched proudly despite their large losses and were enthusiastically singing an anti-Semitic song, obviously relieved that the day's fighting was over.

But it was not. On Smocza, near Nowolipie in the Productive Ghetto, a huge bomb lay hidden in the doorway of a factory, set to go off the second the troops passed by. David Nowodworski's ZOB

111

group, which was based at Nowolipie 67 on the corner of Smocza, had checked the bomb every day for weeks to make sure that it was in working order.

Now, at last, late in the afternoon of the first day of the uprising, the fighters in the Productive Ghetto would have the opportunity to strike. As soon as the bomb exploded, they would fire furiously into the presumably shattered German ranks.

Among the most impatient fighters was Jacob Putermilch, whose brooding Semitic face reflected the bitter disappointment he had felt all day. Why hadn't he received the order to fire at the Germans as they had marched past his post on their way to the Central Ghetto that morning? Jacob's post then had been at Leszno 76, a street divided down the middle by the ghetto wall.

Jacob, standing at a window, had grasped a grenade in an upraised hand, but he couldn't unleash it because the signal never came. Damn Eliezer, he swore to himself, though he loved Eliezer Geller, the ZOB commander in the Productive Ghetto. Eliezer was to give the signal by hurling the first grenade, but he played with his missile until it was too late. Was Eliezer acting on what he mistakenly thought was the order of Yitzhak Zuckerman—not to join in the battle?

Anyway, the chance was missed, and all day the fighters in the Productive Ghetto had been nervously listening to the explosions and gunfire in the Central Ghetto, wondering what was happening. The only person they had shot that day was a Jewish Gestapo agent who had been taken prisoner.

Jacob had even found time in the morning to visit his father, who lived nearby, as he was about to descend into a bunker. The old man, though dejected and worried, embraced his son with joy and looked silently into his eyes. For a long while they stood motionless. Then they shook hands and separated, each of them knew, forever.

Nor did Jacob expect to see his sister, Hagit, again. She was with another ZOB group in the Productive Ghetto. And Jacob had little doubt that she would fight to the last bullet. She had always been an activist. It was she who had influenced him to join the Hashomer Hatzair movement under Mordechai Anielewicz before the deportations began. Thus he had automatically become a ZOB fighter.

Jacob had been especially useful while working with his father in a ghetto laundry that washed clothes for German soldiers, having the opportunity to steal items that would permit the fighters to disguise themselves during their varied operations. He had also helped to burn down warehouses full of goods being manufactured for the Germans. Finally he had been assigned to the Productive Ghetto, and he was now eagerly awaiting battle.

At about 5 P.M. word came that the Germans were retiring from the Central Ghetto via Smocza Street. They would march right by the bomb. Eliezer then ordered Jacob's group to leave Leszno 76 and join Nowodworski's group at Nowolipie 67, which overlooked the explosion site. In a few minutes Jacob was watching the Germans approach, dragging their feet but singing vigorously.

At the proper moment, Nowodworski, who had miraculously escaped from Treblinka a few months earlier, gave the signal that would help to avenge those who did not get away. Somebody pulled a switch. . . . But nothing happened. A wet wire had caused a short circuit. As the Germans marched past, Jacob bit his lips, and some of the fighters felt like weeping. Once again, fumed Jacob, fate had cheated them of victims. And after all the preparations, the hopes, the visions of terrible vengeance. . . .

But the Jews then threw grenades and Molotov cocktails, and the explosions enveloped the street in great billowing clouds of smoke and dust. A moment of expectant silence, and when the air cleared, about a score of Germans could be seen lying dead or twisting in pain. The Jews embraced and kissed each other, and tears of joy came to Jacob's eyes. More might have been killed, but the sight of a single dead German was enough to enrapture them.

The enemy reorganized and fired back. But by now the fighters had scattered safely to other positions.[11]

Walther Caspar Többens grew more nervous by the hour as the fighting raged on. The situation was far worse than he had expected. The Jews in the Central Ghetto were battling ferociously and had even attacked SS troops in the Productive Ghetto. Not only might all his workers die in the struggle, but his factories, with their millions of marks' worth of equipment, might vanish with them.

He had rushed to the ghetto at 4 A.M., shortly before the *Aktion* began, and posted notices on the doors of the factories and workers' quarters ordering all employees to show up for work the next morning. They would not be harmed, he promised. But those

113

who hid, he warned, would be taking a great risk since the police would search everywhere.

Többens intended to haul all the workers who showed up directly to Umschlagplatz. There he would pile them on trains that would carry the younger, stronger Jews to his new factories in Lublin, the others to Treblinka. But so few people came to work that he decided to wait until he could lure more out of their hiding places. He didn't want to frighten them into still greater resistance.

In the afternoon, while General Stroop was attacking along Nalewki Street, Többens thought the time might be ripe to pluck at least some of the workers from their hideouts, especially in the Brushmakers' District, which adjoined the Central Ghetto. Certainly, hearing the storm of artillery and machine gun fire must have given the workers food for thought. So he sent Heinrich Lauts, director of the brush factory, into the Central Ghetto to see Stroop.

Lauts stumbled through the debris of battle and found Stroop at a command post on Nalewki Street.

"General," he said, "would you please cease fire for a short time so that I can persuade the brushworkers to come out and transfer to Lublin."

Stroop shrugged his shoulders. "The Jews are throwing Molotov cocktails at us and you expect me to cease fire?"

"It's important for the war effort to transfer the workers. Everything is prepared. I need just half an hour to go in and ask them to report to Umschlagplatz."

Lauts knew, of course, that only those volunteers considered the fittest would be sent to work while the others were doomed. This was unfortunate, he apparently felt, being more humane than Többens, but better the good workers than none at all.

Stroop reconsidered. He would, after all, send most of them to Treblinka.

"All right," he said, "I'll give you one half-hour. But you go at your own risk."

Lauts realized the Jews might kill him. And he was frightened. Yet he felt strangely confident. Had he not always treated his workers fairly? He had not permitted brutality like some of his colleagues had. And he had tried to save as many as possible from the gas chambers. Besides, so much was at stake. The whole ghetto industrial complex was, in a sense, his baby. Assigned by the

114

German government to organize it, he had brought into the ghetto his old friend and partner, Többens, as well as other ambitious businessmen. Was it his fault if the SS kept interfering and sending more and more workers to Treblinka?

No, he was a friend of the Jews and they would listen to him.

Stroop ordered his men to cease fire, and guards opened the gate in the wall separating the Brushmakers' District from the Central Ghetto to let Lauts enter. He hurried into the courtyard of the nearest factory building and shouted, "This is Lauts. I want to help you. Everything is prepared. I can save your lives. I beg you to report to Umschlagplatz."

An eerie silence greeted his appeal. Unperturbed, Lauts then ran to several other courtyards and shouted the same message. Finally a handful of Jews emerged.

"Where are the others?" he asked one of them.

"In the bunkers," was the answer. "They don't hear you. Anyway, they are afraid they will be killed."

Lauts hurried back to Stroop and said breathlessly, "Everybody is hiding in bunkers. Please extend the cease-fire and I think I can get them out."

Stroop agreed, and Lauts returned to the Brushmakers' District and continued to shout his appeal. But again only a few Jews emerged. Finally Stroop began his attack on Muranowski Square, and Lauts led his small catch to Umschlagplatz. He was disappointed that he had not persuaded more to come. . . .

Meanwhile, at about 5 P.M., Többens made a fiery speech to a group of workers in the courtyard of one of his factories in the Productive Ghetto. The Jews in the Central Ghetto were behaving very badly, he fretted. They were being led, he assured his listeners, by "bandits" and "terrorists."

"But their actions," he said, "have nothing to do with you. Do not follow the example of the Central Ghetto."

He then suggested that all the workers volunteer for transfer to Lublin, where they would live comfortably and in safety.

That evening, Lauts was conferring with Többens at his headquarters in the Small Ghetto when he was called to the telephone. It was one of the brushworkers. He was sorry that he and some of his comrades had not heard Lauts' appeal but had learned about it afterward. Would Lauts return to the Brushmakers' District the next morning to collect them?

Lauts and Többens were delighted. Perhaps the workers had

115

begun to see the light and now realized that it was better to work for them than to die; though, of course, some would die anyway.

The two men could not have imagined the welcome that the fighters in the Brushmakers' District were preparing for them.[12]

Another industrialist who urged his workers to transfer to Lublin was Karl George Schultz, called Little Schultz to distinguish him from Fritz Schultz, who owned more factories. The owner of a textile firm at Leszno 74–76 in the Productive Ghetto—as well as one on the Aryan side—K. G. Schultz managed to persuade most of his eight hundred workers to show up at about 6 P.M. in the Leszno factory courtyard to listen to his appeal.

The workers had believed him when, on April 15, he assured them, "I am not God and cannot know what will happen, but one thing is certain: You'll remain here at least three more weeks. . . . You'll all leave together with me and under my care."

Now, only four days later, Schultz told them, "Unfortunately I cannot keep my word to you. Unforeseen things have happened. You can thank your people for it—the bandits, who by their behavior have brought matters to such a state."

At 5 A.M., he announced, all his workers would be leaving for Poniatow. The machines were already on the way. When he finished speaking, the workers headed back to their apartments or bunkers, either to pack for the next day's trip (they were told they could take fifteen kilograms of luggage) or to hide.

Michael L., Schultz's technical director, and Yitzhak Gitler, his administrator, couldn't make up their minds. Perhaps they should transfer; the workers might be treated decently in Poniatow. Anyway, they did not have a bunker to hide in, since they had planned earlier to flee with their families to the Aryan side as soon as proper arrangements could be made.

Now there seemed to be no way to escape from the ghetto, and people who had spent time and money building bunkers were not offering to share valuable breathing space with people who had not.

But Michael's wife, Maria, was adamant when the two men returned to Michael's apartment.

"We must not fall into their trap," she said. "We must find a place to hide."

The two men exchanged rather sheepish looks. She was right.

They would hide. But where? Each residence block was isolated, and they had to stay within it—unless the guards accepted a bribe, which seemed unlikely now that the uprising had broken out. Michael decided to try anyway.

Risking a bullet in the head, he strode into a nearby guardhouse at about 10 P.M. and bluntly offered the guards a bribe to let him, his family, and some friends cross to the Aryan side. The guards consulted, then agreed, to Michael's great joy and astonishment. Feeling he could save still more people, he then suggested that additional groups he permitted to leave—if they paid suitable sums, of course.

"Very well," one of the policemen said. "You may go in groups of five until the change of guard at 2 A.M."

Michael rushed back to his apartment, and shortly people streamed out of the building toward the gate. Having arranged everything, Michael thought that the women in his party of eight—his wife and daughter and Gitler's wife, daughter, and mother—were entitled to be in the first group, and that he, Gitler, and the fiancé of Gitler's daughter should be in the second group. But the others panicked and pushed toward the gate, refusing to heed Michael's plea for order.

"We all go at once or nobody goes," cried one.

The guards, frightened by the massive assault on the gate, started to fire. And so nobody went.

Where would they hide now? Perhaps in the building next to their own. The trouble was, it was only partially constructed. It did not even have a stairway yet. There was only one way to enter. Michael, Gitler, and their families returned to their apartment building and climbed to the attic. There, they placed a stool on a table and helped each other climb through a narrow opening in the ceiling that led to the slanted roof.

The last person left was Gitler's elderly mother. Shaking with fear, she insisted that she could never make it. And as the men sweated and slipped on the roof, frantically pulling her, they were almost ready to agree, though she finally squeezed through.

Their real troubles now began. How were they to cross over to the roof of the neighboring house, about four yards away? The only answer lay in a wooden plank already placed between the two roofs, apparently by other people who had earlier crossed over. Michael peeked over the roof's edge. He chilled as he stared at the street, six floors down.

One by one the Jews inched their way over the narrow board, pausing precariously in the center when it began to bounce. Finally it was the turn of Gitler's mother, and she began sobbing hysterically that "we're going to be killed." But supported by one man in front of her and her son to the rear, she was finally prodded ahead. When they reached the center, the board creaked and seemed ready to crack under the combined weight. The three figures froze, silhouetted in suspension like grotesque statues against the starlit sky.

"Just a little farther," whispered Michael, who had already crossed. "Just a little farther. . . ."

How clear was the spring sky. What a beautiful night. . . . Just a little farther. . . .

Finally they were across. Everyone climbed through another opening into the attic of the new building, where at last they could catch their breath and rest.

"What are you doing here?" a voice cried out in the dark.

What *chutzpah* to intrude into the bunker of others, threatening them all! The newcomers collapsed on the concrete floor. Suddenly they realized that in their desperation they had neglected to bring food or water. And those who had arrived earlier were not in a sharing mood.

Gitler's daughter started to weep. "What can we do? I'm only sixteen. I want to live."

Her father and Michael could not answer her. They had blundered into a death trap.[13]

Shortly after the first German troops marched into the Central Ghetto, several SS men called at Rettungskommando headquarters and selected ten Jewish first aid orderlies, including Sewek Toporek, for a special mission.

"Jewish Communists are revolting against the Germans," one of the SS men explained. "And you are going to help us find them."

The day before, Sewek had told a Gestapo officer that he didn't know where the Jews were hiding. But the Nazis would make sure that Sewek and his fellows searched every house in the Warsaw Ghetto if necessary. The Gestapo had not given them status for nothing. The chosen ten were divided into twos and teamed with two or three SS men. Then the various teams went their different ways.

Sewek's two guards ordered him and his companion to enter a half-destroyed house and bring out any Jews hiding in it. Sewek was desperate. If he refused, they would shoot him on the spot. If he obeyed, he would be leading his own people to death. He thought of what his boss, the Gestapo agent Lolek, had told him: "If only a thousand Jews remain alive, we will be among them."

But what was a man who lived with a dead soul?

The Germans, noting Sewek's reluctance, prodded him with their submachine guns and followed him and his companion into the house. There they found four ailing elderly people who apparently had no bunker to hide in. The Germans ordered their two Jewish helpers to take their "quarry" out, and the group marched to the Judenrat building at Zamenhof and Gensia.

Sewek gasped as they entered the courtyard that Lieutenant Brandt had a few days earlier suggested be turned into a children's playground. While SS men milled around, weapons in hand, hundreds of Jews arrested that morning lay dead, their blood still fresh on the ground. The four elderly captives began to scream, and Sewek, feeling the clammy hand of fear and guilt on his throat, pondered the wages to be paid by the "last thousand survivors."

General Stroop, meanwhile, personally selected many of the people to be executed as he stood in the front square where he had set up headquarters and stopped columns of Jews being marched to Umschlagplatz. There was simply too much chaos at the overcrowded railhead. Some would have to die here and now. After choosing his victims—including all redheads, for some reason, and others whose faces he least liked—he led them into the courtyard, and in the shade of a clump of ancient trees, he watched while his men mowed them down and piled up the corpses in neat stacks to leave room for others.

How would he dispose of the bodies? Perhaps, he suggested to his aides, they could be steamrollered into the ground. But he decided later that it was more practical to burn them.

Between executions, while the machine guns were cooling off, Sewek saw his brother, who had also been forced to guide Jews into the courtyard. They managed to meet alone and, in whispers, decided on a plan to evade further service for the Gestapo.

Since their own house lay only a few buildings away, perhaps the Germans would let them go home for breakfast before continuing on their strenuous mission. To their surprise, the Germans agreed. Well-fed Jewish helpers were, after all, more cooperative. A guard escorted them home and left them there with their father, saying he would come back for them.

Sewek and his brother clung to the hope that in the confusion of the uprising they would somehow be forgotten.

But they had no hope at all of ever forgetting.[14]

It was 8:30 A.M., less than half an hour after Stroop ordered his troops into the Central Ghetto, when Dr. Israel Rotbalsam heard the tramp of boots in the courtyard of the Czyste-Berson-Bauman Hospital at Gensia 6–8. Since going to bed after the bridge game, he had lain awake on his sweaty mattress in the secret second-floor room where many of the doctors and hospital workers were hiding. Like the bells in a madman's mind, every nocturnal noise had echoed with deafening resonance as he strained to detect the dreaded sound. The sound he now heard. The Germans were coming.

January 18! Images of the hospital massacre he had witnessed during the first revolt still flashed through his mind. Now, again, the patients who could not be moved were lying in the wards downstairs, waiting to be killed in their beds. Rotbalsam could hear doors crashing open and guttural voices roaring like beasts. Then shots. Screams. . . . January 18. . . . What a dreadful game of bridge he had played last night. . . . Was it his fault if the patients couldn't be moved? Oh, God!

Minutes later the shooting stopped. Voices. Footsteps. This was it. But then the sounds receded. Silence. Rotbalsam and his fellows waited, barely breathing. Hours passed. Still, they waited. No one wanted to go down . . . to see. Rotbalsam tried to sleep. He was tired, drained. But the echoes persisted even in the silence.

Finally he and the others went down. They stepped over bodies sprawled on the staircase; some of the patients had found the strength to try to flee. Most, about fifty, still lay in their beds, drenched in blood.

They had been too sick to be moved.[15]

Against the rumble of thunder from the Central Ghetto a pleasant tune echoed through the Productive Ghetto. It blared from a loudspeaker installed on a German truck parked near the ghetto gate on the Aryan side of Leszno Street. It was interrupted only by sporadic appeals for workers to register for transfer to the Lublin labor camps.

Two men dressed in firemen's uniforms suddenly walked over to the SS officer standing by the truck. Captain Henryk Empacher and Major Wladyslaw Grzankowski, members of Captain Iwanski's Home Army underground unit, addressed him solemnly. Would he permit them to drive a fire engine into the ghetto to put out a fire near the Church of the Virgin Mary on the Jewish side of Leszno, the only church behind the wall? Noting that the Nazi looked drunk, they handed him money to buy more liquor. The German accepted it.

Soon a fire truck with its siren whining screeched into the ghetto, and a short time later it roared out. Within an hour it had made three more round trips. Thus did nearly fifty Jews escape, hidden amid the fire extinguishing equipment.

And there were still more Jews where these came from—a vault under the crypt of the church. They had reached the vault by entering a building near the church and crawling through a tunnel. Normally they would climb from the vault into the crypt and from there run down a short stairway to the Aryan side of Leszno, where Iwanski's agents would meet them and hustle them away. But with the SS guarding every inch of the wall since the uprising started, only the fire engine could get them out of the ghetto.

It was Iwanski and his ZZW comrades who had designed this escape route. But not without the help of Father Marceli Godlewski, a most unlikely benefactor of the Jews. Before the Germans arrived in Warsaw, Godlewski had been openly anti-Semitic. The Jews dominated the economic life of Poland, he had preached time and again from his pulpit, and their domination must end.

Father Godlewski's preachings had not been unusual. Most Polish clergymen had shown little sympathy for the Jews, even under the Nazi regime, at least until extermination began. But as soon as the Germans stormed into Warsaw, Father Godlewski began a transformation. A Jew who had converted to Christianity, Father Fodor, had had a powerful influence on him, and soon Father Godlewski was devoting himself entirely to helping the Jews at great risk to himself.

One of the Jews under Godlewski's wing was a member of the ZZW, and he introduced the prelate to Iwanski. Soon, with Godlewski's blessing, Iwanski's men were digging the tunnel under the crypt. The tunnel and bunker would be used not only to save Jews but to smuggle arms and supplies to the ZZW.

When the fire engine sped out of the ghetto for the fourth time, a suspicious German guard stopped it. He found the Jews. Captain Empacher, sitting at the wheel, smiled and removed his gold watch. He also offered the guard three liters of the finest vodka. The German returned his smile, and the fire engine zoomed ahead.

Next time, thought Empacher, there would have to be a much bigger fire.[16]

While Iwanski's group continued to help the Jews after the uprising began without consulting Home Army leaders, some of these leaders met in a Warsaw apartment to decide whether such help was "practical." General Tadeusz Bor-Komorowski, the bald, mustachioed deputy Home Army commander, asked Warsaw Commander Colonel Chrusciel his opinion.

Chrusciel had already examined this question with his chief of staff, Major Weber, who claimed to have suggested giving the Jews ample support. According to Weber, Chrusciel replied, "If we put our troops on the alert and start fighting, we will be finished. A million people will die."

"But they're fighting alone, and no one is helping."

"Tell me how to help and we will."

Now Chrusciel would tell Bor-Komorowski how. He had been preparing for two months to help them, he said. Sabotage units under Major Josef Pszenny would try to blow holes in the ghetto wall to divert the Germans and permit at least some Jews to escape. Others would be led to safety through the sewers.

Chrusciel's colleagues looked surprised. True, his plan was in line with the Home Army decision not to help the Jews fight the Germans (Yitzhak Zuckerman had gotten nowhere trying to obtain more arms). It was designed only to help them escape from the ghetto. But should they offer even this aid? Should Poles risk their lives to save Jews?

After some argument the command agreed to Chrusciel's proposal, though it was too late to coordinate it with Jewish plans. How would history judge them otherwise? They decided, however, not to publicize their decision in their underground publications. As Chrusciel would explain later, "There were . . . certain sections of the public whose attitude toward actions in favor of the Jews was reluctant or directly hostile."

Too many Poles, it seemed, would like to see the Germans keep their promise to settle the Jewish problem for them.[17]

On receiving the go-ahead from Colonel Chrusciel, Major Pszenny, who strongly favored helping the Jews, rushed to his men to organize an immediate attack. But they, too, debated the agonizing question: Should they risk their lives for the Jews? There was no time to argue, Pszenny exclaimed. It was 4 P.M. At six they would blow a hole in the northeastern part of the wall on Bonifraterska Street. Who would volunteer?

But the debate continued as the sounds of battle in Muranowski Square, just behind that section of wall, shook the building. The danger was great, some pointed out. German forces were concentrated in the area of attack. And only Jews, after all, were being killed. But Jews were human beings, were they not? And weren't the Germans the common enemy? Finally most of Pszenny's men—thirty-one—volunteered. Jews or no Jews, this was undeniably a good chance to strike at the Germans.

Pszenny was relieved. He then reported that Bonifraterska Street was full of people watching the battle in the ghetto. The Germans were doing nothing to disperse them, apparently calculating that these spectators would serve as a shield against an underground attack. But Pszenny said hopefully that they would actually facilitate such an attack since the volunteers could lose themselves in the crowd and more easily take up their positions.

Within an hour the volunteers, except for ten who did not show up after all, were mingling with the excited throngs who were witnessing, as if at an outdoor theater, a life-and-death struggle safely confined to another world on the other side of the wall.

While some of the partisans wormed their way to positions along the wall or across from it, several sidled into the courtyard of a house on Sapiezynska Street, which ran perpendicular to Bonifraterska, and began preparing the explosives: two specially designed mines mounted on crossed wooden boards. These mines would be hooked onto the ghetto wall and would presumably blow a huge hole in it.

Meanwhile Pszenny stood nearby, waiting for the proper moment to fire into the air and thereby signal his men to start shooting at the guards standing by and atop the wall and at windows of buildings overlooking the ghetto. In the midst of the confusion four men would run to the wall and attach the mines to it.

But before all the partisans were in position, a car loaded with Polish policemen suddenly careened into Bonifraterska Street and came to an abrupt halt. As the first policeman jumped out, one of the saboteurs fired at him, and the others, mistakenly thinking this shot was Pszenny's signal, began shooting at every guard and policeman in sight.

While the crowd scattered in panic, the men with the mines, covered by their comrades, dashed toward the wall, but two were killed and one wounded by guards. With the enemy now firing from all directions, Pszenny ran to the mines, which lay on the street, and detonated them himself, then shouted for a retreat. A great blast shook the earth, and screened by the sooty clouds that enveloped the area, Pszenny and his men scrambled into hiding, carrying their wounded with them.

The attackers suffered two dead and four wounded while killing about a dozen Nazis. Because they were so few and their objective was so limited, their action had been doomed to failure before it began. Even if they had blown a hole in the wall, not many Jews could have come out.

Having little practical value, the attack was an act of conscience on the part of some men and an act to ease the conscience on the part of others.[18]

At nightfall Zivia Lubetkin and Zachariah Artstein crawled half-alive, together with the rest of Zachariah's group, from the jam-packed, almost airless bunker at Kurza 3 into the courtyard and greedily inhaled the smoky air for several ecstatic minutes. Although bullets and shells still ravaged the Central Ghetto, they came from buildings on the Aryan side; the Germans did not dare remain in the ghetto after dark for fear of being attacked from every shadowy corner. And so the people in the bunkers came out of their holes like gophers to breathe the tainted air, search for food, and visit relatives and comrades in other shelters if they knew where to find them.

When his group had settled upstairs in a room at Kurza 3, Zachariah immediately sent his deputy, Tuvia Borzykowski, to find some flashlight batteries. Tuvia ran across the street to Kurza 4 and began searching the abandoned apartments. He found that one was occupied. Rabbi Eliezer Itzhak Mayzel had come up from his bunker with a number of people to conduct the Seder, fighting or no fighting.

The rabbi's one-room apartment looked as if a cyclone had struck it. The bedding was jumbled together, the chairs lay overturned, and the floor was strewn with household objects and broken window glass. But amid this chaos, with fires nearby providing the only light, Rabbi Mayzel and his companions sat around a festive table. In the reflection of the flames the wine in the goblets looked as red to Tuvia as the blood of the Jews who would die in the uprising.

The rabbi invited Tuvia to join them and resumed reading aloud the *Haggadah*, the prayer book for Passover, to the accompaniment of shooting and explosions. In the flickering glow the tears of Mayzel and his guests shone like polished beads. Their spirits fluctuated from sentence to sentence. A miracle might yet happen, as it once had in Egypt, said the rabbi. But then, they were a deserted generation doomed to perish. He grew more gloomy as he went on. He was tired from sitting in the bunker all day, numb from the gunfire, stirred and confused by each bit of news about the fighting.

He finally laid the *Haggadah* down in despair and lowered his head over the table, raising it only to speak occasionally with Tuvia, to learn about the battles that day, about plans for the future. Tuvia, a sensitive intellectual, felt strange in the dismal, oppressive atmosphere. Even news of the day's victories could not dispel the despondency and hopelessness revealed in the rabbi's face by the bright flashes of light from the broken windows. He represented, Tuvia felt, the tragedy of the older generation, which had not the strength to die fighting.

When Tuvia rose to leave, the rabbi gave him a few packages of matzos and wished him and his comrades success.

"I myself," he said, "am too old and weak. But you are young people. Fight successfully and don't give up, and may the Lord be with you!"[19]

Kalman Friedman gambled that the Lord was with him that evening when he decided to leave the relative safety of his cellar shelter and go upstairs to another Seder. Kalman, a short, gentle, soft-spoken man, lived at Nowolipie 53 in the Productive Ghetto. Throughout the day he had listened to the murderous sounds of war reverberating in the Central Ghetto and to the blare of loudspeakers nearby demanding that workers like himself volunteer for transfer to Lublin. At any moment the Germans might come and search the buildings for prey.

Still, Kalman had to keep his word to his neighbors, Jacob Nussbaum and his eight-year-old nephew, Izio. He had promised to attend their Seder. Nussbaum was paralyzed and refused to hide in a bunker and become a burden on others, and Izio refused to go into hiding without him.

"Whatever happens to you," the child said, "will happen to me as well."

Kalman entered Nussbaum's apartment and was greeted with joy by his two friends. Then he and the boy moved the table close to the bed in which Jacob helplessly lay. They spread a white tablecloth on it and, as tradition required, wrapped three matzos in a towel.

"*Ha Lachma Anya*," Nussbaum wailed, sitting up in bed, as he started reading the *Haggadah*.

Memories crowded Kalman's heart. He thought of past Seders—family celebrations throbbing with joy and grandeur. Now he had no family. One day, some months earlier, he had returned home from work and found that his mother, father, and four sisters had all been deported. He had been left shatteringly alone, except for these two dear neighbors.

They, too, were crushed with grief and loneliness. Under Nussbaum's pillow lay a photograph of his wife—a beautiful woman with a face carved in crystal and glowing with charm. During a roundup in September 1942 she had remained in the house with him, even though all Jews who failed to report and were found in their homes were automatically shot. He was unable to move, but he begged her to go. She was young and strong. Perhaps they would only send her to work. If she remained, she would certainly be killed. As for him, he was doomed anyway.

"No," she had said, "I cannot leave you."

She would serve him until her last moments. Who else would do it? If they came for him, she would appeal to their conscience, plead with them, kiss their hands. After all, she said, the German was a human being with a heart and mind and trace of conscience. As she sat by his bed, they continued to argue.

126

"Please go."

"Allow me to remain."

"You are still young. Your life is still ahead of you."

"No, only with you! Only with you!"

Nussbaum felt faint. If she did not leave, he thought, he would go mad. Finally, with tears in her eyes, she began to pack. And when she had finished, she prepared clothing and food for him, moved their elegant furniture into a corner, and scattered dirt and pieces of glass on the floor to give the apartment an abandoned look. Then she went into the kitchen and neatly laid the silverware, several gold rings, and her wristwatch on the table. Perhaps when the murderers found these valuables in the kitchen they would not continue searching the apartment.

When everything had been arranged, she departed without saying good-bye, unable to face the moment of parting. She left the door wide open, apparently to reduce SS suspicions that someone might be hiding inside.

Two days later Nussbaum heard footsteps. The Nazis were going from house to house, looking for Jews in hiding. Shooting and screaming wildly, they broke down every door that was locked. Then they entered Nussbaum's flat and he trembled as he heard them in the kitchen, banging on the walls and opening the closets and drawers. They barely glanced in the bedroom and apparently did not see him. Finally they left.

"My God," Nussbaum later told Kalman, "I am a criminal. I drove her out and I saved myself! She, my wife, the pure woman, sacrificed herself for me."

Some days later, as Nussbaum and Kalman sat consoling each other in their common misery, the door opened, and a frightened child entered. He ran to the bed and fell upon it weeping.

"Izio!" cried Nussbaum, and his stifled sobbing mingled with that of his nephew.

"Uncle," the child said with bursting heart, "you know, they took mother and father."

Only the day before, he told his uncle, his mother had stroked his head, kissed his eyes, and gently warned him, "Now it is forbidden for chidren to run about in the streets."

She took him to the attic and put him in a corner shielded from wind and rain, next to a barrel.

"When you hear footsteps," she whispered, "hide in the barrel and wait. In the evening we will return and take you."

Izio then went on, swallowing his tears: "I sat until late at night and waited; I was cold. I wasn't hungry. I didn't even open the bundle of food that mother had left for me. Below, it was quiet; no voice could be heard. But I was filled with fear. I was so tired and afraid that I fell asleep in the barrel. I woke at noon and found that mother had not yet come."

His words stuck in his throat as he related that he then understood why his mother and father had not come to take him. And so he had made his way through the glass-strewn empty streets, past smashed storefronts with axed doors, past corpses sprawled in the gutter, to his uncle's home.

"Izio," Nussbaum said, "calm down. You will remain with me. It is good that no one saw you. It is a real miracle. Be calm, my child."

Soon Izio was taking care of all his uncle's needs. He cleaned, cooked, and served, and became his nurse. He risked his life going out to search for food. He comforted his uncle with rumors that all the Jews would soon become American citizens, and when some German soldiers marched by, he said, "They are not looking for you, uncle. They are searching for healthy Jews."

It was for his uncle that Izio lived. He had become an adult overnight, a child without a childhood.

Kalman filled the Seder glasses with wine, and Izio began to ask the Four Questions traditionally asked by children at the Seder meal to define the meaning of Passover. The child chanted the questions in singsong Yiddish. One was: "*Far vos iz gevorn farendert die dozike nacht fon alle nacht*" ("Why is this night different from all other nights?")

Izio showed no sign that this question had any special significance to him. But Kalman and Nussbaum exchanged agonized glances.[20]

To Mordechai Anielewicz and his fighters, the answer to that Biblical question was simple. This night symbolized not only the miracle of Moses but the miracle of the ghetto. This was a night of redemption. A euphoric night. Yet there was one nagging question. Who would live to tell the story of this new miracle?

Mordechai wondered. Perhaps more people than he had imagined. The fighters were confronted by a new and strange situation. They had expected to fall in battle that day. But the day had ended, and they were still alive. They had actually beaten the German Army. Might they survive after all? Would the Germans have any better luck the next day, or the day after that? But this flash of optimism was short-lived. Mordechai could not be optimistic after objectively analyzing the ZOB position with his deputies as they sat in a corner of their bunker in Mila 29.

Except for the grenades, Molotov cocktails, and the few rifles the ZOB owned, its fighting power had been more illusory than real. The pistol, which every member proudly carried, had actually proved almost useless. Mordechai had expected his fighters to confront the Germans face to face on stairways and in attics, narrow passages, tunnels, and doorways. In such close-range clashes, the pistol would have been adequate. But the Germans were careful to keep their distance, employing tanks, artillery, flamethrowers, and large assault units. What could a pistol do in such a battle?

Moreover, the day's struggle had confirmed the ultimate objective of this *Aktion*: complete annihilation of the Jews remaining in the Warsaw Ghetto. The Germans, it was clear, would throw in all they needed to achieve this end. Thus, Mordechai and the other ZOB leaders still did not doubt that they would all die in the ghetto. They could only hope to prolong the battle. But to do even this they would have to get help from the Polish Home Army.

That evening Mordechai learned of their chances from Yitzhak Zuckerman, who had managed to send a message to him through a gravedigger who worked in the Jewish cemetery at the western edge of the ghetto. The Home Army would provide no more arms. When Yitzhak had asked to meet with Colonel Chrusciel, the Warsaw commander replied, under orders from the national command: "The Warsaw Military salutes the heroes of the Warsaw Ghetto who have shown that they can fight. I believe that a meeting is not expedient now."

Nor was there any response yet from the London government-in-exile to a request for weapons and an appeal to the Polish people to help the Jews in any way they could. Mordechai did not know that the government-in-exile, while doing nothing about the arms, had ordered the Home Army to broadcast a message on its secret radio that day, lauding the heroic actions of the ZOB: "The people of Warsaw are following this unequal struggle with admiration and with manifest sympathies for the ghetto in its death throes."

Although this message did not even ask the Poles to help the

Jews, it would be broadcast only after the uprising was over and the Jews had been destroyed.

The best news from the Aryan side was that Yitzhak had managed to get twenty-five rifles from the Communist PPR. But the trouble was, with the guards covering the entire length of wall, there seemed no way to get the rifles into the ghetto. (The ZOB still did not know about the underground passages dug by the ZZW, which might have been used for the purpose.)

Unless arms and ammunition could be smuggled in immediately, Mordechai decided, the ZOB would have to change its tactics. With even pistol ammunition running out, his fighters would be unable to defend their positions much longer. They would have to fight in small partisan units; to hit and run, making every bullet count, then disappear into the bunkers.

It would not be the kind of fighting he had envisaged when he had refused to build special bunkers or dig underground escape passages for his fighters. He could not afford heroic face-to-face encounters with an enemy that was attacking as if it were being challenged by a full-fledged army.

The Poles, Mordechai bitterly concluded, had decided to let the Jews die.[21]

"Excellent! I congratulate you, Herr General. You extricated us from an embarrassing situation."

Colonel Hahn put down his French apéritif and rose from an armchair to greet General Stroop, in whose suite he had been waiting.

"Don't take a bath," Hahn said. "Just wash your hands and sit down to eat the dumplings before they get cold. They were brought in a minute ago."

In a few moments the two men were sitting at the table, silently stuffing themselves with dumplings. Hahn paused only to tell Stroop that he, too, was very fond of this dish—a remark, thought Stroop, intended simply to please him.

They both knew that the German performance that day, even after Stroop had taken command, had been far from excellent, that their troops had been humiliated by a handful of amateur Jewish fighters, including women. Scores of the general's troops had been killed or wounded, and what had been achieved? Only about four hundred Jews, all civilians, had been captured, while all the fighters got away. And though the Germans had managed to destroy a few houses, they had been unable to penetrate Muranowski Square.

Nor could Stroop's troops hold the area they did conquer. The general had withdrawn every one of his men after dark, fearing Jewish counterattacks in the unfamiliar ghetto labyrinths. He could only make sure that the Jews could not get out, or the Polish partisans in, by replacing the 120 *Askari* guards surrounding the ghetto with 250 Waffen SS soldiers.

In terms of the National Socialist theory of Aryan racial superiority, how could Stroop and Hahn explain the disaster to each other, to their superiors, to themselves?

When the two Germans started on the crispy venison and truffles, they finally began to exchange views and information. Hahn was concerned that two of his own men had been wounded. The front line, he delicately suggested, was no place for security men. Stroop promised he would try his best to prevent such misfortunes in the future.

After dinner Stroop telephoned General Krüger in Cracow, then Himmler in Berlin to report briefly on the results of the fighting after he had taken command that morning. He had "defeated" the Jewish "bandits," he said, though, unfortunately, they managed to escape over the roofs and through the sewers. None of his men had been killed, even while under von Sammern-Frankenegg's command, he lied; and only twenty-four had been wounded.

Himmler expressed satisfaction and congratulated Stroop. The general had not disappointed him, he said in his "soft and pleasant" voice. But he should be careful not to fall into a trap of exaggerated optimism in the following days.

The Reichsführer gave Stroop a free hand to employ all necessary means to destroy the ghetto. But he should not burn or blow up houses before all industrial, especially military, enterprises had been evacuated. The German managers, as well as the machinery, tools, raw materials, and manufactured goods, must be fully protected from fire, shooting, and explosions, Himmler stressed.

After talking with Krüger and Himmler, Stroop met with his personal staff and the commanders of all his units. Then, when they had left, he worked on a report, drank a glass of Burgundy, and went to bed. He had almost fallen asleep when one of the telephones near his bed began ringing.

"*Donnerwetter!*" ("Damn it!") he roared into the mouthpiece. "How dare you wake me up! Are you so stupid that you don't know that in a few hours I must command the ghetto operation and that I must sleep three or four hours before that!"

His caller cleared his throat and, when he began to speak, sent a spasm of shock through the general. It was Himmler!

Stroop sat up in bed and began to apologize, but Himmler gently replied, choking with laughter, "Do not be angry at me, my dear Stroop, for waking you up and interrupting your precious rest. But after thinking over your reports and Krüger's telephone messages, I have arrived at some general conclusions. You should realize that you have passed only the preliminary phase of the *Grossaktion.* April nineteenth is only the overture to the historical event which will be named *Grossaktion in Warschau.*

"You conducted the overture magnificently. It came out extremely well, especially against the background of the clumsy attempts of that bungler, von Sammern. Since I am fond of Wagner's operas and the contemporary National Socialist musical conductors, permit me to tell you: Maestro, continue to play thus, and our Führer and I shall never forget it."

When the conversation ended, Stroop put down the telephone and happily lay back. So he was a maestro! Yes, he had taught those Jews a lesson for daring to challenge the invincible German Army. Tomorrow, April 20, was the Führer's birthday, and Stroop would orchestrate a special musical treat for him: the death wail of the Warsaw Ghetto.[22]

On the first day of the uprising, the American and British governments sent representatives to Bermuda to decide how to help war refugees. The Americans were instructed not to discuss Jewish refugees only, or to raise questions of religious faith or race in appealing for public support or promising U.S. funds.

In his opening speech Richard Kidston Law, of Britain, declared that only victory in the war would solve the refugee problem and that the persecuted people "should not be betrayed . . . into a belief that aid is coming to them, when, in fact, we are unable to give them immediate succor."

Dr. Harold Willis Dodds, president of Princeton University, said on behalf of the Americans, "The problem is too great for solution by the two governments here represented."

And Breckinridge Long, the U.S. assistant secretary of state in charge of refugee affairs, wrote in his diary the following day, April 20, referring to American Jewish leaders who were trying to pressure their government to do something to save the Jews: "One danger in it all is that their activities may lend color to the charges of Hitler that we are fighting this war on account of and at the instigation and direction of our Jewish citizens."

Didn't they realize that they were playing into Hitler's hands by trying to save their people from mass extermination?[23]

The Second Day

April 20

Mordechai Anielewicz awoke after only a few hours' sleep and stared into the lamplit bleakness of the bunker in Mila 29. It had not been a dream after all. This was the day after the uprising had started. A new day. A day he had never expected to see. And there were Mira and all the other fighters, some still asleep, others getting ready for battle. No, not a dream. Another day of life!

Mordechai breathed in the grimy air with the same boundless appreciation he had felt in the summer of 1939, when he, Mira, and new members of his organization had camped amidst the breathless beauty of the Carpathian Mountains. That had been his last summer of reckless freedom, of pure joy. Other instructors on the trip had even accused him of performing irresponsible pranks and showing no discipline. He encouraged the youngsters to forget the world and the burdens it imposed on them, they complained.

Now many of the same youngsters were here with him in this dark tomblike bunker, stooped under the burdens of a Samson. And it was the world that had forgotten them. The same boys and girls who had badgered him to take them for a hike in the woods, for a swim in a mountain stream. They were still impatient. Still determined to drain joy from every moment of life.

How many Germans would they kill today?[1]

* * *

General Stroop had also awakened after little sleep. He was nervous and uncertain. The euphoric optimism that engulfed him following Himmler's late-night telephone call had dissipated. As he shaved, he stared approvingly into the mirror at his fair Nordic face and reflected on the uncertainties. Would the Jews resist as strongly as they had yesterday? Would the Polish underground attack in strength? Perhaps his SS men would lack the courage to fight hand to hand.

Stroop gulped down his breakfast, still pondering the dangers; and when he was about to leave his suite to supervise the destruction of the Jews, he paused to cross himself, as his Catholic mother had taught him to do. He was, after all, alone in the room. When he had gone downstairs and climbed into his car, he breathed in the warm spring air and felt calm again, even serene.

The driver drew the car to a halt just outside the ghetto wall, where troops were gathered. Stroop got out and ordered Major Sternhagel, his new second in command, to split his force of thirteen hundred into detachments of thirty-six men, each led by an officer, and to reoccupy the area captured the preceding day. Sternhagel was then to seize the rest of the Central Ghetto, as well as the adjoining Brushmakers' District to the east, and to search every square foot of the captured terrain for Jews in hiding.

His troops would certainly crack the backbone of the Jewish defense that day, Stroop felt. The next two days they would mop up the last-ditch defenders. His confidence had returned. But there was no use taking unnecessary risks. Maybe he could still lure at least some of the Jews out of their hiding places by peaceful means. Before attacking, he would give Heinrich Lauts, the director of the brush factory, another chance to persuade his four thousand workers to volunteer for transfer to Lublin.

He glanced at his watch: 6 A.M. In one hour he would move into the ghetto.[2]

Lauts was waiting at the gate at 6 A.M., as he had promised the Jewish worker who telephoned him the night before from the brush factory. He hoped he would have greater success than he had had the previous day in persuading his workers to emerge from hiding and go to Umschlagplatz. This time, he did not enter

135

alone. Two of Stroop's men escorted him, wearing white "truce" rosettes on their lapels and holding their rifles over their heads to demonstrate their "peaceful intentions."

When Lauts and his guards entered the courtyard of Walowa 6, the ZOB fighters hiding behind windows permitted them to advance, listening to Lauts cry, "You have fifteen minutes to come out. I shall guide you to the trains that will take you to labor camps in Lublin. You will be safe. Come out, I beg you!"

Silence. The fighters had been given orders to hold their fire until large units appeared. They did not have enough bullets to waste on individuals. Finally, twenty-eight workers trickled out of the buildings around the courtyard. Lauts despaired. Twenty-eight out of four thousand! They were still being stubborn. He shouted again. Suddenly several shots rang out. One of his guards fell. Then Lauts himself slumped to earth, a bullet in his leg.

The Jews, he felt, were not playing fair.[3]

General Stroop was enraged by the reception accorded Lauts, and at 7 A.M. he ordered his troops, Germans and Ukrainians, to enter the ghetto via the Nalewki Street entrance. To get there some marched northward along Zelazna Street and turned east on Leszno along the Aryan side of the street bordering the Productive Ghetto.

But the dividing wall did not block the view of the Jewish fighters perched at windows in buildings along the Jewish side of Leszno. Jacob Putermilch, whose group had returned to Leszno 76, was still rejoicing in the Nazi carnage he and his comrades had caused the previous day with the barrage from Nowolipie 67 (even though their huge bomb had failed to go off) when his eyes gleamed at the sight of this new prospect for vengeance. The enemy column, about fifty men led by motorcyclists and followed by two armored cars, was much larger than the one he had seen the day before.

Eliezer Geller rushed into Jacob's apartment on the third floor and ordered the fighters to attack with gunfire and grenades as soon as he gave the signal with two grenade explosions.

When the SS men passed the building, they were greeted by a storm of gunfire and explosions. Smoke engulfed the street, and the soldiers, screaming in panic, flattened themselves on the ground against the Aryan side of the wall or ran into nearby houses, leaving behind the dead and wounded, about a third of the force.

When the Germans recovered from their shock, they machine-gunned all the buildings along the ghetto side of Leszno—including Leszno 72, the area headquarters of Walther Casper Többens. Többens, who was in his office at the time, ran to a window to see what was happening when a bullet struck him in the hand. One of his faithful aides pulled out a pistol in anger and fired through the window, shouting, "Do not shoot! There are only Germans here!"

When the firing on both sides stopped, Jacob and his comrades raced through the attics to neighboring buildings. The German survivors gathered their casualties and trudged on toward the Central Ghetto—only to receive another murderous welcome from two more ZOB groups based at Leszno 36. After a fifteen-minute battle, ten more Germans lay dead or wounded on the street.

Meanwhile, ZZW fighters entrenched in a house on Smocza and Nowolipie, a block east of Leszno, tossed grenades at about a hundred Germans marching toward the Central Ghetto via Nowolipie, killing or wounding about ten and forcing the rest to retreat.

When the fighting had ended, Jacob and the others on Leszno gathered to exchange stories of their victory.

"How many opportunities like this are we going to have before we die?" Eliezer asked.

"I agree to live just one week," said Jacob, "if we have the possibility of doing every day what we have done today."

Another fighter, Shalom Sufit, was more demanding: "I won't sleep peacefully in my grave unless I kill at least ten Nazis."

Less scornful of death than the Jewish combatants were the shaken German survivors, who would be tested again in the Brushmaker's District and the Central Ghetto.[4]

"If only I could breathe in the scent of the trees and flowers instead of the buildings burning in the ghetto."

Dvora Baron gazed nostalgically at the park in Krasinski Square on the Aryan side of the wall running along Swientojerska Street. She was standing at a third-floor window of Walowa 6 in the Brushmakers' District, chatting with her comrade, Shlomo Shuster. To the west, in the Central Ghetto, was a ghastly world of smoke and flame; to the east, a sunlit world of trees and flowers. Dvora, the daughter of a well-to-do textile merchant, remembered the leisurely days of her childhood when she had played in Krasinski park.

"I love flowers so much," she sighed.

Shlomo glanced at her beautiful oval face and was silent for a moment. "Yes," he finally said, "in my town, too, there was a park with trees, flowers, and grass. I remember. . . ."

Shlomo was only seventeen, but his blue eyes reflected an older man's maturity. The son of an impoverished shoemaker, he had smuggled bread into the ghetto many times to keep his family and himself alive. But his delicate features betrayed his youth and camouflaged his toughness and tenacity.

He and Dvora were restless, impatient. They had been on guard at the window for a day and half, and the Germans had not yet attacked the Brushmakers' District, where five ZOB groups were scattered in buildings on Swientojerska and Walowa, which extended from Swientojerska at an angle. Only Lauts had come with his silly promises. What a surprise awaited the enemy.

"Why don't the Germans come?" Shlomo asked. "When will we get the chance to show them?"

"Don't worry, they'll come," Dvora assured him. "After their defeat yesterday, they're careful about opening a second front. . . . But it won't help them."

"My hand is itching. I want to throw something at them."

"The time will come. In the meantime, we can rejoice in yesterday's victories. . . . Their screams were louder than the Jews' on their way to die."

As they stared at the trees and flowers, they could hear the fierce fighting going on in the Central Ghetto.[5]

The Nazis that morning had attacked through Nalewki gate and driven toward Muranowski Square again, accompanied by a tank and a flamethrower. At the corner of Nalewki and Muranowska streets the ZZW fighters had opened fire and knocked out the tank with Molotov cocktails. But the attackers, far superior in number and firepower than on the previous day, this time managed to reach Muranowska 7, ZZW headquarters.

They were desperately trying to enter the building and capture the two bullet-riddled flags still fluttering at the top, but the machine gun flanking them took a terrible toll. Finally Stroop's men used a flamethrower, and the fighters were forced to flee to other buildings, from which they continued to fire. Some were caught and shot on the spot.

But despite their gains, the Nazis failed to seize the headquarters and take the flags, which continued to wave even as the fire burned itself out.

Nevertheless, by noon Stroop had control of the square. And now he would take the Brushmakers' District, where a bullet had struck Lauts hours before.[6]

"Perhaps we'll manage to get out of the ghetto and hide until the end of the war. We can make our way to the Russian front. After all, we are not very far away, only some hundreds of kilometers."

Shlomo shrugged, his blue eyes skeptical. Dvora, he felt, had a lively imagination.

"I don't believe this will happen," Shlomo said, "though it's a lovely dream."

"It is a dream, but sometimes dreams come true. I can imagine myself sitting by the Sea of Galilee and telling our friends. . . . "

Dvora began to sing a Zionist song when suddenly, at 3 P.M., they saw enemy troops turn into Walowa from Franciszkanska. As the force emerged from the black clouds that had settled over the Central Ghetto, Dvora rushed to report the news to Hanoch Gutman, her group leader (no relation to Israel Guttman, the security guard in the bunker at Franciszkanska 30), who immediately sent a messenger to Marek Edelman, the ZOB area commander.

Marek, too, had been gazing at the Aryan side—people going about their normal lives to the rhythm of music and traffic noises. Were those people returning his gaze? The wall reached up to the height of only one story and was not very thick, yet Marek feared that the outside world could not see over it or hear the shooting, the explosions, the cries for help on the other side. Would history even record what was happening here?

On seeing the Germans approach, Marek suppressed his excitement. His dark eyes, set in a thin, pale, Semitic face with prominent nose and thick lips, perpetually reflected a hard cynicism; and his normally disheveled appearance somehow seemed to accentuate this quality. Even his red angora wool sweater, which he had found in an abandoned apartment and now proudly wore under crisscrossed leather bandoliers, could not brighten the somber image.

Marek's parents, both of them leading Bundists, had died when he was still a boy, leaving him entirely alone. Thus, since his early youth his only devotion had been to the Bund, to the welfare and defense of Polish Jews. And the Bund had rewarded him, at the age of twenty-two, with the top position in its military command. He was a good commander: unsentimental, unemotional, pragmatic.

During the first deportations in the summer of 1942, when the Germans were trying to deceive the ghetto population into believing they would snatch only a relatively small number of Jews, Marek had been the perfect man to help useful Jews escape the Nazi dragnet. As an employee of the hospital then operating in Umschlagplatz, he managed to lead selected individuals to safety by claiming they were ill, an excuse that the Germans accepted at that time. One woman begged him to take out her fourteen-year-old daughter, thrusting some diamonds into his hand. But he rejected her pleas. He could take out only one person, and he chose a ZOB girl who was a valuable messenger. It was the practical thing to do.

So cool was he that when the uprising started in the neighboring Central Ghetto the previous day, he didn't bother to get up from bed till noon. After all, it was a cold morning, and the Germans weren't attacking his area yet. But they *were* attacking now, and his objective was to shoot at them and explode bombs. He didn't especially care how many Germans were hit. The idea was to shoot. For shooting was, in the eyes of the world, the clearest assertion of honor and heroism.

Marek himself scoffed at this view. What was so honorable or heroic about choosing the way one was to be killed? He chose to fight mainly as a gesture of solidarity with his comrades and as a concession to the pride and reputation of future Jewish generations. After all, with death decreed for all Jews anyway, there was nothing to lose. But he did not agree with those who regarded resistance to the negation of life as inextricably linked with honor. Resistance in hopeless circumstances offered little more to him than the fleeting satisfaction of revenge, which he felt had no real value.

Real honor? Real heroism? Marek recalled the youth who had

voluntarily jumped aboard a boxcar bound for Treblinka so that his mother would not have to travel alone: an action, however noble, that most of the fighters viewed as craven submission to genocide. But Marek would not defy his comrades or disappoint the world. He would, by all means, shoot. Not as a matter of conscience or honor but of pragmatism.

Actually Marek felt somewhat guilty for not having fired the previous day. When he had finally risen from bed and led a patrol to observe the situation in the neighborhood, he noticed several Germans and should have ordered his men to shoot at them. But he had to admit that he was still burdened with the traditional fear of his people: that violence would breed greater violence. It was one thing to prepare for battle, another to leap into its midst. Now, however, he would make up for his error.

Meanwhile, Hanoch Gutman rushed down to the cellar of Walowa 6 to join Simcha Rathajzer, or Kazik, as he was known. Simcha, a handsome blond youth of nineteen who disguised himself in an SS uniform, was in charge of the welcoming committee. He and Hanoch would set off the biggest bomb to be manufactured in the ghetto, a mine buried under the gate to the courtyard shared by Walowa 6 and Swientojerska 32.

Several members of Simcha's family had been killed when a bomb hit his home during the Nazi siege of Warsaw in 1939, though he himself, despite serious wounds, had managed to crawl out of the debris. God had saved him for this moment, he felt. From a small window, Simcha could see about three hundred Germans approaching. As Hanoch seized the switch that would trigger the electrically detonated mine, Simcha pressed the alarm-bell button to alert the fighters. They waited. . . . When the Nazis reached the gate to the courtyard, Hanoch pulled the switch.

The whole area convulsed thunderously, and Simcha saw parts of bodies grotesquely flying in the air together with bits of pavement and fragments of masonry. When the smoke cleared, he gloried at the sight of about eighty soldiers lying dead or wounded in the street. The others streaked away in panic through a hail of grenades and bullets.

Stroop, who was standing some distance away, boiled in humiliation. He greeted with contempt the survivors who came panting by, and he ordered them to go back and not to return without the dead and wounded.

The Jews were jubilant. They had scored their biggest single blow against their would-be murderers. The principal hero was Michal Klepfisz, the Bund engineer who had supervised the manufacture of the Molotov cocktails and then of this devastating mine. Although Michal had in recent weeks spent most of his time acquiring arms on the Aryan side, he had smuggled himself—and several pistols—into the ghetto on April 17, his birthday.

Feigele Peltel and Jacob Celemenski had visited Michal in his apartment that day and found him caressing and playing with one of the pistols like a little boy.

"If only I could keep it!" he sighed.

Although Michal was slated to smuggle the weapons into the ghetto, the visitors suggested that, since it was his birthday, one of them should do it instead. But Michal insisted on going.

"Who knows," he said, "perhaps I will teach them a lesson with this little instrument."

And so Michal returned to the ghetto and was trapped there by the *Aktion*. He considered himself very fortunate. He was now able to see for himself what his precious creation, the mine, could do.

As Dvora stared from a window at the ravaged flesh of the "human beasts" strewn around the bloodstained street, she, too, saw what the mine could do.

"Now I can die happy," she mused. But she added, with some puzzlement, "Yet somehow my desire to live has grown."[7]

The Jews in the Brushmakers' District waited eagerly at their posts. Certainly the Germans would be back, and another surprise was awaiting them in the same courtyard. An hour, two hours, passed. Finally the word spread. A car followed by two files of soldiers was heading toward them. Would these Nazis enter through the debris-cluttered gateway? The tension grew.

The car, with three high-ranking officers sitting in it, halted in front of the gate. Simcha and his comrades, hiding behind windows, could hear them speaking. Then came the tramp of many boots. German soldiers trotted in, hugging the house walls. When the first six had entered, about two dozen more tagged behind.

Simcha hurled a grenade from his window into their midst, and missiles then poured down upon the trapped, screaming enemy from almost every window overlooking the courtyard. The survivors, some of them afire, fled, leaving the courtyard littered with

142

dead and wounded. A sharpshooter on the roof fired at them, and six more fell dead. Only two escaped unscathed. Nazi morale plummeted, and Stroop had to deny a rumor among his men that he himself had been killed.

Half an hour later, at about 5 P.M., the Germans put the Brush-makers' District under deadly siege, raking every building from the Aryan side with three antiaircraft guns, flamethrowers, and machine guns. It was now the Jews who were desperate. They were helpless targets who could not find any Germans at whom to fire back. Finally, Walowa 6 and the neighboring buildings burst into flame.

Since the fighters had not prepared for a withdrawal, expecting to remain at their posts and fight to the death, they did not know where to flee. So Simcha volunteered to seek a new shelter. He would stand the best chance since he had an Aryan appearance and was wearing an SS uniform, though there was a danger that Jews from other groups might fire at him. . . .

Simcha's gentile features had always proved a useful asset to the ZOB. Once, in late 1942, he entered a ghetto police station un-masked—in order to draw attention to himself—while several of his masked comrades took over the station and freed a number of Jewish prisoners. Word soon spread that the Polish underground was actively helping to liberate Jews from the Gestapo.

Another time Simcha donned an elegant leather coat of the type that many Gestapo agents wore and, at gunpoint, brashly marched the daughter of a wealthy Jew through the ghetto streets while frightened residents scampered for safety. He took her to the ZOB jail, then called for her father, who had refused to pay "taxes" to the ZOB. When the man arrived, Simcha loaded his pis-tol and gave him two minutes to pay or be "executed." The man paid up, and on learning that the threat would not have been car-ried out, he congratulated Simcha on his performance. . . .

Now Simcha would again use his Aryan appearance in the ser-vice of the Jews. After a long search, he at last found a bunker and began to climb down into it when he heard the hysterical cries of the occupants as they saw first his German boots, then his uni-form. Simcha jumped all the way down and succeeded in calming them. But clearly the fighters would not be welcome in that shel-ter, and so Simcha went looking for another.

Finally, after Shlomo Shuster cleared the way by running from Walowa 6 while throwing grenades in all directions, Simcha led his comrades to a bunker in Swientojerska 34. There they were warmly greeted.

One fighter who remained at his post until the last minute was Abraham Diamant, who at forty-three was among the oldest ZOB members. After his wife and daughter had been deported in July 1942, he became a fanatical supporter of armed resistance. And though some ZOB commanders thought he was too old to fight, fellow members of his Poalei Zion Left Party knew differently.

"When the time comes to speak with the rifle," he told the skeptics, "we'll see who is young and who is old."

Now the time had come, and Abraham's rifle, first used in the Russo-Japanese War of 1904, took a heavy toll as he stood behind several mattresses and fired from a small fourth-floor window at Swientojerska 32. He then jumped from place to place, shooting still more Germans.

"Now they're learning how the Jews feel," he cried gleefully after hitting six.

When a flamethrower set the building on fire, the Germans infiltrated to the first floor, and Abraham's group began to retreat through the attics. But Abraham pleaded with his group leader, Hersh Berlinski, to let him stay so he could knock out a machine gun that was creating havoc. He opened fire through the smoke of the approaching flames, and the machine gun fell silent. Finally Abraham agreed to withdraw.

A few Jews stayed at their posts too long. Trapped by the flames, they jumped through windows only to be shot to the last man, either in the air or after hitting the ground. When the smoke reached one bunker on Swientojerska Street, about fifty occupants, including some children, began to trickle out and were captured. They were taken to Umschlagplatz and shipped off to death camps—except for the children, who were shot on the spot.

Marek Edelman, the zone commander, was leading one group of fighters through the attics when suddenly they heard footsteps. Germans! At that moment a fighter who had crawled up a stairway behind the enemy threw a grenade. One of the Nazis replied with automatic-pistol fire from behind a chimney. Then . . . silence. A fighter in Marek's group had leaped on him in a suicidal attack.

The other Germans scattered chaotically, and Marek, who in the darkness was completely ignorant of what was happening, saw only that the path through the attics was clear. Shortly, he and his men were crowding into the bunker at Swientojerska 34, where they joined Simcha and his companions.

At 11 P.M., Marek, Simcha, and Hanoch Gutman returned to the attics to retrieve the body of the man who had been killed leaping on the German with the pistol. They found him lying where he had fallen, perforated with bullets. His own cherished pistol was missing.

Michal Klepfisz had not survived his day of triumph.[8]

While the battle in the Brushmakers' District was raging, the Communist PPR on the Aryan side ordered its military arm, the People's Guard, to attack a heavy machine gun post at the wall on Nowiniarska Street, near Bonifraterska, which was pinning down Marek Edelman's fighters. The Jews could not knock out the gun by themselves since they were too exposed to the fire.

Earlier that day the PPR had delivered twenty-five rifles to Yitzhak Zuckerman, the ZOB agent on the Aryan side. This was an enormous arsenal by ghetto standards, but the rifles could not be smuggled past the tight ring of ghetto guards. The PPR would now try to help the beleaguered Jews with direct military action. They would do so even though they had not yet fully recovered from the effects of the now defunct Nazi-Soviet alliance and, more recently, from the arrest of most PPR leaders in May 1942.

Four Poles led by a Jewish commander—one of the few in the Polish Resistance—would attack the German machine gun post. Among them was Jerzy Duracz, a young Pole who was especially enthusiastic about helping the ghetto because of his interest in a young Jewish PPR partisan, Anna Maczkowski, whom he would eventually marry. In September 1942, her PPR superiors in the ghetto had sent Anna to the Aryan side to make contact with surviving leaders of the Polish segment of the party, who had been forced deep underground after the May arrests. The last words she had been told before she departed were engraved in her memory: "Remember, you must get to them. You must get weapons. We don't want to die without fighting. They must give us weapons."

But misfortune had dogged Anna from the moment she crossed to the Aryan side with a group of workers. On leaving the group she was immediately surrounded by a band of Polish black-mailers, one of many such bands that were constantly searching

145

for Jews in hiding. She was stripped of everything but her dress and coat (she successfully implored them to let her keep her coat).* Through some contacts she searched for the party leaders, but they had burrowed so far underground that she could not find them.

Finally, after several weeks, she made contact with the People's Guard leader, Francisze Jozwiak, code name Witold. In his secret flat, Anna accused the party of abandoning its ghetto branch. She found Francisze sympathetic as he explained the danger of ghetto ties following the May arrests. His desire to help the Jews now seemed to echo the sentiment of most Polish Communists, particularly in the rank and file, though some were motivated more by Moscow's order to fight the Nazis wherever possible than by a compulsion to save the Jews as a matter of conscience and human duty.

But Anna soon learned that not all party leaders shared this desire. In their concern for party security, some opposed any contact with Jews on either side of the wall. Nor did they want to send Jews to fight with the Communist partisans in the forests for fear of antagonizing the peasants.†

Indeed, even Josef Lewartowski, the guiding light of the ghetto PPR who had worked hand in hand with the captured Pinya Kartin and was himself a longtime Soviet agent, was considered too marked a man to deal with. During one intensive roundup, in September 1942, he telephoned party leaders on the Aryan side and asked them to help him escape, and they curtly replied that he must look after himself. The following day Lewartowski was shoved into a boxcar bound for Treblinka.

Anna herself was something of an exception. Francisze ordered her to remain on the Aryan side to acquire weapons, which she obtained mainly by grabbing pistols from the holsters of police-

---

*After many pleas by the Jewish underground, the Polish *Komitet Walki Cywilnej* (Committee for Civilian Struggle) issued a warning to blackmailers (published in the clandestine journal, *Biuletyn Informacyjny*, April 18, 1943), and consequently about 10 blackmailers were executed. The Jews felt this represented only a token Polish effort, and indeed it did little to deter the blackmailers. By contrast, the Home Army executed about 2,000 informers and agents who collaborated with the Nazis or worked for them from January 1943 to June 1944.

†One top PPR official who opposed giving armed support to the Jews when the April uprising broke out was Wladyslaw Gomulka, who was to lead Communist Poland after the war. Such action, he avowed, would be cited by anti-Semitic nationalists as "proof" that the PPR was controlled.

146

men before they could react. She soon met Jerzy Duracz, who was eager to help the Jews, even at great risk. And now Jerzy would take the biggest risk yet.

At about 6 P.M. he and his three comrades gathered on Krasinski Square and circled the area where the action was to take place. From Nowiniarska Street they could see the heavy machine gun nest which was manned by two Waffen SS soldiers with Polish police standing behind them. While the gun fired in bursts, people casually sauntered along the street; some stopped and watched.

Suddenly a Polish civilian, recognizing the commander of Jerzy's detachment as a Jew, approached him and tried to blackmail him. The commander pretended to reach for his wallet but pulled out a pistol instead and shot the blackmailer. He then threw several grenades at the machine gun, while Jerzy and the other two men shot at the policemen behind it. The SS men and the policemen fell, but so did the Jewish commander, though his men, including Jerzy, managed to withdraw without a loss.

The machine gun was knocked out, giving the fighters in the Brushmakers' District a brief breathing spell and a chance to escape the fires consuming the area.[9]

Meanwhile, a few blocks away, other Poles were helping the Nazis solve the Jewish problem. A Jew who managed to escape from the ghetto through the sewers was immediately denounced by someone who saw his soot-blackened figure emerge from a manhole. The police captured him and ordered him to face the wall of a building with his hands up. For several moments, the Jew stood trembling with fear and cold.

Suddenly, he somehow distracted the attention of his captors and fled. The Germans closed in but could not find him. They were about to give up the search when a Polish street sweeper went up to them and pointed toward the Jew, who was crouching behind a tree.

The Germans dragged the fugitive away.[10]

At 11 A.M., Governor-General Hans Frank met with his staff in the great hall of Cracow's royal palace, his headquarters, to discuss the security situation in Poland and to celebrate the Führer's birthday. Frank thanked Providence for giving Germany such a

147

leader as Adolf Hitler, then proposed a toast to the Führer. Everybody sipped a glass of wine and tried to look cheerful on this happy occasion. But the smiles were strained, especially Frank's.

All was not going well in the Warsaw Ghetto. And in Berlin, the difficulties might reflect on him, even though the fault, Frank felt, lay with Himmler and his top representative in the General Government, Krüger. Frank was already having trouble enough with Himmler, who wanted to usurp his functions in this Polish region.

The Führer should have listened to *him*, not to Himmler. He, Frank, understood the situation in Poland better than the meddling SS chief. For months he had been calling for a policy of relative moderation toward the Poles in order to induce them not to join or support Jewish resistance or to interfere with operations against the Jews. But Himmler favored a tough policy, fearing that the Poles would interpret moderation as weakness, and Hitler agreed with him.

So now the Warsaw Jews were rebelling, and there was a grave danger that the Poles might rise up in their support. And since Warsaw was a key point for the transfer of German supplies to the east, what a disaster that would be!

And what an irony. In this very hall, on December 16, 1941, Frank had delivered his historic speech revealing for the first time to his officers what was in store for the Jews:

> The Jews must be done away with in one way or another. . . . I know that many of the measures carried out against the Jews . . . are being criticized. There are deliberate attempts . . . to talk about cruelty, harshness, etc. . . . On principle we will have pity on the German people only, and on nobody else in the whole world. The others, too, had no pity on us. . . . This war would only be a partial success if the Jewish clan survived it while we shed our best blood in order to save Europe. My attitude toward the Jews will, therefore, be based only on the expectation that they must disappear.

Now, more than a year later, Frank was realizing his expectation. But would it backfire?

Various speakers stood up and delivered reports. Wilhelm Ohlenbusch, propaganda chief for the General Government, supported Frank's view that German policy toward the Poles should be eased for practical purposes. Then Eberhard Schöngarth, General Krüger's deputy, agreed, even though Krüger himself

148

had always backed Himmler's "tough" policy. Frank was surprised. Himmler, it probably seemed to him, had finally seen the light—now that German security in Poland was being undermined by the Warsaw Jews.

In the middle of the meeting a messenger entered and handed a telegram to Krüger. It was a report from General Stroop. After scanning it, Krüger read aloud the details of the previous day's battle in the Warsaw Ghetto. When he finished, silence pervaded the hall. No one else had the heart to speak.

So everyone started drinking, and toasting the Führer again on his birthday.

After the meeting Frank went to his office and dictated a letter to Reichsminister Lammers, one of Hitler's aides. It read in part: "Since yesterday we have in Warsaw a well-organized uprising in the ghetto, and we have already had to use machine guns. The killing of Germans is continuing and reaching dangerous dimensions."

He needed, said Frank, the support of all national and party authorities, and he "must not be a target for insults and attacks." Since he had not been given a free hand in dealing with the security situation in Poland, he could not take responsibility for the mess in Warsaw. Why had Himmler refused to discuss the problem with him? he asked.

Perhaps Hitler would now listen to him. Certainly the Führer would see that it was Himmler, and not Frank, who had pushed a policy that might permit the Jews to trigger a catastrophe that could seriously jeopardize the whole German position in the east.

The question was, would the Poles help the Jews, and perhaps even rise up with them?[11]

"You must stop fighting, and we will help you leave the ghetto," the tall Pole said after introducing himself as Grenadier Karol.

Yitzhak Zuckerman, still seeking arms for the ghetto even though he had not yet found a way to smuggle them in, was meeting with the man, whose real name was Janiszewski, in an apartment on the Aryan side. Janiszewski, a Home Army secret service agent, had been brought there by another Polish underground officer called Hajduk, who was sympathetic to the Jewish cause.

The ZOB must stop the revolt at once, Janiszewski repeated. And if it refused, the Home Army would not only withhold help

149

from the organization but would fight it. The ZOB was little more than a band of Communists and agents of Moscow, he fumed.

Yitzhak was stunned. The day before, Colonel Chrusciel had refused to supply him with arms, but at least he had praised the fighters. Now Janiszewski was calling them all Communists and threatening them. The Zionists and the Bundists could hardly be described as Communists, Yitzhak bitterly replied.

"And anyway," he said, "you can't investigate the political ideas of everybody in an army, neither in yours nor in ours. . . . Only six months ago we were criticized for not resisting the Germans. Now, when we are resisting, we are asked to stop.

"We cannot agree. I ask you to give us the weapons we need. We will fight, regardless, as long as we can. When we are unable to fight any longer, then you can help us to leave the ghetto."

Janiszewski reiterated sternly, "We will not give you any arms. And if we should find that your fighters are Communists, we will fight them."

Unknown to Yitzhak at the time, Janiszewski, who earlier had been captured and then released by the Gestapo, was now a Gestapo agent. Hajduk, on learning this some time later, raided Janiszewski's house with several men and killed him.

Actually the Gestapo did not need Janiszewski to frustrate Jewish efforts to obtain arms. There were enough Polish patriots, the Jews were convinced, to do the job.[12]

Early in the evening, General Stroop met with Walther Caspar Többens (whose wound apparently was not very serious) and the other German industrialists in Többens' Prosta Street office in the Small Ghetto. The general was in an ugly mood. Despite all his efforts he had failed to crack the Jewish defense system or capture any Jewish fighters. He had seized some enemy territory and burned down a few buildings, but since he could not risk leaving his men in the ghetto after dark, the Jews could reoccupy the captured zones, and he would have to fight for them all over again the next day. Moreover, he had rounded up only five hundred civilians on this day—hardly more than on the previous day.

What a birthday gift for the Führer.

From now on there would be no more coddling of these greedy businessmen who thought only of saving the Jews they needed to keep their shops going. They wanted to phase out their businesses slowly and send their workers and machinery to the Lublin labor camps at a leisurely pace to make sure that not a day's profit would be lost, that not a factory was damaged. Now Stroop would lay down the law. He would clean out the whole Productive Ghetto immediately.

All Jewish workers, he ordered, must assemble at six the following morning, April 21, for transfer out of Warsaw. At Umschlagplatz a selection would be made: Those fit for work would be sent to the Lublin camps, the rest, "elsewhere." Only a handful could remain temporarily to help move the machinery. All factory operations would come to a halt at once.

Többens and his colleagues were shocked. How could five hundred workers, hundreds of machines, and warehouses full of goods be moved overnight—and in the middle of an uprising? The workers would resist and sabotage the whole huge investment before being killed themselves. Then there would be neither labor force nor machinery nor finished goods. And the German Army urgently needed these goods.

Stroop did not argue. He removed his pistol from his holster and threatened to shoot Többens and his colleagues. They were persuaded.

Többens then issued a formal proclamation and spread the word through the factory managers that all workers, except the handful who would be given special passes, must report to assembly points by 6 A.M. The workers would be transferred to the Lublin camps, where they would be safe and comfortable. They would be allowed fifteen kilograms of baggage and would be supplied food for two days. Anyone found without passes after 6 A.M. would be executed.

He was sorry about this order, Többens told the managers. His main concern had always been his workers' welfare. But could he help it if they chose to follow the orders of "bandits" and "criminals"? So now they had only two options: to transfer or to die. When the managers pointed out that the Jews feared they would die anyway, Többens scoffed, "What nonsense. Nobody ever killed a person who wanted to work."[13]

The bunker at Franciszkanska 30 in the Central Ghetto was bustling with life that night. Scouts had returned with the report that there wasn't a Nazi in sight. The sound of footsteps and

151

voices could be heard only near the wall, and lights blinked here and there; but the enemy clearly feared to face the Jews in the ghetto at night.

So after waiting about two hours just to make sure, most of the occupants climbed out of the bunker, like cadavers rising from the grave, to fill their lungs with fresh air and visit their apartments to cook, wash, and take back whatever they needed. Guards were posted, and it was estimated that if an alert were given, everybody would be back in the bunker within ten minutes. Only the ill, the elderly, and mothers with small children stayed below, profiting from the tranquillity and luxury of space provided by the exodus.

But the other occupants soon trickled back, many weighed down with sacks of food. Abraham Gepner, former head of the Ghetto Supply Department, had instructed the others to break into the warehouses and bring the flour, groats, and other items stored there. In the dim lamplight the sight of the sacks being carried in reinforced the joyous feeling of most occupants that they would live for at least a few more days.

Israel Guttman, the chief of security in the bunker, longed to see his comrades in Mila 29, a few blocks away. Despite the dangers he decided to go. Arie Wilner, the former ZOB agent on the Aryan side who was still suffering from the wounds inflicted on him by his Gestapo torturers, handed him notes for Mordechai Anielewicz and Tosia Altman, who was so dear to him.

Guttman knew that Arie was suffering less from the pain in his crippled feet than from the agony of missing the battle—the battle he had vowed to take part in before he had been disabled. . . .

"Don't try to persuade me. I am doomed here. I cannot hold on. Let me go back to the ghetto." Arie's sister Halina was desperate. She would not listen to him or to her sister Guta or to her parents, all of whom were hiding with her on the Aryan side. Every time she walked down the street, she saw people staring at her. They knew, despite her "good appearance." They knew she was a Jew. The Poles always knew. It was better to take her chances in the ghetto, among her people.

But there would be another *Aktion* soon, Arie argued. It was insane to go back. Halina kissed her dear ones on the face and hands.

"Forgive me. Forgive me for anything I might have done to

hurt you. I know that sometimes I made you suffer. I did not mean it. I love you so much. . . . It was only my nerves. Forgive me."

Arie brought Halina back to the ghetto. And a few days later she was deported.

"I wanted so much to save all of you," Arie told Guta afterwards.

"And yourself?"

Arie nodded his head and pointed toward the ghetto. "There is my place, to fight with them to the end. . . ."

And now, to die without fighting.

Guttman made his way through the ghetto ruins, passing shadows of other frightened men, to Mila 29. This bunker, too, was vibrantly alive. People were entering and leaving constantly, and in one corner a crowd of fighters surrounded Mordechai, bombarding him with questions and receiving orders from him. Occasionally Mordechai took someone aside to speak with him.

Guttman was at first unnoticed. Everyone was too busy discussing the glorious victory at Mila and Zamenhof the previous day; there had been little fighting in the area on this second day of the revolt. Finally several comrades sat down with Guttman and described once again every detail of the battle. It was impossible to talk about tomorrow. They thought of nothing except yesterday. They reveled in repeating the story over and over again. No matter what happened tomorrow, they could now die with a smile on their lips.

Tosia appeared, and Guttman gave her Arie's note. She read it wistfully. She would come to visit Arie, she promised.

Guttman soon returned to Franciszkanska 30, arriving after everyone else had come back. Sitting beside Arie's cot, he gave him a full description of everything he had seen and heard. Arie excitedly absorbed every word, smoking one cigarette after another. He laughed when Guttman told him that while Arie had been on the Aryan side, members of Hashomer Hatzair had conducted heated discussions on whether, under the circumstances, they were permitted to break their strict code prohibiting smoking, among other pleasures, before they reached the Holy Land.

Cheered by the news Guttman had brought, Arie became more talkative than usual. He spoke about his experiences on the Aryan side: the arms deals, the people he had met, the prison.

Tosia? She would soon come to visit him.
The night passed quietly.[14]

General Stroop was in a quandary. He knew that most of the
Jews in the Productive Ghetto were no more likely to volunteer
for transfer than were those in the Brushmakers' District. And he
could not continue to suffer big casualties in return for limited
territory, which he had to abandon after dark anyway. He had
been sending false reports to Himmler. Only two of his men had
been killed and nine wounded in the two days of fighting, he
wrote, when actually there had been hundreds of casualties. If the
Jews were not crushed soon, the truth might become known, and
then he could lose forever his chance of getting an estate in the
Ukraine.

Stroop noted that only when buildings had been set afire did
the Jews come out of their holes in large numbers. He discussed
the matter with his officers, and they agreed that fire seemed the
best way to clean out the ghetto. Would it be feasible, Stroop pondered, to set the whole ghetto on fire? That would mean destroying the German factories and warehouses with everything else;
turning into ash, if necessary, equipment and goods worth millions of marks. He had no choice, Stroop finally concluded. To
hell with Többens, Schultz, and the rest.

That night, Stroop asked Himmler for special powers. Could he
take whatever measures were necessary to "clean out" the ghetto,
even if German property and goods had to be sacrificed? Yes,
Himmler replied. Stroop was delighted. He would burn down the
ghetto, building by building, while seeking out and destroying all
hidden bunkers and underground passages.

He would trap the Jews like rats, starting the next day, April 21,
with the Brushmakers' District.[15]

The Third Day

April 21

In the dawn light streaming through a shattered window in Leszno 76, Eliezer Geller, ZOB commander in the Productive Ghetto, urgently met with his group leaders. How could they foil the enemy plan to grab all the workers in this area in one great swoop? Többens' ultimatum was simple: Transfer to Lublin or die. The deadline for reporting was noon. But had not the workers in the Brushmakers' District held out the previous day? Those in the Productive Ghetto must now emulate them—or be rescued if they were captured or driven by fear to obey the order voluntarily.

Eliezer's commanders were not sure how these people could be saved, but they were confident that if there was a way, Eliezer would find it. Tall and slender with light blue eyes and a delicate complexion that flushed when he felt the slightest emotion, Eliezer had operated as an agent on the Aryan side some months earlier and had manged to fool even the most perceptive Pole and German into believing that he was an arrogant Polish dandy. He had dressed garishly and, more important, learned to gaze straight ahead confidently; most Jews on the Aryan side betrayed themselves by staring with frightened eyes at the ground. Yet Eliezer expected to be exposed and killed. He wrote a friend on January 14, 1943, referring to himself in the third person: "He is

155

carrying on a love affair with Mavetski, and who knows if he will not marry her."

Mavet means "death" in Hebrew.

The Germans had captured Eliezer when he fought with the Polish defenders of Warsaw in 1939, but eventually they released him, convinced he was a gentile. He then organized a Warsaw branch of Gordonia, a small but militant Zionist organization dedicated to the principle that manual labor almost mystically purifies man. When the deportations from Warsaw started in September 1942 and most Jews were praying for deliverance from the ghetto, Eliezer raced back from the provinces and risked instant death to get back in. He sneaked past some guards while they were busy checking other people.

Since the Nazis at that time were not yet rounding up registered workers, Eliezer ingeniously organized a "factory" in which his fighters could pose in that role. And though the Germans refused to authorize the factory and padlocked the door, the fighters found it useful anyway—as a hideout. The Nazis never searched the premises because of the padlock, permitting the Jews to come and go through a secret door. Almost all of Eliezer's fighters had thus survived.

Would he now be able to save the workers?

Eliezer decided that his fighters had two options: They could mingle with the deportees in the designated assembly areas and, before reaching Umschlagplatz, open fire on the Nazis, or they could shoot from their present posts at the trucks taking the Jews to the boxcars. Before making up his mind Eliezer sent scouts to find out how many people were reporting voluntarily to the assembly areas.

By 7 A.M. the first volunteers, carrying knapsacks on their backs, were plodding toward their uncertain destiny, too tired to fight, too frightened to hide. As they emerged from their apartments where they had stayed the night, the Nazis took advantage of the relative peace to enter the abandoned lodgings and loot whatever remained, firing into each door before breaking in.

At about 9 A.M. the fighters saw a group of them enter their own building, Leszno 76. Eliezer decided to let the Germans climb part way to the third floor, which the fighters occupied, before ordering an attack. From the cautious, quiet way the Nazis were moving up the stairs, Eliezer guessed they were not seeking loot but acting on the basis of information a traitor had given them.

156

At that moment a messenger, Lea Korn, burst into the apartment and reported that the Germans had surrounded the building and were climbing up several staircases. The fighters rushed to the attic, and within minutes the Nazis entered the hastily abandoned flat, hurling grenades, firing automatic guns, and crying wildly. When they found the place vacant, one of them shouted, "Destroy the damned gang!" and they furiously sprang toward the attic.

Slowly they pushed open the door. Three entered. In the darkness a shot rang out. One of the fighters, Kuba Gutreiman, standing flat against the wall, watched ecstatically as his target crumbled to the floor. The other two SS men withdrew, carrying their casualty with them.

Kuba, short and broad-shouldered, leaped up and kissed the other fighters, his eyes laughing behind his spectacles. But almost immediately they heard approaching footsteps and the command "Forward!" sounding from two staircases. The fighters ran to a connecting attic toward a bunker prepared for such an emergency.

On the way, they were startled to see what looked like a ghost. A civilian lay in a corner, covered with feathers from ripped bedding. Jacob Putermilch grabbed the man and led him to the bunker, a walled-off room that could be reached only by lowering a ladder from the attic. Here the fighters joined ten civilians, so crowding the room that people had to crawl over the beds lined up along the walls in order to move about.

Eliezer immediately began to interrogate the stranger. Had he betrayed the fighters? Julek, as the youth called himself, claimed that the Germans had captured him and were taking him to an assembly area when he managed to escape and ran up to the attic where the fighters found him.

Eliezer did not believe him and ordered that he be executed. In a quivering voice Julek again denied his guilt. Silence reigned in the bunker as everyone focused their eyes on the youth. To trust him could be to risk the lives of them all.

"I see," said Julek, "that you are members of an organization. I was, too, before the war. I was a member of Hashomer Hatzair. During the war I lost touch with them. It's true I did not look for them, but I had to take care of my family."

Eliezer asked Julek to name his acquaintances in Hashomer Hatzair, and the youth called off several names. But was that

157

proof of his innocence? Eliezer stared at Julek, plumbing his heart.

Another chilling moment of silence.

Very well, said Eliezer, Julek could join his men.

Julek smiled, though his eyes remained sad, and the fighters and civilians sighed with relief. With millions dying, saving one Jew was like saving a thousand.

But the problem remained: How would the fighters save several thousand this day?[1]

Fritz Schultz, known as "Big Schultz" to distinguish him from K.G., was frantic. The most important industrialist in the ghetto after Többens, he was bitterly resentful of Stroop for his monstrous deportation order. Did he have to deport the workers so swiftly? Couldn't he wait until the industrialists were able to transfer all their equipment and goods safely, without loss or damage? What a cruel way to treat those who had made such sacrifices for the war effort.

Schultz lamented in his diary that Többens, in charge of the massive move to the Lublin labor camps, would allow him only one hundred Jews to pack and load on trucks everything in his more than fifty factories, which normally employed eight thousand persons. This was ridiculous. The absolute minimum he needed was 140. He called Többens and pleaded for forty more. Többens reluctantly agreed.

Before 7 A.M. Schultz was peering from a window of his office at Nowolipie 44. So few people were heading toward the assembly area in his compound. This he felt was understandable. Though his Jews were to go to the Trawniki labor camp (the Többens workers to Poniatow), they were naturally afraid that they might be shipped elsewhere. They wanted to work only for him because he was kind to them. The Jews, after all, *were* human beings, and they knew he realized this.

Schultz sat down at his desk and checked over the special permits from Többens. No, 140 Jews were not enough after all. He needed another twenty-three. And he wanted to exchange thirteen for others who were more skilled. Schultz asked one of his managers to telephone Többens again. The manager and Többens haggled. Finally Többens gave in. All right, Schultz could have his twenty-three Jews and exchange thirteen others. But Stroop might not appreciate such generosity. Schultz felt relieved. He gazed from his window again. More Jews were trickling into the assembly area. Hopeful that the trickle would turn into a flood, he requested the SS to send additional guards to help keep order. The street was already cluttered with baggage that Többens had promised would be sent along separately.

But by morning's end even the trickle had dried up.[2]

One worker Többens could not coax into reporting was Kalman Friedman, who had come up from his bunker on Nowolipie Street to spend the first Seder night, April 19, with the crippled Jacob Nussbaum and his devoted eight-year-old nephew, Izio. Kalman had stayed that night in Nussbaum's apartment, then descended to the bunker the following morning. He did not bid farewell to his dear neighbor because he intended to see him again later that day. But gunfire and explosions nearby made it impossible for him to leave the shelter. And after hearing heavy footsteps in the yard at night, he decided to wait until the next morning to go upstairs again.

Shortly after dawn on this third day of the uprising, he heard more gunfire mingled with savage cries. Nazis were storming into the courtyard and up the stairways to ransack the apartments. Kalman and his companions silently huddled together, terror-stricken. But finally the danger passed.

Terrible anxiety gripped Kalman. What had happened to Nussbaum and Izio? Fearing that Nazis were still in the area, Kalman removed his shoes, then left the bunker, slowly climbed the stairs and darted past creaking open doors to his neighbor's flat. He stopped in shock at the bedroom door. Amid household items strewn on the floor stood the bed, mussed and bloody. Under the bed lay Jacob Nussbaum, dead.

Kalman was paralyzed, unable for a moment to comprehend what had happened. Then he thought of Izio, the loyal guardian. Where was he? He whispered his name, as if the murderers might hear him. He searched for the boy in the kitchen, in the bathroom. Izio had vanished. Kalman grew frightened by his own footsteps in the heavy silence and returned to the bunker, overcome with sorrow and depression.

Poor Nussbaum. Poor Izio. And Kalman had not even managed to say good-bye.[3]

Just before noon, the deadline for the workers to report for transfer, Eliezer Geller and his fighters climbed from their bunker to the attic again and took positions at windows overlooking a large assembly area. Eliezer had made up his mind. It would be foolhardy for the fighters to accompany the civilians to Umschlagplatz. They would attack from their posts instead.

Exactly at noon, as trucks loaded with several hundred volunteers began to move off toward the railhead, Jacob Putermilch and the other fighters tautly waited the word to fire at the drivers. But Eliezer now saw that the danger of hitting the Jews in the trucks was too great. He had to veto that option, too. Instead he ordered his fighters to fire only at the Nazis who were gathering Jewish stragglers in the streets and courtyards and looting the vacated buildings.

Everyone started shooting, including the sole rifleman, Shimon Heller, a tall, pale, dark-haired youth. Though from a rich, assimilated Cracow family, he had become an ardent Zionist, fanatically dedicated to revenge. He had the honor of being armed with the group's only rifle because he was the best ZOB marksman. Scoring a bull's eye with every bullet, Shimon kissed the rifle and pressed it to his heart after each hit. But though some Germans fell from ZOB gunfire, Eliezer realized that his men could not save many Jews.

Later he sent Jacob and his comrades to Nowolipie 67, where they joined David Nowodworski's group to await the Germans returning from the Central Ghetto, as they had on the first day of the revolt when the bomb on Smocza Street had failed to go off. This time the Germans did not march past singing but rode by in swiftly moving trucks, all the easier to kill. The Jews threw grenades and Molotov cocktails, and from the storm of thunder and flame rose the cries of Germans afire. Jumping from their blazing vehicles, they ran in all directions, prime targets for the Jews.

Another Jewish victory—except for those piled into the boxcars, some heading for immediate death, others for a precarious stay of execution in the labor camps. But now the real test would come for the Jews in the Productive Ghetto; for those who remained, the great majority, had defied Többens—and Stroop. And the general now ordered that they be found and dealt with mercilessly.[4]

In the Brushmakers' District, ZOB commander Marek Edelman and his fighters in Swientojerska 34 were hoping for a breathing spell this day. Marek's idea was to make the enemy think that the Jews had either fled or been killed and then surprise them the following day, April 22.

But General Stroop had a plan of his own. He, too, would play possum. He would not strike until noon. Thus he would lull the Jews into thinking the Germans had no stomach left for infantry attacks but would satisfy themselves with sporadic artillery blasts from the Aryan side.

So Marek got his breathing spell—but a short one. At noon sharp, Nazi trucks began drawing up in front of the buildings on Walowa, Swientojerska, and Franciszkanska, and SS men placed drums of gasoline in front of the house gates. Then, just before the trucks pulled away, they set fire to the drums, and soon the entire section had turned into a raging inferno under a bloodred sky streaked with pillars of swirling smoke.

Suddenly hundreds of people on the upper floors of the buildings burst out of their hiding places, only, in many cases, to be overcome by flame and smoke. Others were trapped when Nazis flung grenades into the doorways, blowing up the wooden staircases that were not already on fire. Many, finding no escape route, leaped from windows—easy targets for cocked German rifles. One man crashed on a burning beam in a courtyard on Swientojerska and remained alive. In his agony he begged people running by to kill him, but nobody had the time—or the heart—to perform this act of mercy.

Pleading for refuge, people began to knock on the entrance to the cellar door at Swientojerska 34, where most of the fighters were holed up. But as dusk dissolved into darkness, smoke also filled this bunker; and the fighters, coughing and choking, realized they had to get out. But how? The Germans had blown up the stairs leading down to the cellar, and from this gap, flames lashed out like serpents' tongues.

There was only one way to escape. If they threw a board across

161

the fiery gap, they could perhaps climb out. A plank was found, and the fighters lined up to leave. They would clear the way for the civilians, who would follow and then seek refuge in whatever bunkers they could find. The wounded would have to stay behind . . . to burn alive. There was no choice. They could not possibly be carried through the flames to safety. Some of them wept; others pleaded to be taken. Most remained silent, in a state of shocked, horrified resignation.

The fighters dampened their clothing with water and heaved the plank into place. Holding wet handkerchiefs to their faces, they raced through the flames to the ground floor and out the front door. As Simcha Rathajzer, one of the first, stumbled into the courtyard, he was overwhelmed by the sight. Although it was night, the whole area was lit up as if it were high noon. All around him towered sheets of flame that crackled like devilish laughter as they greedily consumed everything in their path.

Fire clung to clothes, which started smoldering. The pavement melted into a black gooey substance overspread with sticky liquefied pieces of broken glass that stuck like glue to burning soles.

"One after another we stagger through the conflagration," Marek Edelman later wrote. "From house to house, from courtyard to courtyard, with no air to breathe, with a hundred hammers clanging in our heads, with burning rafters continuously falling over us. . . ."

Simcha, still holding a wet handkerchief to his face, felt in the unbearable heat as if he had been flung into a furnace. He could not endure it a second longer. . . . Then gradually the heat diminished, and the glowing sky faded. He and his comrades had reached their immediate destination: the courtyard of Franciszkanska 21, which was not yet on fire. Now they would try to cross into the adjoining Central Ghetto.

Marek Edelman sent out a patrol to find a way through the wall separating the two zones at Franciszkanska, and they soon returned with grim news. Part of the wall had been demolished, but the breach was well-guarded and targeted by a heavy machine gun. Trying to go through it would be suicide. But so would remaining in the path of the flames that were hungrily stalking them.

Marek conferred with his commanders. Everybody agreed that it was better to die trying to get through the wall.[5]

* * *

As General Stroop had planned, bunker after bunker fell in the Brushmakers' District that day, with Jews being smoked out or betrayed by captured victims frightened into committing treason. Some bunkers were so well-hidden and well-ventilated that they remained intact even in this inferno. Among them was the shelter at Swientojerska 35, area headquarters of the ZZW, where fighters led by Josef Lepata safely retired after the bitter fighting.

But some bunkers were less sturdy and threatened to crumble. Thus, the people in a shelter at Swientojerska 28 were convinced that they would either be crushed under collapsing timber and masonry or asphyxiated by the smoke seeping in from the burning building above. Many had already lost consciousness from the intense heat. One occupant, Simcha Holzberg, suggested fleeing to the ruins of another building about a block away, Franciszkanska 27, which had already burned in the 1939 attack.

Holzberg, a young Orthodox Jew who always had a small Bible in his pocket, did not belong to any fighting organization but was one of the "wild ones," or independent fighters. He carried a pistol and, with several comrades, made hit-and-run attacks on the SS forces. Before the uprising he had worked as an orderly in a German Army hospital on the Aryan side, where he was able to steal weapons from wounded soldiers.

When night fell, Holzberg slid open the hatch of the bunker and, followed by more than a hundred men, women, and children, streaked across a crazy quilt of courtyards to the skeletal remains of Franciszkanska 27. Many arrived with severe burns, while others did not make it at all through the storm of bullets and sparkling embers.

Breathlessly, Holzberg and his companions sought to hide in the ruins. But they could find little cover. What easy prey for the Germans scouring the area for survivors, thought Holzberg. He knelt and prayed to a God that seemed to have abandoned even the faithful.[6]

That afternoon the flames spread to the adjoining Central Ghetto. Noemi Judkowski was hiding in a cellar at Nalewki 36 when she smelled smoke. A man on guard outside suddenly rushed down and cried, "Our house is burning!"

163

All Noemi's efforts would soon be reduced to ashes. As an architectural student, she had designed the bunker she was sharing with about fifty other people. It was elaborately equipped with electricity, plumbing, and other conveniences that would make conditions bearable for a few months. But as in most bunkers, the occupants became irritable as they waited for either death or a miracle to deliver them. Not only were they cramped and hardly able to breathe, they were obsessed with the fear of discovery.

Their obsession began to focus on a ten-year-old mentally retarded boy who cried incessantly, threatening to give them away to Nazis who were combing the area for hideouts. A bitter argument broke out. Should the boy's mother take him out of the bunker? To leave would mean almost certain death, Noemi and others pointed out. The occupants could not be that cruel. Either all would live or all would die. But why, some persisted, should everyone have to be sacrificed to prolong the lives of two of them who would die anyway if the crying brought the Nazis to the bunker?

It was finally agreed: The boy must leave. Noemi was distraught. This was the Nazis' greatest crime: what they had done to people who were normally kind and compassionate. How savage the will to survive could be. So the day before the house above them began burning, the mother, leaving her twelve-year-old girl behind, climbed with her son from the bunker to a room upstairs to await their fate.

Now, with the building on fire, the same fate threatened to engulf those still in the bunker. When the smoke and heat had nearly overcome them, Noemi and the others scrambled out to the courtyard of the building, coughing violently, and reeled through a blizzard of soot toward another bunker farther removed from the fires raging around them. But one refugee left the fleeing column: the little girl.

Seeing her brother lying on the ground after he had apparently jumped from the third floor of the blazing building, she ran to him and found that both his legs had been broken. She gently dragged him to a tree that stood in the courtyard, then snapped off some branches, which she fashioned into a triangular shelter covered with large leaves. She pulled her brother into the shelter in a pathetic effort to shield him from smoke, fire, wind, and sun, and stayed to care for him amid the smoldering carnage.

By the time Noemi reached the second bunker, the two children had vanished behind a screen of smoke.[7]

At about noon, Chaim Frimer, who had been on a combat mission that morning, was returning to his base, Mila 29, in the Central Ghetto, when he noticed from afar that flames were engulfing the building. His heart sank. Mila 29 was Mordechai Anielewicz's headquarters. If the ZOB command perished, the uprising would probably be over.

Chaim was already in a state of shock, having learned that morning from another fighter that his own apartment building had burned down. His father had been caught by the Germans when he left the bunker in the cellar after announcing that he refused to die like a rat in a hole. As for his sister Krysia, her fate was unknown.

Now Mila 29 was burning. Fearful that those in the bunker under it were not aware of the danger, he and his group rushed to it and found that Mordechai had already prepared for a hasty departure.

Mordechai was determined to remain as long as possible—at least until dark—because of the danger of seeking new shelter in broad daylight while SS patrols were hunting everywhere. But when the smoke grew thicker and the heat more intense, he ordered about a score of fighters to get ready to leave with him, among them Israel Kanal, Berl Broide, Chaim Frimer, and apparently Mira Fuchrer. They would seek another hideout while the more than one hundred other occupants, including civilians who had crowded in, would try to stay until dark—longer if the danger subsided.

Lutek Rotblatt would be left in command of the bunker and would lead the rest of the people to safety. He had been directing night attacks from Mila 29 since the first day of the uprising, when his group had fought at Nalewki and Gensia. Lutek was burdened with more than the fate of those in his bunker. His heart was heavy with thoughts of his wife, Hela, his mother, Maria, and her adopted daughter, who were hiding elsewhere. Had their bunker been set afire? Were they alive? He wanted to run out and see, to help them. But now he had a new responsibility he could not shirk.

165

Mordechai and the others were sorry to be leaving such an excellent base. Mila 29 was well-camouflaged and large enough to house a number of groups, permitting Mordechai to send several at a time to fight in different places. The fighters had slept by day, when complete silence was necessary, but had been feverishly active at night. They prepared food, cleaned their weapons, and went out on dangerous missions after bidding a wordless farewell to comrades with glances of affection and anxiety.

Then the return—a shattering fusion of joy and despair as some came back and some did not. The radio was turned on at lowest volume. How strange it always was to hear news from the outside world, music from another planet. Had not all Creation ended? Was there still life somewhere?

Night had blended into day and then into night again, and only the cock the fighters kept in the bunker made them aware of time. When it lay down to sleep, night was falling; time to go out and fight. When it crowed, day was dawning; time to seal the entrances and go to sleep. The fighters envied the cock, for it was unable to grasp the danger threatening them. Mordechai often feared that it would give away their position, but he did not have the heart to kill it. There was too much death already. Only the Nazis and their helpers deserved to die.

The cock was not crowing now, apparently as choked from the smoke as the other inhabitants of Mila 29. But Mordechai knew the time. It was time to find a new corner of refuge in the diminishing ghetto, perhaps the last.

He led his fighters out of the bunker and formed them into a column in the courtyard. Then, after an exchange of shots with a German patrol passing nearby, they sprinted through the courtyard gate and down Mila Street toward Nalewki, hoping to join other groups based there if they could get through. En route they stopped at Mila 17, where Mordechai decided they would stay the night.

Mordechai now seemed to realize more clearly than ever that he had made a serious mistake when, unlike the ZZW leaders, he had refused to build special bunkers for his fighters before the uprising for fear of weakening their will to fight. He and his men would have to depend on the goodwill of others to find bases as they were forced to move from one to another.

Meanwhile he was a commander without a command post.[8]

* * *

At day's end, General Stroop felt relieved as he climbed into his car and left behind the stench of the ghetto. What a lovely spring evening, he reflected as he passed Lazienki Park, noting with delight the first April flowers. Yes, it had been a good day.

He was finally making headway. His men had trapped a few thousand Jews that day, either rooted out of the bunkers or talked into giving themselves up. He had found the way: Burn them out! How they cried when they started to fry. Some preferred to kill themselves jumping from windows rather than fall into German hands, but that was fine with him. These "parachutists" provided his men with excellent target practice.

Still, Stroop was a bit concerned about the morale of his troops. Some of them had asked him what to do about captured Jewish infants. They obviously had qualms. These men, Stroop lamented, did not seem to understand that Jewish infants would grow up to be monsters, that they would perpetuate the subhuman race. So he had told them to take the babies by the legs and smash their heads against the wall. And with satisfaction Stroop watched them taking his advice.

But then Colonel Hahn gently protested. The Germans, Hahn said, shouldn't soil their hands by touching Jewish flesh. It would be better to shoot the infants. This argument made sense to Stroop. The hands of an SS man should be as clean and pure as his heart.

Tomorrow, the general was sure, morale would reach its peak. True, after bitter fighting today at Muranowski Square his men had still been unable to reach the two flags that fluttered defiantly over the ruins. But tomorrow he would rip them down at any cost and show his troops—and the Poles, whom he still feared might attack—that no one could resist Nazi power for long.[9]

The Fourth Day

April 22

There was no other way. In order to survive, the ZZW force defending Muranowski Square would have to attack—despite its weakened condition, despite the Nazi hordes closing in on the half-destroyed buildings in the square, despite the artillery and the flamethrowers and the iron determination of General Stroop to capture the flags that humiliatingly symbolized Jewish resistance.

The ZZW defense system had all but disintegrated on this morning, especially after an artillery shell demolished one of the two heavy machine guns and wounded the crew. The few fighters left were weary from days of battle, and there were no others to relieve them. Now all that stood between the Nazis and control of the square was one heavy machine gun, still perched atop Muranowska 7, flanked by the two flags.

Meeting in the sooty cellar headquarters in the building, the ZZW leaders, among them Pawel Frenkel, David Appelbojm, and Leon Rodal, decided on a desperate plan. The ZZW would draw individual German units into the labyrinth of alleys stretching away from the square, where they could be trapped and annihilated. But would the Nazis fall into the trap?

To entice them the Jews pretended that their defense had completely crumbled. They removed the machine gun from the roof

168

of Muranowska 7, ceased firing, and hid from view. The square grew eerily silent, with only the flags left in place as part of the lure.

The fighters knelt at windows, waiting for the Germans to make a move. One of the most impatient was sixteen-year-old Jurek Plonski, the former smuggler, who was based in a small factory with a ZZW group. Minutes passed, but the enemy remained in place, too cunning and experienced, it seemed to grab the bait. Suddenly several German officers darted to a doorway across the street, leaving their men waiting in the square while they consulted.

Shortly, a man in an SS uniform walked over to the soldiers in the square. They should come with him, he said. They would capture the flags. Then he ran into the courtyard of Muranowska 7 and up a flight of stairs to the first floor, where he dashed to a window and dropped a grenade on the Germans who were about to climb the stairs after him.

A ZZW fighter had made good use of his SS uniform.

The Jews began firing and throwing grenades from every window, and they hit many Germans before they could retreat into the street.

Stroop was enraged when he saw the flags still fluttering. He sent a special SS task force under First Lieutenant Otto Dehmke to take Muranowska 7 and pull down the banners. Dehmke led his men into the building but was killed when a grenade he was holding exploded from Jewish fire.

Stroop's rage grew. Dehmke had been one of his finest officers. He ordered the immediate execution of several hundred captured Jews in reprisal. He also decided on a new policy. Until now he had been rather selective in choosing what to burn down, trying to spare streets with German factories and storehouses. But this was no time for nitpicking, especially with his men showing signs of fear.

Soon the Nazis set afire the buildings bordering on Muranowski Square, including Muranowska 7, where the two flags still brazenly flew. As the fire spread, the ZZW fighters fled through the smoke and ash, and many were either shot or captured and sent to Umschlagplatz. But the ZZW commanders, among others, managed to escape, and they relayed word to some of their scattered units to leave the ghetto through the secret ZZW passages and make their way to a forest outside Warsaw, where they could continue fighting as partisans. One unit had already tried to leave the previous day but had been trapped and destroyed in the passage leading to Muranowska 6 on the Aryan side.

At his base in the factory, Jurek Plonski found a working telephone and dialed a Polish contact on the Aryan side.

"Can you organize help to get the civilians out of the ghetto?" he shouted.

No, came the answer, the ghetto was too tightly surrounded.

"If you can change into mice," the Pole said, "maybe you can escape."

Jurek put down the phone and peered through a window toward the smoking remains of Muranowska 7. He wanted to cry. The two tattered flags were finally gone.[1]

Sitting on a stool in the entrance of a building on Niska Street, northwest of Muranowski Square, General Stroop gazed at the same ruins, but with joy. Now that the flags were gone he could relax and savor the sight of his attackers burning and blowing up the buildings with daring proficiency. He was intrigued, even enthralled, by the spectacular scenes flashing before his eyes.

From his post, Stroop could see and hear it all as he chatted with his staff. The confusion was "unbelievable," he would later relate. Fire, smoke, dust, the red sky, mattress feathers, the smell of burning wood and bodies, the roar of artillery, the blast of grenades, sparks flying in the wind, and the "parachutists" leaping to their deaths from buildings aflame.

But they did not jump immediately. He saw them in the windows, on the balconies, atop the roofs. Some fired on his men below or scurried along the cornices, seeking to escape somehow. A few even sang songs—probably the Psalms, Stroop thought. Others shouted, "Hitler *kaputt!*"; "Down with the Nazis!"; or "Long live Poland!"

Stroop grudgingly admired their ingenuity. When the flames drew unbearably close, before jumping they would throw down mattresses, quilts, and pillows, hoping to land on them. But they weren't clever enough, for while they were in midair, his men would pick them off.

"Poof! Poof!" he would exclaim later, simulating a hunter shooting ducks.

170

The Nazis found other ways to amuse themselves. Before the fire reached them, some of the Jews swallowed vials of poison they had kept for such an occasion. Whole families would consume poison simultaneously, with mothers sometimes spoon-feeding their infants. They had but one fear: that they wouldn't die soon enough, that they would suffer first and perhaps be burned alive. And lucky was the SS man who came upon a Jew writhing in agony from poison that worked too slowly.

When the Nazis entered the burning Brauer factory, they found a distinguished Jewish physician, Dr. Kapotzowski, lying on the floor screaming with pain. He had taken defectively packaged poison that was not strong enough to kill him instantly. The Germans picked him up and threw him on a pile of garbage. When he begged them to end his suffering, they simply stood around, laughing and joking, until finally he died.

From a window of his second-floor bunker in the Czyste-Berson-Bauman Hospital on Gensia Street, Dr. Israel Rotbalsam watched as fire raged through a building just across the street and prepared to lead his comrades in search of a new shelter if the flames reached the hospital.

While Germans surrounded the blazing structure, firing at Jews who tried to run into the street, Rotbalsam heard amid the screams a familiar wailing sound. Through the shattered basement windows of the building he could see a number of elderly Jews praying, skull caps on their bobbing heads, prayer shawls around their shoulders, until finally they vanished in a cloud of death.

Many of those Jews who managed to escape from the burning buildings or could not stand the heat in the underground bunkers desperately tried to reach the Aryan side through the sewers. Hundreds drowned or were asphyxiated in these putrid channels, which Stroop had filled with water and gas, while others climbed over the bodies hoping to escape the same fate.

Still, Stroop was not satisfied. Reports kept coming in that Jews were, in fact, escaping through the sewers. It was simply impossible to flood and gas every channel. But such troublesome flaws did not dilute his pleasure as he sat observing his new strategy for destroying the ghetto. Suddenly his eyes focused on one particular balcony nearby, from which a strange, almost ghostly voice emanated, amplified by the gusty wind. A young woman, who shared the balcony with three other adults and a small child, was calling out to Stroop. Through the engulfing flames she lamented that a great nation, one that had produced such a man as Goethe, could commit such a crime.

"I myself am not asking for mercy," she cried, "because I know I cannot expect any from you. But remember that you will pay for what is happening to us. You will have to stand trial for this."

In a moment the balcony was consumed in fire, and the people jumped to the ground, the child cradled in the young woman's arms. Stroop immediately rose from his stool and ordered several of his men to finish off any "parachutists" who might have survived the fall from that balcony.

Goethe? No, Nietzsche was the true German. Stroop remembered his words: "Blessed be that which makes the man hard!"[2]

At Mila 17, their temporary refuge, Mordechai Anielewicz, Chaim Frimer, and the other fighters who had left Mila 29 the previous day awoke early to the crackle and roar of catastrophe. Wild flames raged all around, buildings tumbled thunderously, and billows of smoke spiraled into the heavens. The whole area was afire. Mordechai sent out a patrol. Soon it reported back: SS troops were gathering nearby to trap Jews fleeing from their hideouts.

Mordechai ordered his fighters to stand by windows overlooking the courtyard and wait for the Germans to enter. The Nazis came, and the fighters mowed them down, then withdrew to a neighboring building. When night fell, Mordechai led his small force toward Nalewki, still hoping to link up with other groups, but this force was pinned down by enemy gunfire from the courtyard of Mila 5.

The fighters could neither advance nor retreat, and fire licked at them from every direction while civilians poured into the courtyard from the flaming buildings all around. If anyone tried to leave through the courtyard gate, he was shot by Germans roaming the streets. Even the wooden gate was soon blazing, sealing the trap completely.

Mordechai was faced with a grim choice. Should he and his fighters die as fuel for the flames or as targets for the Germans? He preferred to face the Germans. But the civilians, feeling some protection from the mere presence of armed Jews, surrounded the fighters. No, they insisted, the fighters must remain. Mordechai and the others tried to explain that they were soldiers on duty, but their explanations were in vain. Frenzy then seized the civilians. They hugged and kissed each other, cried, and begged God to forgive them for their sins. They pleaded with Mordechai and his group to save them from certain death, unable to imagine that these fighters, though disciplined, were as desperate and helpless as themselves.

Chaim Frimer later wrote that his "heart cried." It was "the most terrible scene I can remember from the uprising." But the battle had to go on. To the last man. One fighter fired into the air, and the civilians wildly dispersed. Then Mordechai and his fighters charged through the burning gate, certain they would be riddled by Germans waiting for them on the street.[3]

Shortly before dawn, Simcha Rathajzer cautiously made his way along the wall separating the Brushmakers' District from the Central Ghetto toward the breach in the barrier. Simcha and another fighter, serving as scouts, would lead Marek Edelman's three groups of survivors through the breach into the Central Ghetto, which was not yet completely aflame.

Simcha crawled over the bricks in the opening and looked around. Although he knew a German machine gun was nestled in the ruins nearby, the way looked clear for the moment. He signaled for the first group, led by Hanoch Gutman, to advance; and within minutes all these fighters, their feet wrapped in rags to stifle their footsteps, had crawled through the breach and were running from courtyard to courtyard inside the Central Ghetto.

But as the second group emerged, led by Hersh Berlinski, a Nazi patrol passing on the Brushmakers' side apparently observed something and a German called through the breach, "*Ist jemand da?*" ("Is anybody there?")

He was greeted with silence, of course, and in a moment Berlinski's group, which had taken cover in nearby debris, started moving farther into the Central Ghetto.

The last unit of fighters were led by Marek Edelman and Jurek Blones. As they were crawling over the bricks, a German searchlight suddenly illuminated the entire wall. Exposed to enemy observation as if in daylight, the fighters froze, expecting to die in a hail of bullets. They heard a sharp crack, and suddenly the light flashed out. A fighter had pulled the trigger first and hit his target. The entire group was thus able to escape before the Germans could gather their wits.

At about 5 A.M. Marek and his fighters, shocked and exhausted, began trickling into the bunker at Franciszkanska 30. All arrived safely except one, a youth named Krzepicki, who had been wounded and had died on the way—after he had successfully escaped from Treblinka. Arie Wilner and the other inhabitants of the shelter embraced the newcomers, astonished that anyone could have emerged alive from the inferno sweeping the Brushmakers' District.

After a hot meal washed down with a little vodka, the survivors lay down and went to sleep, while the flames they had escaped followed relentlessly in their footsteps.[4]

Still trapped in the Brushmakers' District were scores of Jews either hiding underground or running from one hideout to another, frantically trying to escape incineration. Among them were Simcha Holzberg, the Orthodox "wild one," and his companions, who the day before had fled from their ovenlike dwelling at Swientojerska 28 to a bombed-out shelter a block away.

With SS troops seeking out every last surviving Jew, Holzberg and his group realized they had blundered. It was better to risk being roasted alive in their concealed bunker than to fall almost certain prey to the Germans in the exposed ruins of their new hiding place. They decided, therefore, to return to Swientojerska 28.

After dark they set out, stumbling through the fiery wasteland, darting behind charred barriers every time an SS patrol passed, taking temporary refuge in gassed-out bunkers. Shots rang out. A loudspeaker in the wilderness called on survivors to report for transfer to the labor camps. Gradually Holzberg's group dwindled. Some were caught; some gave themselves up. But Holzberg and about twenty others staggered on with the mindless stealth of hunted animals.

Suddenly the dim dancing serpents of light cast down by the glowing night sky revealed a human figure lying in their path. Holzberg knelt down and stared into the pleading blue eyes of a young girl about twenty years old. A doctor in the group examined the girl. Both of her legs were broken, and she was paralyzed, unable even to speak. There was no hope for her, the doctor said; but Holzberg insisted on taking her along with them despite the difficulty of carrying her through flames, over rubble, and past Germans. Some of his companions protested: She would die anyway, so why jeopardize the lives of them all?

"She is coming with us," Holzberg repeated.

He and two others then carried her to the bunker.

Holzberg was relieved to find that, with the building overhead already a blackened skeleton, the shelter underneath had cooled and was, at least, livable. He sat in a corner, took out his prayer book, and began mumbling a Passover prayer, thanking God for his deliverance as the Jews of Moses' time had done thousands of years earlier. Soon others joined him in prayer, and their wails mingled with the terrible moans of the wounded girl.

The moans persisted long after the wails, throbbing hammer-blows upon minds already half-crazed by heat and fright. The Germans had sound-detection devices. They had dogs. They were searching everywhere for hidden bunkers. The noise would sure-ly lead them to this one. Everybody would die because of this girl, who was doomed anyway. All eyes turned to Holzberg, who just before had been leading them in prayer. *He* was responsible. *He* had insisted on bringing the girl here.

One man walked up to him with a cord and formed a loop in the center. Holzberg understood.

"No, I can't do it!" he cried.

The man looked contemptuously at him, then turned to two other youths. They also refused. Holzberg gazed into the girl's eyes, as he had when he found her. He saw fear. He saw agony. He saw God.

Finally the man put down the cord, picked up a pillow, and placing it on the girl's face, pressed down. He stared at Holzberg. Holzberg hesitated. Yes, it was true. Better one than all. In a mo-ment he was helping to tie the cord around the pillow. Then he pulled it tight, pausing only to wipe away his tears.[5]

Trapped in the courtyard of Mila 5 by flame and gunfire, Mor-dechai Anielewicz and his fighters burst through the burning courtyard gate expecting to die as they emerged. They found corpses littering the street, which glowed from the fire like a car-pet leading to hell. But the Germans, who had minutes before been guarding the gate, had miraculously vanished. Another re-prieve!

175

Mordechai led his fighters to Mila 16, one of the few buildings not yet afire on that street, and they entered an abandoned apartment, collapsed on the floor, and went to sleep. Chaim Frimer was so tired that when his group moved on after dark, he stumbled along in a state of semiconsciousness, his eyes almost shut. He and the others passed through several cellars and emerged in the courtyard of Mila 18, a jumble of ruins since the 1939 German attack.

Mordechai had learned that under the ruins was perhaps the largest and most elaborate bunker in the ghetto. But he wasn't sure whether the owners, a band of wealthy thieves, would welcome them. They had guns, but so did the fighters. Anyway, it was no time to worry about the temperament of one's landlord.

A civilian they found who knew the way squeezed through a camouflaged opening in a shattered section of wall and uttered the password. The others followed and, on their bellies, wormed through a narrow passage that led to a small room where a guard sat. Receiving permission to move on, the fighters crawled through another passage to a final concealed opening, from which a ladder led down to the bunker. The hideout had four such entrances.

When the fighters had climbed down the ladder, they were met by a man with a huge belly and a thick red neck. He was Shmuel Asher, alias Shmuel Izhakel, the underworld figure who had built this "luxury" bunker for his family, friends, and gang of thieves known in the Warsaw vernacular as the *Chompes*.

"Welcome," Asher said to Mordechai with a handshake and a smile on his fat, jovial face. "Whatever is ours is yours, and we are at your disposal. We are alert and agile and well-trained in breaking locks, in sneaking silently and unnoticed in the night, and in climbing fences and walls. And we are well-acquainted with all the paths and holes in the destroyed ghetto. You will see that we will be useful to you."[6]

Jacob Putermilch had an acute stomachache as he stood guard at a window of Nowolipie 67 in the Productive Ghetto. The previous night he and his comrades had rummaged through some abandoned apartments and found a few groats and beans in the corners of kitchen cupboards. While they were cooking this precious bit of food, a German patrol noticed sparks and smoke coming from the chimney and began firing through the windows. As Jacob dashed for cover, he gulped down the beans half-cooked, just in case he couldn't get back to them. The stomachache followed.

At about eight in the morning, however, it suddenly disappeared. This was no time to dwell on petty discomforts. A large unit of Germans—no mere patrol this time—was about to attack through the courtyard gate. Jacob and the other defenders on the fourth floor began firing, but the Germans broke through the gate and ran into a doorway. As they clambered up the stairs, smashing into every flat, Jacob could hear an SS officer shouting, "Before you shoot a Jew, show him to me!"

When the intruders stormed into the apartments on the floor below, Jacob and the other fighters pitched grenades from their windows into the windows on that floor. The cries and screams that filtered through the smoke were gratifying.

Minutes later, scores of Germans swarmed into the courtyard to reinforce their comrades. But as grenades and Molotov cocktails exploded in their midst, panic ensued, and the survivors ran in all directions, like "poisoned rats," in Jacob's words.

"Fire! Annihilate the goddamn gang!" shouted the SS commander.

But the fighters wouldn't cooperate. They raced to the bunker just beneath the attic where, the day before, Eliezer Geller had judged the young stranger innocent of treason. There they joined comrades who had arrived from other buildings also under attack.

The fighters exchanged a few words. Any casualties? No, but one man was missing: Izio Lewski. Jacob Putermilch felt a stab of shock. He knew Lewski well. But there was no time for emotional meditation, especially since Germans had reached the attic just above the bunker and were shooting from the window. A grenade then exploded, and plaster rained from the ceiling.

Silence. Hardly anyone dared to breathe while German boots clapped overhead. Jacob recognized again the hysterical voice of the SS officer who had demanded their annihilation. The Germans searched the attic. An hour passed. Could the Germans fail to find the camouflaged opening to the bunker?

Finally the Germans left, and the fighters relaxed. Now they could think . . . and consider poor Izio Lewski's fate. But then, more footsteps. Closer and closer.

Three knocks on the hatch, then a muted voice: "Jerusalem."

The password! In a moment Jacob climbed the ladder, his pistol ready, and he opened the hatch. There stood a grotesque figure with blackened face and feathers clinging to him from head to foot. Izio Lewski!

Lewski stumbled down and sat on a ladder rung, breathing heavily. He removed his glasses and then took his cap off and began cleaning the lenses with it. As he silently polished, a smile broadened his sooty face. Someone handed him a glass of water, which soon had feathers floating in it. Lewski blew away the feathers and drank the water; then, taking a deep breath, he wiped his mouth with his sleeve and said, "Comrades, I experienced something that I just can't believe I lived through."

Still polishing his glasses, he continued, "While I was at my observation post, I suddenly heard heavy footsteps, and when I turned around, several Germans were standing there. Before I could think, I heard a call: 'Hands up!' I leaped to the side and hid myself behind a wall. They opened fire and ordered me to drop my pistol. When I refused, they started shooting again and tried to get closer. I fired twice and jumped to another position.

"They followed and I stalled them, firing once or twice. Then I realized I had only one bullet left. Well, I told myself, this bullet is for me. I'll blow my brains out with it. What else could I do? I was cornered. But then the Germans themselves saved me by throwing a grenade. I caught it before it went off and threw it back at them. WHAM!"

When Lewski finished his story, some of the civilians in the bunker cried for joy and kissed him.

All in all, a good day, thought Jacob. Until he left the bunker that night to seek food and saw that the sky had turned red from the fire consuming the Central Ghetto.

His stomachache did not return.[7]

"Kill me! Kill me and my child!"

Pola Elster watched in horror as the woman pleaded with the Ukrainian guard in the large stinking room overlooking Umschlagplatz. The room had once been a ward in a hospital. Now the hospital was a seething madhouse for Jews being shipped to labor and death camps.

Pola, a ZOB fighter who had been captured the previous day in a bunker in the Brushmakers' District, now could barely move in the tangle of human flesh writhing on the floor, which was covered with excrement because no one was permitted to use the lavatory. People screamed as guards indiscriminately beat heads with rifle butts. Children pleaded for water in the stifling heat, only to be kicked in the face. Bearded religious men were forced to perform Hassidic dances amid Nazi laughter before being shot on the spot. Young women were dragged out and raped, then sent back with blood dripping down their legs. A doctor lucky enough to have a bottle of cyanide poured the precious solution into the feverish mouths of some children—a great sacrifice, since these children were strangers.

Pola stared at the grotesquely burned faces of a sister and two brothers who were sitting nearby. It was impossible to see their eyes. Then she saw the infant. His tiny hands and feet had been almost carbonized, but he didn't have the strength to cry. His face, however, reflected indescribable agony, while his eyes expressed an adult's understanding of what was happening to his people. He lay in the filth beside his mother, whose face and hands were so severely burned that she could not hold him in her arms. Thus she appealed to the Ukrainian to end her own suffering and that of her baby.

Without hesitating, the guard aimed his rifle at the woman and fired. But he would not shoot the infant as he lay next to his dead mother. One humanitarian act was enough, he explained to the others.

Then came the turn of five Judenrat leaders who were still alive, including the president, Marek Lichtenbaum. Shortly after they had been brought to the hospital building, an SS officer called out their names and led them to a garbage dump where Walther Caspar Többens was waiting for them. The officer lined up the five men and checked their names once again. Then he raised his submachine gun and fired several short bursts. Lichtenbaum and two others fell to the ground.

The fourth man in line, Dr. Wielkowski, pulled a document from his pocket, and with a trembling hand he held it out to the officer, who glanced at it briefly. It was an official letter from the German governor of Warsaw indicating that Wielkowski was not to be harassed by the police. The officer grabbed the document and slapped Wielkowski across the face with it. Then he tore it to pieces and shot the doctor. Többens now ordered the fifth victim

179

out of line and led him to a boxcar. This man apparently looked strong enough to work for him in Poniatow.

Pola would have to wait to learn her destination. The boxcars were too overloaded to take her this day.[8]

From the time the uprising started, Feigele Peltel had been trying to persuade some Polish policemen and firemen to help her smuggle arms to the fighters. But her efforts were in vain. The ghetto had become virtually impenetrable. Even so, she would explore other possibilities.

On this morning, Feigele succeeded in passing through a German outpost to the Aryan side of Swientojerska Street, which faced the wall sealing off the Brushmakers' District. Feigele pleaded that she only wanted to see her sick mother, who lived on Swientojerska; and the guard let her pass, though this area was officially barred to civilians.

The street was seething with military activity. Units of Nazi soldiers marched in both directions. Trucks and ambulances raced through the ghetto gates. SS automobiles stood parked by the wall. Though trembling, Feigele walked on, bluffing her way past several other sentries until she finally came to the partially destroyed building where Stanislaw Dubiel lived.

Standing outside in the dust and debris were Dubiel and his wife. They were among those brave Poles willing to risk their lives to save their Jewish brethren. As they greeted Feigele, they were frightened. Some Germans had just searched the house, and by some miracle they had failed to find the ten-year-old twin Jewish girls hiding there.

As Feigele entered the Dubiels' apartment, she saw the two children, Nellie and Vlodka, peeping with silent, anxious faces through a curtained window toward burning Walowa Street in the Brushmakers' District. They had stopped eating and even refused to speak to anyone. Throughout the day they stood at the window, waiting . . . waiting for just a glimpse of their mother. What had happened to her? Until shortly before the uprising, the little girls had seen her every day.

After Dubiel had sneaked into the ghetto one day and told the girls' mother where the apartment was, she haunted Walowa Street. She would look about cautiously, then slacken her pace

180

and stare lovingly at the window overlooking the wall, from which she knew her children would be watching her. Sometimes, when there were no Nazis around, they would even exchange a few endearing words across the wall or the girls would drop a note.

Now Walowa Street, reflecting a deadly glow, was deserted. But the little girls still waited.

Feigele was startled when firing suddenly broke out, it seemed, from the Dubiels' apartment.

"The shooting comes from our roof," Dubiel said. "The Germans mounted a machine gun up there. It's been going on all night. Today it's been a bit quieter than usual."

"Would it be possible to contact the ghetto through this house?" Feigele asked him.

"No, the area swarms with Germans. You could hardly escape their notice. At any rate, stay here for the night, and you'll see for yourself."

Feigele watched through the window as Germans walked along Walowa Street, sprinkling the buiding entrances with liquid from cans and then retreating. In a few moments the structures burst into flame.

"Look over there!" Dubiel cried, pointing.

On the balcony of a building stood a woman wringing her hands. She suddenly ran into her apartment but soon returned carrying a child and dragging a mattress. She threw the mattress to the ground to break her fall and began to climb over the railing, clutching her child. But a bullet caught her. The child dropped to the street while the mother's body dangled from the railing.

Feigele turned from the window, horrified. Smoke drifted in from the ghetto. No one said a word. Then she returned to the window.

"All night," she later recounted, "I stood before the open window as if in shock, my face feeling the heat of the fires, my eyes smarting from the smoke, watching the entire ghetto go up in flames."[9]

That day, also, on the Aryan side of Swientojerska Street, six Jews climbed out of a manhole. A little boy riding by on a scooter, having been taught at home that "a Jew will come and put you in a sack," informed a band of Polish blackmailers, who immediately pounced on the six. The Jews bought themselves off for five thousand zlotys. But another blackmailer came along and handed them over to the Gestapo, which paid him a similar sum.

Meanwhile, during the battles in the Productive Ghetto, a group of about twenty Jewish workers marching down Leszno Street bribed their German escort to let them break away and cross to the Aryan side. Hardly had they set foot there when they were surrounded by blackmailers and driven back into the ghetto because they had nothing to offer in return for their freedom.[10]

The Fifth Day

Mordechai Anielewicz found Mila 18 a self-contained world within a world as Shmuel Asher guided him through a long narrow corridor and into numerous rooms on either side. Asher's gang of thieves had excavated this gigantic bunker under three large adjoining buildings.

Electricity, a well, a fully equipped kitchen, and a recreation room helped to make life comfortable for the bunker's several dozen inhabitants. And lending to a homey atmosphere were brightly colored sofas and other decorative items. Mila 18 was a veritable underground palace.

Shmuel Asher was the undisputed ruler of this kingdom. A roly-poly foulmouthed man who reminded the fighters of a character out of a Bialik tale, he presided over all aspects of bunker life with an iron though benevolent hand. He determined the menus, the sleeping arrangements, and the schedule for trips outside the bunker to steal food.

But Asher readily agreed to grant the fighters full autonomy under Mordechai. Indeed, he treated them with almost embarrassing respect and demanded that his henchmen do likewise. When Mordechai and his group arrived, each of the thieves and his family had a separate room. But Asher offered to impinge on his own privacy and that of his men in order to accommodate the newcomers.

183

Mordechai, however, politely rejected the offer. He wanted his fighters to have their own place, so he ordered them to dig out a large room for themselves. They spread the excavated earth on the floor of the room, leaving enough space only for crawling and lying down. Who needed embroidered sofas? After all, for them this was simply a base from which they would fight to the death.

As his fighters settled into Mila 18, Mordechai felt renewed confidence, even euphoria. The uprising, he was certain, had far from run its course. He sat down in a corner and scribbled a note to his friend and deputy, Yitzhak Zuckerman, who was still trying to obtain arms and find a way to get them into the ghetto. The note would be smuggled to the Aryan side through the Jewish cemetery, just before this artery of contact with the outside world was to be cut.

"I don't know what to write to you," Mordechai started. "Excuse me if this time I do not write to you of personal matters. To express what I and my friends feel, I will say that we have succeeded beyond our wildest dreams."

Mordechai described the fighting of the previous four days and announced that the fighters were beginning to adopt partisan tactics.

"This evening three groups will go into action. They have a twofold mission: to locate and capture weapons. Remember, a revolver has no value for us; its use is limited. We have urgent need of hand grenades, submachine guns, and explosives."

Mordechai then came to grips with reality, though incredibly his euphoria persisted, undiminished.

"It is impossible to describe the conditions reigning in the ghetto. Very few could bear all this. All the others are destined to perish sooner or later. Their fate has been sealed. In most of the bunkers where thousands of Jews are hiding it is impossible to light a candle because of the lack of air.

"I greet you, my dear friend. Who knows whether we shall meet again? My life's dream has now been realized: Jewish self-defense in the ghetto is now an accomplished fact. Armed resistance by the Jews has been realized."[1]

Michael L. and Yitzhak Gitler were growing weaker each minute from the lack of food and water. And so were their families.

184

The eight of them had been hiding since April 19 in the attic of a new, partly completed building in the Productive Ghetto after having reached this isolated stairless haven by crossing a narrow plank from the roof of a neighboring building.

In their haste to hide they had neglected to bring food, except for a bottle of vitamin pills, which was keeping them alive. And the forty or so other Jews in the bunker refused to share their food with these "interlopers." What business did these people have barging into *their* hideout?

Their families, Michael and Gitler knew, could not last much longer, especially Gitler's sixty-year-old mother, who had still not recovered from the horrifying experience of crossing the plank. And Gitler's teenage daughter, Nina, who kept sobbing, "I want to live!" seemed near the breaking point. Only Michael's wife, Maria, steadfastly refused to exhibit any doubt that they would survive.

But even she had to agree that to remain there much longer would be to die from hunger or thirst, if the Germans didn't find them first. During the day they peered through cracks in the wall and observed Nazis entering buildings nearby and dragging out Jews, sometimes shooting them on the spot. At night they cowered on the concrete floor as Germans on neighboring rooftops turned searchlights on every building. And they were trapped six floors up. At least in an underground bunker the people could scavenge for food and water at night.

Thus Michael and Gitler decided to leave their shelter and seek another. At about 2 A.M. on April 23 they climbed through an opening to the roof and grabbed the plank they had used to cross over to this unfinished building. The original occupants of the attic had pulled the plank in to prevent more "intruders" from joining them, so now the two men would have to put it back in place again. It if fell, they and the others would inevitably die here.

As a searchlight scanned the area, they sweated, groaned, and prayed while holding the plank at one end and maneuvering it across the chasm to the roof-edge of the next building. When the board was finally in place, they rushed across it and reached the neighboring roof just as the Germans began firing at them. They crawled to the opening in the attic, and Gitler began lowering himself through it when somebody inside grabbed him. As a gun poked into his ribs, a voice demanded in Polish, "Who are you?"

185

Realizing this was no German, Gitler identified himself and explained his mission; and two men—ZOB fighters—embraced and kissed him.

"We thought you were Germans," one of them said.

Several other fighters came up, and four agreed to return to the unfinished building with Michael and Gitler to help bring across their families, who would stay in an underground bunker used by the ZOB. But when the rescue party had crossed the plank and was about to come back with the two families, the other Jews, feeling they were being left to die, tried to keep them from going.

"Nobody leaves unless we all leave!" a man declared.

The fighters brandished their pistols, and one warned, "Anybody who tries to interfere will be shot. We'll return for all of you as soon as we find a place."

When a desperate youth then tried unsuccessfully to kick the plank off the roof, Gitler barely prevented one of the fighters from shooting him.

Finally the evacuees precariously threaded their way across to the other building, reaching it just before Gitler's daughter, Nina, fainted. They were then led to a bunker at Leszno 76, where they joined fighters of Eliezer Geller.[2]

Later that day Eliezer visited the bunker at Nowolipie 67, where Jacob Putermilch and his group were now based, and Eliezer sat down on a bunk to talk with them. Clean-shaven and freshly washed, Eliezer smiled and exuded confidence. Jacob, who was exhausted from a day of hit-and-run fighting, could hardly believe that the area commander had been in battle for several days. But Eliezer's words were less cheerful than his appearance.

"Children," he said affectionately, "it's bad. The ammunition is almost exhausted, and there is no possibility of getting new arms."

He ordered them to stop all attacks and to shoot only in self-defense—and only when the bullet was almost certain to hit its mark. And be sure, he added, to keep the last bullet for oneself.

Jacob and the others were glum. They were fighters, but they were no longer able to fight. They must simply run and hide. Was this the end of the uprising?

"We have fulfilled our task," Eliezer said, trying to raise their spirits. "We have done enough. The results will be felt later. I am proud of our fighters and their deeds."

Then he asked about the food supply. Aharon Chmielnicki, who had worked in his father's bakery before the war, replied, "We're going to bake bread tonight. Tomorrow everybody in the bunkers will be able to stuff themselves."

Eliezer's eyes brightened in amusement, and he smiled, then licked his lips mockingly.

"No, it's true," Aharon insisted, explaining that he would bake the bread in a bakery he had found in the courtyard of the building, complete with several sacks of flour and enough dry wood to make a fire. There was also plenty of water. All that was missing was yeast.

"You've whetted my appetite already," Eliezer said. "Anyway, I'm glad your morale is high. I'll pay a thousand zlotys for every loaf of fresh bread you bake."

Later that night, Aharon left to produce one of the miracles of the uprising: fresh bread for the ghetto.[3]

Walther Caspar Többens stepped out of his chauffeured car on his way to Umschlagplatz, where he would conduct a new "selection," and confronted three Jews who had just been dragged out of a house by a Gestapo man. The luck of Sewek Toporek and his father and brother had run out. The two brothers, who had been forced to take captured Jews to the Judenrat building for execution on the first day of the uprising, had managed through a ruse to return home and join their father. But now their privileged position would no longer serve them.

Noting their peaked red caps, which members of the Rettungskommando wore, Többens remarked almost benevolently, "You won't need your caps anymore. You're going to Poniatow to work for me."

Then he drove off while the Toporeks started on foot toward Umschlagplatz, escorted by the Gestapo man. En route they met a party of SS officers led by General Stroop himself.

"Who are these Jews?" Stroop wanted to know.

"Members of the Rettungskommando, sir," the Gestapo man replied.

"Our aim is to destroy Jews," snapped Stroop, "not to heal their wounds."

187

As the family moved on, Sewek, who had overhead Stroop's remark, shuddered. They would certainly be sent to their deaths. When they reached Umschlagplatz, where a long line of empty boxcars was waiting to swallow up thousands of Jews packed into the square, Többens ordered them to advance to the first car and climb in. As they moved on, Sewek instinctively felt that the first car was going to Treblinka, despite Többens' earlier reassurance. Amid the massive, hysterical confusion in the jammed square, the three jumped into the *last* car.

Playing Russian roulette with the boxcars, Sewek judged from experience that it was safest to believe the opposite of what the Nazis promised. Sewek's car ended up in Lublin Airport. There he posed as a tailor and was sent to a labor camp, while his father and brother continued on to a death camp.[4]

Meanwhile, some five thousand other "privileged" Jews were being lined up on Niska Street, the sealed-off zone where Lieutenant Franz Konrad ran the Warsaw branch of the Werterfassung like a giant private enterprise. This organization, which collected abandoned Jewish property, had until now been left undisturbed. After all, the goods stolen from the Jews—furs, jewelry, art pieces, furniture (often with money and valuables hidden in the upholstery)—could help the Reich finance the war. Every bit counted.

Konrad firmly supported this logic. And if he personally grew rich in the process, he would simply be earning a normal agent's fee for all his efforts. Little wonder that Konrad usually beamed with good humor.

But on this morning Konrad looked glum as he stood on the street, facing his workers and hundreds of Jews from other parts of the ghetto who had managed to sneak into the Werterfassung area and pose as workers. Up to now, Konrad had succeeded in keeping his labor force—and his profits—intact, despite the efforts of his civilian competitor, Walther Caspar Többens, to strangle his enterprise. With few Jews in the Productive Ghetto volunteering to come out of hiding and transfer to Poniatow, Többens needed more workers for his own factories there. Thus he had his eye on the qualified Werterfassung workers. Since they saw no reason to hide, they would be easy to grab.

On the second day of the uprising Többens had tried playing a little trick on Konrad. He asked him to send his workers to German headquarters in the square facing the Judenrat building to receive new work registration numbers. When Konrad led his workers there, Többens demanded that five hundred of them be transferred to Poniatow. No, Konrad angrily replied. He had too few workers as it was.

The Jews heard a loud exchange of words, a few muttered curses. Then Konrad jumped into his car and zoomed away, returning shortly with General Stroop's approval of his stand. Triumphantly, he sent all the workers back to Niska Street even before Többens could issue them new registration numbers. The Jews laughed and cried for joy, and some even celebrated by getting drunk. Konrad had refused to part with a single worker. Henceforth they would trust him completely.

Therefore, they did not hesitate now to line up on the street, together with all their baggage. They would, Konrad told them, simply be moving to the isolated Small Ghetto in the south. There they would continue to work peacefully at their same tasks. Only a group of fighters who had infiltrated this area decided to remain behind, suspecting a trick.

Among the workers was Jonas Turkow, the Yiddish actor who had hidden in the bunker of Lutek Rotblatt and his doomed orphans some months earlier. He did not like the gloomy look on Konrad's face as he assured the Jews that they need not worry, that they were in no danger whatsoever. Konrad said that before going to the Small Ghetto, everybody would receive the new registration numbers that should have been issued at the Judenrat building a few days earlier. Jonas and the others felt a sense of relief, until the lieutenant added, "The numbers will be distributed at Umschlagplatz."

A long shuddering silence followed.

"We are finished," Jonas thought.

Többens, it seemed, had won after all. He would get his five hundred workers. And the rest would die.[5]

Flanked by several SS officers, including Konrad, Többens stood talking in a corner of Umschlagplatz while the frightened, bedraggled crowd tried to read something of their fate in the faces of the officers. The group of Nazis began laughing and slapping each other on the shoulder. Someone, it seemed, had told a joke. Then back to the business of the day.

Többens returned to his vehicle, and his driver helped him remove two blackboards supported on sticks and carry them to a place near the boxcars. On each was chalked the name of a different company. The Jews who had been working for these firms were to gather by the sign designating their particular one.

Többens, whip in hand, waited by the blackboards for several minutes, but no one emerged from the distrustful crowd. Többens then shouted in German, "All skilled carpenters step forward, together with their families."

Someone translated the call into Polish, but there was still no response.

Többens then smashed his whip into his hand and yelled, "I advise those who have been called to step forward in their own interest. Otherwise they will regret it."

Treblinka! Several dozen people responded.

"Skilled artisans step out!"

Then tailors.

The score who scrambled to the various assembly areas increased to hundreds, then thousands. Almost everybody, it seemed, was a carpenter, an artisan, a tailor. Husbands left wives, parents left children, children left parents. For if their claims were believed, they might be sent to a labor camp and live a little longer.

Többens, almost surrounded by guards, moved from one assembly area to the other, glancing indifferently at each claimant as he or she stepped forward from the throng. If his whip pointed toward the train, the claim was accepted. The designated car would supposedly head toward the Lublin labor camps. The guards pushed the others back into the crowd.

But as the Jews became more panicky, Többens appeared to grow frightened. He gave a signal, and machine gunners posted on the roofs and at other strategic points around the square began firing into the hysterical crowd from every direction, killing and wounding scores of people.

Meanwhile Többens ordered the Jewish policemen who had escorted Konrad's huge group from the Werterfassung to separate them from the rest of the people in the square. They linked arms,

190

forming a chain around these workers, and were joined by SS reinforcements. Then, with the help of Konrad's deputies, Többens tried to pick out skilled individuals who would remain behind to work for him in the Small Ghetto (and be sent later to Poniatow), but in the frenzied chaos he had to settle for about five hundred selected mainly at random.

An SS man then announced to those still unchosen that three hundred metalworkers would also remain in Warsaw. The rest would be deported, despite Konrad's promises that all would stay behind. His lust for profits had to give way to Stroop's lust for blood, and Többens, as he had shrewdly planned, was able to pick up the human leftovers. Jonas Turkow later described the scene that followed: "Everyone tried to find himself in the front rows in order not to be excluded, God forbid, from the group of three hundred. They simply leaped over each other. Women, children, and elderly people were trampled underfoot. The machine guns did not cease to fire and sowed death right and left. Apparently the Germans wanted to diminish the number of Jews."

Suddenly an aging SS officer with gray hair and a sympathetic face approached a man who lay on the ground writhing in pain and asked him in a concerned manner what had happened. The Jew pointed to a wound in his leg.

"Poor, poor man," the officer responded.

He slowly drew his pistol from his holster and fired into the man's head, then sought out other wounded people to show his sympathy in the same way.

When the Werterfassung workers had finally been whipped into formation, two SS men walked down the rows, selecting and counting. Jonas, who was several rows back, felt certain they would count to three hundred before they reached him. He trembled with each number called out: "two-eighty . . . two-eighty-one . . . two-eighty-two . . ." Only a few more would be saved. And he was among them.

As soon as number three hundred was called out, Nazi guards beat and pushed the remaining people, including the Jewish policemen, whose services were no longer needed, into the rest of the crowd, and then drove the whole human mass toward the boxcars with whip and bullet. People dropped bags, haversacks, bundles, but in the crush nobody could bend to pick them up. Besides, what was the point? Were they not going to their death?

191

Some Jews tried to smash through the police cordons into the assembly areas of those privileged groups staying behind, but were shot. Konrad personally ordered an SS man to kill one woman, who without permission tried to join such a group. Suddenly, loud, almost hysterical laughter sounded over the screams and wails. Többens was watching these scenes of murder and terror with uncontrollable glee.

"Yes," he cried, "the Jews thought they were smarter than I!"[6]

Among those caught in the crush was Pola Elster, who had suffered through the horrors of the hospital building for three days. Instinctively she tried to drop back in the crowd. Perhaps the cars would fill up and she would have another few hours of life. But she was carried forward by the throng to a boxcar and crammed in with about seventy others. The car was bolted from the outside, and her fate, Pola surmised, was sealed.

People stepped on each other's feet and on bodies that had collapsed. They cursed, wept, and begged for water in the scorching heat. Germans standing guard outside ignored these cries, though occasionally one would place a bottle of water in a grasping hand thrust out of the tiny barred window—for fifty zlotys a quart. First the children would drink a few drops, then the women, finally the men.

But there wasn't enough. Pola did not think about food. Nor did anybody have any. To drink, drink. . . . Thirst was consuming her and the others. The tongue and the throat dried up. Even a cube of sugar would not melt in the mouth. Finally mothers forced their children to drink their own urine. But this only increased their thirst or gave them convulsions.

Hours passed. Why didn't the train move? Fierce quarrels broke out over trifles: Who stepped on whom? Whose turn was it to stand by the window? Who drank too much of the precious water? Pola infuriated most when she suggested she would file the window bars and try to escape. Had not the Nazis threatened to shoot everyone in the car if one tried to flee? And escape was impossible anyway. Guards were stationed on the roof and between cars. But Pola had made up her mind.

Finally, at about 9 P.M., a whistle blew and the train lurched forward. A great moan went up. People forgot their petty quarrels.

192

Yes, they were moving. All her life Pola had loved trains. As a child she used to walk to the railroad station and watch them pull out. Each departure filled her young heart with fantasies of far-away places, people with different customs, high mountains and green valleys and ancient cities throbbing with life.

Now she was in a train that she was sure would take her to death. But her final destination was the labor camp at Poniatow.[7]

Jonas Turkow and the other "metalworkers" marched from the site of agony in silence. Jonas glanced around and saw dozens of familiar faces following the column with envious expressions. He kept tripping over corpses, for if he tried to walk around them he would feel the burning lash of the guard's whip. When the column had emerged from Umschlagplatz and was walking along Dzika Street on the Aryan side of the ghetto wall, an SS man shouted, *"Halt!"*

Jonas trembled. Were they going to lead the group back to Umschlagplatz?

"Lie down on your bellies along the wall!"

It now seemed obvious. The Germans would shoot all of them dead.

Jonas heard the click of a rifle bolt over him. He closed his eyes and pressed his head to the ground, waiting to die. But nothing happened. He opened his eyes and glanced from side to side without lifting his head. The world on this side of the wall looked so peaceful. Neat houses, grass, an air of sleepy silence. On the other side he could hear screams, groans, shots. For hours he listened . . . and waited for the final shot.

"Get up!"

As he rose Jonas saw standing nearby about a hundred soldiers, each armed with a submachine gun and holding the chain leash of a giant wolfhound. An officer stepped out of his car and approached the Jews. Who among them, he asked, was a tailor or a cobbler? There was a hush as the prisoners tried to calculate which response would mean life and which, death. The German repeated the question and added, "Tailors and cobblers to the right. All others remain where you are."

Now almost all of the three hundred Jews stampeded to the right, converting themselves from metalworkers into tailors and

193

cobblers. They pushed and trampled each other in their eagerness for "salvation." The Germans, apparently fearing a mutiny, unleashed the dogs, which leaped upon the people, tearing at their flesh. One of them sank its teeth into Jonas' buttocks. After managing to kick the beast away Jonas fell to the ground in agony amid a thunderous crescendo of screams, barks, and guttural bellows. Finally several shots were fired into the air, and a semblance of order was restored. Two separate columns were formed, and the Jews, limping and gasping, began marching through Warsaw.

As Jonas' group staggered ahead under heavy guard, Poles gathered along the streets to watch the motley spectacle. One woman, wringing her hands, exclaimed, "Jesus, Mary, what do they want from the poor!"

But a hooligan called, "To Palestine!" and others also jeered, ignoring an elderly woman who scolded them.

At Casimir Square one of the guards stopped in front of a small butcher shop and asked the vendor for a piece of meat for his dog. A Polish worker passing by remarked, "Our people are dying of hunger, and you want to feed your dogs with meat?"

The German turned to him and said, "Just come here, you hero." And before the Pole could react, he brutally slapped him.

As the Jews marched on, an elegantly dressed Pole walked up to a guard and, pointing at them, said, "You are doing the right thing leading those kikes to their death. They are all Bolsheviks. . . . Let God punish all of them."

The guard, listening calmly as the Pole continued to incite him against his prisoners, nodded his head: "Ja, Ja."

Suddenly the Pole noted Jonas' look of contempt and fell upon him with clenched fists. But Jonas, discovering in himself an unexpected strength, hit him between the eyes and knocked him to the ground. Panic broke out among the Jews, who feared that the Germans would open fire. The Pole got to his feet, and entering the column, he began to look for Jonas, who had moved on. But the other Jews pummeled him.

The guards began cursing and quarreling, blaming each other for the uproar. Some even unleashed their dogs to restore order, but they only loped alongside the column, barking loudly. A guard's bullet pierced the air, and suddenly complete silence reigned.

Some Poles were sympathetic, some were not. It seemed incred-

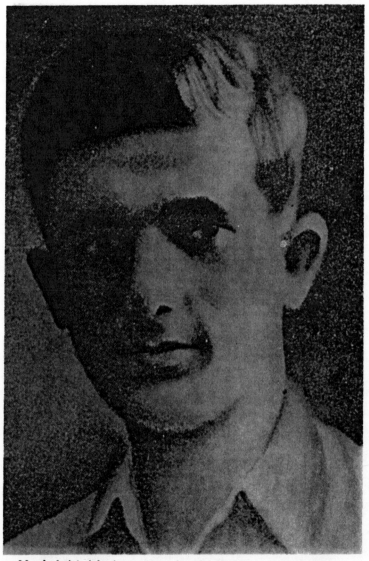

Mordechai Anielewicz, commander of the ZOB *(Yad Vashem)*

General Jürgen Stroop, SS commander of the Warsaw Ghetto operation,
after his capture   *(Yad Vashem)*

Collecting the ghetto dead   *(Yad Vashem)*

Ghetto children cry for food   *(Centralna Agencja Fotograficzna)*

Strollers pass starving man   *(Yad Vashem)*

Smugglers climb wall to Aryan side   *(Centralna Agencja Fotograficzna)*

General Stroop, *right*, confers with his officers   *(Yad Vashem)*

Jewish police report for duty   *(Yad Vashem)*

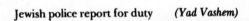

The destruction on Mila Street
(Yehiel Kirshbaum)

Jew jumps from burning ghetto
building   *(Yad Vashem)*

Jew climbs through camouflaged door into bunker   *(Yad Vashem)*

Yitzhak Zuckerman, ZOB
second-in-command
(Yad Vashem)

Zivia Lubetkin, a ZOB
commander *(Beit Lohamei Haghetaot)*

Mira Fuchrer, ZOB fighter
in Central Ghetto
(Beit Lohamei Haghetaot)

Captain Henryk Iwanski,
Home Army officer who
helped Jews *(Henryk Iwanski)*

Eliezer Geller, ZOB
commander in Productive
Ghetto *(Yad Vashem)*

Arie Wilner, ZOB representative on Aryan side *(Yad Vashem)*

Jacob Putermilch, ZOB fighter in Productive Ghetto *(Jacob Putermilch)*

Chaim Frimer, ZOB fighter in Central Ghetto *(Beit Lohamei Haghetaot)*

Lutek Rotblatt, ZOB fighter in Central Ghetto *(Beit Lohamei Haghetaot)*

Regina Fuden, ZOB fighter in Productive Ghetto *(Beit Lohamei Haghetaot)*

Hela Schipper, *left*,
ZOB fighter in Central
Ghetto, with
unidentified woman
(Beit Lohamei Haghetaot)

Tuvia Borzykowski,
ZOB fighter in Central
Ghetto
(Yad Vashem)

Simcha Rathajzer,
ZOB fighter, *left,* with
Polish partisan;
Yitzhak Zuckerman
follows
(Simcha Rathajzer)

Marek Edelman,
center, ZOB
commander in
Brushmakers' District
(Beit Lohamei Haghetaot)

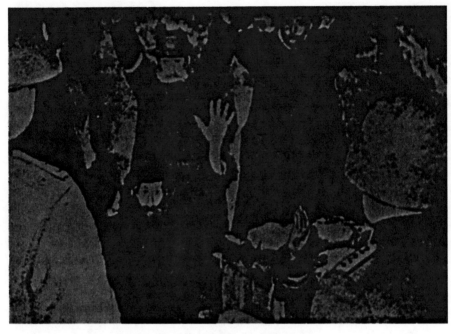

Nazis find Jews in bunker *(Yad Vashem)*

Nazis strip women prisoners *(Beit Lohamei Haghetaot)*

Nazis round up Jews; German soldier at right is Josef Blösche, known as "Frankenstein" *(Yad Vashem)*

Nazis capture Jews *(Yad Vashem)*

Captured Jews herded toward Umschlagplatz   *(Yad Vashem)*

Umschlagplatz, railhead for the run to Treblinka   *(Centralna Agencja Fotograficzna)*

Jews pile into boxcars   *(Centralna Agencja Fotograficzna)*

Ruins of Warsaw synagogue   *(Yad Vashem)*

Dvora Baron, ZOB fighter in Brushmakers' District *(Beit Lohamei Haghetaot)*

Artur Zygielbojm, Jewish representative in Polish government-in-exile *(Beit Lohamei Haghetaot)*

Michal Klepfisz, ZOB fighter in Brushmakers' District *(Beit Lohamei Haghetaot)*

Tosia Altman, ZOB fighter in Central Ghetto *(Yad Vashem)*

False identification card of Feigele Peltel, ZOB agent on Aryan side *(Beit Lohamei Haghetaot)*

Sewek Toporek, member of Rettungskommando *(Sewek Toporek)*

Aharon Chmielnicki, ZOB fighter (and baker) in Productive Ghetto *(Aharon Chmielnicki)*

Josef Pzenny, Home Army officer who helped Jews *(Yad Vashem)*

Zachariah Artstein, a ZOB commander in Central Ghetto *(Beit Lohamei Haghetaot)*

Pola Elster, ZOB fighter in Central Ghetto *(Beit Lohamei Haghetaot)*

Israel Kanal, a ZOB commander in Central Ghetto *(Beit Lohamei Haghetaot)*

Jonas Turkow, Yiddish actor *(Beit Lohamei Haghetaot)*

Leon Feiner, ZOB representative on Aryan side *(Beit Lohamei Haghetaot)*

Masha Glytman, ZOB fighter in Central Ghetto *(Masha Glytman)*

Mordechai Growas, ZOB fighter in Central Ghetto *(Beit Lohamei Haghetaot)*

Abrasha Blum, Bund political leader *(Beit Lohamei Haghetaot)*

Josef Lewartowski, PPR leader in ghetto *(Yad Vashem)*

Pinhas Kartin, Soviet agent in ghetto *(Beit Lohamei Haghetaot)*

ible to Jonas that human beings could be divided in their attitude toward unspeakable atrocities.

Finally the Jews reached a small labor camp just outside Warsaw. Jonas, though still limping in pain from the dog bite, could hardly believe his luck. He had survived a "selection," he had remained in Warsaw, and he had had a unique personal opportunity to strike at those who would murder his people.[8]

That day, while thousands of Jews were being piled into the boxcars, others were brought to Umschlagplatz to fill up the vacated hospital building and await their turn. One of these newly captured Jews was Kalman Friedman, who had celebrated the first Seder with crippled Jacob Nussbaum and his eight-year-old nephew, Izio, and later found Nussbaum dead in his apartment and Izio missing. Kalman's bunker, the cellar of the same building, had been discovered that morning and the occupants routed out with grenades.

Now Kalman sat on the slimy floor of the depot of death, listening to the sounds of genocide: human beasts roaring, their victims screaming, a locomotive whistling. He tried to prepare himself for the fatal moment. He sat silently in a state of shock, meditating. Suddenly he felt something pulling at him from behind. He looked around and stared incredulously.

"Izio!"

Kalman had wanted to shout, but the word barely trickled out. As Izio laid his head against his friend's shoulder, Kalman felt the child's quivering limbs and burning cheeks. He stroked his face, which was wet with tears, and lifted his head to look at him. Izio's eyes had deepened, and his lips were pale. The two hugged each other.

"What happened?" Kalman asked. "Tell me everything."

"They struggled with my uncle," Izio said. "They wanted him to get up, and finally they threw him to the floor. All this time they fired at the bedding, the closet, and even the stove. They took me downstairs. Outside, a German came to me with a belt in his hands. His face was red, and I thought he would whip me. But he lifted me up and smiled at me. He took out a biscuit and gave it to me, and then let me down. I didn't understand anything he said. I don't know what they did with my uncle, but I think they shot him. . . ."

When Izio had finished his story, he lay quietly against Kalman, who felt numb. If only this moment could stretch into eternity, thought Kalman, so that he would never feel anything again.[9]

In midafternoon Jacob Putermilch and several other fighters were standing guard by the windows of the attic at Nowolipie 67 in the Productive Ghetto when they saw about fifty Germans and Ukrainians enter the courtyard. They walked without hesitation, apparently knowing just where to go as in previous intrusions. Once more, it seemed, a traitor had been at work. Jacob and his comrades immediately climbed into their hideout under the attic.

Hardly had they bolted the hatch when they heard boots tramping. Then automatic fire. The Nazis were spraying the attics as they advanced. The Jews in the bunker sat with their eyes riveted on the hatch, ready to follow their plan. First the civilians would leave; then the fighters, posing as civilians, would follow and suddenly open fire. But the shooting soon stopped. The Nazis had gone. Everybody sighed with relief.

After dark there was a knock on the hatch, and a woman's voice uttered the password. Regina Fuden, known as Lilit, was making her nightly call. Everybody's spirits rose. As the liaison among the various posts in the Productive Ghetto, Regina moved from bunker to bunker, cellar to cellar, attic to attic, always on an urgent mission, bringing news and orders. Without her, every post would be isolated. She was strong, devoted, and brave—a "visiting angel," as the fighters called her—with lively gray eyes, curly blond hair, and a low, haunting voice. She almost always arrived with a smile.

But not this time. Regina's grimy face was hard, her hair unruly and full of feathers, as she pulled along a young boy about twelve years old. She had caught him in an attic, hiding in a pile of feathers, after seeing him lead the Germans to several bunkers, including this one. As Jacob and the other fighters questioned the boy, he turned pale and trembled in fear, cowering on the floor and refusing to speak.

Finally the fighters threatened him, and he broke down. It was true, he admitted. The Germans had sent him to spy on the Jews and reveal this and other hideouts. They had said they would feed him well if he agreed. And kill him if he didn't.

"Using my information," the boy confessed, "a group of Germans came to find you. When they returned, they yelled and cursed me because they said my information was wrong."

Shortly, Eliezer Geller, the area commander, and Hershel Kawe, the commander of another group, stopped by the bunker and debated what to do with the young traitor. They could not keep him prisoner since they were constantly on the move, but if they let him go he might continue giving away bunkers.

The fighters agonized. Twelve years old: an age when, in normal times, a boy prepared for his *bar mitzvah*, his entry into manhood at thirteen; when he frolicked in the fields, playing football or chasing butterflies; when he wove dreams of a heroic future full of splendor and exotic adventure.

The youth must be shot, Eliezer decided. Hershel agreed that he should be executed. But every bullet counted. There was another way. Hershel grabbed the terror-stricken boy and dragged him upstairs to the attic.

He then shoved him out a window.[10]

At dawn Feigele Peltel was still standing at the window in the home of Stanislaw Dubiel on the Aryan side of Swientojerska Street overlooking the blazing Brushmakers' District. A ghastly, lifeless silence had descended over the ghetto when suddenly she saw a human form crawling toward a pile of ruins. A spray of fire, and the figure blended motionlessly into the scorched wasteland. As the sun grew brighter, there was a knock on the door. Feigele lurched away from the window as Dubiel let in two German officers.

"Anyone outside of your family living here?"

"No, I do not harbor any Jews."

Without bothering to search the house, the Germans rushed to the window and put their cameras to their eyes.

"It's a good site," one remarked, "if it weren't for those damned fires."

They snapped photo after photo for about half an hour, joking about the "comical Jewish clowns" as they jumped to their deaths.

When they had finally gone, Mrs. Dubiel, crossing herself and mumbling prayers, begged Feigele to leave, too. Bidding goodbye to the Dubiels and the little twin sisters they were hiding, Feigele emerged into the street and walked past swarms of Germans. She did not dare to look toward the window where the twins stood, still hoping for a miraculous glimpse of their mother through the smoke and fire.[11]

Also watching in agony from the Aryan side as the black shroud of genocide settled over the ghetto was Yitzhak Zuckerman. In despair he issued a manifesto to the Polish underground and the inhabitants of Warsaw:

> Poles, citizens, soldiers of Freedom! Through the din of German cannons destroying the homes of our mothers, wives and children; through the noise of their machine guns, seized by us in the fight against the cowardly German police and SS men; through the smoke of the ghetto that was set on fire, and the blood of its mercilessly murdered defenders, we, the slaves of the ghetto, convey heartfelt greetings to you. We are well aware that you have been witnessing breathlessly, with broken hearts, with tears of compassion, with horror and enthusiasm, the war that we have been waging against the brutal occupier these past few days.
>
> Every doorstep in the ghetto has become a stronghold and shall remain a fortress until the end. All of us will probably perish in the fight, but we shall never surrender. We, as well as you, are burning with the desire to punish the enemy for all his crimes, with a desire for vengeance. It is a fight for our freedom, as well as yours; for our human dignity and national honor, as well as yours. We shall avenge the gory deeds of Auschwitz, Treblinka, Belzec, and Majdanek!
>
> Long live the fraternity of blood and weapons in a fighting Poland!
>
> Long live Freedom!
>
> Death to the hangmen and the killers!
>
> We must continue our mutual struggle against the occupier until the very end!
>
> Jewish Fighting Organization

General Stroop was furious when he read the manifesto. This was a call to the Poles to rise up in a general revolt. And his fury grew when he learned that General Krüger in Cracow had received a cable from Himmler that day, saying, "The combing out of the Warsaw Ghetto is to be carried out with greater toughness and . . . tenacity. . . . The tougher the measures used, the better it will be. The incidents just show how dangerous these Jews are."

198

Stroop now decided to send aircraft to drop incendiary bombs on the ghetto and issued a manifesto of his own: "Entrance to the former Jewish quarter is most strictly forbidden. . . . Whoever will be caught in [it] without a new valid permit will be shot."

To show he meant business, he ordered his men to set ablaze a Polish house on Casimir Square and shoot an entire family for hiding a Jew.

Still, some Poles courageously responded to the ZOB appeal. That day Colonel Chrusciel ordered his men to stage "a maximum effort" to help the ghetto fighters. Within hours one Home Army unit attacked SS patrols in the Jewish cemetery area, killing two Germans, while another assaulted German posts on Leszno Street. Most Home Army newspapers praised the Jews for their courage but did not mention that Poles had risked their lives to help them. The Home Army might lose popular support.

However, three groups of the PPR attacked and killed several Nazis on the street, and PPR publications trumpeted the details. Meanwhile the PPR central committee, though split over the question of helping the Jews, united to draw up a coded message addressed to the Soviet government. As recalled by a PPR member who helped to compose it, the message read:

> Warsaw is in flames. The Germans have started to bestially exterminate the remnants of the Jewish population in the Warsaw Ghetto. It is impossible for the organization to gain access to Jews defending themselves in the ghetto. The PPR organizes resistance against the liquidation of the ghetto and assists the fighters.
> . . . Retaliation in the form of bombing a number of military objectives and part of the German quarter in Warsaw is desirable.

A PPR signalman transmitted the message to a Communist partisan base, which relayed it to Moscow. A Soviet bombing might create sufficient chaos to permit a mass breakout from the ghetto.[12]

The Sixth Day

Aharon Chmielnicki, the baker's son, was only a common soldier at the battlefront; but now, in the courtyard bakery at Nowolipie 67, he wielded the authority of a general. As he had promised Eliezer Geller, he was baking fresh bread for the Productive Ghetto on the night of April 23. Jacob Putermilch heated the oven, a second man carried water, and a third kneaded dough. Meanwhile several girls searched the apartments for onions as a replacement for yeast.

His helpers worked swiftly, realizing that the bread had to be out of the oven before dawn, when the Germans would certainly come. But they showed no respect at all for Aharon's exalted status, symbolized by the white apron he wore. They joked about every order.

"Mamzarim!" ("Bastards!") muttered Aharon.

No one worked harder or faster than Aharon himself. He feared that even though the courtyard gates were well-guarded, the Germans might suddenly appear while his hands were full of dough, and he would be incapable of reaching for the pistol in his belt. With sleeves rolled up he sweated through the night at his old profession, immersing himself in the past, when he had worked in his father's bakery; remembering the people who would come in and inquire about the family's health while his father weighed the bread. . . . His family—all had been shipped to

200

Treblinka, where he would have ended up, too, if he had not leaped from the window of the boxcar taking them there.

Aharon was abruptly shaken back to the present. How stupid! Why was he putting chunks of dough on a scale? As if it mattered now how much a loaf of bread weighed. When a helper had shaped the dough into loaves, Aharon, like a skilled juggler, spun them into the oven. Then he and his assistants went outside to check whether the smoke spiraling from the chimney was noticeable. They chilled on seeing a black pillar rising into the night sky. Well, at least they would die on a full stomach.

Finally, near dawn, the bakers removed the bread from the oven: about three hundred loaves of various sizes, each almost as flat as a pizza because of the lack of yeast. They inhaled the odor with the ecstasy of a dope addict sniffing his favorite narcotic. As they put the loaves into sacks, they suddenly remembered it was Saturday morning: the Sabbath. Since observant Jews would not light fires on the Sabbath, it was their custom to bake in advance a vegetable dish called *cholent,* a mix of potatoes, beans, and groats. The fighters had found these ingredients in the apartments, so why let a hot oven go to waste? It was already the Sabbath, but in time of war even the observant felt free to work.

Soon several girls were peeling potatoes while Aharon showed the others how to make *cholent,* urging, scolding them on. Dawn was breaking. Did they want to die before they even tasted his delicious creations?

When pots of *cholent* had been thrown into the oven, Aharon and his aides rushed to nearby bunkers to distribute the bread. They hid the remaining bread in a pile of feathers in the attic, hoping that the feathers would keep the odor from reaching the nostrils of the enemy.

The people in the bunkers were so hungry that they stuffed themselves while the bread was still hot, rinsing it down with water, complete with floating feathers. And Aharon stuffed his pockets with the money Eliezer had promised him if he baked the bread.

The Jews then lay back and patted their shriveled stomachs, dreaming of the next course. Soon the *cholent* would be ready.[1]

In the Central Ghetto that morning, flames began reaching into every bunker.

Since the uprising started, Dr. Israel Rotbalsam and other medical personnel had been hiding in a concealed room on the second floor of the Czyste-Benson-Bauman Hospital on Gensia Street. But now, about twenty Germans entered the hospital courtyard and set the building on fire. Rotbalsam and his companions ran into the courtyard and joined hundreds of other Jews fleeing insanely in all directions while German machine guns blazed away at them.

The doctor and about ten other survivors in his group managed to make it into the courtyard of a neighboring burnt-out building, where they hid in the ruins.[2]

At about the same time, disaster stalked some one hundred fighters and civilians still entombed in the underground bunker at Mila 29, former ZOB headquarters. Lutek Rotblatt, who had been put in charge when Mordechai Anielewicz had left with about twenty fighters on April 21, remained here with the others, since the fire devouring the building above had gone out shortly after Mordechai's departure. But now the building was once more a raging furnace, with flames shooting out from the top floor.

However, since the fire would take some time to spread to the bunker, Lutek decided to try waiting until dark before evacuating it in order to avoid a battle in broad daylight. Tension rose as the people waited under the burning house, and about every half-hour someone would go out to see how fast the fire was spreading. At 3 P.M. the second story was aflame; at five, the ground floor. The bunker inhabitants assembled at the exit, ready to leave. Could they hold out until nightfall? Lutek soon realized they could not.

The bunker turned into an oven, and the smoke became so thick and dark that the inhabitants could not see each other. The civilians began to panic, pushing toward the exit, and the narrow passage leading to the surface was soon clogged with squirming bodies, creating a bottleneck of flesh. Then debris from the burning building began to fall, blocking the passage from the outside.

But even in the face of disaster, Lutek and the other fighters remained cool. While some squeezed their way to the surface and removed the debris, others untangled the huge knot of bodies inside. Soon the people were lined up and climbing out of the bunker one by one. Although many were wounded from the crush

202

and others half suffocated, there was no time to care for them. Nor was any first aid equipment available. In their desperation even the seriously wounded stumbled along unaided.

While Lutek led the people in search of buildings where they could stay until dark, more and more refugees scrambled from scorched ruins in every courtyard to join the motley convoy. The fighters tried to organize the civilians into three files, but they lacked all discipline. Some were so loaded down with possessions that they could hardly walk; others would not move because a loved one was missing.

Lutek went from bunker to bunker, hole to hole, dragging out those who were afraid to emerge, warning them that the convoy would start without them. One girl, about ten years old and suffering from severe burns, crawled out of a tunnel and pleaded with the fighters to save her mother, who was trapped inside with her clothes on fire. Several fighters ran to her aid but arrived too late. The mother had been buried under smoking wreckage. The girl screamed, refusing to believe that her mother was dead. She had to be taken by force.

With fighters leading the way, bringing up the rear, and flanking the crowd of hundreds of civilians, the convoy plodded toward Nalewki Street, finally reaching an oasis in the desert of fire—Mila 9. Here, in its three adjoining courtyards, they were absorbed into a mob of thousands who, flinging themselves through flame and gunfire, had fled here from dozens of smoked-out bunkers.

The fear-ridden multitude, loaded down with pots, blankets, bundles, fought for every square foot of space. People pushing from both directions met in the middle of passages connecting the courtyards, where they clawed at each other, swore, screamed, sobbed, and threw themselves against solid walls of battered flesh.

Milling among the thousands were hundreds of fighters without a base, without a plan, most of the ZOB men and women from the Central Ghetto who were not hiding in the few bunkers—like Mila 18 and Franciszkanska 30—that were relatively impervious to heat and fire. In the midst of the chaos, Lutek Rotblatt met with other ZOB leaders, among them Zivia Lubetkin and Zachariah Artstein, who had fled from their shelter at Kurza 4.

Soon the civilians surrounded them, clinging as if to their last hope. If the Germans had failed to destroy them with all their guns and tanks, they were succeeding with a diabolic weapon the Jews had not counted on: fire.

Zivia gazed at the civilians clustered around them as they murmered, trembled, waited for the fighters to perform a miracle.

"*Tierinke, vuhin?*" ("Dear ones, where to?")

"But we ourselves were perplexed," Zivia later reflected. "What should we tell them? What did we ourselves know? How horrible was the responsibility to the last of the Hebrew fighters! We would not be able to stand fast in the face of the destructive fire without food, without water, without our equipment. There had to be a fast way out; but where to? And how?"

Suddenly a young man walked up to the leaders and said that he knew of a passage through the sewers to the Aryan side. Maybe the Jews could break through in groups. Zivia, Lutek, and the other commanders debated the idea. What was left to depend on but a miracle? After some hesitation they agreed to try. Death awaited them on the Aryan side, too. But perhaps some would escape. Here there was no chance at all. The civilians agreed. All wanted to go with the fighters.

Was it not absurd? Zivia asked herself. An exodus to the Aryan side of thousands of men, women, and children! Even Moses could not succeed in such a mission. But the people insisted. So the leaders decided that four fighters with Aryan-looking faces would be sent the next morning to test the route. Once on the Aryan side, they would ask Yitzhak Zuckerman for help in evacuating as many Jews as possible—and let him know that his wife, Zivia, was still alive. Since the previous day, all contact with Yitzhak had been broken. No more messages could be carried through the tightly guarded Jewish cemetery, and all telephones were dead.[3]

At 7:40 A.M. a powerful blast in the Productive Ghetto shook Jacob Putermilch and the other fighters in the bunker at Nowolipie 67 out of their slumber. They had been sleeping for less than an hour and a half after having filled themselves with Aharon Chmielnicki's freshly baked bread, but now they were wide awake and ready for action. Quiet prevailed again. But the fighters were alarmed. It was an unusual blast. Were the Germans using a new type of bomb?

Suddenly there were cries in Yiddish: "Jews, come out! There is no sense hiding. Come out and stay alive! This is your last chance. They are going to blow up the bunkers!"

There would be amnesty for those who volunteered to work in Lublin.

Another Jewish traitor! The fighters would never come out, except to kill Germans. But some civilians were now more pliable. It was better, they thought, to take their chances than to be destroyed in the bunkers. Perhaps they would be sent to work after all. Hundreds thus streamed out from underground, from attics and hidden rooms. Though most civilians still chose to remain in the bunkers, Többens now scored his first major triumph.

As Jews suddenly appeared on the street, carrying with them their pitiful belongings, Fritz Schultz, Többens' most important business competitor, recorded in his diary: "We are amazed on learning what a huge number of people had been in hiding."

Now he would have workers for his plants in the Trawniki labor camp in Lublin. Of course, not all were strong enough to work. How unfortunate. To show his human feeling, he served his employees bread and coffee as they entered Umschlagplatz. He then ordered those few who were remaining behind to remove the goods from his ghetto shops. The deadline for the transfer was 10 A.M., April 26—two days later, when all factories were to be blown up.

The fighters, meanwhile, stayed in their bunkers. They could not attack now because the Nazis were mingling with the Jews on their way to the assembly areas. And after the experience with the boy who was executed the previous night, they feared that other traitors would point them out if they exposed themselves. Finally, at about 12:30 P.M., Eliezer Geller ordered Jacob and another fighter to reconnoiter the area and bring back the precious food supply—the bread hidden under a pile of feathers in a nearby attic and the *cholent* left in the bakery oven.

Jacob and his companion climbed into the attic and stood motionless for several moments as they glanced around in the silence. Fear seized Jacob. He suddenly felt as if he were in a jungle full of wild beasts. The two fighters then moved swiftly from attic to attic, leaping through the openings in each brick wall.

As they approached the corner where the bread had been hidden, Jacob's fear grew. If the Germans had found the bread, perhaps drawn to it by the strong odor, they might be waiting for someone to fetch it. At that moment Jacob stumbled over a body partially covered by feathers. He aimed his pistol at the form, then pushed it with his foot. But it did not move. He pulled it out of the feathers and recognized one of the fighters: young, pretty Alma Kornblum. A bullet had pierced her head.

The two men moved her body into a corner and covered it again with feathers. Soon it would be his turn, thought Jacob, the turn of them all. With bowed heads the two stood over Alma's body and swore to avenge her. Then they moved on toward the place where the bread was hidden.

On arriving they looked under the feathers. The bread was gone! They had walked into a trap! Automatically they flung themselves into the feathers, expecting to hear a volley as they fell. But there was still only silence. Then they heard shooting and explosions outside. The Germans had found some bunkers. Should they continue on to the bakery in the courtyard? Was it worth risking their lives for a few pots of *cholent?* Hell, yes. It was all there was to eat.

They crawled through another attic toward the stairway leading to the courtyard. Quiet again. Like in a cemetery. Not even a fly was buzzing. They slowly walked down the stairs, one behind the other, pistols tightly gripped. The doors to the flats were open, and they creaked as the wind blew through the windows. Jacob, who was leading, peeked in as he passed each apartment and saw overturned furniture, with papers and objects of every sort scattered on the floor. Only a few days before, these apartments had been bristling with life. Now they were desolate, unless Jews were hiding behind concealed walls. Never had he seen the catastrophe befalling his people in more vivid focus.

When Jacob reached the second floor, he smelled something burning. He halted at a half-opened door and was about to look in. But feeling intuitively that he should not, he paused for a second. Just then a burst of gunfire ripped through the door.

Jacob leaped up the stairs after his companion. Several Germans were on his heels, shouting and firing. He stopped at the attic door, turned, and hurled a grenade, then followed his comrade through the attics. The two Jews threw themselves behind a camouflaged wall and, after waiting until dark, returned to their bunker with the devastating news.

No bread. No *cholent.* [4]

206

* * *

At Umschlagplatz that afternoon, Kalman Friedman and little Izio joined hundreds of other Jews being driven from the hospital building into the square, where a new row of boxcars stood with doors gaping. Kalman held Izio's hand as they reeled down the stairs under a flurry of rifle-butt blows and whiplashes. They stepped over people who had fallen, over luggage that would never be delivered, and finally stumbled toward the boxcars between two lines of Nazis who again beat, kicked, and insulted them.

Kalman and the boy were the last two Jews to be shoved into one of the cars. As they edged their way toward the window, the door slid shut, and a Ukrainian soldier shouting, "One hundred!" locked the carriage.

Sighs, shouts, curses, prayers. The sweat burned, the heat maddened. Kalman admonished God. Why did the sun shine upon the SS man standing outside the car? Why was the air free for him? Why was he not consumed by fire together with them? Why did not an earthquake bury the whole world?

Izio looked faint as he stood next to Kalman and licked the droplets on the iron window bars. Kalman looked into his eyes and saw the end of the Jewish people.

That night the train began to move. And the rumble of the wheels drowned out the noise of desperate people at work on the door and window, pounding, bending, cutting, wrenching. Suddenly air gushed in and bullets whizzed by.

Caught in a great human tide, Kalman found himself tumbling into space—free—while the train raced on, carrying Izio and others to their final destination.[5]

That evening General Stroop returned to the Central Ghetto to watch his men at work. He was drawn, as if by an invisible magnet, to the periphery of the inferno, where, surrounded by his personal guard, he thrilled to the spectacle of his making: crashing rafters, acrid smoke, crumbling walls, falling balconies, and of course, the "parachutists." If only Himmler were there to see how meticulously he was carrying out orders.

Stroop observed his men trying to root out some Jews entrenched in the block of Werterfassung buildings on Niska

Street—the fighters who had stayed behind when Lieutenant Konrad had led his Jewish workers to Umschlagplatz the previous day. Konrad's men had just finished removing all the confiscated goods that had been stored in the buildings. The lieutenant was relieved; his main source of illegal profits had been saved. Stroop was relieved, too; his troops could now clean out the fighters.

The general wasted no time. He sent an assault unit to surround and enter the buildings. But gunfire from the windows drove the Germans back, and even Nazi artillery had little effect. So Stroop turned to his foolproof weapon: fire. Flamethrowers went into action, and soon the buildings were ablaze. But the battle went on.

Stroop was impressed by the defenders' zeal and courage. He watched incredulously as one Jew burst out of a building, his clothes on fire, his face blackened, his body scorched, and stood calmly for several moments breathing the hot but fresh air. Suddenly seeing the Germans, the man shouted something, threatened with his fist, and made an indecent gesture. He then fired at a Nazi and ran back into the flames instead of surrendering.

Such "maniacs"—the Jewish "elite"—Stroop regretted, had been holding up the whole ghetto operation. But he was finally making good progress. He was driving the Jews from their holes, not only with fire but with grenades and gas. He had scattered twenty-four assault units throughout the ghetto to systematically comb it out, to look under every stone, behind every wall. They had even managed to stop the Jews from sneaking out of the ghetto amid the corpses that were piled into hearses heading for the cemetery. Every hearse was now being inspected. All his men had needed was a little experience fighting a sly, treacherous foe. Now they were gaining confidence with each Jew they found.

Perhaps, Stroop felt, he should do what Colonel Hahn jokingly suggested: give a special battlefront decoration to the bravest "bunker masters," those who captured the most bunkers. On the other hand, the general was transferring the weaklings in his force out of the ghetto.

He was especially disappointed in the *Askaris*—the Ukrainian, Latvian, and Lithuanian Fascists. How spineless and undisciplined many had turned out to be. The Latvian he had met on the eve of the *Aktion* at the ghetto gate, the blond Nordic type who had been so keen on killing Jews, proved to be a "complete fool."

He had encountered this Latvian again after the fighting started and found him weeping and mumbling something about not being able to kill women and children. He couldn't look at the blood, the corpses. Stroop was unable to restrain himself. He slapped the young man in the face and ordered him out of the ghetto, together with another 150 *Askaris*. Cowards! All of them!

But not the SS men he was now watching as they fired at the Jews dying in the fire. No, they were brave men who fought like true Nazis. Finally, after eight hours of fighting, they rushed the Werterfassung buildings under a cover of concentrated rifle and machine gun fire and cleaned out the whole compound.

Stroop glanced at his watch. After midnight. It was Easter Sunday. He scanned the flaming ghetto and was cheered by the sparks in the sky. What a wonderful way to celebrate the Resurrection.[6]

The Seventh Day

April 25

Easter morning blossomed bright, sunny, and gay on the Aryan side. In crowded Krasinski Square, right outside the ghetto wall, the tinkling melodies of a carousel echoed festively, mingling with the joyous voices of youngsters riding wooden horses, the gossipy chatter of women dressed in white holiday finery, the gruff shouts of vendors selling flowers, vodka, and trinkets in colorfully draped stalls . . . and the explosions, gunfire, and hysterical cries of people burning alive on the other side of the wall.

People stood in clusters watching the spectacular show. While some seemed frozen with horror, others grinned in fascination. They lifted their children up so that they could see, too, feeding them candies and pointing to a particular balcony or roof from which Jews, trapped by the flames, were flinging themselves to the scorched pavement below.

Some of the spectators expressed regret about the destruction of so much property. To others such a show was appropriate on this day. It was Easter, and were not the Jews responsible for Jesus' suffering? For the sufferings, too, of Poland? Initially the uprising had thrilled the Poles. But now many wondered whether the Germans might have been right when they charged day and night over the radio, in the newspapers, and in posters that the "Jewish Bolsheviks" had murdered over ten thousand Polish officers. The Red Army had captured these Poles during the German-Russian invasion of Poland in September 1939. Their mass graves had just been discovered near the Soviet town of Katyn, and Russia and Germany, which had successively occupied the area, were pinning guilt for the atrocity on each other. (Evidence later indicated that the Russians were responsible and that some of the victims were Jews.)

Anyway, many Poles had read that morning's edition of the official underground organ of the fascistic National Party, which stated that the fate of the murdered Jews was a "hundredfold merited."[1]*

Not far from the festivities, General Stroop brimmed with optimism as he rose from bed in his apartment, which was located in a palatial building on Aleje (Alley) Ujazdowskie. He had moved into the apartment after taking over the Warsaw command from Colonel von Sammern-Frankenegg. It had been a long nasty night. Not until 2 A.M. had the "bandits" in the Werterfassung been overcome by flame and gunfire. His men were exhausted. He would let them sleep late on this Easter morning, starting his main attack only at 1 P.M. They deserved the rest.

But Stroop himself would not rest. He was determined to end all resistance in the ghetto by the following day. And he was sure he would. The Jews had no way to combat the flames. By tomorrow a ring of fire would force all of them to withdraw to a narrow strip of unburned territory, and at that stage the antiaircraft guns and howitzers would provide the final squeeze.

After witnessing the holocaust the previous day and conferring with his experts, Stroop was, in fact, convinced that all the leaders of the revolt were already dead. He telexed General Krüger that morning that it could be assumed the leaders had been killed. But as reports of bitter resistance continued to pour in, he began to

*Maksymilian Tauchner, who witnessed the scenes of horror with other Poles, wrote in his memoirs: "There were fine, touching, heartwarming words. . . . But these words, alas were few. . . . There was the voice of an indignant fireman saying, 'They're not people, they're cattle,' because when he called to a Jew standing on the roof of a burning house with a child in his arms and asked him to give him his valuables before he jumped into the abyss of fire, the Jew only spat. . . . People stood near the ghetto for hours on end, looking on at this unique spectacle. People were burning, children were burning. If even the sight of these children could not move hearts hardened with hate, apparently there were no hearts there at all. . . ."

have second thoughts—and deep regrets. Especially when Krüger and Himmler expressed doubts about his claim.

Colonel Hahn invited the downcast general to lunch this day, and over generous portions of dumplings, turkey, and mushrooms, he gave him some brotherly advice: Listen always, but never act on the opinions of so-called specialists and experts.

"They are, on the whole, shithouse experts," Hahn said. "I keep them because I must. We are short of intelligent police experts. Before you send another important written report, would you please, General, be kind enough to ask my opinion, too?"

Stroop promised that he would. Then the two men sipped black coffee and cognac, and Stroop rose to leave for the ghetto. He felt better after talking with Hahn and consuming so delicious a meal. But one problem still rankled him: If he did crush the uprising by the following day, thousands, perhaps tens of thousands of Jews still in hiding might emerge all at once. And he was already short of trains, as Umschlagplatz was overflowing.

He would have to start killing more Jews in the ghetto itself. Early that morning he had already given orders, apparently to Hahn, that more than five hundred be taken to Pawiak Prison in the Wild Ghetto and shot. Most of them should be dead by now.[2]

Leon Wanat was a Polish prisoner who worked in the Pawiak Prison office. Shortly before noon he gazed out the window toward Dzielna Street and saw hundreds of Jews—men, women, and children—huddling together on the street along the wall enclosing the prison courtyard. They formed an almost solid carpet of humanity, stretching from the closed prison gate all the way down the block.

Wanat was puzzled. Why so many Jews? Previously the Nazis had always brought them in small batches, enough to fill the underground dungeons as other Jews were removed to be shot in the ghetto ruins. Now they brought hundreds. Where would they fit them all? But after seeing the daily horrors perpetrated in this gray concrete slaughterhouse, Wanat felt he was prepared for anything. He was still haunted by the grisly murder of Pogorielow, the world-renowned chess champion, and his family. An SS man had hanged him and his wife in their cell, then strangled their infant.

212

Shortly the guards opened the prison gate and herded the Jews into the courtyard. After ordering them to lie down, they began taking small groups, from five to eight, outside the wall again and across the street into another courtyard shared by two abandoned buildings. Wanat then heard screams and a volley of shots, and a few minutes later, the same sounds.

At about that time, Alphons Czapp, of the German 22nd Police Regiment, happened to be walking by, and he wondered what was going on in the courtyard across the road from the prison. He entered, passing a guard whose attention was elsewhere, just as a machine gun mowed down a group of Jews. He left quickly.

Czapp was recovering from a bullet wound inflicted by a Jewish sniper a few days earlier and was still off duty. He belonged to a regular police force, not an SS unit, and wasn't supposed to see what was happening in the Gestapo prisons. Hahn would have his head for this if he knew. His unit's job was to search the buildings for Jews and turn them over to the SS, and what fate these Jews ultimately met was strictly SS business. Not every German was considered capable of understanding the ideology of racial genocide. It had to be history's great secret.

According to Czapp, he was sickened. Though he himself had led a squad of Germans in mopping up the Jews, he claims he did not intend to kill any, except in self-defense, and that he could not have refused to obey orders without risking his own execution.

Group after group were led to the mass-murder site to be shot, while SS men neatly piled up the bodies of those who had been killed earlier. Leon Wanat could not see the actual massacre from his window, but he watched the victims waiting in the prison courtyard. With every scream and volley, they raised their heads slightly and seemed to converse with each other, perhaps, he thought, speculating who would be next, how many more minutes of life remained. When a guard motioned for a new group to get up, they obeyed, sobbing and pleading for mercy. But there would be none.

Finally, at about 4 P.M., the prison courtyard was empty, and silence prevailed. Wanat was dazed. No, despite the atrocities he had witnessed daily, he was not prepared for this. He returned, shaken, to his desk. He had much work to do, for the Germans found his handwriting exceptional and very impressive in reports he sent back to Berlin about the activities in Pawiak Prison.[3]

* * *

General Stroop's plan to burn and smoke the Jews out of their bunkers and trap them in isolated, unburned areas was already working. Mila 9, whose three connecting courtyards were seething with refugees and fighters from surrounding blocks, was the biggest trap. Sealed in by fire, ringed by Nazi troops, these Jews, including Zivia Lubetkin, Lutek Rotblatt, Zachariah Artstein, and other ZOB chiefs, saw only one slim chance for escape: the plan for a mass exodus through the sewers to the Aryan side.

Early Easter morning four fighters with Aryan-looking faces— two men and two women—made their way from Mila 9 to the manhole they were to enter. Before the day ended, they were convinced, they would either die or return with help from Yitzhak Zuckerman to lead the people out of the ghetto. Led by Tuvia Borzykowski, the fighter who had attended the melancholy Seder of Rabbi Mayzel on the first night of the uprising, the group climbed into the sewer to find itself in a subterranean madhouse. Tuvia later recounted:

> Masses of refugees were huddling in the filth and the stink, in pipes so low and narrow that only one person could pass at a time, walking in a low crouch. They lay on the ground in the excrement and other filth, pressed to each other. Some of the elderly people and children had fainted, with no one paying any attention. The stream of sewage washed away the bodies of the dead, making room for the living. The wounded lay there bleeding, their blood mixing with the sewage.

Tuvia and his companions struggled to get through the human dam created by the huddled refugees, worming and clawing their way forward inch by inch until finally, after several hours, they reached a manhole they thought opened on the Aryan side. They quietly pushed aside the heavy iron cover, and one of them poked his head out. They were still in the ghetto! The grotesque march continued. Another manhole. The cover was lifted. This *must* be the Aryan side. But before they could emerge, they heard German voices. Then no sound at all. The fighters waited, agonizingly standing in a crouched position, nauseous from the stinking air. No, they would wait no longer—Germans or no Germans.

The two girls climbed out first, followed by one of the men. Suddenly several Polish policemen appeared, grabbed the girls, and turned them over to the Germans. The man tried to run but collapsed with a bullet in the head. Tuvia, who was just lifting himself out, now realized that this exit opened on the border of the ghetto, the most heavily guarded of all places. Before he could react, he felt a bullet graze his cheek, then heard a scream behind him. The bullet, entering the manhole at an angle, had hit a civilian who was right behind Tuvia, wounding him in the throat. Tuvia instinctively dropped back into the sewer a split second before another bullet whizzed by, and he fell on the wounded man.

He stood up and dragged the man through the filth toward the ghetto, moving just fast enough to avoid a shower of grenade splinters in the manhole area. Despite his feeble condition he began running through the slime with his burden, driven by the sheer momentum of frenzy and will. No bodies now blocked his path. All that remained were wet rags, shoes, a pair of glasses. The refugees had either been discovered and removed by the Germans, or had been washed away by the sewage.[4]

In Mila 18 Mordechai Anielewicz, unaware of Tuvia's mission, decided on a plan of his own to contact Yitzhak Zuckerman on the Aryan side. Perhaps Yitzhak could help at least some Jews escape.

Mordechai again wished he had dug tunnels to the Aryan side before the uprising. With the whole ghetto burning down, what was the purpose of sitting and waiting to die in the flames or fall into Nazi hands? Would it not be better to reach the forests, where they could at least fight? Now the sewer was their only hope.

Ironically, Mordechai saw possible salvation in the fires. He learned from his scouts that as the flames had spread southward to the uninhabited Wild Ghetto and threatened an important factory there, the Germans had sent Polish firemen to save the plant. If the fighters made contact with these Poles, perhaps they could bribe them to deliver a message to Yitzhak and return with a reply.

Mordechai chose Chaim Frimer and two others for the mission, and they left at once. In the darkness the three men threaded their way through the smoking ruins on Mila Street. They saw shadows emerging from burnt-out houses on both sides of the street—Jews coming out of their hiding places like hunted animals to search for food and breathe some fresh air. One man lifted a manhole cover and disappeared into the cavity. As they passed Mila 46, which was aflame, refugees informed them that a group of fighters were hiding in the cellar.

Chaim and his two comrades rushed in and found the Bund group led by Levi Gruzalc, who had been out of contact with ZOB headquarters since the first day of the uprising. Chaim was joyous to see old friends, among them Masha Glytman and Melech Perlman, whom he had thought dead. He was on a special mission and had to continue on immediately, Chaim told the ten fighters. They should leave the bunker before the fire above reached them, he advised, and he would meet them in a neighboring courtyard on his way back and lead them to a new hideout.

Chaim and his two companions then raced on to the Wild Ghetto, where they hid in the ruins of a destroyed building near the factory that was on fire. When they saw the Polish firemen fighting to extinguish the inferno, Chaim sent his men to capture one of them. Shortly they returned with a prisoner.

"Please don't kill me," he begged. "I'm not responsible for what is going on."

They would not harm him, Chaim promised. All they wanted him to do was help to get some people out of the ghetto, with the cooperation of his superior, if possible. Both, of course, would be paid handsomely.

The Pole agreed. He would meet his captors at this same place the next day to make final arrangements.

Their spirits buoyed, Chaim and his men hurried back to the group of Bund fighters and led them to a courtyard near Mila 18. Then Chaim reported to Mordechai. Where should the Bundists hide now? In the burned-out bunker at Mila 29, Mordechai replied, until room could be made in overcrowded Mila 18. Chaim then shepherded the group there and found to his surprise that the bunker had hardly been touched by the fire that had devoured the building overhead. Since day was breaking and the Nazis were on the hunt again, he decided to stay with the others until nightfall.

Chaim felt they were relatively safe. There was nothing left to burn above ground, and the bunker was hidden under a thick layer of ash and debris.[5]

Bunker after bunker fell as Stroop's men relentlessly tracked the fighters down in the scorched path of the flames, using dogs,

216

traitors, and detection devices. In one underground hideout at Muranowska 29, where some ZZW fighters had joined about a hundred civilians, panic broke out when a voice from outside shouted in Yiddish, "You have a quarter of an hour to come out."

The inhabitants were almost boiling in the intense heat caused by a fire that had just burned down the building above them. They had hung some soaking blankets by an air hole so that the outside air would cool the bunker, but debris covered up the opening. Adam Halperin and several other ZZW men had then dug another air hole leading to an adjacent cellar. But now, it seemed, their labors had all been in vain.

The fighters urged the people to ignore the ultimatum, to die in the bunker, if necessary, rather than in Treblinka. All agreed. But then they smelled gas. While women screamed and children cried, everybody ran toward the newly dug air hole. In desperation some tried to crawl through but could not advance because the passage was so narrow. Finally Adam and two other men tried, pushing and pulling each other along. Once in the adjoining cellar, they started pulling the others through.

The first person to follow was a stout woman who wriggled to the middle of the passage but then couldn't move either way. Those in the bunker pushed her, while on the other side, Adam, braced by his two comrades, gripped her hands and pulled her. A few inches more. . . . The woman's hysterical cries were suddenly drowned in a tremendous explosion. Adam barely escaped as tons of earth buried the woman alive, together with all the others still in the bunker.[6]

Jacob Putermilch and his group were still in their bunker under the attic of Nowolipie 67 in the Productive Ghetto. At about 8 A.M. they were shaken by a blast of static from a loudspeaker in the courtyard. An announcement followed: "Today is a day of free movement. The possibility is offered to report voluntarily until 2 P.M. Those who report will be transferred to the labor camps in Trawniki and Poniatow. Those who do not report will be burned in their hiding places. All houses in the ghetto will be set on fire."

General Stroop would not spare the Productive Ghetto. He was determined to end the uprising the next day in a great final orgy of destruction that would devour everything, including the factories and warehouses. Even if the industrialists did not remove their machinery and goods in time.

After the announcement Eliezer Geller decided to use the "free movement" to send Hancia Plotnicka, a high-spirited, courageous young girl, to the Aryan side with messages for ZOB comrades there. He chose three fighters to escort her to a sewer-opening leading to the Aryan side.

The trouble was that the sewer entrance—at Karmelicka 5, ZZW area headquarters—lay in the opposite direction from the assembly point for the workers. And any movement away from there was likely to arouse suspicion. Thus, Hancia and her three escorts—Meir Schwartz, Heniek Kleinweis, and Adek Himmelfarb—scrambled through the attics as far as they could but then had to descend to the street for the final stretch. Through the corners of their eyes they could almost feel the inquisitive stares of Germans posted in front of the house gates as they passed other Jews struggling along with their pitiful bundles toward the assembly area.

Finally an SS man stopped them. Where were they going? Heniek, known as an "idea man" who could ingeniously extricate himself from almost any threatening situation, replied, "We are volunteers going to report for transfer to the labor camps. We're just stopping at Karmelicka 5 to pick up baggage we left there."

The German, looking skeptical, said, "I'll go with you to make sure no one bothers you."

Heniek was concerned but not alarmed. They would manage somehow to get rid of the German in the courtyard. But when the group reached Karmelicka 5, they met two other Germans at the gate. The play had to go on. The four Jews, tailed by the three Germans, entered the building and walked up to the third floor. They would break away and escape through the attic. But there the stairway ended. No attic! They were trapped. Heniek peered into an abandoned flat where everything was overturned, and to his immense relief he saw several valises on the floor. The fighters entered, and Heniek gave each one a bag. When he went out the door, Heniek looked back nostalgically, as if parting from his home with sorrow. Then the group walked toward the assembly area.

Playing for time, the fighters stopped every so often and put down their bags. Awfully heavy, they sighed. Every moment was vital to figure out a way to escape. But as they moved on, the num-

218

ber of German escorts swelled while their chances of getting away dwindled. One hope remained: Maybe the ZOB fighters at Leszno 74 and 76 would see them and engineer a rescue. However, when they passed these buildings, there was no one in sight. The last hope was gone. They were guided into a large courtyard surrounded by Germans with submachine guns—the assembly area.

Once inside, the four fighters abandoned their baggage and continued contemplating how to escape. Suddenly a German officer appeared before them and asked, "Where did you come from?"

"From a hiding place," replied Heniek. "I heard that nothing would happen to those reporting voluntarily, so I came. There were other Jews in the hideout who would also have come," he added, "but they feared they would be shot."

Would Heniek be willing to show him the place?

"Yes, but on condition that you promise you won't shoot the people."

The German gave his word. Then Adek and Meir offered to take him to their bunker, too. It was overflowing with Jews, they said.

The officer left the fighters for a moment and returned with about ten Germans. The four Jews then started walking. At first Hancia tried to draw away from the group, apparently fearing that her comrades had turned traitor, but she soon realized it was only a trick. Heniek and the officer marched in front, side by side, followed by the other Jews and German soldiers.

How could they get away from these beasts? Heniek pondered. The officer interrupted his thoughts.

"Are there many Jews in the bunker?"

"Fifteen."

"Are they armed?"

Heniek began to sweat. The German would certainly search him! He instinctively felt under his jacket for his pistol, which was hanging from a cord tied around his neck. No, Heniek replied calmly, there were no arms in the bunker. The officer stared at him suspiciously. Heniek stared back, and they searched each other's eyes. They were almost at Leszno 74, where another German was on guard. What should he do? Heniek feverishly asked himself.

A few steps away from Leszno 76 he casually unbuttoned his jacket. Then he quickly drew out his pistol, aimed it at the officer, and pulled the trigger. As the German slumped to the ground, the guard by the gate, in his shock and confusion, dropped his rifle instead of firing it.

At that moment Heniek dashed through the gate and across the courtyard toward an entrance to the building, with Adek and Meir close behind. The Nazis ran after them, firing with automatic weapons. But all three fighters miraculously made it to the entrance, though Meir was wounded in the hand. Racing up the stairs, they paused for a moment to look out a window, hoping to see Hancia. But they did not. The Germans had apparently shot her in the street. Heavyheartedly the three survivors continued on to the attic and made their way through the attic system to the bunker at Nowolipie 67.

Hardly had they told their tale to Eliezer, Jacob, and the other fighters, who had nervously awaited their return for hours, when the Jews heard boots clapping above the hatch. Then the sound of voices and a familiar shout in Yiddish: "Come out, Jews! You will not be shot! You'll be sent to Poniatow, where you will work and be fed well."

No reply. The voice then called out to the civilian owner of the bunker: "Dorn, I have come to rescue you. Don't be afraid. I am speaking to you as to a good friend. Come out. We'll go together. There are many volunteers."

After more silence: "Dorn, come out before the bunker is blown up. You ought to know that everything will be burned down here. Not a single house will remain. Come out!"

It was the building janitor. He had betrayed them.

The bunker seemed doomed.[7]

Fritz Schultz, the industrialist, could not recall a more miserable Easter. By ten o'clock the next morning, April 26, all goods and machinery had to be removed from the ghetto factories, which would then be blown up. Yet he had only a handful of Jews to do the job. He would certainly miss the deadline. Didn't Stroop realize he would be harming the war effort if all this material was destroyed?

And how many of his Jews would live to work in Trawniki? Stroop didn't seem to understand his need for manpower. His poor, unfortunate workers. Schultz could never manage without them. Since they needed strength—in case they lived—he sent a supply of food to Umschlagplatz for those penned up in the hospital building awaiting trains to transfer them to his labor camp. But when he tried to send a second supply column, the guards blocked their entry.

Later that day Schultz wrote in his diary:

> An understandable commotion took place . . . which prompted me to go myself to Umschlagplatz and put things in order. Once I got there I was given permission to enter the hospital. . . . My appearance gave rise to moving scenes. Thanks to my . . . assurances that the people would certainly go to our Trawniki camp and nowhere else, I succeeded, to a certain extent, in calming them. I also received permission to supply them with bread and coffee again.

But Schultz was not as optimistic as he seemed. After visiting his workers, he telephoned SS troop leader Bartecko, his associate in Trawniki, who would presumably enjoy a share of the profits. Would Bartecko please come to Warsaw immediately and use his influence to save the machinery, goods, and workers.

Schultz was not the only one worried about Stroop's intentions. His colleague Többens, who was in charge of the whole evacuation to Poniatow and Trawniki, was also concerned. Unless Stroop extended the deadline for the transfer of the ghetto factories and sent the able workers to the Lublin camps instead of to death camps, he, too, could lose a fortune. So he, too, cried for help. Certainly, he felt, he could count on General Globocnik, who, like himself, had a big financial stake in the Poniatow enterprises.

That Easter Sunday, Többens went to Lublin to talk with Globocnik. The general listened and fumed. Stroop, he felt, was an ambitious fool who refused to play the game. He considered telephoning Himmler or Field Marshal Hermann Göring to explain how Stroop's policy could damage the war effort. Göring, especially, wanted war industries strengthened.

But first, Globocnik decided, he would go to Warsaw the following day to see Stroop. And to press his point he would take with him about thirty loyal SS men. But Stroop would not be easy to persuade, considering the momentum of murder he was generating. That night Stroop optimistically wrote in his daily report to General Krüger, "With this bag of Jews today, we have, in my opinion, caught a very considerable part of the bandits and lowest elements of the ghetto."[8]

Jacob Putermilch and his fellows waited with pistols drawn for the Germans to break through the hatch on the ceiling of their bunker at Nowolipie 67. Even though the captive janitor of the building had warned the occupants of dire consequences if they refused to come out, no one had obeyed. How many seconds to death? How many minutes? But the minutes passed, and quiet prevailed. The Nazis had apparently gone. But they would be back.

David Nowodworski, fondling a grenade, climbed the ladder to the hatch, cautiously opened it, and got out. Seeing that the way was clear, he motioned for the others to follow. The occupants had to find other quarters before the enemy returned. Several fighters left, including Meir Schwartz, who, because of his wounded hand, had to be pulled through the hatch.

No sooner had this group departed than Germans fired through the heavily draped window of the bunker, forcing Jacob and everyone else still there to lie flat on the floor. When the firing stopped, Jacob rose and darted through the smoke to the ladder, then lifted himself through the hatch just as a grenade exploded in the attic. Caught in a swirling storm of feathers and dust, Jacob groped around for those who had emerged before him but discovered he was alone.

The evening light reflected on the slowly settling dust like the sun bathing a gray cloud. Jacob, barely able to breathe, waited for more people to come out of the shelter, but no one else did. He then decided to head for the bunker that served as a hospital for the fighters in the Productive Ghetto, just across the courtyard in Leszno 76. To avoid being heard he slid down the banisters as he had in his childhood, then raced across the courtyard toward the entrance leading to the hospital bunker.

"Stay where you are!" a German shouted.

But Jacob managed to reach the doorway and leap up the stairs. From a second-floor window he could see and hear a German appealing to him. He should come out, the German cried, and report for transfer to Lublin before the building was set afire. Jacob laughed bitterly to himself and continued on to the hospital bunker, a walled-off room in a three-room flat.

Jacob knocked on a tile stove and uttered the code word; then, when a door in the stove was opened, he slid through on his back into the bunker. The occupants welcomed him as they might the Messiah, having been sealed off from the outside world for two days. Almost all were wounded and critically in need of medical care. While Jacob reported on the recent fighting, a number of his missing friends crept in, among them Meir Schwartz, who was feverish from his wound.

That night Jacob returned to the attic of Nowolipie 67 with several comrades to bring two other wounded fighters to the hospital bunker. They found the victims, Shalom Sufit and Hana Grauman, buried in a pile of feathers. The couple were lovers, and now they clung to each other, their bodies seemingly glued together with the blood flowing from deep wounds.

With difficulty they were carried on improvised stretchers through the attics and across the courtyard, both of them brutally biting their lips to keep from moaning in their agony. When the group reached the hospital bunker, a young doctor was brought from a nearby hideout to perform a double operation. Although weary from treating wounded Jews around the clock, the doctor, under a dim light, calmly began to cut into raw flesh. No anesthetic was available, but the patients did not utter a sound. Afterward, despite the pain, they fell asleep, once more in each other's arms.

Jacob collapsed into an armchair and reflected on the day's events. The Nazis had rooted the fighters out of their hideout. And soon they would find this hospital bunker, too, if the building was not burned down first. Had the doctor done the wounded a favor, saving them for the more ghastly death that would surely follow?[9]

Later that night Mordechai and Tosia Altman led a group of fighters from Mila 18 to Franciszkanska 30 for a reunion with the crippled Arie Wilner and other ZOB members, including those who had escaped from the burning Brushmakers' District three days earlier. They were greeted joyously. Mordechai spoke little, but his eyes said much as he shook hands with his comrades, lingering especially with the wounded.

Tosia kissed Arie on the cheek and sat by his bunk, telling him the latest news. Things weren't going so well. But better than expected. After six days of battle they were still alive, weren't they?

Arie said he wanted to spend his last days with Tosia and his old comrades now in Mila 18. Although the bunker was already packed with people, Mordechai agreed to make room for Arie. They would all die together.[10]

As Easter Sunday came to a fiery end, ZOB representatives on the Aryan side sent an urgent plea for arms in a memorandum to the Polish government delegate in Warsaw:

> The tragic and heroic battle of the Warsaw Ghetto has aroused the admiration of the entire thinking Polish population. These feelings of sympathy, however, have not yet found concrete expression among the military circles of the Polish underground. Despite calls and demands by the . . . Jewish Fighting Organization . . . the embattled ghetto has not yet received any . . . ammunition or firearms.
>
> We therefore turn to you once again—at the very last moment, in the midst of raging fires, through the din of night-fighting—with an urgent cry to expedite military assistance.

But the government delegate did not respond with weapons. Instead he sent a glowing report to London. The uprising had been admirably prepared, he wrote, and the action had borne the stamp of military operations. The Germans had, in fact, been driven out of the ghetto several times. The delegate also issued a proclamation to the Polish people, calling upon them "to show sympathy for the suffering of the Jews and extend assistance to them"—a call that Prime Minister Sikorski himself had still not made.

The "thinking" Poles were indeed sympathetic, even as some lifted up their children to watch the Jews burn alive. Arming the Jews, however, was another matter. Too many of them were, after all, Communists.[11]

The Eighth Day

April 26

At about 1 A.M. Tuvia Borzykowski staggered into the boiling caldron of Mila 9 after having plodded back through the sewer from his abortive mission to the Aryan side, where three of his comrades had been either captured or killed. He was still supporting the man wounded at the sewer exit, whom he had dragged all the way through the slime.

The great crowd filling the three courtyards of Mila 9 had been waiting in a hushed but electric atmosphere throughout the previous day and evening. Only the cries of children, the moans of the dying, the prayers of the faithful, and the low, singing voices of the fighters had broken the silence, though the refugees had briefly exploded into life when someone arrived with a loaf of bread. They pounced upon him to grab a crumb.

Now they crowded around Tuvia as he gasped out his experience to Zivia and the other fighters. Silence again. But now the silence of overwhelming despair, of utter hopelessness.

The plan for a mass exodus was canceled. The people were told that they would have to remain in the burning ghetto and hide in whatever shelter they could find. The fighters would crowd into Mila 18, which they had learned about from Mordechai's messengers.

"What was there left to say to the fighters, to the anxious Jews around us?" Zivia later lamented.[1]

* * *

While this ZOB plan for a mass escape failed and another—
Mordechai Anielewicz's—hinged on the response of a couple of
Polish firemen, the ZZW was desperately trying to save the people
in its own area. This organization had been splintered, separated,
and almost decimated in the heavy fighting that had shaken Muranowski Square in the first days of battle. Now the leaders—Pawel Frenkel, David Appelbojm, and Leon Rodal—planned a new
operation that hopefully would permit a large-scale exodus of
fighters and refugees through the still usable tunnel connecting
Muranowska 7, which now lay in ruins, and Muranowska 6 on the
Aryan side. The trouble was that the ZZW would probably have to
fight to keep the passage open, and it lacked weapons.

But on this morning three fighters, the Lopata brothers and
their sister, had managed to get some. Dressed in Nazi uniforms
and speaking fluent German, the two brothers cursed their sister
as they prodded her with rifle butts across Muranowski Square toward a building in which the SS stored arms—a normal scene of
soldiers brutalizing a Jewish prisoner. When they reached the
building, the men pushed her aside and stormed in with guns
blazing. In the confusion the family managed to haul away several
crates of arms and ammunition, while the Germans, uncertain
who was a friend and who an enemy, fired at each other. ZZW
fighters then collected the arms of those killed to add further to
their arsenal.

These weapons, however, were not enough to clear the way for
a large exodus of Jews. So everything, it seemed, depended on
Captain Iwanski.

Two messengers trudged through the sewers from the ghetto
and reported to Iwanski with a message from Appelbojm: He had
been wounded, and he needed arms and ammunition urgently.
The note ended, "I am signing this message with my blood to
show you how tragic our situation is. My personal situation is even
more hopeless."

Iwanski wasted no time. He ordered his deputy, Lieutenant
Zajdler, to prepare a combat unit to enter the ghetto with supplies
and bring back the wounded and all the women and children it
could find.[2]

* * *

At about 8 A.M. a man guarding the bunker at Mila 29 heard strange noises outside. He nervously awakened Chaim Frimer, who had shepherded the Bund squad there the night before. Chaim listened carefully. Footsteps. . . . The Germans were in the courtyard above the bunker. Then a loud knock on the hatch. Chaim and his comrades leaped from their bunkers and grabbed their pistols.

"Hide under your bunks!" Chaim ordered.

If the Germans looked in and saw nothing, perhaps they would go away. As Chaim lay under the bunk nearest the entrance, he watched with alarm while somebody in the courtyard lifted the hatch. A face peeped inside and a voice cried in Yiddish, "Jews, come out of there! If you leave now you won't be hurt."

No response. Then a German appeared at the entrance and shouted, *"Juden, raus!"* ("Jews, out!")

The German dropped a grenade through the opening, but no one was wounded in the explosion. Under cover of smoke the fighters crawled out from their hiding places. What should they do? Suddenly they heard the sound of people running. They hid again, just as a much greater explosion blew a huge hole in the asphalt roof of the bunker, exposing the inhabitants. One fighter, David Hochberg, was gravely wounded, and he gave his pistol to a comrade as he took his last breath.

Through the jagged opening the fighters could see a cluster of Germans standing some distance away with their rifles pointed at them.

"Raus!" they shouted.

There was only one thing to do: Spring a surprise attack. With weapons hidden under their clothes, they would climb out and open fire. Levi Gruzalc volunteered to go first. But as he was lifting himself out, a bullet struck him dead.

Now the Jews would have to fight it out in the bunker. When Mila 29 had served as ZOB headquarters, the fighters had built under the courtyard a small dugout with a narrow passage that led to the main bunker. Chaim now ordered everybody to squirm into the dugout. When all but he had jammed in, he found there was no room for himself. So he lay in the passage facing the main bunker. Soon he saw a dog sniffing around the hole in the ceiling.

"This is the end," he muttered to himself.

He held his breath. But to his astonishment the dog moved on, apparently unable to smell his quarry because of the smoke and dust.

Soon all was quiet. The Germans had gone away. And when darkness fell, Chaim led the survivors to Mila 18.[3]

Tuvia Borzykowski had not yet recovered from his exhausting trek through the sewer when he was awakened before dawn at Mila 9 and ordered to join a group of fighters going to Kurza 3 nearby. The Germans were likely to pass that building soon on the way to Mila 9, and they had to be stopped before reaching this massive center of refuge.

Shortly after daybreak, as expected, a large SS detachment marched into the courtyard of Kurza 3 and was greeted by volleys of bullets. As the Germans fled in panic, leaving many dead behind, Tuvia and his companions slipped away to Mila 5. They had little time to rejoice over their victory. One wing of Mila 5 was ablaze and the other threatened. Diving into a basement bunker in the still-unburned wing, the fighters found themselves crushed between refugees from the burning sector, who also wanted to get in, and those already in the bunker, trying to get out.

Though machine guns sputtered relentlessly and explosions shook the scorched earth, Tuvia and his fellows were literally squeezed out into the deadly open and could not find other shelter. Finally the group split in two, and Tuvia's section wormed its way into an overflowing bunker just before the Germans trod into the courtyard.

When the guard left outside failed to report after some time, Tuvia climbed out and found him dead. He grabbed the guard's pistol and crawled back into the bunker just as the Germans sent a hail of bullets his way. The situation was desperate, Tuvia told his group. The only thing to do was to get out and fight.

When the fighters started to leave, the other bunker dwellers demanded to be taken along. Or else, they said, they would not let them go. But they were going to fight, the ZOB men explained, and the civilians would only burden them. The people would not listen. They were convinced that the fighters had discovered a way to save themselves and were concealing it from them. Screaming in protest, they formed a human wall blocking the exit.

One fighter armed with an old hunting rifle suddenly rushed the civilians. Using his gun as a barrier, he pushed them away from the exit while his comrades scrambled through it. The crowd attacked the fighter and tried to snatch his rifle, but he held on until his whole group had departed. He then let go of the gun suddenly, and those who were clutching it fell backward to the ground as he scampered to join his comrades.

Tuvia and the others ran into a portion of the building that was still standing and unleashed bullets and grenades from the windows for about half an hour, hitting many Germans. Finally the Nazis threw incendiary bombs and set the remains of the building on fire.

The fighters then fled to Mila 7, but that building, too, was soon in flames. Civilians raced through the corridors and down the staircases like stampeding cattle. Some carried children and bundles. Others ran amok, screaming with their clothes afire. Those who scurried outside were mowed down by machine gun fire.

In the midst of the massacre Tuvia and his companions found themselves trapped on the first floor while burning debris fell on them, singeing their hair and clothes. They were blinded by the smoke as the floor under them, about to burn, began to collapse, with only the girders intact.

One girl, Salka, suggested that they all commit suicide, since fighting the enemy no longer seemed possible. It was better than burning to death or being shot. Some agreed, but Tuvia protested. They should, he said, hold out as long as possible. It was almost dark. Perhaps the Germans would leave soon, as they did every night when darkness fell.

While the flames edged closer, the fighters argued. Most of them were now swinging toward Salka's view, but Tuvia begged his comrades to at least wait fifteen minutes. And to make sure Salka would, he grabbed her weapon.

At that moment the floor under them began to burn.[4]

In the Productive Ghetto, Jacob Putermilch awoke about 6 A.M., stiff from sleeping in a chair all night in the hospital bunker at Leszno 76. He went up to the attic with other fighters to observe the enemy's movements. But Leszno and Nowolipie streets were desolate, with not an enemy patrol in sight, though on other days at this time the SS was already searching for Jews. The only noises came from the Aryan side of Leszno—the normal sounds of daily life—and from the more distant Central Ghetto, where machine guns rattled and dynamite exploded under a canopy of thick black smoke. But the Productive Ghetto was deathly silent. An ominous sign.

Suddenly, a little after 8 A.M., the fighters noticed a young civilian guiding a unit of Germans into Nowolipie 67, where, in the bunker under the attic, Jacob's unit had hidden before the hideout was discovered the previous day. At the same time a group of about twenty Germans split up and started up the various staircases of Leszno 76, including the one leading to the hospital bunker. They knew where the fighters were, Jacob was sure.

The fighters, scrambling to posts by the windows, helplessly watched while the Germans stormed upstairs, firing volleys into every door as they moved toward the attics. How could the Jews resist such a powerful, concerted attack? They must try to break through the siege. Eliezer Geller divided his fighters into three groups and ordered each to slip out a different way. Perhaps some would get through.

Eliezer himself led a group of twelve men, including Jacob, through the attics toward a staircase he thought might still be free of Germans. They ran down the stairs one by one, but when they got to the floor beneath the attic they were greeted by automatic fire. One fighter threw a grenade, filling the staircase with dust, and amid the cries of enemy wounded all managed to reach the next floor down. But then the dust began to settle, and while bullets continued to fly, the fighters could hear Germans shouting from above and below.

Here, on this staircase, Jacob was sure death would come. But even as this thought raced through his mind, he dashed with the others through a metal door and slammed it shut. The fighters found themselves in a huge room that had served as a Többens workshop. They grabbed several sewing machines and heavy wooden tables and placed them against the door, then explored the two other smaller rooms in the apartment. They would make their stand from room to room, killing as many Germans as possible before they themselves died.

As hundreds of bullets pierced the front door, the fighters retreated to the second room. Finally the Germans broke down the door, smashed through the barricade, and sprayed the room with bullets. The fighters then opened the door of the second room and tossed a grenade at the Germans. After an explosion the attackers withdrew with their casualties.

With this respite, Eliezer tramped from room to room, rubbing his forehead as he desperately sought a way out of the trap. Every few seconds he would stop, wave his hand as if he were about to suggest a solution, then continue pacing. Soon the Germans struck again with even greater force. Bullets riddled the wooden door leading to the second room, which the fighters had barricaded with furniture.

Jacob and his fellows lay flat on the floor to avoid being hit, while plaster from the ceiling showered them. Each man counted his bullets. Each bullet would be made to count. The last one would pierce his own brain. They lay there waiting for the door to be torn from its hinges, their pistols aimed. . . .[5]

Meanwhile, in the Central Ghetto, Tuvia Borzykowski and his group were also convinced the end had come. They were trapped in the flaming horror of Mila 7, with the floor burning beneath them and the Germans outside shooting everyone who tried to escape. Though Tuvia had pleaded with his comrades to wait fifteen minutes before committing suicide, even he now saw that there was no other way out.

But at that moment of resignation, the shooting outside suddenly stopped. The fighters were puzzled. One by one they started to crawl through the ruins toward the front door, suspecting that the lull was merely a maneuver to lure the Jews out. But with darkness descending, the Germans had indeed gone. In a state of shock, Tuvia and his fellows looked around. Corpses lay everywhere in the charred courtyards. Tuvia could hardly believe that he was alive. Why had God chosen him? The fighters fell into each other's arms and wept.

Then they walked to Mila 18.[6]

Lutek Rotblatt, one of the other newcomers to Mila 18 that night, stayed only long enough to greet Mordechai Anielewicz and gather three comrades to help him find his wife, mother, and sister—if they were still alive. He wanted to bring them to the relative safety of this bunker.

Unknown to Lutek, the three had moved from the attic of their home at Muranowska 44 to a neighboring underground bunker owned by Dr. Tulo Nussenblatt, a famous scholar and Zionist historian. They had been there only a short time when the people in the bunker, about thirty of them, began to smell smoke and hear footsteps above. An infant started crying.

"Shut him up!" someone yelled.

The father then came to Lutek's wife, Hela, with a hypodermic needle and asked her to inject an unidentified substance into the child to quiet him. When Hela refused, the father injected it himself, and the baby stopped crying and went to sleep. Soon the occupants realized that the footsteps were actually those of Jews fleeing the flames. The parents tried to awaken their baby but could not. The child was dead. Now all that could be heard were the hysterical sobs of the distraught young couple. They had killed their infant—for nothing.

Soon, it seemed, everybody was sobbing, everybody but Maria—Lutek's mother. Perhaps she had already seen too many children die—her whole orphanage. She sat on her cot in silent despair. Where was Lutek? Was he dead, too? She would not want to live if he was. She refused to eat anything and clutched a little box from which she would occasionally spill several lethal pills into the palm of her hand and stare at them longingly.

When the smoke grew thicker and flames licked at the hatch, the people began crowding out of the bunker and scattering to find other, safer ones. Hela, Maria, and Maria's adopted daughter, Dolcia, joined with Nussenblatt's family; and as they hobbled through the wasteland, the flames followed while bullets sang by.

From cellar to cellar, staircase to staircase, they ran. There was no room anywhere. Nussenblatt puffed along with a heavy briefcase in hand. In it was a precious collection of rare documents, the archives for a book he was writing on Theodor Herzl, the founder of Zionism. A father might kill his child, but Nussenblatt would not part with the briefcase. Finally they took refuge in a cellar.

And it was here Lutek and his three comrades found them. Hela fell into Lutek's arms with joy, while Maria simply stared at him unbelievingly. Lutek apologized to the others in the cellar for not rescuing them as well; Mila 18 was already overcrowded. But he would try to return for them when room could be made. Then, with fires still raging all around, the family and their escorts twisted through the flames to that last-ditch bunker.[7]

The Germans fired relentlessly through the second door in the apartment, where Eliezer Geller, Jacob Putermilch, and ten other defenders of the Productive Ghetto lay on the floor with weapons aimed. Suddenly Eliezer leaped to his feet. He ran into the third room and peered over a balcony. In the courtyard three floors below he saw a large pile of garbage.

"Our only chance," he cried, "is to jump down on the heap of rubbish!"

Eliezer ordered Shimon Heller, the sharpshooter with a rifle, to remain in the room and cover the retreat of the others. Then he pulled the sheet from a bed in the room and ripped it into several strips while his men knotted them together and tied the improvised rope to the balcony railing.

As a flurry of bullets swept the last two rooms, Shimon groaned. He had been hit in the hand. Nevertheless he managed to fire back. Others asked to take his place, but he refused even to let them bandage the wound. He vowed not to die until he killed at least five Germans.

"Don't give me trouble!" Shimon replied. "Go on and jump!"

Then, while Shimon continued to fire, Eliezer slid down the rope but had to jump part of the way because it was too short, spraining his arm as he landed in the garbage. Jacob and the others did not bother to use the rope. They simply jumped down.

As soon as each fighter landed, he took up a firing position in the courtyard. Jacob listened with a pounding heart to the single shots coming from the apartment. Shimon was still alive. Finally it was Shimon's turn to jump. But the others could neither see nor hear him. What had happened?

Suddenly a shot rang out, and Shimon appeared on the balcony. He gazed at his comrades standing around the courtyard, and tears of joy seemed to well in his eyes. Then a burst of fire sounded from inside. Shimon turned, fired back, and began climbing over the railing. At that moment a submachine gun rattled, and Shimon fell dead upon the pile of garbage.

His fellow fighters bowed their heads. Shimon had died so that they might live, but only after keeping his vow to kill at least five Germans.[8]

"These are bad, very bad, Easter days for the enterprise and the people connected with it," industrialist Fritz Schultz wrote in his diary that day.

Bad indeed. True, General Stroop had agreed to extend the deadline for evacuating most of his factories in the Productive Ghetto from 10 A.M. to 2 P.M. But the few Jewish workers left to Schultz had time to transfer his equipment to storehouses on the Aryan side in only the most haphazard manner. Everything was mixed up—finished and half-finished goods, materials, machines. It would cost him a fortune to reorganize everything, to replace damaged equipment.

"I cannot possibly assume any responsibility," he angrily recorded, "for the army goods entrusted to me, or for an orderly winding up of the process."

Stroop, however, couldn't have cared less. His task was to burn Jews, and he would not let the greedy industrialists and Wehrmacht supply officers put him off. Their factories would go up in flames after 2 P.M. The remaining Jews were getting tougher to capture. They were no longer volunteering for transfer. He was now facing the fighting elite, and only fire could drive them out. He would raze the whole ghetto to the ground, factories and all.

That morning he visited a factory where he found only a few obsolete machines and a small number of finished products. Yet the place was swarming with Jews. In a frenzy he called together the officers who ran the plant and charged that they were *shabbes goyim.** He then sent the Jewish workers to Umschlagplatz and closed down the factory. Saboteurs!

General Globocnik arrived in Warsaw just before the 2 P.M. deadline, as his "business partner," Többens, had advised, and strutted into Stroop's office, surrounded by thirty of his own SS men. The shops should not be burned down, Globocnik urged Stroop, until all goods and equipment were moved out. Furthermore, he pleaded, Jewish workers must be spared. After all, they helped to fill Germany's war needs. Not to mention—and he didn't—his own financial needs.

Perhaps the size of Globocnik's entourage impressed Stroop, for he approved every request. But no sooner had the visitor stepped out the door than Stroop picked up the telephone and called Globocnik's bitter foe, General Krüger, in Cracow. When

---

Shabbes goy is a Yiddish term for a gentile who, on the Sabbath, switches on lights, builds a fire, or performs other tasks on behalf of Jews whose observance of the Sabbath prohibits such activities.

Krüger heard what had happened, he immediately left for Warsaw and stormed into Stroop's office. Ignore the profiteer Globocnik, Krüger screamed. Stroop must keep to his own schedule. What was more important than killing Jews? Money? Some extra supplies to pamper the Wehrmacht? In fact, Krüger would send Stroop more troops to finish the job. Stroop beamed.

And even while the two Nazi officers talked, the Productive Ghetto was being set afire.[9]

At about 3 P.M. Leon Wanat, the Polish prisoner in Pawiak Prison, was passing through a corridor when he saw a familiar scene from the window. Clusters of Jews—fifty-nine men and two women—were being herded into the prison courtyard. Just the day before he had witnessed a bloody massacre. Would there be another today? But this group was different. It was composed of blue-capped Jewish police, the ones who seemed to relish rounding up their fellow Jews for deportation.

Lieutenant Brandt, Hahn's Gestapo specialist on Jewish affairs, greeted the policemen and commanded them to stand in two ranks. He then ordered the guards to make sure that all prisoners in Pawiak were confined to their cells for the next few hours, though nobody bothered Wanat since he worked in Brandt's office.

Finally the policemen were told to lie down on their stomachs. A guard motioned to the first in one of the files, and he was led into the courtyard of the two buildings across the street, where the previous day's slaughter had occurred. A shot sounded, and a second man was led out. Then another and another. When those who remained began to talk among themselves, a guard ordered them to be silent. They obeyed. If they themselves had ignored pleas for mercy, could they expect the Nazis to be more merciful?

Yet they had served the SS with unstinting loyalty, sometimes betraying even members of their own families. Didn't they deserve to live? To start a new life with the wealth they had gained from bribes? Had they sold their souls for nothing? They waited quietly.

After all the bodies from the two-day massacre had been piled into the two buildings across the street, the Nazis set the structures ablaze and watched the smoke curl into the sky.

Leon Wanat, numbed, then went to write a new report for Brandt in his splendid handwriting.[10]

By the end of the day Mordechai Anielewicz's command bunker at Mila 18 was jammed with more than three hundred people. Among those streaming in were Chaim Frimer's group of survivors from Mila 29, Tuvia Borzykowski's men, Lutek Rotblatt's family, Zivia Lubetkin, and scores of other fighters and civilians burned out of their own bunkers. Nobody could be turned away. It was too dangerous to leave outside anyone who knew where the shelter was.

Though he feigned high spirits, Mordechai was discouraged. It was no longer possible to fight in the ghetto. Nor to escape from the ghetto so his fighters could carry on the battle in the forests. Tuvia's mission through the sewers, he learned, had failed. Now everything seemed to depend on the dubious inclinations of the Polish firemen who were to meet with his fighters that night. And even if they sought help from Yitzhak Zuckerman, the Polish Home Army would probably refuse to cooperate with him.

Mira Fuchrer, who alone understood her beloved Mordechai's private torment, tried to console him. The fighting could go on, she assured him. If necessary, in the rubble. Mira herself went on daring operations almost every night, seeking food in abandoned or destroyed buildings, news about Nazi movements, or simply German blood. And each time she returned, Mordechai greeted her with the same warm embrace his other fighters had come to expect—no more, no less. He would greet her many more times, she insisted. They had only begun to fight.

The fighters actually looked forward to their nightly forays from Mila 18, for this once-luxurious refuge had turned into a gigantic hall of horrors. Fittingly, each of its rooms was named after a concentration camp or death camp. "Treblinka," built for eight to ten people, now overflowed with thirty, none of whom could stretch their legs when lying down. One could only turn over if one's neighbor sat up. The intense heat from the kitchen nearby and the lack of air made sleep almost impossible. People soaked in their sweat and were constantly drying their bodies with dirty towels. "Trawniki" and "Poniatow" were cooler but just as crowded, and "Piaski," the room dug out by the fighters, was the worst of all

236

because the ceiling was so low that the occupants could only move on their bellies and had to lie down all the time. Even the connecting corridors were so packed that those passing through would have to climb over a carpet of bodies. One had to stand in line for hours to get to the single water tap, which barely trickled, and since nobody could wash, lice soon infested every garment. The line was just as long in front of the single toilet, encouraging people to relieve themselves almost anywhere, and thereby to add to the terrible stench pervading the bunker.

But food was the gravest problem of all. For the telltale smoke would not permit cooking in the light of day, and the blackness of night disappeared before more than half the dwellers could be fed. Ironically, there was no shortage of food yet. Piles of flour, cereal, and beans still remained, and Shmuel Asher's band of thieves, lithe as cats and well-trained in their profession, never failed to return at night with food snatched from ruined bunkers.

Asher himself would often lead these food-seeking expeditions, and always in style. He put on boots which were kept highly polished by a faithful subject, and he strapped two pistols to his huge belly. Then he wriggled through the exit tunnel, finding the opening less snug as his great bulk gradually diminished.

Despite his discouragement, Mordechai kept his fighters disciplined and selfless in the midst of the chaos and deprivation. Each one watched over the other as if he were his brother's keeper. Nothing was done unless it would benefit all. Mordechai himself was constantly in motion, giving orders, welcoming newcomers, personally raising each fighter's spirits. Then he would sit with Mira to raise his own.

On this night Mordechai sent several fighters on the fateful mission to meet the Polish firemen. While awaiting their return, with Mira beside him, he bitterly scribbled a last appeal to be smuggled out to Yitzhak if the firemen agreed to cooperate. It was apparently to be shown to Home Army leaders:

For a week we have been involved in a life-and-death struggle. . . . Our losses are enormous, taking into account the number of victims of shooting and of the fires in which men, women, and children perished. Our end is imminent, but while we are in possession of arms we shall continue to resist. . . .

As we feel our last days approaching, we ask you to remember how we have been betrayed. The day will come for us to be avenged for the shedding of our innocent blood. Help those who at the last moment will slip through the enemy's hands to carry on the struggle.

According to Hela Schipper, who was present, after composing the letter Mordechai read it aloud to his fighters. They approved every word.

As the night passed, the men sent to meet with the Polish firemen failed to return. No one, it seemed, would slip through the enemy's hands to carry on the struggle.[11]

The Ninth Day

April 27

"Well, Vladek, so we're going out to dance with the Germans today, are we?" joked Edward Zaremba across the counter in his pharmacy.

"Sure," replied Lieutenant Zajdler, who was to accompany Captain Iwanski's force into the ghetto to help the beleaguered ZZW fighters. "Get some of your stuff ready. You'll probably be having some visitors today. And don't you forget a quart of vodka."

It was 7 A.M. Soon Zaremba, a member of Iwanski's unit, was helping to load arms onto a wagon. And by 10 A.M. these weapons, as well as others collected elsewhere, were in burlap sacks tied to the backs of Iwanski and seventeen of his men. They were ready to leave the cellar of Muranowska 6 on the Aryan side and cross through the tunnel to Muranowska 7 in the ghetto. Among them were Iwanski's younger son, sixteen-year-old Roman, and two brothers, Waclaw and Edward.

A contingent of ZZW fighters already on the Aryan side and some Polish partisans—about sixty in all—would remain hiding in an upstairs apartment at Muranowska 6 to keep the tunnel open and to cover those fighters and civilians who would return with the rescuers.

With Iwanski leading the way, the men plodded along in single file, shielding their Sten guns and grenades from the sand that

239

sifted down constantly from the ceiling and walls of the narrow rubble-strewn passage. Finally they reached the cellar of Muranowska 7 and climbed through the exit on all fours. Several ZZW fighters embraced them, their unshaven faces grimy and swollen with the smoke and tension of battle.

But no sooner had the last man climbed into the cellar when a messenger rushed in. Nazi soldiers, he gasped, were moving up Nalewki Street with tanks! There was no time to waste. Guided by a fighter wearing an SS uniform, Iwanski and his men hurried through subterranean passages and holes in the walls, stumbling over twisted iron, bricks, barbed wire, collapsed masonry. Shortly they came to the courtyard of an abandoned building.

From behind some ruins emerged David Appelbojm, a dirty bandage around his head and his arm in a sling. As he hobbled toward his old friend, supported by an aide, tears came to his eyes.

"We are all dying," he said, hugging Iwanski. "We need ammunition and grenades. Thank God you've come."

ZZW forces, Appelbojm explained, had reoccupied the ruins of Muranowska 7. They were struggling to keep the escape tunnel to the Aryan side open for the fighters, who would continue the battle in the forests, and for as many civilians as could be saved. Some ZOB units, he said, were tying down Nazi troops with diversionary fire on Niska Street to the west. ZZW fighters poised on rooftops along Muranowska Street would use the automatic rifles and two machine guns that Iwanski had just brought in to support an attack on the SS troops marching up Nalewki Street. The Nazis had already cut off some units on this street, but these isolated groups could still snipe at them.

Iwanski's men would stay and fight, even though their mission was simply to deliver the arms and ammunition. They would relieve a few dozen ZZW fighters to enable them to evacuate their wounded. Iwanski split his group into two platoons, one under his own command, the other under Zajdler's, each reinforced with Jews. He and his men, among them his son Roman and his brother Edward, then scrambled into the rubble of Muranowska 7; and Zajdler's men moved into ruined buildings on Nalewki Street adjoining Muranowski Square.

Around noon the fighters heard the rumble of trucks and halftracks. The Nazis were almost at the square. Iwanski silently watched them approach as he lay alongside his son and his broth-

240

er. He trembled slightly at the sight of the raw German power, suddenly realizing that this was suicide. Why had he brought his loved ones to share his fate? Unlike the Jews, he and his family did not *have* to fight in order to survive. Yet strangely he was glad they were there.

As the rumble grew louder, he smiled at his son.[1]

The defenders nervously held their fire as two half-tracks followed by a column of Latvian SS troops inched their way up Nalewki Street. The guttural voice of an officer thundered, "Mop up the Jews hiding in the square!" The men instantly started searching for Jews.

Zajdler later wrote, describing the scene:

> They were so close we could almost have touched them. They looked in through the gaping windows and sent occasional bursts of fire into the buildings. My group, which was concealed behind a large gate, let them pass. Our orders were to attack them from the rear as soon as Bystry [Iwanski] had opened fire.
> The moments seemed to creep by. My hands clutched my gun impatiently. I felt drops of sweat roll down my back, my hands were moist. But not yet, not yet, I whispered to myself.

Suddenly a grenade exploded under the treads of the first half-track. Another blast followed, and the Nazis ran for cover behind a pall of smoke. But they could not escape a deadly crossfire that trapped and killed many of them.

Wearing a stolen SS uniform, Leon Rodal, the "officer" who had ordered them into the square, had played his role perfectly.

Soon, however, the Latvians recovered from their surprise and machine-gunned the area from one of the half-tracks while a German force moved in to help them. Zajdler's group was now cut off from Iwanski's. As Zajdler began to despair, a young Jewish messenger, Yankele, the twelve-year-old son of a ZZW fighter, came running up to him.

"*Poruchnik* [Lieutenant]," he cried. "Down through this cellar you can get up to the attic, where you'll be able to attack them from behind. And when you give it to them, the sons of bitches, they'll all be *kaputt*. I'll take you there."

Zajdler and several of his men followed Yankele to an attic of a

241

half-demolished building. They peered out a window and saw seven Germans clustered in the gateway of the debris-filled courtyard. What a target! Zajdler whispered an order to his men, and four Sten guns sputtered. As the Germans bolted out the gate, they were greeted with more fire from other fighters. But simultaneously, the half-tracks rained shells on Zajdler and his group.

"What is left of the walls crumbles and collapses," wrote Zajdler. "I lie low behind a ruined wall, with fragments of brick and mortar raining down on my head and back. The air is filled with a dark, suffocating cloud of smoke. Firing a few more bursts, the half-tracks withdraw. I hear the rattling of their traction treads."

Zajdler got up and found two of his men lying dead in each other's arms. Another was unconscious. The lieutenant ordered Yankele, who was pale but unhurt, to bring the rest of his platoon to his position to carry on the fight. The situation could not be worse, thought Zajdler. His platoon had been gravely depleted. And the Nazis were getting ready to attack again. What in blazes happened to Iwanski? he wondered.[2]

Shortly after he had been cut off from Zajdler's force, Iwanski, together with his son Roman, his brother Edward, and some Jewish fighters, crawled over the rubble and through several cellars, trying desperately to close the gap. Finally they succeeded, but hardly had they taken up their new positions when Edward was struck by a bullet. As he collapsed, a huge chunk of masonry from a shattered wall fell on his back, crushing him to death. Another piece fell on Roman, who was lying nearby, and gravely wounded him.

Iwanski was hiding behind some rubble only a short distance away but was totally unaware of what had happened. Suddenly a ZZW fighter called to him, "Captain, things aren't going so well with your family."

Iwanski turned around and saw his brother sprawled under a block of stone, blood oozing from his mouth. He then saw his son, his head bloody and his legs buried under another heavy piece of masonry. As he stumbled toward Roman to free him and administer medical aid, he wanted to weep. But he thought of his men. A soldier could not afford to blur his vision with tears.

After ordering one of his fighters to take his son to the rear, Iwanski sent a messenger to Zajdler. What was his situation? The messenger returned with a note from the lieutenant. Several of Zajdler's men had been killed and wounded, and he himself had been badly bruised. Worried that this force could not hold—he did not know that his other brother, Waclaw, was among the wounded—Iwanski crawled upon a mound of rubble to observe Zajdler's sector. At that moment a bullet hit him in the head, penetrating the top of his skull. As he was losing consciousness, he ordered one of his ZZW men, referring to Zajdler by his code name, "Tell Zarski I'm wounded. He must take over the command and hold the tunnel entrance at all costs."[3]

Minutes later, about 4 p.m., Zajdler was reading Iwanski's message. Deeply shaken, he ran to Appelbojm to consult with him. He had only eight unwounded men. Could they bar the enemy from Muranowski Square? They had to. As these men scrambled to new positions in the ruins of Nalewki Street, they heard a heavy rumbling. Some armored cars were chugging up the street, sputtering fire from side to side, with the infantry marching close behind. The Nazis peeped into every entrance, looking for Jews. All at once Zajdler's men sprayed them with bullets. The armored cars ground to a halt, and the infantry responded with merciless fire.

A few of the defenders managed to crawl around to the enemy's rear and surprise them. But a half-track then moved up, followed by more infantry, and spit lead into the ruins. Then mortar shells began pouring down on Zajdler's men, while two aircraft strafed them.

Zajdler was desperate. The SS had thrown into the battle what may have been the most powerful striking force of the uprising. And his handful of men were trapped in a narrow street facing a moving wall of armor and a storm of automatic fire. The steel wall moved closer and closer. . . .

Suddenly a shadowy figure darted from behind a charred wall toward the half-track and threw a bottle. Flames licked the steel sides and poked into the interior. Another bottle, and the flames shot higher. Zajdler's men fired heavy bursts to cover the heroic figure, but an SS bullet punctured him. He almost fell under the tread of the half-track as the German crew jumped out and scurried for cover in a ruined building.

Zajdler later wrote: "He lies, gray, his legs buckled up beneath

243

him, under the sacred halo, as it were, of the flaming tank. The fire leaps up to the pennant fluttering above the burning monster—the hateful black and white flag."

Twelve-year-old Yankele lay dead.

When the boy's father realized who the figure was, he started to dash toward him in crazed anguish but was stopped by his comrades. The battle had to go on. And it did, in a swirl of smoke from the flaming half-track that turned the street into an invisible alley of death.

Finally the fighters were forced to leave the scene as the enemy fired bursts at every moving shadow. By this time every fighter had been wounded; Appelbojm, a second time, now in the lungs. Even so, the defenders kept fighting as they retreated. Then, at about 5 P.M., the Germans stopped shooting and slipped away, while ambulances screeched into the battle zone to pick up their dead and wounded.

As the fighters stumbled into the wrecked bunker at Muranowska 7, they were greeted by Captain Iwanski, wearing a bloodstained rag around his head. He had regained consciousness, but he stood feebly and unsteadily, supported by one of his men, as he listened to the fighters tell their battle tales. The situation was hopeless. All of them, said Iwanski, must escape with him to the Aryan side. Appelbojm shook his head as he lay on the ground, while his girl friend, Wladka Cykow, tended his wounds. No, he would not leave. Some of the less severely wounded fighters, including Pawel Frenkel, also protested.

"But, Mietek," Zajdler said, calling Appelbojm by his code name, "why don't you come along with us?"

"Look, dear friend," Appelbojm answered, "I may be wounded, but my mind is functioning normally. I know my people. I can't just leave them here. I have lived to see the most beautiful moment in my life, the moment to which I have devoted everything. I've seen my people fighting in battle. And this battle, in spite of everything, is going to end in our victory. I want to remain in this fight to the very end."

But Iwanski was insistent. Hadn't the plan been for the fighters to leave? "You're coming with us," he said. "We'll put you on your feet again. I have a whole hospital at my disposal."

"No, no. I won't go."

"If you don't come with us you're going to die."

"I know I'm going to die, and soon. But I want you to tell the world what has gone on here, to let the world know that we fought to the end."

Iwanski gave up. He promised to deliver the message. And he would try to come back for the civilians who were still alive in the bunkers.

Then, with the lightly wounded helping the seriously wounded—among them Iwanski's son Roman and Leon Rodal, both fated to die from their injuries—about fifty fighters climbed into the underground passage and hobbled to Muranowska 6 on the Aryan side. Several hearses were waiting for them. They crawled in and lay on three tiers of boards; above them rested some coffins decorated with flowers. After reaching the Jewish cemetery, they hid in tombs until they could be spirited away to Iwanski's underground hospital.[4]

Iwanski's group managed to escape shortly after a Nazi force had attacked the sixty-odd ZZW and Polish fighters whom the captain had left in Muranowska 6 to cover the exodus from the ghetto. An informer had that day sent an anonymous letter to Colonel Hahn, the Gestapo chief, reporting the presence of this group. Hahn immediately notified Stroop. Was the Polish resistance joining the revolt? they wondered. Stroop acted at once. He sent a special assault unit headed by one of his toughest fighters, Lieutenant Diehl, to wipe out the enemy concentration.

But the Jews and Poles fired from the windows and roofs of Muranowska 6 and adjacent buildings, bitterly resisting the attack, and soon Hahn had to bring in reinforcements. When Diehl reported that "German" soldiers in Wehrmacht uniforms were helping the enemy, Stroop thought the lieutenant was having hallucinations. Neither realized that these Germans were really Jews in SS disguise.

Nazi fear and confusion grew. Stroop urgently called Himmler in Berlin. The Reichsführer agreed: The Poles might be rising in revolt. A call then to General Krüger in Cracow: Wipe out the enemy concentration, he fumed. Finally, a conference with Hahn and his deputy, Dr. Kah: Act prudently, Kah warned. Wait until nightfall. Then block off the area around Muranowska 6.

"The fire," Kah argued, "could spread from the ghetto to the rest of Warsaw and cause terrible trouble."

Stroop approved this plan. In his daily report to Krüger, he claimed that his men had destroyed twenty-four of the "bandits" and arrested fifty-four others and that they would mop up the rest the next day.

"The external appearance of the Jews caught," Stroop wrote, "indicates that the turn has now come of those who led the entire resistance movement. Cursing Germany and the Führer and the German soldiers, they leaped from the burning windows and balconies. . . .

"Among the bandits who were caught or killed there were some who were definitely identified as being Polish terrorists."

Meanwhile, other Poles chose sides.[5]

At about seven that evening a guard rushed into Mila 18 and breathlessly reported to Mordechai Anielewicz: A lone, unidentified figure was crawling in the street toward the bunker. Mordechai was shaken. Was it one of his own men? Or was it a Nazi or a Jewish informer leading the Germans to this underground refuge? He picked his way through the clutter of human wreckage in the dark corridor until he found Chaim Frimer. Mordechai ordered him to check out the man. He had to know whether a German attack was imminent.

Chaim left immediately with Masha Glytman, one of the Bund fighters he had brought here from Mila 29. Emerging from the bunker the two cautiously crawled through the ruins until they saw the mysterious figure. Masha instantly recognized him. It was Melech Perlman, a Bund member and an old school chum who had left the night before, together with three other fighters, for a rendezvous with the Polish firemen at the edge of the Wild Ghetto. Melech's clothes were bloody, and his face looked ghostly white in the pale moonlight. He was gripping his stomach.

"Melech, what happened?" Masha asked, kneeling beside him.

When he had been dragged into the courtyard of Mila 18, Melech gasped a reply. They had gone to the ruined building at Gensia 80 for the meeting with the firemen and had just begun to talk—when it happened. The Germans attacked. The Poles had led the fighters into a trap. During the battle all the Jews were killed except himself. And he was hit in the stomach.

The Germans finally left, thinking all of them dead, and he waited in a pile of feathers until dark. Then he hid his own pistol

246

and those of his dead comrades in a stove, and despite his agonizing pain, he crawled all the way back to Mila 18.

"I had to come back," Melech groaned, "to tell you where the pistols are."

Chaim and Masha decided that Melech was in no condition to be dragged through the narrow passage leading into Mila 18. He would certainly die on the way. So with great difficulty they carried him through the rubble to an upstairs bunker at Muranowska 33.

Chaim returned to Mila 18, but Masha stayed with Melech all night, nursing his wound, feeding him food and tea. She recalled how, as a student, Melech had sung arias so beautifully and written such fine essays for the Bund newspaper. He was a delicate intellectual who hadn't seemed to hold much promise as a fighter.

Just before dawn, Masha was about to leave Melech when he told her how happy he would be if only he had a weapon with which to kill himself, since he expected to die anyway. He had been stupid to leave his pistol behind after the battle.

"Now," he said, "I will die an ugly death, either struck by a German bullet or burned alive."

Masha departed with a feeling of dread. And indeed, upon her return the following night she would find his charred body. The bunker's survivors said that they had heard his screams as flames lashed at his body.[6]

While the treachery of the Polish firemen seemed to crush Mordechai's last hope for a mass escape from the Central Ghetto, the fighters in the Productive Ghetto were planning a breakout of their own. General Stroop was rigidly enforcing his order that the whole sector go up in flames that day, whether or not the industrialists had removed their equipment and goods. And to remain would mean almost certain death.

In fact, thirty-six ZZW fighters had already left the night before. From their base at Karmelicka 5, which led into an underground passage connected to the sewer system, they started toward the Aryan side, where they would be met by Captain Iwanski's men. They would then escape to the forest. But they got lost in the maze of sewer tunnels and dragged themselves through the slime for thirteen hours before finally reaching a manhole exit.

Their rejoicing was short-lived. Overhead they heard shooting and shouting. They had wound their way not to the Aryan side but to Muranowski Square in the Central Ghetto, right in the middle of the battle their ZZW comrades were waging. Desperately they tried to lift the cover so they could leave the filthy sewer and join in the fighting. But it would not budge.

"If only someone would lift it from the outside," Simcha Korngold later wrote. "Wedged down here, we can neither live nor die, nor are we able to give a helping hand to our comrades who are fighting just overhead. . . . Are we to die like rats in these narrow, slimy catacombs?"

Two of Iwanski's men made sure that they wouldn't. After a long search they found the fighters and led them to the Aryan side. The group were taken to an apartment at Gryzybowska 13, from which they would be spirited out of Warsaw to the forest.[7]

The ZOB fighters in the Productive Ghetto had waited too long to escape the trap, it seemed. Now fire was sweeping their sector, and they had to flee from bunker to bunker. By evening Jacob Putermilch, hiding in the hospital shelter, was resigned to a fiery death. He almost envied the wounded, for they did not yet know that the whole area was being set aflame, and they could harbor at least a breath of hope.

As Jacob awaited the worst, Eliezer Geller and several of his fighters crawled into the bunker through the tiny entrance and urgently took him aside. All the fighters, he said in a quiet but excited voice, would escape from the ghetto that night, together with as many civilians as possible. They would leave from an underground bunker at Leszno 56, which opened to a passage that led to the sewer network. They must assemble in that bunker immediately.

A moment of joy. Then doubt. Leszno 56 was about ten buildings away. They couldn't use the attic system because of the fires, and if they went into the street, German patrols would be waiting for them. But they had to try.

Not yet aware of the spreading flames, the wounded suspected that all the able-bodied people would be leaving the shelter but not the ghetto. Still they sensed that the end was near for them. The two wounded lovers, Hana Grauman and Shalom Sufit, clung to each other in desperation as they lay side by side, seeking some solace in the certainty that they would die together.

Eliezer could see the apprehension in the eyes of the wounded as they stared at him, silently seeking reassurance. When one seriously injured fighter who had tried to commit suicide complained that his comrades had taken his pistol from him, Eliezer ordered that it be returned immediately. Suicide would be a merciful act. He then asked the less severely wounded to come with him. Among those he considered too handicapped to leave was Meir Schwartz, who had been shot in the hand while escaping the Germans the previous day. The suspicions of the remaining people grew.

Why were some leaving? one asked. Eliezer answered vaguely that they were moving to buildings farther away but that he would maintain contact with the hospital. Why was the smell of smoke getting stronger? another asked. Just smoke carried by the wind from the Central Ghetto, was Eliezer's answer.

Eliezer's heart wept. He had no choice. He must abandon the wounded. But he couldn't let them know this. He couldn't make them suffer with this knowledge; they should be spared until the last moment. They needn't worry, he said reassuringly. One girl would stay to care for them.

When the departing group had crept into the next room, he turned to a young woman who had proved herself among the bravest fighters, and said, "Guta, you must stay here and look after them."

A heavy silence followed. Then Guta burst into tears.

"No, I do not want to," she cried. "Do you think that because I am a girl I can't fight like a man? I'm strong, young, and can still fight. And I want to live!"

When Eliezer insisted she remain, Guta argued that by staying she would not help the wounded to survive.

"Their fate is sealed," she sobbed, "while we still have a chance."

Jacob and the others remained stonily silent. They feared that a single word from them might decide the fate of a comrade, and they dreaded this responsibility. They sympathized with Guta. They agonized with Eliezer. Never could a human being be faced with a more terrible dilemma. Eliezer felt morally bound not to abandon the wounded. Yet, was it a moral decision to condemn an additional person to death to keep a moral commitment, especially against her will?

Eliezer had made up his mind. His face pale, his voice faltering, he refused to back down. The wounded could not be left alone, he insisted. And there was no time to argue. Every minute was precious and could be decisive.

At that anguished moment, another girl's voice sounded: "Eliezer, I shall stay with the wounded."

Eliezer turned to Lea Korn, whose soft, gentle manner screened an iron will, and stared at her in mute shock.

"Don't lose any time," Lea urged. "Try to save yourselves from death. Continue your struggle on the other side of the ghetto wall."

She added, "After losing Yehuda I have nothing left to lose."

Lea's comrades understood. Her beloved Yehuda Konski had been betrayed to the Gestapo about a month earlier, while trying to buy arms, and had died on the torture rack without talking. Since then her only purpose in life was to fight until death. She now walked over to Guta, brushed away her tears, and embraced her. Then she returned to the hospital bunker to die with the wounded.[8]

The Tenth Day

When daylight broke, an eerie stillness pervaded Muranowski Square. The ZZW had abandoned it to the Germans. David Appelbojm and Pawel Frenkel, who had refused to leave the ghetto with Captain Iwanski, took their small band of fighters and left the ruins of Muranowska 7. They could no longer hold the entrance to the tunnel there since they knew that the Nazis would overwhelm them in a new attack. So the two ZZW leaders wove their way through the charcoal wasteland toward the Productive Ghetto. They felt they could more easily keep open the tunnel at Karmelicka 5 as a pipeline for arms from Iwanski and as an escape route for civilian survivors, and perhaps eventually for themselves. Unlike the strategic Muranowski Square, the Karmelicka zone was not a magnet for Nazi attack and occupation; the enemy did not yet know about the tunnel there.

Supported by one of his men, Appelbojm stumbled forward at the head of his fighters, who soon found themselves in a running battle with the Germans. He apparently got as far as Stawki and Smocza streets, where he and some of his fighters set up a base in the Transavia factory compound. He died soon afterward from loss of blood.

Frenkel, meanwhile, pressed on with most of the fighters along Smocza to the corner of Nowolipki Street at the edge of the Productive Ghetto, where they set up a stronghold in the ruins about

251

a block away from the Karmelicka tunnel. Soon they were battling the enemy from building to blazing building, though wounded, bleeding, and exhausted.

They had to keep the tunnel open.[1]

Only a few blocks away, at Leszno 56, ZOB fighters huddled by the entrance of another tunnel leading to the sewer system. Eliezer Geller, Jacob Putermilch, and their comrades had zigzagged for about two hours from the hospital bunker to Leszno 56, breathlessly arriving at about 2 A.M. They would start through the passage as soon as all fighters who could be reached arrived.

The bunker was a walled-off three-room cellar with a tiny camouflaged door that blended in with the rest of the wall. It had been built by smugglers who had brought food and other goods through the tunnel before the uprising. Soon the shelter was crowded with people—the original occupants and the fighters in the area—and one could hardly move or even sit down.

Eliezer sent ten men to burn down Többens' headquarters at Leszno 72 in a final act of revenge, though Stroop was ready to set it on fire anyway, together with the rest of the Productive Ghetto. Then, at about 10 A.M., Eliezer ordered Jacob to go back to the hospital bunker with Regina Fuden, the courageous liaison between the various groups, who knew intimately every attic and pathway in this fighting zone. Eliezer had inadvertently left there a bagful of false documents and money, and the fighters would urgently need them to survive on the Aryan side.

As the two fighters leaped from roof to roof and tore across debris-choked courtyards with bullets zinging around them, Jacob thought to himself, Is it worth taking such a risk for the sake of documents and money? The answer had to be yes, for many lives depended on their success. When they finally reached the hospital bunker, the people there greeted them with an explosion of joy. They were not being abandoned after all! They bombarded the couple with questions and for several minutes forgot their sufferings. Jacob felt that the risk of the mission had been justified if only to see the look in their eyes.

But the visitors had no time to linger. As Jacob grabbed the bag of money and documents and was about to leave with Regina, Meir Schwartz blocked the exit. He raised his bandaged hand in front of him and said firmly, "I'm going with you."

252

Meir was nervous and pale, and his eyes reflected his deep dejection. After a long pause he stammered in a low voice, so that he would not be overheard by the others, "As long as I can walk I should not be left behind. I cannot be compared with those unable to move. I know it is difficult to do anything with a bandaged hand. I know that I'll be a burden. But this is not a good enough reason to leave me behind to be burned alive."

As he waited for a reply, Meir bit his lips and covered his eyes with his unwounded hand.

"Meir," Jacob said, "you are right, but you can't come with us now. The way through the attics is almost completely destroyed. And one has to run through streets guarded by the Germans and jump from one roof to another. In your condition, especially in daylight, you can't do it. But as soon as I return I'll tell Eliezer about your request, and you'll probably be taken out at night."

Another wounded fighter, Sara Feigenblat, also wanted to leave with Jacob and Regina.

"I am young and healthy enough," she said. "Why shouldn't I be together with you?"

She asked Jacob to tell her brother Jacek, who was Jacob's group leader, to do everything in his power to rescue her. Jacob kissed her and left the bunker with Regina.

The area was still swarming with Germans. While running through the ruins of one attic, Regina accidentally dropped her pistol in a pile of feathers. While she searched for it, footsteps approached.

"Forget the pistol and come on!" Jacob urged.

"No," Regina replied as she knelt in the feathers, bathed in sweat, feeling everywhere for the weapon. "I will not return without my pistol."

Jacob stood by the attic door with his own pistol drawn and saw a German climbing the stairs.

"Remain where you are!" the Nazi bellowed.

Jacob fired and heard the German's body tumble down the stairs. When he turned toward Regina, he noticed she was smiling and shaking the feathers off the pistol she had managed to recover. They streaked toward Leszno 56 through a hail of bullets and, on arriving, handed their precious bag to Eliezer. Yes, he would send a couple men to the hospital bunker that evening to bring back Meir Schwartz and Sara Feigenblat.

Meanwhile, though exhausted, Regina was assigned to explore

the tunnel winding to the sewer so that she could later lead the way. When she returned, she would search for fighters who might not have received word of the exodus, since only she was familiar with every building and passage in the area. Anyway, she wanted this mission; her fiancé was among the missing.

As Jacob saw Regina off, he was apprehensive, for she would also be looking for his sister, Hagit. He decided that before leaving for the Aryan side he would try himself to rescue his father, who was hiding in a bunker several blocks away.

The hazardous trek through the sewers was delayed until ten the next morning, April 29. Anyone who had not shown up by then would have to be left behind.[2]

Yitzhak Gitler had managed the impossible. He had brought order out of the chaos of his bunker at Leszno 76. He and Michael L. and their families had been living there since April 23, when ZOB partisans had helped them escape from the attic of a partially constructed, stairless building. Despite the horrors of five days and nights in this hermetically sealed, almost airless shelter, they had made the best of the situation. Gitler, appointed bunker commander by the ZOB fighters based there, forced people at gunpoint to give the sick and elderly choice places on the mattresses and blankets that covered the floor, and he made everybody share in the chores as well.

Once, Nazi footsteps could be heard overhead, and it appeared that all was over when an infant started to cry. The mother pressed a pillow over the child's face, inadvertently smothering it to death. The Germans had learned the approximate locations of this bunker and others from a small boy, about eight years old, whom one of the fighters had caught and brought to this shelter.

"What shall we do with him?" Gitler asked.

"I thought of killing him on the spot," the fighter said. "But it is a pity to kill youngsters now. However, if he tries to get away, you'll have to shoot him."

Now, at about 8 A.M., more footsteps sounded above. This time somebody knocked on the camouflaged ceiling door. All seemed lost. Then Gitler and Michael heard the voice of a friend.

"Two delegates must come out for a very important meeting. There will be no danger during the next two hours."

Gitler and Michael, who like all the others in the steaming hideout were in their underwear, dressed silently, climbed out, and hurried to the designated meeting place, where they joined representatives from other bunkers. Their friend explained amid the ruins that Többens was offering another amnesty. The factories would be burned that day, the friend said, and the workers were needed to evacuate all the machinery and goods in the next few hours. Then all of them would be transferred safely to Poniatow. Go back to the bunkers, the friend urged, and spread the word: The deadline to report was 1 P.M. After that the bunkers would be blown up.

Returning to their shelter, Gitler, Michael, and the others called everyone out. There was no choice. As hundreds of Jews began gathering in the courtyard of Leszno 76, Michael decided on a daring move, one that had almost worked on the first day of the uprising. He walked over to a German guard and said, "I have a thousand zlotys. Let ten of us pass and you shall have it."

The guard looked surprised at this brazen attempt at bribery. "That is not possible," he replied.

"Then let five go."

"I still cannot."

"Just three, then, three souls."

The soldier paused. "Very well, but *schnell!*"

Barely able to believe his luck, Michael rushed back to his group and said, "He's agreed to let three go. No more. But from the other side I'll do all I can to save the rest of you."

Michael and his wife and daughter were then permitted to slip through a gate to the Aryan side.

No sooner had they gone than Többens appeared in the courtyard. He was in a fierce mood. First, his business partner, General Globocnik, had failed to frighten General Stroop into stretching the deadline for evacuating the factories and saving the qualified workers. Then the underground had set afire his headquarters in the Productive Ghetto, even before Stroop could act, and much of his capital was going up in smoke. Now Stroop had given him a new order: The Jews were *not* to help evacuate any more shops, after all. They were to assemble in a designated courtyard and then march directly to Umschlagplatz.

Többens had found Stroop in a rage, which would be reflected in the general's official report the following day: "Some of the armament factories are being evacuated very slowly. In several cases one gains the impression that this is done intentionally." The industrialists must finish the job *immediately*. But they would not be permitted to use Jews to help them do it.

Többens walked up to Gitler, who he knew was the manager of a factory, and fumed. Why were there still people in the bunkers? He glanced at his watch. It was about 11 A.M. The deadline for reporting to the assembly point would be advanced to noon, he shouted. In one hour the bunkers would be blown up and those hiding elsewhere would be hunted down and shot.

Többens then moved on, leaving Gitler petrified. One hour! One hour to follow Michael out of the ghetto!

Gitler pleaded with every guard he could find to let his family go. Finally one agreed to help for ten thousand zlotys. In a panic, Gitler tried to round up the cash but found that his family group had only nine thousand zlotys in all. The soldier would not take it.

The deadline passed, and most of the Jews, including the Gitlers, had chosen to ignore it, realizing that they would not be put to work in the ghetto as they had been told. It was still best, they felt, to hide in the bunkers and pray for a miracle, though Gitler lingered in the courtyard of Leszno 76, feverishly looking for another guard who might make a deal before it was too late.

At 12:40 P.M., Többens approached Gitler again. He agreed to extend the deadline to 1 P.M.

"Tell your people," he stormed, "that they will die in twenty minutes if they don't go to the assembly point. Are they so stupid? Can't they understand that?"

Gitler now concluded that there was no alternative. He began yelling in the nearly empty courtyard for the Jews to come out of hiding. But his call went unheeded. He explained to Többens that the people were packing and would soon emerge but were afraid of being sent to die. Többens gripped his riding crop with both hands and stared at Gitler with an insulted look.

"Nonsense!" he exclaimed. "Nobody who wants to work will be killed. They will all be sent to Poniatow."

"May I tell them that Többens guarantees that?" Gitler asked.

"Yes! Go quickly!"

Gitler walked away and began shouting again but still without success. Suddenly he heard another voice calling. The words sounded like "Hitler! Hitler! Hitler!" Some German, it seemed, was crying the praises of the murderous Führer. But then he realized that someone was calling *his* name—*Gitler*. It was the guard whom Michael had bribed to win freedom for himself and his family. Michael had sent him back for the Gitlers as well.

The guard accepted the money already raised by Gitler, but once more he agreed to take only three people. Gitler's wife, mother, and daughter would leave, but he and his daughter's fiancé would have to stay. Gitler accompanied the three women to the gate, then managed to slip out with them.

Twelve minutes later, while they were on their way to hiding places on the Aryan side, hundreds of their companions who had remained behind were dead or en route to Umschlagplatz, where Többens, with a flick of his whip, would keep faith with only a restricted number of Jews he considered fit enough to be his slaves.[3]

On the same day, ZOB agents on the Aryan side sent a cable to London through the Polish underground communications network. Addressed to Shmuel Zygielbojm and Isaac Schwarzbart, the Jewish representatives in the Polish government-in-exile, the letter read:

> Today is the ninth day that the ghetto fights back. SS and Wehrmacht formations are laying siege to the ghetto. Artillery and flamethrowers are employed and airplanes shower high explosives and incendiary bombs on the forty thousand Jews who still remain in the ghetto. The Germans mine and blast blocks of houses where the residents put up resistance. The ghetto is burning and smoke covers the whole city of Warsaw. . . .
>
> Only the power of the Allied nations can offer immediate and active help now. On behalf of the millions of Jews murdered and burned alive, on behalf of those fighting back and all of us condemned to die we call on the whole world: It is imperative that the powerful retaliation of the Allies shall fall upon the bloodthirsty enemy immediately and not in some distant future, so that it will be quite clear what the retaliation is for.
>
> Our closest allies must at last understand the degree of responsibility which arises from such apathy in the face of an unparalleled crime committed by the Nazis against a whole nation, the tragic epilogue of which is now being enacted. The heroic rising, without precedent in history, of the doomed sons of the ghetto should at last awaken the world to deeds commensurate with the gravity of the hour.

For some unexplained reason, the Polish underground did not deliver this letter until May 21, more than three weeks after it was transmitted—when it no longer mattered much.[4]

The Eleventh Day

April 29

Jacob Putermilch was ecstatic. Shortly after 2 A.M. Regina Fud-
en returned to the bunker at Leszno 56, accompanied by a dozen
fighters she had found wandering in the ruins—among them Hagit, Jacob's sister. Another euphoric brother was Jacek Feigenblat,
Jacob's group leader, who had gone to the hospital bunker to
bring back his sister Sara as well as Meir Schwartz.

But Regina could not share in the joy of reunion with a loved
one. She had failed to find any trace of her fiancé, and the torment of leaving him behind was etched in her pale, delicate face.
She must go back and find him, she told Eliezer. But Eliezer shook
his head. The time for departure was near, and since she had explored the sewer and was best qualified to lead the exodus to the
Aryan side, he could not take a chance on something happening
to her.

Jacob silently embraced his sister for several moments amid the
chaos of people preparing to depart. The bunker was crammed
with refugees and fighters. Yet Jacob might have been in the Garden of Eden. After all the horror of the past few days, the two had
survived and found each other.

But joy suddenly dissolved into apprehension. What of their father? If he stayed behind, he would be burned alive. They must
try to rescue him from his bunker. At about 4 A.M. they went to

258

Eliezer and asked to leave on this personal mission. Eliezer looked at the time and skeptically wrinkled his forehead.

"I'm not opposed to your going," he said, "but it will soon be daylight. In an hour or two we'll start getting ready. Will you have time to do it?"

"We'll leave immediately," Hagit replied. "It won't take us more than an hour."

When Eliezer nodded his approval, Jacob and Hagit pushed through the crowd to the exit and cautiously wound their way through the ruins, using still-existing attic passages and avoiding spots where Germans were posted. Finally they reached Leszno 40, only two buildings away from Leszno 36, where their father was hiding. But the structure was ablaze, and behind it stood rows of soldiers. The two fighters tried to skirt the building, regardless; but smoke choked them, and fire singed their hair and clothes. So close to their father, yet a million miles away. They had to go back.

Returning to Leszno 56 at about 9 A.M., they were plagued by the feeling that they had abandoned their father, even though it had been impossible to get through to him. They joined about forty fighters and civilians who silently stood amid their bundles and rucksacks, their faces sunken, their eyes dazed, people who had not eaten or slept for days, who had suffered unbearably. Yet as they tensely waited to descend into the unknown, Jacob could detect a pulse beat of hope.

Yes, perhaps they would survive after all. . . . Only two buildings away![1]

As the Central Ghetto continued to burn, Mordechai Anielewicz, undiscouraged by past failures, called a meeting of the ZOB command at Mila 18 to explore every possibility for leaving alive. Squatting on the dirt floor with his comrades, Mordechai, as usual, appeared calm and serene. He was resigned to death; yet every remaining moment of life was precious. The aim of his fighters, he still believed, should not be to survive the battle but to live as long as possible in order to exact every last pound of Nazi flesh. And since they were no longer able to kill many Germans in the ghetto, it now seemed logical to fight as partisans in the forest, if they could find a way to get there.

So far the ZOB in the Central Ghetto had failed to do so partly because Mordechai had not prepared escape routes. He had thought the Germans would fight by bullet and not by fire, but he had been proved wrong. Now it seemed there might be a way out after all. Mordechai had sent out a patrol to seek underground routes, and while exploring the abandoned ruins of Muranowska 7, the former ZZW headquarters, they had found the tunnel opening there. The ZOB commander was delighted but apparently shocked that the ZZW leaders had never told him about it so that his organization could use it, too, though he had visited Muranowska 7 before the uprising.

At the command meeting Mordechai suggested that the ZOB now use this tunnel. No, he did not know exactly where it led, but it seemed to snake toward the Aryan side. Two men should be sent through it. It would be easier than trying one's luck again through the sewers, though perhaps riskier if the Germans had discovered the passage.

Zivia Lubetkin, Marek Edelman, and the others agreed. Who would be the best men for this mission? Marek, who had come from Franciszkanska 30 for the meeting, recommended two of his fighters: Simcha Rathajzer and Zolman Frydrich. Both won overwhelming approval since they had gentile faces and had had much experience on the Aryan side before the uprising. And Marek, who had commanded both during the battle in the Brushmakers' District, could vouch for their courage and ingenuity.

Simcha had helped to set off the great bomb that had killed dozens of Germans, and he had scouted the way during the breakout to the Central Ghetto. Zolman, a tall Bundist sportsman, had smuggled arms into the ghetto before the uprising, and he was the fighter who first learned about the mass gassings at Treblinka from Jews who had escaped the camp in the summer of 1942. Although he was thirty-two, thirteen years older than Simcha, he looked almost as youthful and had, like his comrade, blond hair and blue eyes.

The two would depart that evening on their mission.

Meanwhile, coincidentally, the remnants of Pawel Frenkel's ZZW band, after battling with the Germans at the edge of the Productive Ghetto, apparently decided to return to Muranowska 7 on this same day, also to get to the forest on the Aryan side.[2]

* * *

At about 10 A.M. Jacob Putermilch crawled into the narrow passage leading from the bunker at Leszno 56 to the sewer system about fifty yards away. He had to back in feetfirst while lying on his stomach, for Regina Fuden had discovered during her exploration trip that the passage led to a hole in the roof of the sewer, and to emerge headfirst from the passage would mean to dive into the sewage and perhaps drown. When Jacob had dropped through the hole into the low and narrow sewer pipe, he had to stand in a crouched position behind others, waiting for his comrades to follow.

The stench of the sewage, which reached up to his knees, nauseated him. Rats leaped over his head, and gushes of filthy water splashed in his face. So narrow was the dark pipe that when Eliezer Geller, who was leading the group, needed someone up front, the person could only advance by swimming in the slime through the legs of those in front of him. Jacob and his comrades, their every muscle aching, felt they were in a torture chamber. But the alternative to crouching was even more disagreeable: sitting up to their chins in excrement and polluted water.

Finally, after about an hour, the order came to move forward. The forty Jews trudged ahead, their bodies still painfully stooped. They advanced 450 feet to a sewer entrance on Ogrodowa Street, one block east of Leszno. There they would climb out and run to Ogrodowa 29, where the *portier* was known to help escaping Jews. But suddenly they all realized what a terrible mistake they had made. In the rush to leave the ghetto before they were discovered or burned to death, they had departed at the worst possible time. It was now noon, when the streets on the Aryan side were crowded with people—Poles and Germans. To emerge now would be suicide. But to remain standing in a stooped position until dark was also impossible.

Eliezer thought he found the answer. Regina had discovered that there were two other manholes nearby, and that under each, one could emerge from the pipe and stand erect on a raised dry island. Everybody could wait on these islands until dark. Jacob and the others thus crowded onto the three islands, pressing against each other until each group formed a solid lump of flesh.

No one dared move for fear of being pushed into the sewage. No one, it seemed, except Eliezer. His comrades watched incredulously as Eliezer, with acrobatic skill, removed his soaking boots, tore up a dry towel, wrapped the strips around his feet, and put on the boots again. Eliezer had been known before the uprising as a meticulous and even elegant dresser, but somehow this performance utterly astonished his companions.

After some time the escapers began to scent the odor of acetone mixed with a strange sweetish smell, and simultaneously they noticed a bank of fog drifting toward them. Someone cried, "Gas!"

As the civilians started to panic, Eliezer shouted, "Back to the bunker!"[3]

When the group had splashed their way back to Leszno 56, they stretched out on the floor, and what they once regarded as a hellish dungeon now seemed like paradise.

At 5 P.M. Regina and another fighter returned from a reconnaissance tour of the sewer with a report on the gas threat.

"At one of the sewer crossings," Regina revealed after catching her breath, "we met two sewer employees. They were going to close a sluice to stop the flow of sewage. Since we knew that by closing it our way would be barred, we told them not to do it. They tried to chase us away and claimed they had to close the sluice. They also had to carry out a disinfection with gas. But we did not let them do it."

Regina paused to catch her breath again, and the fighters eagerly waited for her to continue.

"When we saw that they would not agree to our demand, we had to use force. We drew our pistols and convinced them they should cooperate."

After another pause, Regina added that the Poles had informed them that the disinfectant was damaging to one's health.

"You did the right thing returning to the bunker," she said.

To Jacob and the others, basking in the luxury of dry, flat ground, this remark seemed superfluous. They shuddered at the thought of going through the same ordeal again—standing bent over for hours in sewage water. It was worse than bloody battle. Heniek Kleinweis then went to Eliezer with an idea. Heniek was among the most ingenious fighters. It was he who had engineered his own escape from the Nazis and that of two other fighters by promising to lead the Germans to their bunkers and then firing at the leader.

"I have an idea to make the sewer trip easier," Heniek now told Eliezer. "Each person should be supplied with a board fifty-five centimeters wide to sit on."

When Eliezer looked puzzled, Heniek explained: "Since the sewer pipe is round, we can place across it wooden boards that can serve as seats. Then, when we're not moving, we can sit down."

The fighters rejoiced. Immediately Jacob and three other men accompanied Heniek to the now-destroyed bakery where fresh bread had been baked a few days earlier. They collected the bread shelves, which were just about the right size, and also ripped a couple of barrels apart. When they returned, their arms piled high with boards, Eliezer joked, "What are they for? Are you going to start a fire in the sewer?"

Heniek then distributed a board to each person making the trip, saying, "Remember, you are responsible if you lose it. You won't get another."

Everybody blessed Heniek. Then, at about 9 A.M., the group started crawling once again through the passage leading to the sewer.[4]

The Twelfth Day

Simcha Rathajzer and Zalman Frydrich awoke at dawn with a sense of shock. Instead of finding themselves in a steaming, crowded underground bunker, they were alone in an airy attic. They looked through a shattered window. The sky was blue, not black and red. Were they still dreaming? As Mordechai Anielewicz had ordered, on the previous night they had entered the tunnel at Muranowska 7. After emerging in the cellar of Muranowska 6 on the Aryan side, they climbed to the attic and slept for several hours.

Yes, the sky was blue here; but death had followed them, nevertheless. As they stood by the window, they saw dozens of corpses sprawled on the roof of a lower neighboring building. They ran downstairs to the courtyard, where they saw evidence of a fierce battle. All the windows of the building were broken and the walls were pocked with bullet holes.

A man suddenly came out of an entrance—a Polish streetcar conductor on his way to work. Simcha introduced Zalman and himself as Polish merchants who had entered the ghetto the day before the uprising to smuggle out some old clothes. They had been trapped, Simcha said, and until now they had been unable to escape.

The conductor stared incredulously at the two scrawny, raggedly dressed men, and stretched out his hand.

264

"If that is so," he said, "I want to congratulate you. You can write a book about your experiences."

After vigorous handshakes the conductor described the ZZW stand of April 27 and 28 that Stroop had suspected was a budding Polish rebellion. It had been a bitterly fought battle, he said, in which almost all the Jews were killed. He then escorted the two youths to an underground passage which would lead them to a nearby street. They would thus escape the view of any guards who might be watching Muranowska 6. But no sooner had they set foot in the street when several youths in fancy clothes, obviously blackmailers, started drifting toward them. For although both fighters had Aryan features, their hollow, haunted eyes and tattered clothing betrayed them. Before the blackmailers got too close, however, the two Jews leaped onto a truck that was passing by and jumped off about a block away, unnoticed by the driver.

Then they hurried through side streets until they reached the home of Anna Wacholska, the widow of a Polish Socialist Party leader and the courageous savior of many Jews in the past, who warmly welcomed them. After washing, changing clothes, and eating their first full meal in days, they went to look for Yitzhak Zuckerman to arrange for the rescue of at least some of those still trapped in the ghetto. On arriving at Yitzhak's secret apartment, they found that he was out but were greeted by his pretty sixteen-year-old aide, Frania Beatus, who on the first day of the uprising had told Yitzhak that she was contemplating suicide.

In quiet desperation Frania plied Simcha and Zalman with questions. Was her fiancé still alive? Yes. Her eyes reflected deep, but only momentary, relief. What about the others? Who was dead? How had they died? She wanted a minute-by-minute description of every battle. When she had drained them of information, Frania stared blankly into space, her child's face waxen.

Yitzhak then walked in, and after an emotional reunion, he also demanded to know every last detail of what was happening in the ghetto.

"We must rescue the survivors," Simcha concluded. "The Home Army must help us."

Yitzhak sat back in his chair, his blue eyes filled with anguish, and he said nothing for several moments. Then he pronounced firmly, "We cannot expect any help. We have to rely on our own resources."[1]

* * *

After almost four hours of trudging through the sewer from the bunker at Leszno 56, the Jews of the Productive Ghetto finally reached their destination—the sewer entrance on Ogrodowa Street—for the second time. It was now about 1 A.M. Everyone halted and sat down to rest on his portable bench, not making a sound for fear of being heard on the street above. Eliezer Geller and his deputies discussed what to do next. Two men would climb out and contact the *portier* at Ogrodowa 29, who had always cooperated with the Jews. However, this time he had not been given advance notice of the group's arrival.

Thus, at 2 A.M., David Nowodworski and another fighter mounted an iron ladder, struggled to push aside the manhole cover, and lifted themselves out. They quietly ran the twenty yards to the courtyard gate of Ogrodowa 29 and pressed the bell button. The *portier*, thinking the Germans had come, rushed in his pajamas to open the door and gasped when he saw two figures, soaking wet and covered with filth, facing him with guns drawn.

But when he learned who they were, he agreed to hide them and all the other refugees in an attic room. Within minutes the Jews were helping each other out of the sewer and moving in line to the gate, through the courtyard, and up the staircase leading to the attic, with fighters standing every few yards to guide them in the dark. The wooden stairs creaked, and Jacob wondered how forty people would be able to walk up five flights without being heard by the inhabitants, any one of whom might call the police. But the apartment dwellers slept soundly.

As the survivors breathlessly collapsed on the attic floor, Eliezer told them that two people would have to return to the Productive Ghetto to search for the fighters still remaining there and guide them through the sewer. He chose Hagit Putermilch, Jacob's sister, and another fighter. But when they stood up to leave, Regina Fuden, whose fiancé was still in the ghetto, suddenly intervened, "If anyone returns to the ghetto, it shall be I and nobody else. That is my duty. I began with it and I shall continue. As long as I stay alive, this task is mine."

No, Eliezer argued, she had already taken more than her share of risks. But Regina insisted. She must find the others. She must find her fiancé. Or at least die trying. Finally Eliezer agreed to let

266

her replace Hagit. Two fighters escorted Regina and her companion to the sewer entrance, helped them descend, then put back the manhole cover.

Although Eliezer was caught in the street that day by blackmailers and relieved of all his money and almost all his clothes, he still managed to contact Yitzhak Zuckerman. They arranged for a truck to pick up the fighters the next morning and take them to Lumianki forest, about seven miles from Warsaw, where they would continue the battle as partisans.[2]

While the ZOB group was preparing to leave for Lumianki forest, the ZZW group under Pawel Frenkel had already reached Michalin forest and was battling its way out of German encirclement. These fighters managed to flee back to Warsaw, where that night they entrenched themselves in a bunker at Grzybowska 13. Here they linked up with the ZZW survivors who had escaped from the Productive Ghetto on April 27 and had been unable to reach the forest at all. The two groups then decided to concentrate on evacuating as many Jews as possible from the burning ghetto with Captain Iwanski's help.[3]

In the Productive Ghetto, Regina Fuden and her companion, after trudging back from the Aryan side through the sewer, moved from bunker to bunker, searching for comrades who had remained behind when Eliezer Geller departed with his group of forty. By nightfall the two had found most of them, and Regina was reunited with her fiancé. She gathered the fighters in a shelter at Nowolipie 69 and prepared to lead them before dawn to Leszno 56 for the trek through the sewer, though a curtain of fire now blocked their path.[4]

The Thirteenth Day

It was May Day, and Mordechai Anielewicz was determined to mark the holiday in a special way. After all, he was the leader not only of the ZOB but of the socialist Zionist organization, Hashomer Hatzair. For months he and his fighters had thought of nothing but a battle for death with honor. How distant, even meaningless, had become the battle for life with justice. But then, as they listened to the radio one night, an announcer reminded them that May Day was near. This reminder, coming amid the horror and destruction, at first sounded like a bitter joke. May Day! Suddenly there was elation, nostalgia, visions of a parade, blaring bands, red flags held high.

Mordechai and his fighters remembered. And the memory gave their struggle a deeper dimension. They were fighting not simply to die as human beings but to help others live as human beings. And so they would celebrate this May Day with a burst of defiance against those who would deny man his human identity.

Several groups would leave Mila 18 before dawn, scatter in the ruins, and attack the Germans in broad daylight. Just as they did before the fires forced them to hide underground like insects that only dared to come out at night.

The fighters were delighted. Not only were they eager to celebrate the holiday, but they could hardly wait to see the sun again,

268

even though it shone down on a world of ruins. And to breathe the fresh air and perhaps glimpse a blade of grass on an unscorched patch of earth. No one thought of the risks. To die under a blue sky seemed almost a welcome prospect after the purgatory of Mila 18.

At about midnight a group including Chaim Frimer and Tuvia Borzykowski crept out of Mila 18 and quietly wove their way through the ruins, guided by the pale glow of a half-moon. Two hours later the fighters reached Nalewki 43, a partially destroyed building, and slept for a few hours in one of the flats, undisturbed by the heavy firing from battles already raging. At dawn they rose and squatted by windows, waiting for their turn at the Nazis.

Eight A.M. They heard German voices in the distance. Shortly a civilian entered the courtyard gate, leading several Nazis, and pointed to an entrance. After an exchange of words, the soldiers ordered the man to stand by a wall. A short burst. They no longer needed the informer.

A fighter, the only one with a rifle, exclaimed joyously, "Look, now they are mine!"

He aimed his rifle and fired several times. Three Germans fell. The others fled but returned soon, searching for their tormentors. The fighters now rushed toward another burnt-out building nearby from which they could kill more Nazis. On their way they met a group of Jews scavenging for food in the ruins. Mistaking the ZOB men for Nazis because of their German helmets, the people began running in panic with the fighters on their heels, shouting in Yiddish. One fighter caught a civilian and said, "Look, I'll prove I'm a Jew!" And he pulled down his pants.

Now the people were convinced, and they stopped running. They wept for joy and begged the fighters to save them. The fighters promised to try, then left for battle before they were forced to admit that they had almost no hope of saving even themselves.

After several more firefights, the group returned that evening to Mila 18, exhilarated by its May Day celebration.[1]

Mordechai decided the celebration wasn't over yet. For his next mission he chose his fiancée, Mira Fuchrer. He still would not play favorites. Anyway, with death a certainty for everyone, there was little point in doing so. He wished her good luck in the same comradely manner he reserved for every fighter. And Mira responded with the same sad smile as the others, the same reluctance to exchange looks.

Mira and her comrades soon met their foes, who were waiting for them in the ruins. While the fighters hid in a burning house, the Nazis fired and cursed for about half an hour but were afraid to go deeper into the rubble. Meanwhile, Mira and the others were choking in the smoke as the flames drew closer and chunks of smoldering masonry fell from the ceilings. Mira's dream had been to fall side by side with Mordechai, but now it seemed this would not be.

Suddenly the Germans stopped shooting and withdrew. And Mira and the other fighters were still alive. Later they returned to Mila 18 and excitedly told their battle stories. Mordechai listened with no apparent emotion, even when Mira spoke. But those who were able to look into his evasive eyes knew what was in his heart.[2]

Mordechai's May Day celebration brashly disturbed General Stroop's predawn sleep. Stroop's adjutant kept waking him up with reports. There was heavy shooting in the ghetto. Many SS men and Polish policemen had been killed. Worst of all, the general's troops were growing restive. A rumor was even spreading that although Stroop sent Germans to kill Jews during the day, he was allowing the Jews to reorganize and kill Germans during the night.

Stroop was furious. He would put a stop to this nonsense!

Shortly after dawn he consulted with experts on streetfighting, including a young SS officer from Colonel Oskar Skorzeny's special operations branch who happened to be in Warsaw. This officer, a master of guerrilla tactics, advised Stroop to form special night patrols with his best-trained SS men.

Stroop then telephoned General Krüger, a specialist in streetfighting himself. A good plan, Krüger agreed. Stroop would send into the ghetto five patrols of nine men each and prepare five more for later action. The general called for volunteers, and within a few hours the patrols had been formed and briefed on their duties. That night five of them went to comb the ghetto, including the one that was to ambush Mira Fuchrer's group.

Still, Stroop would long remember this day as deeply disquieting. So sour was his mood that he ordered his men to burn down an industrial plant, equipment and all, because the owner was not evacuating it swiftly enough. And the general warned Fritz Schultz that if he did not meet the deadline for evacuating his headquarters building—10 A.M., May 3—he would be arrested and thrown into prison, though Schultz finally won a four-hour extension.

The trouble was, Stroop felt humiliated. He was even disillusioned. How was it possible that he had been forced to send his best SS men to use refined partisan tactics against a gang of Jews? How were these "subhumans" able to match his own men in skill, tenacity, and fanatical dedication? As he would write in his official report that day, "All the Jews caught today were forcibly pulled out of dugouts. Not a single one gave himself up voluntarily after his dugout had been opened." He added, apparently with both anger and awe, "In one case, the engineers laid a strong concentrated charge and had to proceed to an adjoining entrance where they had something to do. In the meantime, a Jew emerged from the sewer, removed the fuse from the concentrated charge, and appropriated the charge."

One particular incident that day especially disturbed Stroop. He had been in the ghetto, watching prisoners being assembled in a courtyard, when suddenly he heard three dry cracks and saw one of his men collapse. A young Jew had pulled out a pistol and emptied it at the soldier. The other Nazis immediately sprayed the Jew with bullets, and Stroop himself managed to fire his pistol into the prisoner's back before he fell.

The general then strode over to the Jew and stood proudly over him. The man was dying, but Stroop saw vengeance in his eyes. At that moment the victim lifted his head and spat at Stroop. Instantly a guard's submachine gun peppered the defiant Jew. Stroop stared at what resembled a flattened, bloody sack of meat.

He had killed tens of thousands of Jews. But somehow the image of this one haunted him.

Stroop's report that day reflected his mood of dismay and frustration. It was a mood not lost on Josef Goebbels, who recorded in his diary, "Very heavy fighting is going on [in the Warsaw Ghetto]—it has reached the point where the Jewish High Command is issuing daily communiqués. . . . This just shows what you can expect from Jews if they lay hands on weapons."[3]

* * *

Shortly before dawn, Regina Fuden, followed by her group of fighters, darted in one direction, then another, trying to weave a path through the flames that blocked the way from Nowolipie 69 to Leszno 56 and the tunnel of freedom. Leszno 56 was only a few buildings away, but it now seemed as distant and inaccessible as Jupiter.

Suddenly the rattle of automatic guns mingled with the crackle of fire. A German patrol had spotted the group. Regina and the others fought back fiercely in the ruins with pistols and grenades, killing many Germans. But almost all were hit.

The wounded helped to drag each other to the hospital bunker at Leszno 76 nearby, while Hershel Kawa (who had executed the twelve-year-old traitor by pushing him out an attic window) covered their withdrawal. Even after being critically injured, Hershel tossed his last two grenades and fired every bullet he had, enabling many of his comrades to run from the scene. As he lay dying, he removed his gold watch and handed it to another fighter, saying, "I won't need this anymore. Take it and leave. Get the hell out of here and save yourselves."

One of those he helped to save, at least temporarily, was Regina, who had been wounded in the leg but managed to hobble to the hospital bunker.[4]

The Fourteenth Day

May 2

The huge, well-equipped bunker at Franciszkanska 30 was one of only three ZOB bases in the Central Ghetto that had so far escaped the Nazi dragnet. (The others were Mila 18 and Nalewki 37.) But Marek Edelman and his fighters, who had fled here from the burning Brushmakers' District on April 22, expected the enemy to strike at any moment. For the last few days they could hear the loud tramp of German boots overhead. The Nazis obviously knew that a bunker was in this area. But would they find the two skillfully camouflaged entrances in the ruins of the building above it?

Maybe they should leave the bunker and wage an open fight with the Germans. No, Marek told supporters of this plan, they would simply be shot down one by one. Why tempt fate? They would die when their time came. He himself was extraordinarily calm in the face of death. He slept well, even with the sound of enemy footsteps in his ears. Perhaps, he would explain later, because it simply didn't make sense to be nervous. Nothing bigger than death could happen. And death, a constant companion, was no longer frightening because it was so familiar.

Nevertheless Marek sought some security in dispersal, sending a number of fighters to nearby civilian bunkers. He and most of the others, however, remained where they were for lack of room elsewhere.

273

Even after some fighters had gone, the bunker was still bulging with people and was so hot and airless that some died of suffocation and were buried in a dark corner. But on the morning of May 2 the occupants suddenly forgot their misery as they heard once more the sound of boots and guttural conversation.[1]

Overhead several Germans were dragging a mother and her five-year-old child into the courtyard. They beat the woman unmercifully. Where was the bunker? they demanded. But the woman, sobbing, refused to speak. The Germans then turned to the child, gently asking that he persuade his mother to talk. When the child refused, they offered him candy. But he said nothing. Finally one of the Germans began whipping the little boy.

As tears streamed from his eyes and blood stained his frail body, the child crawled under a staircase and pointed to a board that could be lifted from the floor. A German knelt down and removed the board. A Jewish prisoner being held by the Nazis was then forced to shout into the opening in Yiddish, "Comrades, you must come out or die."[2]

Marek Edelman immediately ordered his fighters to leave through the second exit and surprise the Germans from the rear.

"Everyone to the attack!" he cried.

Abrasha Blum, the overage but inspirational Bund political leader, who was physically feeble and did not even have a gun, asked if the order was intended for him, too. In the confusion of the moment, Marek replied, "Yes!"

Abrasha rushed to the exit. He would attack with his bare hands.

Marek and his deputy, Hanoch Gutman, decided on a trick. Dvora Baron would play the major role. Dvora had seen much action since that day (April 20) in the Brushmakers' District when, while waiting for the Germans to attack, she had gazed nostalgically at the flowers in Krasinski Park on the Aryan side.

It was her dream of a new, peaceful world ablaze with flowers that had helped her to survive. But even so powerful an incentive might not serve her on the "Trojan horse" mission she was to undertake now. She would lead the way out of the second exit on the

274

assumption that the Germans might be less inclined to shoot down a girl, especially one with such a demure face. She would pretend that she was surrendering, then throw a grenade in their midst to give her comrades time to climb out and take positions in the courtyard.

Even before she could act, the Germans, seeing no Jews emerge from the first opening, tossed grenades and gas bombs into it. Dvora then lifted herself through the second exit into the ruins of the courtyard. Some Germans nearby immediately spotted her but remained immobile for a moment, perhaps struck by her beauty and daring. Dvora suddenly hurled a grenade, then threw herself behind some debris. Amid the smoke and confusion the other fighters fired at the Germans while scrambling out of the bunker one by one. The first three out, led by forty-three-year-old Abraham Diamant, who had fought so heroically with his ancient rifle in the Brushmakers' District, covered for the rest, dropping German after German with well-aimed bullets.

When most of the fighters had left the bunker, which was now on fire, Abraham was hit. Clutching his chest, he tried to hand his rifle to a comrade, but in an instant he toppled into the bunker to be consumed by the flames.

Bitter fighting then raged in the ruins for hours, with both sides suffering heavy casualties. Finally the Jews were forced to run from the courtyard to the upper floors of a skeletal building, from which they showered missiles upon the enemy. One fighter, Abraham Eiger, was firing a pistol from the second floor when he was severely wounded, but he kept shooting until he ran out of bullets. The Germans below, sensing this, called to him to come down and surrender, promising to spare his life. But Eiger, leaning out the window, shouted in reply, "Murderers! We are being killed by your criminal hands, but you will die like dogs when the world metes out justice!"

The Germans, in their shock and confusion, did not fire at Eiger, even when he continued to condemn Hitler's crimes and spoke about the senselessness of the fight and about the eternal life of the Jewish people. His words echoed powerfully over the smoldering ruins. Finally he was shot dead. Several Germans immediately rushed upstairs and, as if possessed, thrust their bayonets into him, stab after stab. No Jewish bullet could have struck home as effectively as Eiger's bitter, defiant prophecy.

The battle ended when the Germans withdrew at dusk. Marek Edelman then sent a messenger to Mila 18 for help, and Mordechai Anielewicz dispatched Chaim Frimer and several other fighters to the battle zone. They carried the wounded to Nalewki 37, where Zachariah Artstein's group was now based. Hanoch Gutman was one of the injured. He was brought in with his girl friend, Fayche Rabow, who refused to leave his side.

The dead numbered many, including Dr. Tulo Nussenblatt, the Zionist scholar who earlier in the uprising had taken refuge with his family at Franciszkanska 30. He died still clutching his precious briefcase filled with material on Herzl. Another victim was Abraham Gepner, who had headed the Judenrat supply department. The Germans dragged him out of the bunker and executed him on Zamenhof Street.

Some of the fighters were sent to other shelters that night, but Marek and most of his comrades returned to the bunker at Franciszkanska 30 after putting out the fire there. They knew the Germans would attack again in the morning, but they were seized by a supreme fatalism. Anyway, there was nowhere else to go.[3]

Why was it taking so long to destroy the Warsaw Ghetto? General Krüger pondered this question as he journeyed from Cracow to Warsaw. Now he would see for himself—before the delay discredited him in Berlin.

And General Stroop was determined to put on a good show for his boss. He would prove two things to him: that he was crushing the Jews with the greatest speed and mercilessness, and that they were resisting ferociously. Then Krüger—and Himmler—would realize why the uprising was still raging on. The show would start at 10 A.M. A special detachment of SS men would burn down a block of buildings grouped around the Transavia and Wischniewski munitions factories on Stawki Street.

Shortly after Krüger arrived, the two generals drove to the scene. Stroop glanced at Krüger's insignia—three oak leaves and a star on his velvet epaulettes—and regarded his superior with awe. No, Krüger was not afraid to enter the ghetto in the uniform of an SS Obergruppenführer. Little wonder that he was one of the leaders of the National Socialist Party and held such high SS rank. He was a courageous, farsighted man, a true racial expert who had been working with Hitler, Himmler, Göring, and Goebbels from the days of Munich. Stroop could understand why he was always prodding him to kill more Jews, always giving advice, instructions, orders.

On reaching the ghetto, the two generals and their entourage stepped out of their cars and started walking toward the Transavia factory when suddenly they were caught in a heavy burst of gunfire. ZZW fighters had been patiently waiting to welcome Germans since the fighters seized the plant on April 28, after fleeing from Muranowski Square. But they could never have guessed they would be greeting so distinguished a group. Though the Jews hit several Nazis, Stroop apparently was not overly concerned. He had proved one point: that the Jewish fighters could not be easily subdued. Now he would prove his other: that he was dealing with them in the most bestial way.

He ordered his men to set fire to a long row of houses on the street where the factory workers lived. Then he began walking with Krüger and his staff officers along the avenue, enjoying the spectacular view, when a soldier ran up to him. The Jews in one four-story building, the soldier breathlessly reported, were trying to escape the flames by climbing onto the roof through trapdoors and skylights.

The whole party hurried to the building and craned their necks to watch the Jews desperately trying to save themselves from the fire, which was quickly rising toward them. Some had already climbed to the roof. Others, including children barely three years old, crawled along the ledges. Stroop ordered his men to shoot at them, and in a few moments his targets were plunging toward the asphalt below, forming contorted silhouettes against the shimmering wall of fire.

Some of the wounded fell on the protruding spikes of balcony railings on lower floors and hung impaled in midair over a flaming abyss. No merciful bullet should be fired, Stroop ordered. Let them suffer before they died. But volley after volley was loosed at those still trying to escape. Some leaped to their deaths, others preferred to retreat into the engulfing flames.

General Krüger enjoyed the show immensely. He was so impressed with one sharpshooter who scored with every bullet that he later recommended him for a decoration. When the party returned to Stroop's residence, Krüger told his host, flashing a smile, that he was doing a good job under difficult conditions.

"I understand that in this situation, new to us," he said, "it is difficult to achieve lightning successes." And he added, as he was about to depart, "Carry on. It would be good if you could officially terminate the *Grossaktion* on May fifteenth. The end must be accompanied by fireworks. The last tune, of a political propaganda character, will be the blowing up of the Central Warsaw Synagogue. Your chief of staff, Jesuiter, has received the technical plan for drilling holes in the synagogue walls where explosives can be placed. The plan has been worked out by the best army engineer on my Cracow staff."

Krüger also ordered Stroop to photograph everything. "This will be valuable material," he said, "for history, the Führer, Heinrich Himmler, for future historians of the Third Reich, for National Socialist poets and writers, for SS training and schooling purposes, and most important of all, for documentation of our efforts to de-Judenize Europe and the entire world."

Stroop was delighted with Krüger's visit. It had raised the morale of his staff and soldiers, placed him personally in an excellent light, and produced additional troops for his ghetto campaign. Stroop now dreamed of winning a medal for his good work. Such an award would certainly increase his chances of getting that estate in the Ukraine he wanted so badly.[4]

The Fifteenth Day

May 3

In the charred bunker at Franciszkanska 30, Marek Edelman and his fighters listened once more to the sound of stamping boots overhead. The Germans, as they had feared, had returned on this morning to finish the massacre they had started the day before. The fighters now expected to die, but only after taking a terrible toll of the enemy. However, before they could climb out of the bunker to fight, gas bombs exploded, spreading their lethal fumes.

Some of the fighters managed to crawl out an exit, firing as they emerged. A group leader, forty-year-old Berek Snaidmil, one of the oldest ZOB members, was suddenly struck in the stomach by a grenade blast. His comrades tried to carry him with them, but Berek, realizing he was doomed, drew his pistol and waved it at them.

"Don't forget to take this," he shouted. "Keep fighting!"

Then, before anybody could stop him, he thrust the pistol barrel into his mouth and pulled the trigger.

Meanwhile, Hirsh Shaanan, who at seventeen was one of the youngest fighters, shot an SS officer and two soldiers as he plunged ahead through the ruins with other Jews trying to reach safety in some other bunker. When the uprising had begun, his parents had pleaded with him to hide rather than fight. But he had replied, "I don't want to creep into a hiding place like a mouse. I want to fight for the honor of the Jewish people."

Shaanan's father, Lent, was himself an underground activist and had fought the Germans during the invasion of 1939. He understood his son's decision and wished him luck. Now Shaanan's luck ran out as a German bullet mortally wounded him. Like Berek Snaidmil, he refused to be a burden on his comrades, who wanted to carry him, and he handed over his pistol to one of them. Would his friend please shoot him and end his misery? He did.

Among the other fighters killed in the running battle was Dvora Baron, who died while the first spring flowers were beginning to poke through the scorched ruins.

About fifty survivors, including Marek Edelman, made it to a shelter some scouts had found a short distance away—at Franciszkanska 22. It was a five-room bunker built by the ghetto garbage collectors and was in so filthy a state that the fighters wondered if the owners had not used this place to dump their refuse. Smugglers also took refuge here, and not without reason. A passage from this bunker led to the sewer system, and before the uprising, the smugglers had brought their goods from the Aryan side through it.

This channel, Marek Edelman felt, could now be useful to the few fighters still alive. Perhaps even crucial to their survival.[1]

In Cracow, Goebbels' propaganda officer reported to Berlin on this day that "among Poles the opinion being heard is, the fighting in the ghetto has lasted longer than the Polish campaign." But in Warsaw, General Stroop was in a good mood nonetheless. Not only had he made it clear to his superior why the fighting was lasting so long, but he had learned from a Jewish traitor the approximate whereabouts of the "party bunker." This term was used by the Nazis to serve their propaganda line that the ZOB command was made up of Moscow-directed Communists. Stroop would now concentrate on rooting out Jews from this area until he found the leaders.

The fiercely fought two-day battle at Franciszkanska 30 convinced him that he had already reached the hard core of Jewish resistance. He explained later, in his daily report, that some "Jews and bandits fired two pistols at a time," like in a circus. Even the captured ones were defiant, and some women, he found, hid pistols in their "bloomers." While standing in line at Umschlagplatz or while being interrogated, they would suddenly whip out their weapons and fire.

He would take care of that. He ordered that all captured Jews be forced to undress completely and that their clothes be thoroughly examined before being returned to them for the march to Umschlagplatz. Stroop personally went to scrutinize a column of naked Jews—men, women, and children—lined up against the ghetto wall. His eyes focused in particular on one young woman as she stood under the warm spring sun. What a beautiful suntan, he would later recall thinking, feeling rather guilty that he could harbor such a thought about Jewish skin.[2]

On the Aryan side, ZOB representatives cabled an urgent new plea for aid to Artur Zygielbojm and Isaac Schwarzbart, the Jewish delegates to the Polish government-in-exile in London. After detailing the horrors in the ghetto, the message stated, "And the world of freedom and justice is silent. Amazing!"

This cable, transmitted through the government delegate in Warsaw, mysteriously reached its destination only on May 11—eight days after being sent.[3]

The Sixteenth Day

May 4

At about 11 A.M. General Stroop sent his main forces to comb out and destroy the factories of Walther Caspar Többens, Fritz Schultz, and other industrialists. When these buildings had been cordoned off, the Nazis shouted for all Jews to come out—those who had helped evacuate equipment and those who were just hiding. But only a few obeyed.

"Not until the blocks of buildings were well aflame and were about to collapse," Stroop later recorded, "did a further considerable number of Jews emerge, forced to do so by the flames and the smoke. Time and again the Jews tried to escape, even through burning buildings."

Többens and Schultz were enraged. Consumed in the fire with the Jews were many valuable goods, including used furniture, which the thoughtless Stroop had not given them time to remove.[1]

As Captain Iwanski lay in bed, still weak and exhausted, he pondered the new desperate appeals from the ghetto. The battle of Muranowski Square on April 27 had taken a heavy personal toll. He had been badly wounded, and his sixteen-year-old son Roman and his brother Edward had fallen. Yet he knew he could not stop fighting. He was the only human pipeline to the ghetto. He must provide arms and ammunition to the few ZZW fighters still left there and save as many civilians as possible.

His mind made up, Iwanski got out of bed, and with his deputy, Lieutenant Zajdler, he went to Grzybowska 13, where Pawel Frenkel had set up a base after leading a group of his fighters out of the ghetto on April 29. The three men devised a daring plan to save what could be saved in the ghetto. Two missions would go back there—one on May 5, the other on the following day.

Zajdler would lead the first group through the tunnel winding to the Church of the Virgin Mary, where many civilians and wounded fighters were huddled, waiting to be guided to safe hideouts on the Aryan side. The next day Iwanski would trek through the sewers with another group, carrying arms and ammunition for the ZZW fighters still holding out in the ghetto, and he would also return with refugees. The captain could no longer use the passage from Muranowska 6 to Muranowska 7 since the Germans had found it and were guarding it closely. Both groups would take food with them and equipment to drain water out of the main water pipes in the ghetto, since the Germans had cut off all water outlets there.

Among the men with Iwanski would be his elder son, Zbigniew, eighteen, and his surviving brother, Waclaw, who had barely recovered from the wounds he had received in the April 27 battle. Iwanski was reluctant to take them along after losing his other son and brother, but they insisted on going to avenge the deaths of their kinsmen. Iwanski and his wife understood, and with heavy hearts they agreed. A man had to follow his conscience—at all costs.[2]

The Seventeenth Day

May 5

Lieutenant Zajdler's group reached the Church of the Virgin Mary in the evening and found about a hundred women, children, and wounded men waiting to be taken to the Aryan side. Shortly they were all on their way through the tunnel, which opened to the Jewish cemetery. As they began climbing out, they suddenly found themselves the targets of Germans hiding behind Jewish tombstones.

Some fell dead, among them four Polish girls who had been waiting to guide the group out of the tunnel, and many others were wounded. But Zajdler, though struck by a bullet, managed to flee with most of the others to the adjoining Catholic cemetery, where they hid in tombs like mortal ghosts until some hours later they were able to emerge and escape to apartments prepared for them in advance.[1]

After seventeen days of fighting, the Jews hiding in radio-equipped bunkers finally heard Prime Minister Sikorski tell the world that they were bravely defending the ghetto. The extermination of the Polish Jews, said Sikorski, was the greatest crime in the history of mankind, and the Poles should give them any help possible. But why hadn't Sikorski delivered the speech sooner? the Jews wondered. Because, his supporters would explain later, he was too busy with other urgent matters.[2]*

General Stroop was exhilarated when his chief of staff, Max Jesuiter, burst into his office toward midnight and blurted with undisguised enthusiasm the number of Jews seized or killed since the *Grossaktion* began on April 19. But Jesuiter's informal, unmilitary manner disturbed him. Stroop would have to show him his place.

"Go out and come back in again in the manner prescribed by regulations!" he ordered.

Jesuiter, his smile vanishing, sheepishly stalked out, then knocked gently on the door.

"Come in," Stroop said.

Jesuiter marched back in, halted some distance from the general's huge neat desk, clicked his heels, and smartly saluted. He then requested to be allowed to report on an important matter. On Stroop's order Jesuiter advanced toward the desk and handed the general a folder with statistical data. Stroop quickly glanced through it, then looked up and said, "Good, Jesuiter! Forty-five thousand. A nice old Germanic number. Five times nine plus three zeros. The Reichsführer will be pleased."

Stroop invited Jesuiter to sit down in an armchair by the desk and offered him a cigar. Then he put on his monocle and analyzed the figures more carefully. Yes, on this day, May 5, the number of Jews caught or known to have been killed in the ghetto since the *Grossaktion* started was just over forty-five thousand. This figure, of course, did not include those who lay dead in the ruins, who were trapped in the burning buildings, or who perished in the bunkers, which the Germans seldom risked entering.

*Isaac Schwarzbart, the Jewish colleague of Artur Zygielbojm in the Polish government-in-exile, wrote in a pamphlet entitled *The Story of the Warsaw Ghetto Uprising* that "even some of the Polish Government in London officials expressed indignation at the postponement of the appeal from month to month. The reason was obvious. The Polish Prime Minister was apparently afraid to issue a special appeal in time, lest it be met by the predominantly anti-Semitic Polish population with hostile feelings against the Prime Minister and his Government in London."

Forty-five thousand! And it was May 5! A lot of fives. And five was Stroop's lucky number. This was indeed his day. Even the Poles, it seemed, were now on his side. That morning the organ of the right-wing National Democratic Party, *Wielka Polska* (Greater Poland), had stated that "the Jews' struggle has nothing to do with Poland, with Poland's problems."[3]

The Eighteenth Day

May 6

As the first rays of the sun pierced the morning darkness, Captain Iwanski and twenty-eight others, including his remaining son, Zbigniew, and brother Waclaw, descended into the sewer near Iwanski's apartment and struggled through the muck laden with equipment for the ZZW fighters still in the ghetto. Four hours later they arrived at a manhole on Nowolipie Street, where they wearily began climbing to the surface, helped by ZZW men who had been waiting for them.

One after the other, Iwanski's partisans emerged into the carbonized wasteland and immediately took firing positions to protect their comrades as they came out. Suddenly dogs started howling nearby. They had scented the group. Within minutes, before all the Poles had emerged, Germans began shooting from the rubble. The Poles and Jews leaped behind ruins and fired back, with some covering for others who jumped into the sewer again. After about half an hour the battle ended. Many Germans had fallen, but five Poles and Jews had also been killed.

The dead were lowered into the sewer with sacks pulled down over their torsos so that they could more easily be dragged through the slime. Iwanski, who had not climbed out and so did not see the battle, began leading the group on the treacherous route back to the Aryan side.

287

Early that evening, they finally reached the sewer-opening they had entered at dawn and crawled out, their mission a tragic failure. Once in the courtyard of Iwanski's apartment building, the men carrying the corpses gently laid them down. Iwanski's wife, Wiktoria, greeted them with alarm. "What happened?" she cried.

Iwanski told her.

"But who is in the sacks?"

Her husband didn't know.

With a knife, Wiktoria cut open one of the sacks, which was leathery with filth from the sewer. By the glare of a flashlight she stared at the face of the corpse.

"Zbigniew!" she cried. And she fainted.

Iwanski was stunned. He could not speak. His second son. . . .

Then the other sacks were opened, and Iwanski faced the starlit sky and wept. His second brother, too.[1]

General Stroop didn't know what to think when a report of the fighting at the sewer exit on Nowolipie Street reached him. Normally Jews tried to sneak *out of* the ghetto, but now Jews were trying to sneak *in*. Were they carrying out rescue operations? he wondered. If so, they must be getting help from the Poles. He was again haunted by the fear that the Polish underground was getting ready to strike in force and drag all of Warsaw into the uprising.

Stroop telephoned General Krüger in Cracow and expressed his concern. Strengthen the security cordon around the ghetto, Krüger ordered, and move it deeper into the Aryan part of Warsaw.

Stroop obeyed. But he doubted that this measure would work. The Jews—and their Polish friends, he guessed—were trying to help the Jewish leaders still trapped in their bunkers to escape. He must find these leaders. Ludwig Hahn, the Gestapo chief, had the right idea. He was using the services of a captured Jew who had been persuaded to help him. This man had already given away the whereabouts of one command bunker (apparently Franciszkanska 30). Now Stroop assigned a special reinforced unit to accompany Hahn's Gestapo men, who with the help of the traitor were exploring the Central Ghetto for the "party bunker."

The traitor, Stroop was to relate later, was permitted to stuff himself in the German field kitchen until he almost burst. He was plied with schnapps and given a safe-conduct for travel in occupied Poland. The Jew's "sly eyes" shone with satisfaction, the Gestapo men reported. But somehow he could not pinpoint the bunker. He searched in zigzags, trying, he claimed, to remember where it was.

Finally he pointed out one bunker, and the Nazis immediately attacked it. After short-lived resistance by the occupants, the SS found in it only three corpses, one grenade, and one pistol. In anger, the officer commanding Stroop's special unit fired a bullet into the traitor's head.

When Hahn learned about this, he was furious. This Jew obviously knew a lot. He could have been helpful. It was better to have stupid or inefficient Jewish traitors than none at all. But Stroop was not impressed. He had long thought that Hahn's agents were providing him with only the most superficial information, mostly where to find hidden dollars and jewelry. If not, why had it been so difficult since the beginning of the uprising to find bunkers, each of them built with the knowledge of dozens, perhaps hundreds, of people? Once, while sipping cognac with Hahn, Stroop had openly expressed this opinion, and Hahn had replied, "General, what can you do if you cannot find a decent man to inform? You take the first rascal you come across."

This particular Jew might actually have known where the Jewish commanders were. Wasn't this the only thing that counted? Stroop had to admit that it was. He was happy that the Jew, before being killed, had at least led his men to the general area where the "party bunker" might be found. That night he wrote in his report, "We are on the track of the bandits. It is to be hoped that tomorrow we shall succeed in tracing down this so-called 'party directorate.'"[2]

The
Nineteenth Day

May 7

Shmuel Asher, the thief-king of Mila 18, paced sullenly among the prostrate forms carpeting the corridors of the bunker, cursing violently. As conditions worsened, his good humor dissolved— like much of the fat that had bloated his belly. The supplies were gone, and even his most skillful thieves were finding it almost impossible to find food in the abandoned and gassed-out bunkers. The people lay on the floor, almost too weak to move, their pale, thin faces showing signs of emotion only when a child cried for food. They were filled with fear lest the child betray them all.

The fighters, like the civilians, lay stretched out in their underwear on their mats of rags, sweating in the intense heat and nearly suffocating from the lack of air in their smelly, overcrowded rooms. Not only had the food almost run out; so had the ammunition with which to carry on the battle. And to top off their troubles, they suspected that the Germans had found their bunker, though perhaps not yet the entrances to it.

The day before, they had heard the sound of German footsteps and voices just above them—apparently those of the SS unit that had been led to the area by the well-fed Jewish traitor. And on this afternoon they had heard again the tramp of German boots. Only this time, heavy tools banged on the ruins above until pieces of plaster began falling from the ceiling. The occupants held their breaths, some whispering prayers. The Germans finally went away, but the end was clearly in sight, and the fighters and refugees could envisage the bunker turning into a huge mass grave.

In one room Mordechai Anielewicz broke the heavy silence, calling to a girl who sat nearby, "Sing us a song. We should finish life with a song."

The girl began singing a rhythmic Zionist tune. The fighters listened appreciatively, even the anti-Zionist Communists and Bundists. They felt an inner calm despite their misery and imminent danger. Had they not done everything within their means? And had they not been lucky so far? They had expected to die on the first day of battle, but here they were, nineteen days after the uprising started, still alive. They fed briefly on memories of their recent heroic triumphs, talking quietly among themselves.

One recalled how he had struck a German with a Molotov cocktail and turned him into a human torch, screaming and burning. Another described the explosion of a primitive bomb, the exhilarating sight of German arms and legs flying in all directions, of the survivors fleeing in howling panic.

"The horrible memory of this carnage," Zivia Lubetkin would recall later, "inspired us with a certain strange joy, a fulfillment."

Then the conversation turned to escape. Since they could no longer die fighting in the ghetto, having almost nothing left to fight with, they could serve no purpose by staying. Why die uselessly? And with the Germans closing in, they would surely meet such an end if they did not act swiftly. What had happened to Simcha Rathajser and Zalman Frydrich? They had left for the Aryan side to seek help on April 29, more than a week earlier, and had not been heard from since. Could they still be alive? Anyway, scouts had learned that the Nazis were now closely guarding the ZZW tunnel at Muranowska 7, which the two had used to leave the ghetto.

Zivia sat up and began reading aloud a letter written to her in Hebrew by her husband, Yitzhak Zuckerman, early in the uprising. It described his efforts to obtain help for the ghetto, efforts which had not yet borne fruit. Zivia had read it many times before, but somehow she and the others found new hope in each rereading.

When someone remarked on the quality of Yitzhak's Hebrew,

an argument broke out on the relative merits of Yiddish and Hebrew. Since the Communists favored Yiddish and the Zionists Hebrew, the argument soon developed into a shouting match over ideological differences: Communism versus Zionism. Forgetting momentarily their confrontation with starvation and death, they raised their voices in a violent storm of feeling.

Suddenly Shmuel Asher waddled into the room and exclaimed, "You can bring complete destruction down on the bunker!"

The fighters grew silent, returning to the ugly reality they had been trying to escape in a few moments of meaningless ideological passion. Asher then smiled and said, "You'll soon have an opportunity to continue the argument—in the next world."

The fighters laughed and resumed discussing their next step. They and other partisans in the ghetto should leave their bunkers in daylight, attack the guards at the wall, and flee to the forest, Berl Broide suggested. Berl's tough oblong face and bushy-browed grimace reflected his belief in miracles, which had been reinforced when, after being captured by the Germans a few months earlier, he managed to jump from a boxcar taking him to Treblinka. Most might be killed in the attempt, he argued, but maybe a few would survive to fight elsewhere. Here in the ghetto, everybody would die.

Someone replied, "Well, let's assume that we overpowered the Nazi guards. How would we get through the streets of Warsaw to the forest?"

It seemed clear to most of the fighters that a mass breakout could succeed only if the Polish Home Army lent full support, and such support was regarded as only a remote possibility. The ZOB had no Captain Iwanski to help them. In fact, they didn't even know he existed.

Arie Wilner, who had moved here from Franciszkanska 30 shortly before that bunker was attacked, was among the skeptical. The only thing to do, he advised, was to send as many groups of fighters as possible through the sewers. Even if only two out of ten got through, it was better than remaining here, helplessly dying of hunger and suffocation.

Tuvia Borzykowski agreed. And the best way to get to the Aryan side was from the garbagemen's bunker at Franciszkanska 22, where Marek Edelman and the other survivors of Franciszkanska 30 were now hiding. A passage from the bunker, he pointed out, led to the sewer system. And he added, "There is a man in that bunker who knows the way."

Mordechai was gnawed by doubt about all the suggestions. Yet he weighed each one carefully. He realized it was easy to rip them all apart in the light of logic. But what was more logical? Death without battle? Still the main question remained unanswered: How were the fighters to move through the streets of Warsaw? He didn't know, but he finally approved the ideas of Arie and Tuvia.

If they failed, he would have no choice but to assemble in one place all the fighters he could locate and have them storm the wall in a mass breakout attempt, as Berle Broide recommended. They would be forced to do this even without outside help.

That night two groups would try to escape through the sewers, each taking a different route. Perhaps one of them would get through. A group of ten, including Central Ghetto commander Israel Kanal, Tuvia Borzykowski, and Mordechai Growas, would enter a sewer from a bunker at Mila 69 on the corner of Smocza Street. Then several Aryan-looking fighters in this group would go on to the other side while the rest waited for them to return with a message from Yitzhak Zuckerman, which they would immediately relay to Mordechai Anielewicz.

Another group of eleven would leave the ghetto through the bunker at Franciszkanska 22. Chaim Frimer would lead them through the jungle of ruins separating the two bunkers, since he was most familiar with the route. Zivia Lubetkin would go along to arrange with the garbagemen and the sewer guide for the evacuation of the ghetto fighters and as many civilians as possible. Then Chaim would escort her back to Mila 18 to report the situation to Mordechai while the others in their group were tramping through the sewer.

Hela Schipper was asked by Mordechai to go to the Aryan side with this group, but she refused. No, she cried, she would stay and die with her husband, Lutek Rotblatt, and his mother, Maria. But Lutek, hoping that she might be saved, insisted that she go.

"There is a task to fulfill," he said, "and you look like a Pole. You must go."

When Hela finally agreed, Mordechai turned to Mira Fuchrer.

"And you must go, too."

But Mira also refused, and Mordechai could not persuade her. She would remain with him and share his fate.

The designated fighters then prepared to leave, each packing a bundle of clean clothes and submitting to a haircut by a barber so that hopefully, when they got to the Aryan side, they would be taken for typical Poles.

At about 9 P.M. Hela kissed Maria good-bye.

"Don't worry," Hela said. "I'm leaving, but I'll be back. I've always come back. And next time I'll take you with me."

"No," replied Maria. "I'm too old to go. But maybe you young people . . ."

Hela stared at Maria. Too old? Yes, she had gray hair and lines in her face. But she was little more than fifty and still beautiful. A final embrace, and Lutek took Hela by the arm. He was to remain, but he would accompany the group for a few blocks so that he could be with Hela as long as possible.

Mordechai Anielewicz stood by the exit, shaking hands with members of the two groups who were leaving, exchanging smiles and even jokes.

"See you soon."

But nobody really believed it.[1]

In single file the fighters slithered like snakes through the narrow opening of the bunker, bruising their flesh on the sharp stones. When they emerged, they felt somehow disillusioned. So great had been their yearning to see daylight after weeks of night that they actually expected to see the sun shining, though dusk had fallen hours earlier. Even so, they closed their eyes in ecstasy and breathed in the fresh air through open mouths.

Led by Chaim Frimer, the fighters going to Franciszkanska 22 walked silently, with rags wrapped around their feet to muffle their steps, stopping abruptly whenever the crunching of something underfoot sounded too loud. A house nearby still burned, eerily illuminating the night. A window swung in the wind; an iron gate squeaked.

After they had advanced several hundred yards, Lutek halted, embraced Hela, and bid her and the others good-bye. As he walked back, Hela's eyes followed until his figure vanished in the grotesque shadows cast by the moonlit ruins.

The fighters cautiously moved past heaps of rubble and skeletons of burnt-out houses until, on crossing one courtyard, they found the gateway blocked by a great pyramid of iron cots. Chaim began to climb the rusty barrier when a cot fell on him and badly injured his leg. As he fell under a tangle of beds, the others started laughing at this scene of a fallen hero, helmet still on head and pistol in hand. But Zivia rushed to him, helped to pull him out, and treated his wound.

The group then marched on, with Chaim swearing to himself as he limped along, his pride wounded as severely as his leg. Here and there the fighters met Jews wandering in the wasteland who asked, *"Vos tut men?"* ("What is there to do?")

Some described with awe how, earlier that day, a nearby bunker had been discovered and the Jews had defended themselves with arms until the last minute. Zivia sensed a spark of envy in their voices. To them the fighters were happy, invincible, certain to be saved.

After uttering some words of solace, the fighters started on their way again when Chaim suddenly recognized one of the Jews, a young girl who had stayed with his father and his sister, Krysia, in their home.

"Hala!" he cried.

The girl stared at him, finally recognizing him, too. She began to smile, then burst into tears.

"What's the matter?" Chaim said gently. "Aren't you glad to see me?"

When the girl hesitated, he suspected that there was something she did not want to tell him. Finally she spoke, almost incoherently. Fire had forced her and Krysia to leave their bunker. They climbed into a sewer with many other people and made their way to an exit. But when some of them tried to get out, the Germans attacked. Everybody tried to race back through the sewer at once, and in the ensuing panic Krysia stumbled and was trampled to death in the sewage by the others.

Chaim listened to the story with dampened eyes, recalling how his little sister had begged him to let her join the ZOB, how he had refused because of the danger. She had been so proud of him when he had described to her his own heroic adventures. Now Krysia, forbidden to fight back, was dead. And he was alive. . . .

The fighters continued on, stopping off at Nalewki 37 to see Zachariah Artstein's group. Chaim had to lead them to the bunker by way of a circuitous route around the building to avoid having to step over the dozens of Jewish corpses sprawled in the courtyard. After a happy reunion, Zivia and Zachariah briefly reminisced about the magnificent victory they had shared at Nalewki 33 in the first battle of the uprising. As Zivia started to leave, she assured her comrade that she would send a messenger for his group when the time for a mass exodus came.

Once more the Mila 18 group headed toward Franciszkanska 22, finally arriving near midnight to be welcomed warmly by Marek Edelman and his fighters. Zivia and Marek immediately began negotiating with the garbagemen and the guide familiar with the sewer system. The guide agreed to take the fighters through the sewer that night and then return. But Zivia had to promise that when he led the next group of fighters to the Aryan side, he could remain there.

Around midnight Hela and the other ten departing fighters made final preparations. Each was given a cube of sugar and a piece of dry bread. Who knew when and where they would find food in the alien world they would enter? The guide instructed them on how to move in the sewer and how to leave it when they reached the exit, which was right in the middle of Bielanska Street. Except for the guide and two other men who would return to the ghetto, all would hide in some ruins from the 1939 bombardment. Then, when the way was clear, Hela and another fighter would rush to Yitzhak Zuckerman, who would arrange to rescue the others. Zivia repeated Yitzhak's address and telephone number again and again, until Hela and her comrade had them permanently stamped in their memories.

A second group of fighters would follow the next night, arriving at the same manhole at 9 P.M. They would wait there until they heard three consecutive knocks on the cover. That was the signal: The first group was safe, and the second could emerge.

"The heart had much to say to those who were to leave," Zivia would reminisce later. "That they be fortunate, that they reach the beloved land; but words were few. Mutterings of good-bye and handshakes. One after another, the fighters and the guide jumped from the bunker to the floor of the deep canal. A splash of water was heard at each jump. We crowded tensely around the gaping hole. Those who went had candles to light the dark sewer; they disappeared. We listened with great emotion to the gradually fading sound of their steps."[2]

* * *

Israel Kanal and his group of fighters, who had left Mila 18 at about the same time as Hela's group, gingerly threaded their way through the rubble toward Mila 69 at the corner of Smocza Street. From there they would enter a passage leading to the sewer system and then continue on to the Aryan side. However, as they neared Smocza, a hail of bullets suddenly whizzed by. The Germans had heard their footsteps but were firing from a safe distance. Israel, Tuvia Borzykowski, Mordechai Growas, and the others halted and began retreating on their bellies. When the shooting stopped, they stood up and started ambling back to Mila 18.

But nagged by their failure, especially when the lives of all might depend on them, they decided to try a different route, via Gensia Street. True, they would have to sneak past German forces concentrated on Zamenhof Street, but since it would be necessary to cross that street anyway if they were to return to their bunker, they had little to lose.

When the fighters reached the corner of Zamenhof and Wolynska, they silently waited while Mordechai Growas reconnoitered the area, purposely making noise, whistling, throwing stones. If the Germans were around, it was best to draw their fire now. But when nothing happened, Growas signaled the others to follow him.

The group moved ahead in single file, each holding on to the shoulders of the man in front of him to avoid getting lost in the dark. Suddenly, as the fighters were crossing Zamenhof, the Germans, hiding in the ruins, began firing volley after volley in a deadly crossfire.

The Jews, throwing grenades while they scattered, tried to run across the street to hide in other ruins there. But the Germans blocked their way with a wall of bullets. The fighters were trapped. Seven raced through the barrage and miraculously made it to the other side of the street, though four arrived with severe wounds. Their three comrades picked them up and carried them through the ruins toward Mila 18. The three who did not cross—Israel, Tuvia, and Mordechai Growas—started crawling toward Wolynska Street under a storm of fire.

They had no more grenades, no more bullets. Only the blackness of night could save them. They scratched their way forward over hunks of masonry, charred lumber, and dead bodies, their fingers slipping occasionally on partly dried blood.[3]

As Mordechai Anielewicz was seeing off his two groups of fighters bound for the Aryan side, another ZOB team descended into the slimy deep on that side, bound for the ghetto. If things went well, a Jewish fighter and two Polish sewer employees would soon be sitting with Mordechai in Mila 18, planning the big escape. They were being sent by Simcha Rathajser, who with Zygmunt Frydrich had left the ghetto on April 29. It had taken about a week to prepare a rescue expedition.

During this time Yitzhak Zuckerman had finally met with Colonel Chrusciel, the Home Army commander in Warsaw. Earlier in the uprising Chrusciel had refused to see him, enigmatically sending word that this was a time for action, not for talk. But now they were facing each other in an apartment on Slizka Street.

The Home Army could not supply arms to the fighters, the Polish commander said sternly, apparently under pressure from his superiors.

Well, then, what about helping the Jews to get out of the ghetto, as the Home Army had offered to do when the uprising began?

How could the Home Army help?

First of all, by providing a map of the Warsaw sewer system.

The Home Army didn't have such a map. *

What about sewer employees who could lead the way?

The Home Army didn't know any.

Transport from the sewers once the Jews reached the Aryan side?

The Home Army didn't have sufficient trucks.

Then, hiding places for the Jews who came out?

The Home Army didn't know of any. . . .

Yitzhak departed from the meeting feeling sick.

There was only one thing to do. In the apartment used by Feigele Peltel, Simcha and Zygmunt set up their own headquarters

---

*Yitzhak Zuckerman says he learned later that the Home Army did indeed have a map of the sewer system. But it regarded this map as a military secret and apparently felt that the Jews could not be entrusted with it—should any of them happen to survive.

for seeking help. And while Zygmunt went off to see his wife in a hideout on the Aryan side (his six-year-old daughter was in a monastery), Simcha sought contacts with people who *could* help.

Among these people were Polish Socialists and members of the communist PPR. One of the most helpful was a PPR partisan, Constantin Gajek, known as Krzaczek. He was a tall dark-haired youth who posed as a typical Polish dandy, complete with fancy jacket and hat tilted at a rakish angle over his narrow face.

Constantin introduced Simcha to the "king of the blackmailers," whose team of scoundrels ruthlessly fleeced Jews of their possessions. The self-styled king was impressed by their "credentials," which showed them to be members of the Home Army. Not only did the two offer to pay him a tidy sum for his assistance, but they would put in a good word for him after the war if others accused him of treason.

Some Home Army partisans had been trapped in the ghetto, they told him, and a party would be sent in to rescue them. Since the "king" lived in an apartment only about twenty yards from a sewer entrance, could they use it to hide the men when they came out? Of course, said the blackmailer, smiling broadly. As long as no Jews were among them, of course.

However, every effort to organize a rescue trip failed. Once, Simcha barely missed being captured when he returned to the tunnel-opening at Muranowska 6, from which he and Zygmunt had emerged. Another time a smuggler who was to help backed out at the last minute.

But after about a week the two sewer workers were found, and they agreed to go with a fighter to the ghetto. Simcha, Yitzhak, and their comrades now anxiously awaited their return. Would they bring back Mordechai and his fighters? Zivia? Yitzhak would not allow himself to imagine that he might soon be reunited with his wife.

Late that night the team returned. Alone. The Germans were guarding all the sewer exits in the ghetto. The ZOB fighters on the Aryan side were crestfallen. But Simcha, for one, was not discouraged. The next night, May 8, he would try again, and this time he would personally accompany the sewer men.

But even as Simcha prepared a new plan, General Stroop was writing in his daily report, "The location of the dugout used by the so-called 'party directorate' is now known. It is to be forced open tomorrow."[4]

The
Twentieth Day

May 8

All through the deadly night, Israel Kanal, Tuvia Borzykowski,
and Mordechai Growas crawled through the ruins, seeking a safe
refuge. The three fighters, having escaped a German ambush
while en route to the sewer entry on Smocza Street, could barely
raise their heads; for the Germans, though unable to see them in
the dark, relentlessly showered their path with bullets and grenade shrapnel.

When day broke and the Germans were changing guard, the
fugitives managed to rise and stumble ahead in a last feverish
effort to seek a hiding place before being exposed to enemy eyes.
Finally they discovered under one ruin an open cellar already destroyed by the Nazis.

Crawling in and striking a match, they shuddered as they saw
three corpses staring at them. Simultaneously, the stench of rot-
ting flesh assailed their nostrils and feathers clung to their faces. A
succession of flickering matches revealed ripped, bloody bedding,
and kitchenware, clothing, books, and a prayer shawl strewn
about: everything but the food and water they craved. They collapsed on the torn mattresses and wondered how they would ever
rise again. Never had a bed felt so blissfully comfortable.

As Tuvia started to relax, he thought of Mila 18 and felt bitter
pangs of guilt and frustration. His group had been sent on a mis-

300

sion to rescue their comrades—perhaps it was already too late—and here he was lying on a featherbed, helpless to influence fate. He sought relief in fantasy. There were his parents, his relatives, his old comrades who had long since gone to the Land of Israel. Only seconds earlier they had been so far away, in place and in spirit, but now they stood before him in vivid focus, each with his own features, expression, smile.

All at once shots pierced the air outside, and the images dissolved in the dark reality of the cellar. Tuvia now drifted into a new reverie. He saw himself and his two companions lying as dead as the corpses sprawled a few feet away. This time a rustling sound returned him to reality. Someone lit a match, illuminating a horrifying scene. Rats were swarming over the bodies, tearing off pieces of flesh. More and more kept coming out of the holes, gray and yellow, the size of cats.

The fighters beat the ground with sticks; but the rats, with nary a squeal, continued gorging themselves, though some occasionally glanced at the live humans while chewing away on the dead ones. As if to say, in affirmation of Tuvia's vision, Soon it will be your turn.[1]

At about 5 A.M., after a treacherous four-hour march through the sewers, Hela Schipper and her ten companions finally arrived at the opening on Bielanska Street. They would now climb out and hide in nearby ruins while Hela and one comrade would go to Yitzhak Zuckerman's headquarters for help.

The fighters carefully lifted the manhole, and one of them got out. Hela, who was second in line, suddenly heard voices speaking in Polish. The first fighter's pistol holster then dropped into the sewer—a signal that he had been captured. The Polish police!

"They've caught him," Hela told the others. "I'm going up. Maybe I can bribe them. After a few minutes, you follow. But remember, don't give up your weapons."

Hela climbed to the street and began pleading with several Polish policemen, promising to pay them well if they let the Jews escape.

"All right," one said, pointing to a building close by. "We'll let you go. But you must go into that house."

Fearing a trap, Hela refused, and the haggling went on while the others emerged from the sewer, leaving behind the three men who were to return to the ghetto. Suddenly a German soldier approached and started shooting. The Jews fired back and scampered in all directions. Hela ran to some ruins with the fighter who was to accompany her to Yitzhak's headquarters, and the two hid behind a charred pillar.

After about half an hour a German started exploring the ruins and, sighting his quarry, fired his pistol. Hela and her companion started running in opposite directions. Two Polish civilians caught Hela, but she struggled free and escaped into a courtyard, where she hid in some shrubbery, put on the dress she had carried with her, and combed her hair so that she would not be recognizable as a fugitive from the ghetto.

With outward calm she emerged into the street, now filled with morning crowds, and walked to a streetcar stop. As she waited for the car to come, a woman asked her why she looked so deathly pale.

"I just saw a German shoot somebody," Hela replied, "and I'm frightened."

"Yes, I know," said the woman. "I saw it, too."

Hela entered a streetcar, and some time later she found Yitzhak Zuckerman. She urgently explained her mission to him.

What happened to the others who had come with her? Hela didn't know. She would learn later that she was the sole survivor.

"Our people must be helped to get to the forest," Hela said with fierce determination.

Yitzhak nodded. That night, he replied, Simcha Rathajser would leave for the ghetto with two sewer guides to lead the fighters out. Trucks would then take them to the forest.

A terrifying thought gripped Hela: If the Germans knew where the ZOB headquarters bunker was, as its occupants had suspected, her husband, Lutek, and all the others might already be dead.[2]

The guide and two fighters who had remained in the sewer after Hela and the others had climbed out hurried back to the ghetto, and on reaching the bunker at Franciszkanska 22 they breathlessly recounted their story to Zivia Lubetkin and Marek Edelman. When the fighters had emerged, shooting could be

302

heard. Did the fighters escape? The three men couldn't tell. But they *had* heard shots.

Zivia, distraught, wanted to run back to Mila 18 to inform Mordechai Anielewicz that Hela's mission had apparently failed. Perhaps he would want to send out another one immediately. Or perhaps abandon Mila 18 without further delay, before it was too late. But Chaim Frimer, who was responsible for guiding her, protested that dawn was breaking.

"Moving in daylight would be certain death," he said.

"This is not the time to be afraid," Zivia replied.

But when Marek also insisted that she should wait until nightfall, she agonizingly agreed. Overwhelmed by fatigue, she lay down to sleep, only to be aroused some time later by a guard's cry: "They are coming!"

The civilians scrambled to the opening of the sewer, shrieking with terror and panic. Zivia bitterly reproached herself. She should have gone to Mila 18. At least she could die there with her beloved comrades.[3]

It began again at 8 A.M. The same dreaded noise that Mordechai Anielewicz and the other occupants of Mila 18 had heard the day before. The Germans were pounding and drilling into the earth overhead. Mordechai immediately proclaimed an emergency, and fighters scattered to guard the five entrances to the bunker. Mira Fuchrer checked to see that everybody was at his station. Meanwhile the civilians began to panic, and even Shmuel Asher was unable to calm them, though he warned again that the slightest sound could bring death to all. Then, after about two hours, the noise from outside ceased.

The Jews suddenly grew quiet, with everybody straining to hear what was happening overhead. Had the Germans gone? Were they ready to pounce? The answer soon came with a familiar cry in Yiddish. A treacherous Jew called for their surrender. They would all be sent to work; but if they resisted, they would die. Gunfire at one of the entrances was the fighters' reply. The Germans then fired and dropped grenades through the entrance. After the explosions, silence again. A German began to crawl through the smoking tunnel, slowly feeling his way. More shots, and the German collapsed dead. No one else entered.

The Germans then began drilling again through the earthen roof of the bunker. The civilians were now weeping, screaming, praying. Many wanted to leave, but Shmuel Asher and others urged them to wait. Maybe a miracle would happen.

Mordechai, however, didn't expect any miracles. He would not leave alive. Neither would the other fighters. They would stay and fight to the last breath. Isn't that what the uprising was all about? Who among them had expected to live even this long?

A new appeal in Yiddish for surrender. More gunfire in reply. Then, not a sound. Suddenly, a strange odor. Gas! The Germans were funneling gas through a hole they had drilled in the roof of the bunker.

Now even Shmuel Asher decided it was better to surrender than to suffocate to death. As a professional gambler, he played the odds. If he gave up, he would stand at least a one-percent chance of surviving. If he stayed, he would stand no chance at all. So he and about a hundred other civilians—more than half—started crawling through the exit passages, coughing and gasping.

Mordechai understood. But he and his fighters would remain. When he had gathered with his fighters to discuss their options, Arie Wilner, indomitable though crippled, insisted, "We cannot be captured alive!"

Arie thus set the tone for the grim meeting, as he had in September 1942, at the height of the first deportations. At that time a small group of Jews had urgently met, armed only with stones and dreams of the Land of Israel, to seek ways of saving what could be saved. Arie had risen slowly, as if emerging from a trance, straightened his frail body, and said in a quiet voice, "We should do well to hold out . . . but not for our future's sake, nor in hope of a new life. Others who will come after us will probably build the future and a new kind of life. We are no longer a creative vanguard. Our creation now must be the destruction and the end of the enemy—it must be revenge. . . . We must therefore disappear underground, we must hide well, we must prepare, we must train. . . . For the present it is our fate to live. Our purpose demands that we live. . . . Our fate is quite clear."

Now, once more, their fate was clear. And it was no longer to live. They had fulfilled their purpose. They had fought back and humiliated the enemy. They had redeemed the honor of their people. This was their revenge. And so it was time to die.

"Let us all commit suicide," Arie said in the same calm voice that had called his people to arms a few months earlier.

The PPR fighters, led by Michal Rozenfeld, protested. Why should they kill themselves as long as they were able to fight and kill Germans? It was better to be killed while killing.

But the Germans were covering all the entrances, Arie and others replied. There was no way to get out and attack them from the rear. As each fighter emerged he could easily be captured, even if he crawled out firing. And who had enough bullets, except for oneself? No more Germans would enter the bunker to fight it out. They had only to wait for the gas to take effect. So the only real options remaining were to die by gas or die by one's own hand.

Mordechai questioned the proposals of both Arie and the PPR. He opposed leaving the bunker for fear of capture, but he also thought the call to suicide was premature. Perhaps there was a way to conquer the gas. There was no point in killing themselves as long as they stood even one chance in a thousand of surviving. Was it not their duty, after all, to spill as much German blood as possible? If any of them could stay alive to shed a single drop more, this possibility should not be foreclosed by suicide.

He had heard that water could neutralize the effects of gas, Mordechai told his comrades. He proposed that everyone dip a piece of cloth in the puddles that had formed on the floor by the tap and cover his face with it. Nothing, he argued, could be lost by trying this method. It was just conceivable that some might live to carry on the sacred battle.

Although Mira agreed, few other fighters saw merit in this argument, however much they respected Mordechai's views. They were convinced that water could not possibly save them. And they had to decide quickly, as they were growing sicker by the second from the gas, which the Germans were pumping in a little at a time, apparently to prolong the agony of the trapped Jews.

As at Masada, where 2000 years earlier a group of Jews decided to kill themselves rather than surrender to the Romans, most of the 120 fighters at Mila 18 chose the same solution, though it was not imposed on anyone. The more than eighty civilians who remained would either surrender or die of asphyxiation in the bunker.

Lutek Rotblatt left the room where the fighters were gathered and staggered, coughing and choking, to his mother, Maria. He gently seated Maria on a chair and asked her for the cyanide pills she always carried with her. When she produced them, he smiled and kissed her. . . .

The children. Eighty beautiful children. "Let us hope we will live to see the liberation together with the children," he had told his friend Jonas Turkow before the uprising. The children had long since gone, but now their loving protectors would rejoin them. . . .

Slowly Lutek directed Maria's hand to her mouth. Without resisting she swallowed the pills.

After several moments she began convulsing with pain but remained alive. She begged Lutek to shoot her. He hesitated. Then he aimed his pistol at her head and fired. Maria toppled to the ground in a pool of blood but continued to breathe. Lutek fired again. Then twice more. Finally Maria lay dead. And before the sound of the last shot had dissipated, Lutek blew his own brains out.

The sharp cracks of other pistols ripped through the poisoned air as fighter after fighter committed suicide. One girl fired at herself seven times before dying. Another girl didn't have the nerve but pleaded with her best friend, Rivka Pasmanik, to shoot her. Rivka was a tall brunette with dark expressive eyes that did not hint at the iron in her character. She slew her friend, then herself.

Berl Broide wanted to shoot himself but was unable to because he had been wounded in his right hand. He also appealed to a friend, who obliged him.

Arie Wilner dragged himself along on his crippled feet, searching for Tosia Altman, but she was guarding one of the entrances and could not be found. He would not even get to kiss her goodbye. The gas fumes were growing stronger. He, too, shot himself.

And by the water tap, side by side, lay Mordechai and Mira, their faces covered with rags and cradled in shallow puddles. Whether in the end they shot themselves, no one will ever know.

At about noon, some two hours after the Nazis had arrived and only minutes after the final shots had echoed through this massive tomb, someone stumbled along the corridor, crying that he had found a way out. He had discovered an exit that the occupants of Mila 18 had not known existed. But except for a few half-suffocated fighters, the message came too late.[4]

* * *

Israel Kanal, Tuvia Borzykowski, and Mordechai Growas had been hiding for seventeen hours in the rat-infested, half-destroyed bunker they found while fleeing from the Germans. Shortly after dark they stuck their heads out into the black, drizzly night, opening their mouths to catch some precious drops on their parched tongues. Then they climbed out and started back toward Mila 18.

As they neared their destination, they saw what looked like a candle standing on the ground. They drew closer and found that the "candle" was a tiny fire and that a pot was hanging over it. They began looking among the ruins for the person who was cooking, but no one was around. In one shattered room they almost stumbled over a pail full of water. Joyously they fell to their knees and dipped their heads in, one after another, quenching their thirst for the first time in weeks.

But after they had drained the pail, they felt a foul taste in their mouths. They walked back to the fire and told a man who was now tending it about the water, and he exclaimed, "That was not drinking water! That was slops."

They had been so thirsty that they were unable to tell the difference. Though almost overcome with nausea, they moved on and finally arrived at Mila 18. But the bunker did not look the same. The piles of bricks and stones had been rearranged, and the secret paths they knew had vanished. In shock they searched around the ruins and suddenly came upon fourteen people lying together like a jumble of corpses.[5]

At about this time three other figures were approaching Mila 18: Zivia Lubetkin, Chaim Frimer, and Marek Edelman. Although it had appeared that morning that the Germans were about to attack their bunker at Franciszkanska 22, they had mysteriously gone away. Then, after dark, the three fighters left for Mila 18 to report to Mordechai Anielewicz on the apparent fate of Hela Schipper's group. No one knew for certain what had happened to Hela, but Zivia wondered how she would have the heart to tell Lutek that shots had been heard when his wife and the others had emerged from the sewer.

As the three neared Mila 18, their mood lightened. After all, they would be seeing their dear comrades again. They even made plans to play a joke on them while entering. Suddenly they wondered if they had lost their way. Something had changed. Where was the entrance they usually used? And the guard who was always there? Terror seized them. Perhaps the fighters had covered the entrance with stones in order to conceal it.

They checked the other entrances. These, too, had disappeared without a trace, and their guards were also gone. They gave the password. No answer. Then they discerned shadows in a nearby courtyard. Probably some comrades who were about to leave on patrol. They approached the shadows with a sense of relief, recognizing three who were standing: Israel Kanal, Tuvia Borzykowski, and Mordechai Growas. But they froze with horror as they saw a group of people in tattered clothes lying on the ground, their distorted, mud-splattered faces resembling nothing human. One person was unconscious. Another—Dolcia, Maria's adopted orphan daughter—could hardly breathe. Yehuda Wengrower made a gurgling sound, as if choking. Tosia Altman lay moaning with grenade wounds. And others, including Michal Rozenfeld, were in equally critical condition.

Fourteen pitiful figures who had managed to escape through the exit that had been found too late for the others.

The two groups of fighters who had just arrived on the scene stood silently, their hearts torn, unable to comprehend fully what had happened, even as the survivors gasped out fragments of the nightmare. Then they scurried around the entrances to the bunker, clawing at the piles of rocks. Perhaps they could get to the bodies and retrieve the arms. But it was hopeless. The Germans had dynamited everything.

Marek Edelman shook his head, more in dismay than in grief. He had learned to accept death calmly, with complete resignation. Even the deaths of those he loved or deeply respected. With millions of his people dying, this was, after all, the pragmatic attitude. But he hated to see people die before they had to, even minutes before, especially for some uselessly symbolic reason. No symbol was worth a moment of human life.

He would never have committed suicide. He would have tried to leave the bunker, firing as he came out. Let the Germans kill him. Why should he do their job for them? They wouldn't try to capture a man with a blazing gun. The survivors had recounted how one girl had fired at herself seven times before dying. She had wasted six bullets!

Nor could Zivia, the idealist, the dreamer, find solace yet in the immortality of the dead. She would later lament:

> Our lips muttered words of farewell for our loyal and courageous comrades, the glory of our unhappy heroism. Our hopes and dreams were buried here, all that was most precious to us. We walk away stripped, devoid of our dreams, our faith . . . a caravan of bodies moving like spiritless shadows, like ghosts, silent, mourning. . . . Everything was buried here."[6]

After about an hour the "caravan of ghosts" were tied to each other with ropes to prevent the dazed, gassed survivors from falling in the crater-pocked ruins. They staggered into the bunker at Nalewki 37 on the way to Franciszkanska 22. Zachariah Artstein, whose unit was still based there, listened to the gruesome tale. From now on, Zivia told him, ZOB headquarters would be at Franciszkanska 22, with Marek Edelman and herself sharing the top command. The hot-tempered Zachariah flared up: "Then what are we waiting for? Let's all go out and engage the Germans on the open streets in daylight. Let's fire at them and fall ourselves, and that will be the end!"

Zivia calmed him. Why die unnecessarily? Her motley party would continue on to Franciszkanska 22, where she and Marek would try to arrange for all the fighters and as many civilians as possible to escape through the sewers to the Aryan side. They would then continue the battle in the forest. As soon as everything was set, she promised, Zachariah would be notified; and he would lead all those in his bunker, including the walking wounded, to Franciszkanska 22 for the hazardous journey. They would probably leave that night.

When Zachariah seemed skeptical, Zivia reassured him: His fighters would not be left behind.

Zivia's group then continued on to Franciszkanska 22. "There was dumb silence. We all crouched motionless on the ground. Our wills were paralyzed, our hands like stones. We didn't think to bandage wounds, didn't bother to touch the soup that we were served. Darkness prevailed within and without."

But then back to the business of surviving. The fighters were sure the Germans knew about this bunker. In the morning they would certainly come back, as they had at Mila 18. But how would the Jews escape? Through the sewers? Not likely now. A group that followed in the path of Hela and her companions had just returned with bad news. As planned, they had waited under the manhole at Bielanska Street for a signal that the initial group was safe. But the only signal came from the Germans: gunfire.

Nevertheless, another group had to leave for the Aryan side immediately to prepare for a mass exodus. But the fighters were reluctant. They wanted only to sleep, whatever happened. Let all of them die here together. The thought seemed strangely appealing, even to Zivia. But she was their leader. Eight people, she ordered, would leave *now*, guided by two of the men from Hela's group who had returned the day before. Those with Aryan appearances would climb out to the street and seek help from her husband, Yitzhak Zuckerman. Zivia would later say, "At the farewell, numb hearts thawed and tears began to flow, although one was ashamed to cry. Everyone thought: 'What testament will I leave for my family, the world, the future generations, to friends in that distant land?' One after another they mumbled: 'Tell about our fight.' 'Tell about our loneliness.' 'Tell of our stand.' 'Tell!' "

At about midnight, Tuvia Borzykowski, Mordechai Growas, Abrasha Blum, and five other fighters vanished into the bowels of the earth.[7]

A little earlier, at 10:30 P.M., Simcha Rathajzer, a second fighter, and the two Polish sewer employees who had failed to find an unguarded sewer exit in the ghetto the previous night had also descended into the sewer on the Aryan side. Simcha was determined to rescue Mordechai Anielewicz and the other trapped fighters that night.

After trudging through the slime for less than a hundred yards, the guides abruptly stopped and, clearly afraid, announced that they would go no farther. Simcha saw that they had been drinking heavily.

"You must follow my orders!" he angrily replied. "Keep moving!"

The guides stumbled ahead, but every few yards they would

halt and demand vodka and food, which the two fighters carried in their knapsacks. Simcha argued that this was no time to eat and drink. When the Poles persisted in their demands, Simcha finally drew his pistol and ordered them to advance.[8]

That night General Stroop exulted. The battle for Mila 18 had been hard and prolonged, he would later admit. The Jews defended themselves savagely, and his own men were "not too sure of themselves in this direct struggle." But he proudly stated in his daily report:

> We succeeded in forcing open the dugout of the party directorate and in catching about 60 heavily armed bandits. . . . Dispositions speak of 3,000 to 4,000 Jews who still remain in underground holes, sewers, and dugouts. The undersigned is resolved not to terminate the large-scale operation until the last Jew has been destroyed.[9]

The Twenty-first Day

May 9

Persuaded by the pistol in Simcha Rathajzer's hand, the two Polish sewer guides finally led Simcha and the other fighter to a manhole in the ghetto at the corner of Zamenhof and Stawki streets. It was about 2 A.M. Simcha lifted the cover and climbed out, ordering the others to wait for him. With Zamenhof illuminated by a German searchlight, he crept all the way to Muranowska Street, then stealthily moved through the ruins toward the bunker at Franciszkanska 30. He had taken leave of his comrades there on April 29, a few days before that shelter was discovered and destroyed by the Germans.

As he entered the courtyard, he was shocked to find only a heap of debris where the bunker had been. He then saw three shriveled, phantomlike figures lying in the ruins, and they told him of the battle for the bunker. The survivors, they said, had fled to Franciszkanska 22.

Simcha then rushed to this new hideout, but never having been there, he could not find the entrance. He signaled with his flashlight and called out a password. No reply. Then a feeble woman's voice, like the whisper of a ghost, droned from the ruins, "I am here. I will lead you to the bunker. Look for me in the ruins. I have a broken leg and cannot move."

Simcha desperately began searching in the debris, wondering if he had not been hearing things, if he was not going mad. He turned over stones, looked under pieces of masonry, inspected every crack and hole. After about half an hour he gave up. He then ran all the way to Mila 18, stumbling, falling, running again. That bunker, too, had disappeared. He looked around. Nothing but ashes, ruins, corpses, utter desolation.

Simcha suddenly grew calm. Strangely he felt he belonged here in the ghetto amid the dead and the destroyed. Each corpse was a dear comrade, each ruin a living remnant of the heroism of the Jewish soul. Here he would take vengeance and die. Here, too, he would live forever. Then he thought of those waiting for him. He returned to the sewer opening at about 4 A.M., entered it, and pulled the cover over him.

"Let's go," he ordered his comrade and the sewer employees. "Nobody is there."

Although he could not have known, Simcha had arrived just one day too late to save Mordechai Anielewicz and the others in Mila 18.[1]

Since about midnight, Tuvia Borzykowski and his group had been slushing through the sewers, fighting the waves of filthy water that sometimes threatened to drown them, tripping over corpses, feeling as if the slime sticking to their bodies had become part of them. Whatever strength they still had was spent just keeping from being carried away by the foul tide. But they must go on. Zivia and their other comrades were depending on them.

Although the guide supposedly knew the way, he now appeared confused, and at forks in the path he seemed to choose a route mainly by instinct. Tuvia realized that the group was lost. To die in this stinking hell. . . .

Suddenly a bright light in the distance jolted the group. Tuvia could think of only one explanation: The Germans were patrolling the sewers. He had heard that they were doing this. The fighters started to retreat. But retreat to where? To a bunker doomed to destruction? Death lurked everywhere. They halted and decided to await their fate.

The light grew more intense and was soon blinding. Who was carrying the lamp? Somehow it didn't seem to matter. Tuvia and his fellows were completely resigned to death. Then a great echo bounced off the walls of the narrow passage. A single word: "Jan."

Before the echo faded away, someone cried, "That's the password!"

At that moment the beam of light lowered into the canal and there, facing Tuvia and his group, stood Simcha Rathajzer and three other men. The long-separated comrades fell into each other's arms, laughing, sobbing like children, babbling unintelligibly. Simcha offered Tuvia and the others hard candy and lemons, and they started to devour the lemons, their first fresh food in months, without even bothering to peel them.

For a moment, as the fighters stood steeped in sewage, embracing each other, they forgot their suffering, hunger, and exhaustion. They felt they were dreaming. Finally, after the first surge of excitement, Simcha told his comrades of the effort that had been made to save the surviving ghetto fighters. He was now on his way back to the Aryan side, he explained, after failing to find anyone in the ghetto.

Simcha then outlined his rescue plan. Buses would meet the escaping fighters as they emerged from the sewer and take them to safe places. Too good to be true, thought Tuvia and the others. They sensed that Simcha was overly optimistic.

Two men, Simcha suggested, should return to Franciszkanska 22 immediately and lead the remaining fighters through the sewer. The others would continue on to the manhole on Prosta Street, where they would wait for their comrades and then emerge with them to the street.

How much longer to the Prosta Street exit? About two hours. Tuvia chilled. Walking for two more hours in sewage water up to the waist! But now, at least, there was hope. Perhaps in a few days he would have the opportunity to kill more Germans—in the cool green forest, which, after the burning ghetto, he visualized as paradise.[2]

Franciszkanska 22 now resembled a hospital ward. Zivia Lubetkin and other fighters started treating the survivors from Mila 18, washing their wounds with alcohol they found. Zivia then tried to fall asleep, but in spite of her weariness she remained awake, feeling pangs of guilt for having stayed alive while her comrades lay buried under the ruins of Mila 18. Blind fate had saved her and condemned the others to death. Finally she lapsed into a fitful, nightmarish doze.

But she soon awoke with a start, sensing that someone was standing over her. Opening her eyes, she saw two youths. After a blurry moment, she recognized them. But they had left on the trip through the sewer! Zivia was confused. What were they doing here? Was this part of the nightmare? Then her mind grew clearer. Disaster had probably befallen all the others, and these were the only two survivors.

But they were smiling!

The two men excitedly told Zivia of the meeting with Simcha Rathajzer in the sewer. All the fighters and the civilians in the bunker who were capable of making the trip must leave through the sewer without delay, they said. Zivia would later recall:

> This turn of events was stupefying. One could hardly grasp the meaning of this news. The joy at leaving the ghetto didn't penetrate, the horrifying experiences of the day had not yet faded. One was struck by the cruelty of fate; only yesterday the ax had fallen on 100 heroic fighters who could have left with us today. We sat dumb, wordless, frozen to the spot.

But the two messengers persisted. She and the others must leave immediately!

"They won't wait," one said. "And if they go, we are lost."

But they *must* wait! Someone had to tell Zachariah Artstein, as Zivia had promised a few hours earlier on the way from Mila 18. They couldn't leave him and his fighters, or any others, behind.

Didn't she know it was dawn, the messengers exclaimed. If someone tried to reach them in daylight, he would betray both them and the people in Franciszkanska 22. Other fighters gathered around. Go without their comrades? No!

"But it's only logical."

"We will not move from here. If even a single person remains in the ghetto, all of us will remain with him."

The fighters lay motionless on the ground, and many even removed and tossed aside their ammunition pouches.

But it was only logical. . . .[3]

* * *

315

With heavy hearts more than fifty fighters and civilians lowered themselves into the stinking canal.

"Leave me here. I can't go. I won't hold out."

Tosia Altman refused to climb down. She was still suffering from the effects of gas, from the thought of Arie Wilner and the others who died. Why had she not committed suicide, too? She would remain here in the ghetto with them.

But one of the group leaders, Hersh Berlinski, sharply scolded her, then gently helped her into the channel. Were not too many already staying behind? Tosia somehow trudged ahead through the murky water, hunched over with lighted candle in hand, like the others. Then two of her fellow survivors from Mila 18, Yehuda Wengrower and Michal Rozenfeld, also poisoned by gas and weakened, began to sit down every few minutes in sewage up to their necks, holding up the long single file. They, too, begged their comrades to leave them behind so they could die without hindering the chances of the others.

Once more, Hersh shouted orders: "Your words are useless. As long as your hearts are beating, you must continue on! Don't appeal to our consciences. Nothing will help you. We have no other alternative. We cannot carry you because the sewers are too narrow for that. To leave you here means death. Forward, comrades! With your last bit of strength, forward!"

Then Hersh gave each of them several cubes of sugar to give them the strength, and they struggled on. Only Dolcia, Maria's adopted daughter, could not. She fell dead in the sewage, apparently from the gas she had inhaled in Mila 18.

Zivia, at the rear, sought strength in her thoughts as her feet moved automatically in the dark shaft. She heard the echoes of a remote dream. . . . She was on her way to the Land of Israel. Soon she would be meeting her old friends on a kibbutz. But what would she tell them? How would she be able to look them in the eye, to explain to them why she had not remained in the valley of death, why *she* had survived? She hadn't asked to survive, had she? Was it her fault that God had singled her out? As she advanced, the comrades she had left in the ghetto seemed to walk beside her. Zachariah . . . what will happen to you, to the others who are awaiting our call? . . .

The long, snaking file of weary survivors plodded through the narrow passage, which grew smaller the farther they got from the

316

Vistula River, into which the sewer emptied its foul contents. Finally they had to move almost doubled over while holding on to the hips of the person in front for support. Progress further slowed when Yehuda Wengrower began to faint every few yards, holding up the whole line. He could only be revived with a shower of sewer water. But at least the survivors were sure of the way. Some members of Simcha Rathajzer's advance party had chalked arrows on the sewer walls, while others dropped scribbled notes through the manholes above, indicating the right direction.

At midmorning the group reached the manhole opening to Prosta Street, and they joined with Tuvia Borzykowski and other members of the advance party. Simcha had left to arrange for trucks to come and take all of them to the forest. Now they would simply have to wait, crouched over in the sewer, until he returned.

As they counted the passing minutes, the Jews, pressing against each other for support, listened to the sounds of normal daily life sifting in from above. Automobiles honking, the gay voices of children at play. Occasionally a pedestrian would step on the perforated manhole cover and cut off the ribbons of light penetrating the sewer. The sun was shining. The crowds were out. Another world. How could more than fifty Jews, looking more like animals than humans, climb out in their midst and escape in trucks? This question gnawed at everyone. Had they come this far to die in the sunshine, surrounded by children who could still play games and people who could still enjoy a morning stroll?

At about noon a guard standing on the street pushed a note through one of the tiny openings in the manhole cover: The trucks would not be able to come until nightfall!

The Jews trapped in the sewer were thunderstruck. They would have to spend at least eight more hours knee-deep in sewage, cold, bent over, without food or water. And the survivors of Mila 18 were already half-dead. Yet some of the others—especially Zivia, who was ridden with guilt feelings—absorbed the news with relief. Now they could try to save Zachariah Artstein and the other fighters they had left behind in the ghetto. Two men, Shlomo Shuster and Yurek Blones, were sent back on this daring rescue mission.

The rest waited with agonizing resignation for a double miracle: the arrival of the fighters from the ghetto, and the escape of all to the forest. None of them would leave for the forest until their comrades joined them.[4]

When he had emerged from the sewer earlier that morning, Simcha Rathajzer had rushed to the flat of the "king of the blackmailers," where he was to meet two comrades, wash, and change into clean clothes, as planned the previous night. But as he entered the apartment, his body encrusted with filth, the underworld leader and some cronies greeted him suspiciously.

"We have reached the conclusion," said the so-called king, "that you are a Jew."

Simcha froze. Now they might try to blackmail *him*; worse, to foil the mass-escape plan. He decided to act with exaggerated self-assurance.

"I could not care less what you have concluded," he replied. "Please give me a soap and towel so that I can wash up. When I return in the evening, we'll have ample time to discuss whether I am a Jew or not."

The blackmailers were impressed. One of them brought him the soap and towel. While he washed, Simcha discussed arrangements for the sewer escape with the comrades who had been waiting for him: Constantin Gajek, the PPR partisan, and Tadek Szejngut, a ZOB fighter.

Tadek, like Constantin, was one of the most colorful and valuable partisans in Warsaw. Before the uprising he had specialized in smuggling arms into the ghetto and assassinating traitors, and now he helped Jews escape to the Aryan side. A born actor with the tough, blond countenance of a Polish worker, he had learned to imitate the speech mannerisms common to lower-class Warsaw down to the last anti-Semitic curse word. And he was almost never seen without the dusty boots usually worn by Polish smugglers. Thus he consorted easily with smugglers, blackmailers, and Gestapo agents; and the latter, though trained to spot a Jew in any disguise, never imagined that Tadek was one. Nor did Tadek completely suppress his affected personality in the company of his comrades, whom he would entertain with hypnotic, often exaggerated tales of his hairbreadth escapes and heroic adventures.

Tadek and Constantin told Simcha that they had already sent word to the fighters that trucks would come for them after nightfall. But now they felt it was not feasible to send the vehicles until dawn, when the German-imposed curfew would end.

At about 5 P.M., when the street crowds had thinned out with the approach of the curfew, Simcha and Tadek would rush to the sewer opening and deliver a note to the fighters, letting them know of the delay.[5]

Throughout the day the fighters in the sewer wallowed in the muck, chilled to the bone, weak from hunger, parched from thirst. How could the people on the street above laugh, discuss trivialities, play ball, when others were dying a terrible death right under their feet? Yet oddly, the Jews, too, could laugh, even in their suffering.

After listening to the bitter complaints of a civilian, one of the fighters shouted, "Shut up or I'll kill you!"

"That's fine," the civilian replied. "Kill me and put me out of my misery."

"I'd be delighted to fulfill your wish. But you'll have to pay me a hundred zlotys for the bullet."

"I'm rather hard up at the moment. How about fifty zlotys?"

The bargaining went on and on, and everybody laughed, except those who were barely able to remain conscious or were going mad from thirst. Yehuda Wengrower, his thirst enhanced by the effects of poison gas, finally scooped up sewage water and drank it.

Zivia and Marek decided it was too dangerous for all the Jews to be bunched together by the manhole. A single grenade could finish almost everybody. And besides, there was space for only a few people to stand in the raised dry area directly under the manhole. The fighters were thus ordered to scatter to nearby manholes so that everybody could be both safer and more comfortable. After dark, when both the trucks and the fighters still in the ghetto would presumably arrive, someone would be sent to collect all of them.

More than fifteen fighters waded through the slime toward other manholes. But when night fell, neither the trucks nor the fighters in the ghetto arrived. Had the whole complex rescue operation failed? Despair grew from moment to moment, when suddenly footsteps approached. Then a note was dropped from

319

above. All neighboring streets, it said, were full of policemen. They could not come out until morning.

A death sentence, some thought. How could they hold out? They pushed a note through the manhole cover. Please rescue us, they begged. They would come out even if they had to face the Germans in open battle. At least a few might remain alive. But if they stayed in the sewer, all would certainly die.

To Zivia and some others, however, the delay meant a new chance to ease their torment. Maybe now their comrades from the ghetto would arrive in time. Yes, it was just as well that the trucks had not come yet. Otherwise, how could they make the people wait? Zivia scribbled a note of her own and sent it up: Nobody would emerge until the missing fighters arrived.

At about 8 P.M., just before the curfew, the survivors heard footsteps again. The password was given and the manhole cover pushed aside. Suddenly pails of soup, sausages, bread, and lemonade were lowered into outstretched hands. There was barely enough soup for each person to wet his lips, and the bread was hard to swallow because the throat was so dry. But this food would help everybody survive for a few more hours. Before sliding back the manhole cover, a voice assured them, "We're thinking of you. Be patient until morning."

Then a hand placed a note in Zivia's palm. She unfolded it quickly. It was from her husband, Yitzhak Zuckerman: "My dearest, be confident. We are doing everything to find a place where to bring you. If we don't find a place, we'll take you directly to the forest." [6]

The Twenty-second Day

May 10

At 5 A.M. Simcha Rathajzer returned to the manhole. Where were Tadek and Constantin? They were to arrive at the same time with two trucks to take the fighters to the forest. Simcha nervously loitered in the area for about half an hour; then Tadek showed up, but without any trucks. Constantin, Tadek explained, would be coming with the vehicles.

The two men then paced up and down Prosta Street for one hour, two hours. Still no sign of Constantin. People were beginning to fill the streets. It was already too dangerous to let the fighters emerge.

Then, at about 9 A.M., Constantin arrived. He had not been able to obtain the trucks. That was it. Simcha went to the manhole and dropped a note through it: Stay in the sewer until night.

Zivia and Marek read the note with alarm. Shortly before, Shlomo Shuster and Yurek Blones, the two messengers sent to bring Zachariah Artstein and the other fighters still in the ghetto, had returned in deep distress. The Germans were blowing up the sewer entrances in the ghetto, and it was impossible to go back. Now there was no reason to wait.

Zivia and Marek sent up a reply to Simcha: The people were growing weaker and would not survive another day.

Simcha knew he must get them out in daylight, whatever the

risk. He and his two companions quickly agreed on a desperate plan: They would telephone a trucking company and ask that two trucks be sent immediately to this corner to pick up some crates of merchandise. Then they would force the drivers to transport their comrades to the forest.

Simcha sent Tadek and Constantin to telephone for the trucks and bring back several other fighters on the Aryan side in case a battle broke out. Then he waited near the manhole, watching fearfully as the crowds grew, as German soldiers walked by not suspecting that the surviving leaders of the Jewish underground were trapped right under their feet. His heart pounding, he contemplated the next hour. Perhaps his last on earth.[1]

Shortly before 10 A.M. Tadek and Constantin returned with three Aryan-looking Jewish comrades. Soon, they told Simcha, one or two trucks would arrive to pick up the "merchandise." And they had not ignored the security factor. Constantin and one of the ZOB fighters had some minutes earlier entered a tavern near the manhole and confronted a group of Polish policemen who frequented it. Constantin sat down at the Polish policemen's table, drew a pistol from his overcoat pocket, and said quietly, "Gentlemen, we are representatives of the People's Guard [the military arm of the PPR]. We have to carry out a mission on this street. We are notifying and forewarning you. None of you should show up in this section of Prosta Street. Is it clear, gentlemen?"

Then Constantin rose, pistol still in hand, and departed with his comrade, leaving the policemen in a state of shock.

Now Constantin, Simcha, and the other rescuers, laden with boards, began constructing a fence around part of the manhole so that Germans stationed nearby could not see the Jews emerge from the sewer. They worked nonchalantly, as if they were Polish workers doing routine street repairs.

About 10 A.M. a large canvas-covered truck pulled up to the curb on Prosta Street. Constantin walked over, opened the door of the cabin, and sat down next to the driver. Then he whipped out a pistol from one pocket and a bottle of vodka from another.

"Drink this!" he ordered the trembling driver, aiming the pistol at him.

If the driver tried to give the fighters away, they could claim he was drunk. After a gulp the driver backed up to the manhole, as ordered, and Simcha instructed two of his men to lift the cover. Within seconds, dozens of curious Polish passersby began to gather around the opening.

In the sewer Zivia and her comrades heard a clamor overhead, and the canal was suddenly flooded with light. Someone was lifting the cover from the outside. For a moment they were certain that the Germans had discovered them, and they instinctively retreated into the darkness of the tunnel, pistols in hand. But then they heard a voice calling in Polish, "Quickly! Come out quickly!"

It was Simcha. Zivia immediately ordered two men to go and bring back all the people dispersed under the other manholes. But the two refused to leave, arguing that they might return too late. Zivia reproached herself. Why hadn't she sent someone for them earlier? She had lost track of time. She then ordered Shlomo Shuster and Adolf Hochman to go, promising that the truck would wait for them. Both agreed, though Shlomo was still drained from the abortive rescue trip to the ghetto.

Masha Glytman, having just arrived from one of the other manholes with a comrade who virtually had to pull her along, now thanked God that she had come. She had been reluctant to disobey Zivia's order to stay at her outlying position. The exhausting trip had taken more than fifteen minutes. That meant, Masha knew, that it might take over half an hour before the others were found and brought back. Could the rescuers wait that long?

The Jews began climbing out of the sewer, helped by Simcha. "Quick, quick!" he muttered as he ushered them toward the truck, where his men all but threw them inside in their eagerness to get away. The survivors squatted in the vehicle with their heads down so that they would not be seen during the race through the city.

As they emerged from the sewer one by one, the crowd around the manhole grew. The Poles, stunned, stared incredulously at figures that didn't look human, ghostly creatures covered with slime, dressed in rags. Only the burning eyes in the cadaverous faces suggested they were alive. Even the Jews themselves, as they saw each other in the light for the first time in forty-eight hours, could hardly recognize their comrades.

After a few minutes a Polish policeman walked up, and appealing to his patriotic sense, Simcha told him that these were members of the Polish underground who had been on a special mission. They were all armed, he added, to further impress the policeman with the wisdom of moving on. The policeman nodded, as if to say "good luck," and departed.

As Israel Kanal climbed out of the sewer, he asked Simcha in Polish if they were being covered. Simcha took advantage of this question to shout, in another appeal to Polish patriotism, that the whole surrounding crowd was providing them with cover. The Poles remained silent, watching. Did they suspect that these were really Jews? Simcha wondered. He heard someone say, "The cats are coming out." ("Cat" was a derogatory term for "Jew.") If his bluff didn't work, the end would certainly come before all the Jews had time to climb out. He kept looking at his watch. . . . Five minutes, ten, twenty. . . . The cats were still coming out. The Germans were bound to appear at any moment. . . . Twenty-five minutes, half an hour. . . .

More than thirty people had scrambled out, and Zivia remained alone in the sewer. She would not move. Where were the others whom she had sent for? A frenzy seized her. She couldn't leave without them. Especially after having left behind those in the ghetto. Had she not been responsible for scattering them to other manholes? Had she not promised to wait for them, as she had also promised Zachariah? But Simcha, reaching down to her, called, "Hurry! Hurry! There's no time!"

Zivia stared once more into the blackness of the tunnel, praying for a miracle. What should she do? In agony she finally climbed up.

"There are more people down there!" she gasped.*

Simcha replied breathlessly as he pulled her out of the opening. "Get into the truck! Quick!"

Constantin, still sitting beside the driver, noted that no one else was emerging.

"Let's go, or it will be too late," he cried.

Simcha ordered Tadek and another fighter to check if there

---

*Though Zivia says she thus informed Simcha that others were still in the sewer, Simcha says he does not recall being given this information by Zivia until later. It is possible that in the confusion of the moment Simcha did not hear her. In any event, Simcha clearly suspected that others were in the sewer, since he delayed departure of the truck for several minutes.

were any more people in the sewer, and they got down on their knees and shouted into the manhole. There was no reply. At that moment, a second truck pulled up. If there were any more people down there, Simcha told Constantin, this second vehicle could take them.

"But that truck is not ours!" Constantin exclaimed.

Simcha floundered in uncertainty. There might still be a few others. But where were they? Should he wait or should he leave? He feverishly pondered the dangers of waiting. The Germans would come any moment now. And anyway, the survivors were so packed in the truck that they were lying on top of each other.

"The truck is full," he finally told Constantin. "And nobody else is coming out. What are we waiting for?"

He then ordered two other men to replace the manhole cover, and the truck pulled away, with Simcha leaping on at the last moment.

Zivia cried, "Why aren't we waiting for the others? There are about fifteen still down there! Stop! Stop!"

"Where are they?" Simcha asked.

Scattered under other manholes, Zivia answered.

Simcha trembled with fury. Hadn't he told her to be ready to leave with her group that morning? Why had she waited until the last second to get them? No, he replied, they could not wait. A few minutes more and everybody would be killed. He would send the truck back later for the others.

Zivia felt numb in her horror. How many dear comrades had she left to die? She could not grasp that in such desperate circumstances, their fate, the fate of everyone, was in God's hands and not in hers.[2]

As the truck streaked through Warsaw, zigzagging past other vehicles, its occupants were mesmerized by glimpses of the blue sky, the green parks, the spacious squares, the well-dressed people on the broad boulevards. Why had not *they* been fated to live like normal human beings in a sunny, clean, secure world instead of like rats in holes and sewers? They breathed in the fresh air as if it were a priceless perfume, though some, especially Zivia, still smelled the sewer where their comrades remained trapped.

Within minutes they reached a bridge over the Vistula River, which led to Lomianki Forest, their destination, about five miles north of Warsaw. They were about to cross when they saw several German guards standing by the entry, checking identity cards and searching vehicles.

"Get your harmonicas ready!" Constantin shouted through the cabin window, referring to the fighters' pistols.

They obeyed, though they realized their weapons were useless. Not only did they have little ammunition, but what they did have was wet. Constantin then poked his own pistol into the driver's ribs and ordered him to turn the truck around. The driver obeyed, and the vehicle sped along the river to another bridge, which was unguarded. Shortly the vehicle bounced into a forest of thick bushes and white sandhills and trembled to a halt.

As the Jews piled out, they fell into the embraces of living ghosts from the past—the survivors from the Productive Ghetto who had arrived here on April 30, eleven days earlier. Jacob Putermilch and others clasped the new arrivals to their bosoms, ignoring the filth that still clung to them. They had not imagined that anyone from the Central Ghetto had survived. The forest was green, the air fragrant, the spring sun warm. What a joy to be alive.

As someone kissed Zivia, she broke into tears. Tears at last. So many times in recent weeks she had wanted to weep, but the heart had hardened. It had been forbidden to cry; it was not done. But now she wept, finally unburdening the torment in her soul. Others talked, laughed, joked.

Suddenly one of the newcomers slumped to the ground. Yehuda Wengrower, poisoned by gas and apparently by sewer water, faded away at the moment of salvation. His comrades sat in silence for what seemed like hours; finally one man stood up and began digging a grave.

Meanwhile Simcha sent Constantin and two ZOB helpers back to Warsaw with the truck to rescue the fifteen or so people still stranded in the sewer on Prosta Street. But when darkness fell and they had not returned, Simcha boarded a streetcar into town to find out what happened. As the car neared Prosta, he saw a crowd. Instinctively he jumped off while the vehicle was still moving, and he approached the sewer opening. On the street in front of him lay the body of one of the men he had sent. A short distance away was sprawled the corpse of another. Only Constantin had escaped.* Simcha was stunned. And what of the others in the sewer?

The two rescuers, witnesses told him, had gone to the manhole and found Germans surrounding it. A woman had apparently seen them when they helped Simcha rescue the first batch of Jews, and she denounced them. The people left behind had all been killed as they tried to get out of the manhole. The Germans had been waiting for them.[3]

All day long, Yitzhak Zuckerman desperately tried to contact Polish Home Army officers, sending Frania Beatus, his sixteen-year-old chief aide, and other comrades to deliver messages to them. Would they find hiding places for the survivors? Or arrange for them to join partisan units in the woods near Warsaw?

Finally someone rushed back with a note from one of the officers. The note said the survivors should be taken to the forest near Wolin, about four hundred kilometers east of Warsaw, where they would join a Polish partisan group.

Yitzhak was shocked. Poles could travel to Wolin by train or car, but the Germans were constantly stopping traffic to find Jews. Only those few fighters with markedly gentile faces stood a chance of bluffing the inspectors. The others would have to move on foot and would find it equally difficult evading the police. And in any case, they were too weak for such a trek.

The suggestion was an invitation to suicide, Yitzhak answered in a note. The Jews were not ready to make so useless a sacrifice. If the Home Army could not find them hiding places in Warsaw, they should arrange for them to fight as partisans in forests near the city; for example, along the Bug River on the Russian frontier. Actually Yitzhak was skeptical that the Jews could be effective partisans anywhere. For partisans, to succeed, must have the support and sympathy of the local population, and he feared that the Polish peasants, many of them anti-Semitic, would betray them. Nevertheless, he did feel that the Jews would stand a better chance of surviving if they didn't have to travel long distances through open country.

*The Polish driver of the truck who had been forced to take the first group of fighters to the forest disappeared on the return trip. He apparently did not betray the whereabouts of these Jews.

Once more, he reflected bitterly, the Home Army was refusing to help the few Jews who had been fortunate enough to escape from the ghetto. Tomorrow he would go to Lomianki Forest to greet the survivors personally and plan their next step with them. Somehow he would find hideouts for some of them. The rest could perhaps join PPR partisan units or even Soviet partisan units operating nearby. Tomorrow. . . . He still dared not ask himself if his wife, Zivia, was among the survivors. He knew that some of those in the sewer had been killed.

Among them was Frania's fiancé.[4]

"Have someone come to my apartment and take all my things and the thirty thousand zlotys hidden in my clothes. . . . Goodbye, Sara, I am leaving forever."

Sara Biderman, one of the fighters who had escaped from the Productive Ghetto with Eliezer Geller's group, cried into the telephone, "Frania, what are you doing? Frania, don't talk nonsense! Frania! Frania!"

The telephone clicked, and Sara slowly put down the receiver, her face ghostly pale. She began sobbing, and Halina Balicka, a Polish woman in whose home Sara was hiding, ran over to her and asked what had happened. Sara recounted the conversation, explaining that Frania's fiancé had been killed while trying to escape from the sewer.

"Once she told me that if he perished, she would have nothing left to live for, because she has nobody else in this world."

Shortly, Halina was at Frania's apartment, packing the things the young girl had left. She picked up a photograph. Frania's delicate, childlike face smiled for the last time. She had performed her duty as a Jewish fighter, as Yitzhak had ordered when she told him of her wish to kill herself when the uprising began. Now it seemed that the last survivors had come out of the ghetto. And her beloved was not among them. There was no longer any reason to live.

No one ever found Frania's body.[5]

That evening Simcha Rathajzer returned to Lomianki Forest and joined the survivors as they sat around a fire. In a faltering voice he told them what happened to their comrades who had been left in the sewer. Zivia Lubetkin was shattered with grief and rage. If only Simcha had kept the truck there a little longer. . . . She threatened to shoot him.

"Good," Simcha replied. "We can shoot each other."

The tension eased, and everybody silently watched the fire as it crackled in the night, forming images of dear ones, of comrades who had perished. One more day, perhaps one more minute, and you, Mordechai Anielewicz, might be sitting here with us, mourning, as we are, the millions of souls you tried to enshrine.

"The future was shrouded in mists," Zivia would later reflect. "And we, the survivors, were superfluous, lonely, foresaken by God and man. What was there to do that we had not done?"[6]

The same day, in the Productive Ghetto, the Nazis set fire to Leszno 76, burning alive the occupants of the hospital bunker. Among the victims were Regina Fuden, the tireless messenger who had volunteered to return to the ghetto to save her comrades; and Shalom Sufit and Hana Grauman, the lovers who had been wounded together and now died together.[7]

The Last Days

May 11–16

In the ghetto the Nazis continued to clean out whatever bunkers remained, and on May 11 they found the ones that sheltered the staff of the Czyste-Berson-Bauman Hospital. Dr. Israel Rotbalsam was among those caught. When he was herded to Umschlagplatz, he expected, almost with relief, to join the patients he had seen massacred in their beds in both the January and April uprisings.

Captured the same day, after the Germans gassed his bunker in the Brushmakers' District, was Simcha Holzberg, who in his compassion had carried a young wounded girl into the shelter but then helped to smother her to death when her moans threatened to give the shelter away. Now, with his own mental wounds still festering, he wondered if he did not deserve retribution.

On the Aryan side, too, disaster befell the Jews, as well as those who helped them. Almost the whole ZZW force that had escaped from the ghetto had gathered at Grzybowska 13 to await transportation to the forest, which Captain Iwanski's men were to provide on May 12. But on the eve of their departure, the Germans surrounded the building; and in a battle that lasted for hours, they killed the fighters, including Pawel Frenkel, their leader.

Iwanski was in the midst of preparations for the ride to the forest when he received the news. He grieved for his Jewish comrades, among the last ZZW fighters to remain alive, as he had grieved for four members of his own family during the past two weeks.

Iwanski was not to get any respite from personal tragedy. At about the same time that Frenkel's group went down fighting, a messenger rushed into the captain's headquarters and informed him that fourteen Jews and several Poles had been killed when the Gestapo raided a carpentry shop on Dobra Street—the shop where his father worked. When Iwanski checked the report, he found that his father had been among the victims. He had been shot when the Germans found the Jews in the cellar.

Why did Iwanski risk so much to save Jews? He told the author, "When a Jew cries, I cry. When a Jew suffers, I am a Jew. All are of my nation, for I am a man."[1]

At about 11:30 P.M. on May 13, waves of Soviet planes swooped down on Warsaw, guided by the ghetto fires. This was apparently in response to the PPR plea sent out on April 23 for an air raid to help the doomed Jews. They dropped tons of bombs on railroad lines and other strategic areas. Buildings collapsed, scores of people—Germans and Poles—were blown to bits or trapped under the debris, and SS troops based in the city panicked. Amidst the chaos a few Jews managed to escape to the Aryan side through holes blown in the wall, but not many were left to escape.

Then leaflets drifted down upon the momentarily paralyzed city. The rejoicing Jews, some sensing imminent liberation, picked them up and read that Russia "favored the establishment of a free, strong Poland" and that the Polish people should join in partisan actions. Not a word about the ghetto uprising. It was, after all, a small element in the struggle against Fascism.

General Stroop soon brought order to the city and plugged the holes in the ghetto wall.[2]

Shmuel Zygielbojm, one of the two Jewish representatives in the Polish government-in-exile in London, telephoned his friend Isaac Deutscher on May 10 or 11 and excitedly called him over to his residence. Come immediately, he pleaded. Why? Zygielbojm couldn't say over the phone. Shortly, Deutscher arrived.

In an extremely nervous state, Zygielbojm showed him a cable from ZOB agents in Warsaw, relayed to him by Polish authorities. Deutscher read it quickly: The extermination in the Warsaw Ghetto was progressing swiftly. The only thing left to do was to fall fighting. But to fight, they needed arms and ammunition. And all efforts to obtain them had failed.

His own efforts to get help had also been futile, Zygielbojm told his friend. He would now resort to a desperate action: lie down on a hunger strike in front of 10 Downing Street, the British Prime Minister's residence, until the British government used its influence to get arms to the surviving Jews. Would Deutscher do the same?

Deutscher scowled his disapproval. The police, he said, would not permit such a demonstration. And anyway, the censor would not let the press even mention such an incident. This was not a suitable time for emotional gestures, but it was for political moves. Zygielbojm, he advised, should resign from the Polish government-in-exile and inform the British government, members of Parliament, and the press why he did so. Or he should threaten the Polish government with resignation if it did not deliver arms by a specified date.

Even if the British censor prevented the press from disclosing the reason for his resignation, it might be publicized in the United States. And since Prime Minister Sikorski was trying to win American support for his policies, the Polish government would be sensitive to such notorious publicity, perhaps even forced into doing something positive.

But Zygielbojm vigorously dissented. Only a hunger strike, he said, could dramatize the situation sufficiently to force the British and Polish hand. Finally they agreed to send a cable to Prime Minister Churchill. They protested the Polish refusal to give arms to the Jews and asked him to use his influence. Deutscher wrote the cable, and Zygielbojm signed it, though Deutscher never knew whether it was sent.

Zygielbojm could not have known that about this time, on May 10, his wife, Manya, and small son, Artek, who had been hiding in one of the Czyste-Berson-Bauman Hospital bunkers, burned to death when it was set afire.

But this great personal tragedy could only have added to Zygielbojm's overwhelming despair over the murder of his whole

332

people. No, not even going on a hunger strike in front of the Prime Minister's residence was enough to stir the conscience of the Poles and the other peoples of the world. There seemed only one possible way. He sat down at his desk and wrote a letter addressed to the leaders of the government-in-exile, President Wladyslaw Raczkiewicz and Prime Minister Sikorski:

> I am taking the liberty of addressing my last words to you, and through you to the Polish government, to the Polish people, to the governments and peoples of all Allied nations, and to the conscience of the world.
>
> The last news received from Poland makes it clear that the Germans are determined to wipe out, with horrible brutality, the last remnants of the Jews who have survived in Poland. Behind the walls of the ghetto is now going on the last act of a tragedy unequaled in all history.
>
> The murderers themselves bear the primary responsibility for the crime of exterminating the whole Jewish population of Poland, but, indirectly, this responsibility also weighs on all humanity, on the peoples and governments of the Allied nations, because they have not made any attempt to do something drastic to stall the criminal deeds. By looking on indifferently while helpless millions of tortured children, women, and men were murdered, those nations have associated themselves with the criminals.
>
> I wish to declare that the Polish government, although it has sought to influence the public opinion of the world, has not done so sufficiently. It has not taken any steps commensurate with the enormity of the drama that is now happening in Poland. . . .
>
> I cannot be silent. I cannot live while the remnants of the Jewish population of Poland, of whom I am a representative, are perishing. My friends in the Warsaw Ghetto died with weapons in their hands in the last heroic battle. It was not my destiny to die together with them but I belong to them, and in their mass graves.
>
> By my death I wish to make my final protest against the passivity with which the world is looking on and permitting the extermination of the Jewish people.
>
> I know how little human life is worth today, but as I was unable to do anything during my life, perhaps by my death I shall contribute to breaking down the indifference of those who may now at the last moment rescue the few Polish Jews still alive. . . .
>
> I am sure that the President and the Prime Minister will convey my words to whom they are addressed and that the Polish government will soon begin all possible diplomatic action on behalf of

those Polish Jews who are still alive. I bid farewell to everybody and to everything that was dear to me and that I have loved.

Shmuel Zygielbojm

Shortly after noon on May 12, Zygielbojm washed, shaved, put on a clean shirt, and got into bed. He then swallowed a bottleful of sleeping pills and died in protest against a world that stood by indifferently, watching the mass slaughter of his people.[3]

At about 8 P.M. on May 16, General Stroop, surrounded by his aides, stared from a nearby street at the great synagogue. In a few minutes he would observe that hated symbol of Judaism exploding into rubble. Although the synagogue stood on the Aryan side, its destruction would signal the official end of the *Grossaktion*— and the Warsaw Ghetto.

Stroop's statisticians could account for the capture or killing of exactly 56,065 Jews since the uprising started. The general was fascinated by the symmetrical order of the digits in this number. Zero was in the middle, with sixes on both sides and fives at both ends. The fives formed a magnificent constellation. The sixes, of course, were not so favorable, certainly not as favorable as nines. Still, they could be considered inverted nines. The zero, on the other hand, was a symbol of the sun, fertility, life, and eternity. On the whole, a magic number by Germanic astrological standards; though he realized that it did not include thousands of Jews buried in the ghetto debris.

The preparations for the explosion, ordered by General Krüger with his flare for the dramatic, had been difficult and intricate, taking about ten days. It had been necessary not only to empty the interior of the synagogue but also to drill into its foundations and walls several hundred openings in which explosives could be placed. The synagogue was an old building erected in 1877 and designed in neo-Renaissance style by the famous architect Leonard Marconi. It was solidly constructed, and to blow it up with a single blast meant tedious engineering work.

But Stroop felt that the time and money expended were minimal, considering the historical importance of the event. History would long remember Jürgen Stroop for his contribution to the Führer's racial purification program. He would certainly be awarded a medal; he even envisaged a Warsaw street being named after him. And what a perfect theatrical ending to the *Grossaktion.* The great synagogue vanishing with a press of the button while his officers and men, tired and grimy, looked on in the glare of the still-burning ghetto. He would in fact press the button himself, detonating all the explosive charges at once.

It was almost 8:15, the moment of glory. A sapper officer handed Max Jesuiter the electric detonator, and Jesuiter passed it to the general. Stroop felt a great thrill of expectation. Finally, at 8:15 sharp, he shouted, "Heil Hitler!" and pressed the button. A thunderous explosion shook the earth, and fiery clouds rose with leisurely splendor into the evening sky. A fairy-tale symphony of colors. An exquisite allegory of triumph over Jewry. How the Führer and the Reichsführer would enjoy the sight.

Later that evening, after celebrating with fine wine and dumplings, Stroop cabled a momentous announcement to General Krüger in Cracow: "The former Jewish quarter of Warsaw no longer exists."

He could not know that five years later the "Jewish quarter of Warsaw" would exist again—in the spirit of a new nation. That a young troublemaker named Mordechai Anielewicz would return from the "place from which no traveler returns" to steel his people once more in their struggle to survive.[4]

EPILOGUE

Although the Warsaw Ghetto uprising officially ended on May 16, 1943, scattered bands of trapped Jewish fighters continued resisting for several more months. Zachariah Artstein's ZOB group, which Zivia Lubetkin had been forced to leave behind, joined Josef Lopata's ZZW fighters to form the nucleus of the "rubble resistance." The rubble fighters crawled from hole to hole, looking for food and sniping at Nazis.

Zachariah, however, was shot dead in early June while he and another fighter were seeking a passage to the Aryan side. Hanoch Gutman, who had been wounded in the fighting at Franciszkanska 30 on May 2, was also killed, along with his girl friend, Fayche Rabow, who had refused to leave him. Most of the other Jews were slain, but some managed to escape through sewers and over the wall, even as late as September.

Some civilians also held out for months in undetected bunkers. Virtually all starved to death or were killed when they finally emerged to try their luck through the sewers.

Jewish prisoners clearing the rubble found the last survivor on December 13, 1943—a young girl who was burned and barely alive. The prisoners brought her food each day until the Nazis discovered her and took her to Pawiak Prison. The Gestapo was so awed by the miracle of her survival that they ordered her brought back to health and fitted out with a wardrobe. But after a few weeks, SS men tortured her, then took her out to the ruins and shot her.

But even after every Jew had been rooted out of the Warsaw Ghetto, the battle went on—in the ghettos of Vilna, Cracow, Czehstochowa, Bendin, Bialystok, and other Polish towns. Even the Jews in Treblinka revolted, destroying the death camp. Mordechai Anielewicz and his comrades had kindled a spreading and unquenchable flame of resistance.[1]

After the *Grossaktion* had officially ended, General Stroop left the job of mopping up the remnants of Jewish resistance to a single police battalion and prepared plans for constructing a new "model quarter" in the razed area. He studied every detail and even pondered the color and shape of the lettering on the street signs, finally deciding on Gothic letters. He was overjoyed when Himmler personally traced "Jürgen Stroop Avenue" on the blueprint.

Stroop now regretted that he had not kept more Jewish prisoners in Warsaw to work on the project. So he persuaded Himmler to approve the transfer of several thousand Jews from other parts of Europe to a new Warsaw concentration camp set up in the ghetto area on July 19. Meanwhile, Stroop also used the ruins as an execution site for Polish prisoners in order to deceive the Poles, who he still feared might revolt, into thinking that only Jews were being shot.

Stroop's victory won him the Iron Cross, First Class, and a choice post as SS and police commander in Greece, where he served from September to November, 1943. He was then appointed to the same position in Rheine-Westmark, where he lived with his wife, daughter, and son. After a group of German officers failed to assassinate Hitler on July 20, 1944, Stroop hanged the plotters from slaughterhouse hooks, using piano strings to prolong their suffering.

When the Americans pushed into Germany, Stroop, concealing his identity, surrendered to them on May 8, 1945. But soon his captors found his reports on the daily fighting in the Warsaw Ghetto and learned who he was. An American military court tried him and, on March 21, 1947, sentenced him to death for killing American prisoners of war captured in Greece. But in May he was handed over to the Polish military mission in Berlin.

"I was half-conscious, desperate and shattered," he later told a companion. "The Americans had cheated me! Many times they had promised me that I would never be extradited to their Eastern allies."

Stroop was taken to Warsaw, where the Poles began trying him on July 18, 1951, for his crimes in Poland. He claimed he had simply been carrying out orders and blamed his subordinates for any crimes that had been committed. Sentenced once more to death, Stroop remained arrogant and unrepentant to the end. He was hanged in Warsaw's Central Prison on March 6, 1952.[2]

The more than sixty ZOB fighters from the Central and Productive ghettos who had escaped to Lomianki Forest were supplied with food by a loyal Polish peasant who believed them to be members of the Polish underground. But soon they moved to Wyszkow Forest, which was larger and offered more cover. From there they attacked trains, police stations, and other targets, using arms and explosives obtained from Russian partisans. After three months only about half of the fighters remained alive, many of them killed by Polish Fascists.

Mordechai Growas' group of ten fighters, including Izio Lewski and Jacob Putermilch's sister, Hagit, were camping one day by the Bug River when a Fascist unit happened by. Several members sat down with the Jews for a friendly talk when others standing nearby suddenly opened fire, killing Growas and his entire group.

Though members of the Fascist NSZ are believed to have committed the murders, they received no little encouragement from the Home Army leadership itself, which still hoped to incorporate this organization into the Home Army. Thus, in August 1943, the new Home Army Commander, General Bor-Komorowski, prepared for his superiors in London a review of "forms of banditry on Polish soil" in which he lumped Jewish partisans with the outlaw bands terrorizing the countryside in terms reminiscent of Stroop's reports:

> Well-armed bands are constantly on the rampage in towns and villages, attacking manor houses, banks, commercial and industrial enterprises, houses and homes, large peasant farms. . . . Men and women—Jewesses in particular—participate in these attacks. . . . In order to give some assistance and protection to the innocent population, with the Chief Government Delegate's agreement I

have instructed my area and district commanders . . . to take armed action should the need arise against both plundering and subversive elements. I have stressed the need to liquidate the leaders of the bands and not to try to wipe out entire bands.

The Poles who murdered Mordechai Growas' "band" and other groups of Jewish survivors from the ghetto adhered to the spirit of this message, though they disobeyed orders by killing *everybody*.*

When Yitzhak Zuckerman learned of the Bug River massacre from messengers who had spoken with peasant eyewitnesses, he wanted to break contact with the Home Army. But money collected from world Jewry for the relief of the survivors was sent to him by the Polish government-in-exile through the Home Army. Therefore, to cut off relations with the Home Army would be to cut off this vital source of funds. The Home Army had already warned Zuckerman not to use the money for purchasing weapons with which to "arm bandits," and it was delaying payments to him. Yitzhak claimed, in fact, that the Home Army kept part of the money for itself. Anyway, of the million dollars collected for the Polish Jews, not more than $400,000 reached them.[3]†

---

*Some Home Army officers bitterly complained about the anti-Semitism of many of their fellow Poles. An officer known as Kreton wrote to the Polish government-in-exile on January 6, 1942: "It must be said with satisfaction that our people do not in the slightest degree yield to the policy of Germanization. The only headway the Germans make is in fostering their blind and savage anti-Semitism. I really wonder if the attitude of our people toward the Jews does not resemble that of the Germans. This is the only case where the principles of Christian justice based on charity have broken down completely and fail to influence their behavior toward the Jews." Dr. Zygmunt Klukowski wrote in his diary, on November 26, 1942: "Among the 'bandits' are many Jews. The peasants, fearing German reprisals, are hunting down Jews in the countryside; they bring them to the towns, or sometimes they kill them on the spot. Generally speaking, Jews are treated as if they were wild animals; the people here are driven into a kind of psychosis and, disinhibited by the German example, they forget the Jews are human beings; they treat them like rabid dogs, rats, or other vermin which have to be exterminated in any way possible."

†On March 18, 1944, Aleksander Kaminski, editor in chief of the Home Army's office newspaper, *Biuletyn Informacyjny*, wrote in a letter to Jerzy Makowiecki, his superior officer: "Generally speaking, the question of funds collected by American, Palestinian, and British Jews to aid their Polish brethren looks somewhat obscure and troubles me. Apparently, no one has told the Jewish lead-

339

Poles betrayed other fighters who had managed to survive the forest and were trying either to hide or to leave Poland. One group, including Zalman Frydrich and the three Bloneses—Jurek, thirteen-year-old Lusiek, and their sister, Guta—were arrested when a Polish peasant informed on them while they were seeking shelter. They were carted through villages, where peasants were encouraged to beat them; then they were shot. (Zalman's wife was arrested on the Aryan side and died in Majdanek concentration camp. His six-year-old daughter, hiding in a monastery, survived, and after the war she was adopted by a family in New York. In 1962, for unknown reasons, she committed suicide.)

Several ZOB fighters, among them David Nowodworski and Heniek Kleinweis, were killed in a fierce battle after they were also betrayed by a peasant while trying to escape into Hungary.

Even some trusted members of the Polish underground turned against the Jewish fighters. Constantin Gajek, the Communist People's Guard agent who had helped Simcha Rathajzer save Zivia Lubetkin's group from the sewer, guided the fighters from Lomianki to Wyszkow Forest, then reportedly killed several of them for their money and fled. The People's Guard tried him *in absentia* and sentenced him to death. Later, apparently to rehabilitate himself, Constantin daringly tried to free a captured Jew from the Gestapo and was never heard of again.

Another Pole who was helping the fighters, Stefan Pokropek of the Home Army, put Simcha Rathajzer in contact with a young man who claimed he could obtain arms for the fighters. Simcha and Tadek Szejngut, his colorful, storytelling comrade, waited in Pokropek's home for the young man to return with the arms when the Gestapo suddenly showed up. Simcha leaped out a window and escaped, but Tadek was shot dead. The fighters later learned that both Pokropek and the youth he had introduced to Simcha were Gestapo agents.

Another victim believed betrayed by Pokropek was Abrasha Blum, the Bundist political leader who had come through the sewer with Zivia's group. Abrasha was staying in a room with Fei-

---

ership in Warsaw why they are not receiving the proper amounts. . . . Jews have been cut off from any contact with the outside world for five months. I do not know why. I only know that some of the most loyal supporters of the Polish Republic are beginning to suspect some very unsavory machinations. . . ."

gele Peltel, who had been working closely with Pokropek, when the Germans burst in. The intruders, after ransacking the room, said they would be back in a few minutes and departed, locking the door behind them.

The two prisoners tore up some sheets and fashioned a rope which they hung out the window. Abrasha started lowering himself to the street, but the rope snapped and he fell. Severely injured, he was brought back to Feigele's room by Polish policemen, who then took both Jews to the police station. Their comrades were able to bribe the police into releasing Feigele, but they were too late to save Abrasha, who was taken to Gestapo headquarters and killed.[4]

Eliezer Geller (who had returned from the forest on a mission), Tosia Altman, Meir Schwartz, and several other fighters were hiding in the attic of a Warsaw celluloid factory when, on May 24, Tosia, trying to heat a spoonful of ointment to treat her wounds, set fire to some celluloid. In seconds the whole building was aflame. The fighters climbed through an opening to the roof, and as crowds gathered, crying, "The Jews are burning!" Eliezer and Meir managed to escape. But Tosia's dress caught fire; and with severe burns she was dragged away by Germans to a hospital, where she was deprived of treatment and permitted to suffer until she died two days later.

Meir ran into the apartment of a friendly Pole but was soon followed by Germans who began searching the flat for him. When they had left without finding him, the Pole opened the closet where Meir was hiding and found him dead, probably from a heart attack.

Meanwhile, in July, the Gestapo offered to save Jews—those with money to buy a passport issued by a neutral country that would permit the owner to travel abroad as a foreign citizen. The Jews deliberated, argued, struggled with themselves. Was this another trick? Several thousand decided to take a chance and move into Hotel Polski, from which they would be sent to a special camp for foreigners and then abroad.

Among the applicants were Eliezer Geller, who had severely burned his arm in the celluloid factory fire and could no longer fight; Israel Kanal, who was also too ill for combat; Hela Schipper;

and sixteen-year-old Jurek Plonski. Jurek, the young ZZW fighter, had crawled through a sewer to the Aryan side on July 1, after hiding in the ghetto rubble for weeks. Unable to find shelter with Polish friends who now shunned him, he returned to the ghetto twice, rescuing several comrades. But there was nowhere to hide, so Jurek went to Hotel Polski.

The Jews in the hotel were treated well and could come and go as they pleased. Every few days a number would leave and be replaced by others, until one morning the Gestapo surrounded the building. Almost all of the four hundred Jews trapped in the hotel were captured and driven in trucks to Pawiak Prison, where about half were shot and the other half sent to Bergen-Belsen concentration camp to join those Jews who had left the hotel earlier. In this deported group were Eliezer, Israel, and Hela. Of the three, only Hela survived; she was sent from camp to camp until liberation. After the war, she went to Israel, remarried, and today lives in the northern village of Bustan Hagalil with her husband and two children.

Jurek Plonski miraculously escaped from Hotel Polski. He ran to the front entrance and, seeing several milk cans in front of a neighboring grocery store, grabbed one in each hand and calmly walked past the Germans, who thought he was a Polish milkman. He then joined a group of Jewish "cigarette children," young boys from about ten to sixteen years of age who had also escaped from the ghetto and survived by selling cigarettes on streetcorners. At night he took shelter in tombs in the Catholic cemetery.

Eventually he joined the Polish underground and floated across the Vistula River on a wooden plank to contact the Russians—who promptly jailed him as a German spy. He escaped after a week and rejoined the Polish underground. After the war he emigrated to Israel, where today he lives on a kibbutz. But tragedy dogged him even in freedom. His only son was killed in the Yom Kippur War, in October 1973.[5]

When the Polish underground finally revolted against the Nazis on August 1, 1944, Yitzhak Zuckerman ordered all able Jews to join the nearest Polish fighting unit. But Home Army leaders either rejected them or assigned them the most dangerous missions, on which some were shot in the back if they were not killed first by the enemy. At the same time, many Poles hiding in bunkers would not let Jews enter and sometimes shot those asking for help.

Most of the fighters, therefore, fought with the Communist People's Army (once the People's Guard), which accepted them, if also reluctantly. Yitzhak was among them, leading a group of about twelve in the defense of Warsaw's Old City. The group included his wife, Zivia, Marek Edelman, Simcha Rathajzer, and Tuvia Borzykowski. After bitter fighting, the Nazis surrounded the Old City and Yitzhak and his partisans withdrew through a sewer.

As they trudged ahead, they reached a whirlpool and tried to move past it with the help of a rope they fastened to the sewer wall, while the Germans flung grenades into the sewer through a nearby manhole. Zivia fell and nearly drowned but was saved when Tuvia grabbed her by the hair. Tuvia himself then stumbled, but Marek grabbed his head and pulled him and Zivia to safety. All thus survived and made their way into hiding in the modern section of Warsaw.

Yitzhak and Zivia then ordered Simcha to lead a detachment to rescue the ZOB archives on Leszno Street, in what had been the Productive Ghetto. Simcha obeyed reluctantly, claiming that he was being sent on an unnecessary suicide mission. While on this mission, Simcha's party was trapped in a burning house and captured by the Germans. However, the Nazis released Simcha when he explained that he was simply a Polish civilian in hiding.

Meanwhile, Yitzhak and his fighters, after further battle, hid in an abandoned Polish house. Just as the Germans were about to discover them, a People's Army representative, working together with Simcha, found and rescued them.

Among other Jewish fighters who fought in the Warsaw Rising of 1944 were Jacob Putermilch, Masha Glytman, Feigele Peltel, Pola Elster, and Hersh Berlinski.

Yitzhak, Zivia, and Tuvia went to Israel after the war and founded Kibbutz Lochamai Hagetaot (Ghetto Fighters' Kibbutz) in Western Galilee. Today, Yitzhak is in charge of its world-famous documentation center for the ghettos. Tuvia died some years ago. Jacob Putermilch and Masha Glytman also migrated to Israel, where they married. Jacob is an executive for a construction company in Tel Aviv. Chaim Frimer and another ghetto fighter, Pnina Papier, followed suit, marrying and moving to Israel, where Chaim recently died. Simcha Rathajzer settled in Israel, too, and is now a business executive in Jerusalem.

Pola and Hersh were killed in the Warsaw Rising. Jewish and Polish agents had spirited Pola out of Poniatow labor camp, and she remained in hiding in Warsaw until the rising.

Marek Edelman was the only fighter who chose to remain in Poland after the war. Today he is a well-known heart specialist in a hospital in Lodz.

Feigele Peltel eluded the Germans after the surrender of Warsaw and drifted from town to town until liberation. Then she returned to the ghetto with another underground fighter, Benjamin Miedzyrzeck, whom she married. As they walked through Gensia cemetery, seeking her father's grave, they saw "nothing but overturned tombstones, desecrated graves, and scattered skulls—skulls, their dark sockets burning deep into me, their shattered jaws demanding, 'Why? Why has this befallen us?'" Polish ghouls, persecuting the Jews even in their graves, had searched the mouths of the corpses for gold.

Where was her father's grave? "The spot was desolate, destroyed, the soil pitted and strewn with broken skulls and markers. We stood there forelorn. Around our feet lay skull after skull. Was not one of them my own father? How would I ever recognize it? Nothing. Nothing was left me of my past, of my life in the ghetto—not even the grave of my father. . . ."

Feigele now lives with her husband in New York.[6]

Sewek Toporek, the Rettungskommando worker who had been on his way to a death camp but was saved when he posed as a tailor, was sent from camp to camp, ending up in Dachau, where he was liberated. He is now a businessman in Tel Aviv.

Simcha Holzberg, the unaffiliated religious fighter who in a moment of desperation had helped to smother the young wounded girl he had brought into his bunker, was also sent to many camps. In one of them he intended to kill himself but was dissuaded by a companion. The British liberated him from Bergen-Belsen. Now living in Tel Aviv, he has devoted most of his time to caring for and entertaining war invalids, to whom he has become known as Father of the Wounded, a designation that has helped him, in some degree, to overcome the trauma of that agonizing moment in the bunker. In 1976 he won Israel's highest award for humanitarian service.

Others who lived through the Warsaw Ghetto uprising and went to live in Israel include Jonas Turkow, the Yiddish actor; Yitzhak Gitler (Ben-Moshe), now a judge in Tel Aviv; Michael L. and his wife, Maria, Gitler's companions; Jerzy Duracz, the Polish People's Guard fighter, and his Jewish wife, Anna, who abandoned Communism after the war and went to live in Jerusalem (Anna died in 1975); Kalman Friedman, who, after jumping from a boxcar in which he was riding with eight-year-old Izio, hid in Warsaw until liberation, then moved to Jerusalem, where he is a leading official of the Histadrut, the Israeli labor federation; Aharon Chmielnicki (Karmi), today an executive in Israel's bakery cooperative; Israel Guttman, the security guard at Franciszkanska 30 who today works as a researcher and writer for Yad Vashem, the Holocaust documentation center in Jerusalem; Noemi Judkowski, who lives in Kibbutz Lochamei Hagetaot; and Adam Halperin (Harten), a businessman in Tel Aviv.[7]

Although the Warsaw Ghetto workers sent to the Lublin labor camps, Poniatow and Trawniki, hardly found their new life the paradise that Walther Caspar Többens had promised, they lived and worked in relative comfort—until November 4, 1943. That morning, according to Többens, an SS police major stopped him as he was about to enter Poniatow and ordered him to go home, as the camp was to be destroyed. When Többens protested, the officer said he had orders to lock him in the cellar of his home if he caused any trouble.

Meanwhile the fifteen thousand men, women, and children in Poniatow were pushed into a large shed and led out, naked, fifty at a time. Driven by whips to long winding ditches they themselves had dug as "protection against air raids," they were then mowed down. The bodies were thrown into the ditches, and the next batch were led to slaughter, their corpses being heaped upon the previous victims. A few fighters who had been planning a revolt were caught unprepared but nevertheless died while resisting the Nazis.

By midafternoon all the Jews in Poniatow had been shot, joining in death more than thirty-five thousand in other Lublin camps, including the twelve thousand in Trawniki, where Fritz

Schultz was running his enterprises. Himmler had ordered that all the Lublin camps be wiped out within four days. Többens was released, and in shock (so he claims), he telephoned the Wehrmacht in Berlin, for whom his Poniatow factories had been manufacturing goods. Speaking discreetly, for fear the SS might be listening, he reported that he could not produce any more goods since he had no workers. Berlin replied, Produce or face arrest. Többens then flew to Berlin and told the Wehrmacht leaders, who apparently were not informed of the mass murders, why he had no workers.

But Többens was soon in better humor. In no time at all he was opening up new factories in Warsaw and other Polish towns employing Polish workers.

Shortly after the war, American troops captured Többens in Austria. He was being deported for trial in Poland in December 1946 when, like some of his own victims, he jumped from the train and escaped to Bayon. There, under an alias, he founded a new clothing firm with the wealth he had stolen from the Jews. In June 1949 he was sentenced *in absentia* by a West German court to ten years' imprisonment for being a member of the Nazi Party. This sentence was then reduced to five years, and in an appeal hearing in April 1952—at which he finally showed up—the penalty was whittled to the loss of civil rights. Többens was killed in an automobile accident in 1954.[8]

Karl Georg Schultz (Little Schultz) was less fortunate. He was captured by Polish partisans in August 1944 during the Warsaw Rising and executed on the spot. Heinrich Lauts, who had directed the brush factory and failed to persuade the workers to give themselves up during the ghetto uprising, today lives in retirement in Bremen, West Germany.

Ludwig Hahn, the Gestapo and SD chief in Warsaw, was appointed by Stroop district commander of police in Wiesbaden, one of the eight German districts commanded by the general before his capture. Two weeks later Hahn was apprehended by the British, but he escaped and became a "respectable" lawyer in Hamburg. Only in 1960 did the West German war crimes authorities begin investigating him, and for the next seven years he was in custody for short periods totaling three years.

346

Hahn has powerful connections, including his brother-in-law, General Johannes Steinhoff, a former Luftwaffe officer, who has headed the West German Air Force and the NATO military committee. His trial might never have begun if Simon Wiesenthal, head of the Jewish Documentation Center in Vienna, had not protested the delay to Chancellor Willy Brandt. When it did start, in 1972, a lawyer friend secretly passed Hahn the entire record of the investigation. He was finally convicted of war crimes and, in 1975, was sentenced to prison, but he is expected to be released soon because of illness and age.

Governor-General Hans Frank was captured by the Allies after the war. Following the war-crimes trials at Nuremberg in 1945–46, he was hanged. General Krüger left Poland in November 1943 and fought on the Balkan and Finnish fronts. He, too, was captured and hanged after a trial at Nuremberg. Colonel von Sammern-Frankenegg became SS and police commander in a region of Yugoslavia on April 23, 1943, and was killed on September 20, 1944, by Tito's artillery. General Odilo Globocnik left Poland in September 1943 to be SS and police commander on the Adriatic coast. Captured by the British, he committed suicide in May 1945.

In 1951, Franz Konrad was tried simultaneously with Stroop in Warsaw and convicted of war crimes. He was hanged the following year. Karl Brandt was killed during fighting in Posen, Poland, in February 1945. Ewald Sternhagel, Stroop's field commander in the uprising, resides today in Marburg/Lahn, West Germany, inexplicably a free man. Josef Blösche (known as Frankenstein to the Jews), who committed random murders in the ghetto before the uprising and later helped track down bunkers, was recognized in East Germany after the war in a photograph with some captured Jews. He was tried and executed. His partner in murder, Heinrich Klaustermeier, lives in Sennestadt, West Germany, untouched by the law. And Alfons Czapp, who helped to seek out Jews and witnessed the murder of about five hundred in Pawiak Prison, resides in Gelsenkirchen, West Germany.[9]

Captain (later Major) Henryk Iwanski continued to lead rescue missions into the ghetto until August 1943, when he was severely wounded again in the lung, leg, and arm. He was unconscious for four days and out of action for five months. He then fought in the Warsaw Rising in August 1944 and was wounded twice more. After the war, he received his reward: The Communist government in Poland arrested him, together with other Home Army officers, accusing him of fighting not for the workers but only for the "intellectuals and the rich"; he was imprisoned for seven years. Today, Iwanski, nearly destitute and still suffering from his wounds, lives in Warsaw with his wife, Wictoria, who has never recovered from the tubercular condition she contracted while nursing a sick Jewish girl.

Tragically enough—despite their great personal sacrifices and the deaths of Iwanski's two sons, two brothers, and father in the service of the Jews—Iwanski is not fully appreciated by the Jews. He was awarded an Israeli medal as a "righteous gentile," but most Jews know little about his role in the uprising and many do not give him due credit, apparently because he supported the ZZW, which represented the minority Revisionist sector of Zionism. Many also doubt some of his claims, since there are no known Jewish survivors from the ghetto battles in which he says he was involved. However, his deputy, Lieutenant Wladyslaw Zajdler, before dying some years ago, wrote detailed accounts of these battles that support Iwanski's own statements.[10]

Prime Minister Wladyslaw Sikorski died in London on July 2, 1943. Three days earlier, General Stefan Rowecki, the Home Army commander, was captured by the Germans. He was executed in August 1944, after the Warsaw Rising began. General Bor-Komorowski replaced Rowecki upon his capture and led the Poles in the Warsaw Rising, going into exile after the war, when the Communists took over Poland. Colonel (later General) Antoni Chrusciel, the Home Army commander in Warsaw, helped to lead the Warsaw Rising and also fled into exile. Major (later Lieutenant Colonel) Stanislas Weber, his chief of staff, fought in the Warsaw Rising, then settled in London. But he returned to Poland in 1973 "to die at home." Captain Josef Pzenny, who attacked the Germans outside the wall during the ghetto fighting, today lives in Chicago.[11]

NOTES

The following notes indicate the principal sources of the facts presented in this book. Sources of all quotations are included. The identities of interviewees named here are indicated in the Acknowledgments. Further details on publications and documents mentioned here can be found in the Bibliography.

PROLOGUE

1. BACKGROUND TO BATTLE. Meyer Barkai's *The Fighting Ghettos;* Wladyslaw Bartoszewski and Zofia Lewin's *Righteous Among Nations;* Mary Berg's *Warsaw Ghetto;* Tuvia Borzykowski's *Between Tumbling Walls* (incl. quote, "Had the city been dark . . ."); Phillip Friedman's *Martyrs and Fighters;* Nora Levin's *The Holocaust;* Vladka Meed's *On Both Sides of the Wall;** Albert Nirenstein's *A Tower from the Enemy;* Leon Poliakov's *Harvest of Hate;* Emmanuel Ringelblum's *Polish-Jewish Relations During the Second World War* and *Notes from the Warsaw Ghetto;* Leo W. Schwarz's *The Root and the Bough;* Leonard Tushnet's *The Uses of Adversity; Biuletyn Zydowskiego Instytuto Historycznego* (BZIH): No. 26, 1958, "The Smuggling in the Warsaw Ghetto," by M. Passenstein, and No. 55, 1964, "Secret Education in the Warsaw Ghetto" and "House Com-

---

*Vladka Meed's original name was Feigele Peltel, as she is called in this book.

mittees in the Warsaw Ghetto," by Ruta Sakowska; *Collier's*, Feb.. 20, 1943, "Behind the Wall," by Tosha Bialer; *Congress Weekly*, May 12, 1944, "When Jews Settled in Poland " (incl. quote, "My land is open to you . . ."); *Poland*, Jan. 1960, "The City of Death," by Ludwik Herszfeld; Oneg Shabat Archives; interviews with many survivors of the Warsaw Ghetto

THE EVE

1. MORDECHAI ANIELEWICZ AND THE ZOB. Barkai's *The Fighting Ghettos;* Nachman Blumenthal and Joseph Kermish's *Resistance and Uprising in the Warsaw Ghetto;* Friedman's *Martyrs and Fighters;* Israel Guttman's *Revolt of the Besieged;* Shmuel Krakowski's *The Military Aspects of the Warsaw Ghetto Uprising* (unpublished thesis); Bernard Mark's *The PPR and the Jewish Problem During the Hitlerite Occupation* and *Struggle and Destruction of the Warsaw Ghetto;* Nirenstein's *A Tower from the Enemy;* Ringelblum Institute's *Dri; Encyclopaedia Judaica:* Vol. 3, "Mordechai Anielewicz," and Vol. 7, "Hashomer Hatzair"; *Sefer Hashomer Hatzair* (incl. quote from Mira Fuchrer's letter relating to Mordechai); Yuri Suhl's *They Fought Back;* Tushnet's *The Pavement of Hell* and *To Die with Honor;* BZIH, No. 62, 1967, "The Relation of Forces in the Warsaw Ghetto Uprising." by Krakowski; *L'Express*, May 5–11, 1975, "The Warsaw Ghetto Revolt," by Emile Guikovaty; *Jewish Heritage,* Spring 1968, "The Facts about the Jewish Resistance," by Yehuda Bauer; *Jewish Life*, Apr. 1951, "The PPR and Ghetto Resistance," by M. Edin; *Mosty*, Apr. 1947, "He Was My Pupil," by Anna Bayer; *Yad Vashem Bulletin* (YVB): No. 2, 1957, "Facts and Motivations in Jewish Resistance," by A. Z. Braun and Dov Levin, and No. 4–5, Oct. 1959, "Who Organized the Revolt?" by Nachman Blumenthal; *Yad Vashem Studies* (YVS), Vol. 9, "The Genesis of the Resistance in the Warsaw Ghetto," by I. Guttman; *Youth and Nation,* June 1945, "The Commander of the Ghetto Revolt," by Yosef Shamir; Oneg Shabat Archives, "Mordechai Anielewicz and His Movement," by E. Ringelblum (incl. Mordechai's conversation with stranger); Interviews with Marek Edelman, Israel Guttman, Joseph Kermish, Shmuel Krakowski, Zivia Lubetkin (incl. quotes by Mordechai at final briefing), Yitzhak Zuckerman

2. GENERAL STROOP VISITS THE GHETTO. Krakowski's *The Military Aspects of the Warsaw Ghetto Uprising;* Czeslaw Madajczyk's *Pol-*

itics of the Third Reich in Occupied Poland; Nirenstein's *A Tower from the Enemy;* Stanislaw Ploski's *German Materials on the History of the Warsaw Ghetto Uprising; The Report of Jürgen Stroop;* Josef Wulf's *The Third Reich and Its Executives; Odra,* Apr. 1972–Feb. 1974, "Conversations with an Executioner," by Kazimierz Moczarski*; Transcript, Stroop trial; Interviews with Erwin Grosse, Franz Korner, Tadeusz Kur, Kazimierz Moczarski, Franz Stroop

3. ARIE WILNER AND THE POLISH UNDERGROUND. Rachel Auerbach's *The Warsaw Ghetto Uprising;* Bartoszewski and Lewin's *Righteous Among Nations* (incl. dialogue between Grabowski and Wilner); Tatiana Bernstein and Adam Rutkowski's *Help for the Jews in Poland;* Blumenthal and Kermish's *Resistance and Uprising in the Warsaw Ghetto;* Tadeusz Bor-Komorowski's *The Secret Army;* P. Friedman's *Their Brothers' Keepers;* Guttman's *Revolt of the Besieged;* J. S. Hertz' *Zygielbojm Book;* Kazimierz Iranek-Osmecki's *He Who Saves One Life;* Jan Karski's *Story of a Secret State* (incl. dialogue involving Kozielewski, Karski's real name); Stefan Korbonski's *Fighting Poland;* Krakowski's *The Military Aspects of the Warsaw Ghetto Uprising;* Mark's *Struggle and Destruction in the Warsaw Ghetto* and *Uprising in the Warsaw Ghetto* (incl. dialogue between Wilner and Wolinski in Wolinski's report on Polish aid to Jews); Melech Neustadt's *Destruction and Rising;* Nirenstein's *A Tower from the Enemy;* Tadeusz Pelczynski and Adam Ciolkosz' *Armed Resistance in the Warsaw Ghetto in 1943; The Polish Armed Forces in the Second World War,* Vol. 3; Ringelblum's *Polish–Jewish Relations During the Second World War; Sefer Hashomer Hatzair;* Suhl's *They Fought Back; Bleter far Geshikhte,* Vol. 1, No. 2, 1948, "The Polish Democratic Movement and the Insurrection in the Warsaw Ghetto," by R. Gerber; *Jewish Forum,* Aug. 1944, "Polish–Jewish Collaboration in Underground Poland," by Jan Karski; *Jewish Frontier,* Apr. 1967, "Tosya Altman: 1918–1943," by I. M. Biderman; *Midstream,* June 1963, "The Warsaw Ghetto Uprising and the Poles," by Reuben Ainsztein; YVB: No. 3, July 1958, "Arms Used by the Warsaw Ghetto Fighters," by J. Kermish; No. 4–5, "The Jews Fought Alone," by N. Blumenthal; and No. 22, May 1968, "The Poles and the Warsaw Ghetto Uprising," by J. Kermish; *Yalkout Moreshet,* Mar. 1968, "Portrait of a Fighter"; British diplo-

---

*Kazimierz, an officer in the Home Army, was arrested by the Communist regime after the war, as were many Home Army officers, and shared a prison cell with General Stroop for nine months during which Stroop reminisced about the uprising. Kazimierz took detailed notes.

matic messages, Sept. 1942 to start of uprising; Bund letter to government-in-exile, May 11, 1942; Home Delegate report to Polish government-in-exile, Apr. 24, 1943; Stanislaw Weber's reports, "Ghetto Uprising" and "Report of Cooperation Between the Warsaw District of the Home Army and the Jewish Fighting Organization"; Guta and Jacob Wilner's testimony at Yad Vashem; Interviews with Wladyslaw Bartoszewski, Adam Ciolkosz, Edelman, Guttman, Kazimierz Iranek-Osmecki, Joseph Kermish, Emilka Kosower, Lubetkin, Stanislaw Weber (incl. dialogue involving Weber, Chrusciel, Wilner), Zuckerman

4. YITZHAK ZUCKERMAN ON THE ARYAN SIDE. Blumenthal and Kermish's *Resistance and Uprising in the Warsaw Ghetto; Encyclopaedia Judaica:* Vol. 5, "Cukierman" [Zuckerman]; Vol. 8, "Hehalutz"; Vol. 11, "Lubetkin"; Mark's *Struggle and Destruction of the Warsaw Ghetto;* Neustadt's *Destruction and Rising; Commentary,* Jan. 1952, "A Warsaw Fighter in Israel," by Zelda Popkin; Weber reports; Interviews with Lubetkin, Zuckerman (incl. dialogue with Wolinski)

5. HENRYK IWANSKI AND THE ZZW. Bartoszewski and Lewin's *Righteous Among Nations;* Blumenthal and Kermish's *Resistance and Uprising in the Warsaw Ghetto; Encyclopaedia Judaica,* Vol. 4, "Betar"; Alfred Katz's *Poland's Ghettos at War;* Krakowski's *The Military Aspects of the Warsaw Ghetto Uprising;* Chaim Lazar's *Muranowska 7;* Mark's *Struggle and Destruction of the Warsaw Ghetto; The Polish Armed Forces in the Second World War,* Vol. 3; David Wdowinski's *And We Are Not Saved; Express Wieczorny,* Apr. 19/20, 1958, "Memoirs of Wladyslaw Zajdler" (incl. dialogue on sewer trip); *Horizonty,* May 15–July 15, 1968, "Jews in Poland Yesterday and Today"; Iwanski report, "With the Polish Underground of 'Bystry'"; Simcha Korngold's memoirs; Henryk Rolirad's memoirs; Richard Walewski's memoirs; Oneg Shabat Archives (incl. a visit by Ringelblum to ZZW headquarters); Interviews with Adam Halperin, Henryk Iwanski (incl. dialogue with Appelbojm), Simcha Korngold, Lubetkin, Yehoshua Prechner, Henryk Rolirad, Fela Shapsik

6. LUTEK ROTBLATT AND HIS CHILDREN. Neustadt's *Destruction and Rising;* Nirenstein's *A Tower from the Enemy;* Ringelblum's *Notes from the Warsaw Ghetto;* Jonas Turkow's *That's What It Was Like* (incl. Turkow–Rotblatt dialogue); Josef Rode's essay on Jewish police; Ber Warm's memoirs; Interviews with Guttman, Hela Schipper (incl. Schipper–Rotblatt dialogue), Jonas Turkow

7. **CHAIM FRIMER GOES HOME.** Chaim Frimer and Aharon Karmi's *Out of the Fire* (incl. dialogue involving Frimer); Mark's *Struggle and Destruction of the Warsaw Ghetto;* Neustadt's *Destruction and Rising;* Interviews with Josef Barski, Henryk Kotlicki (incl. quote in pistol episode), Lubetkin, Simcha Rathajzer, Schipper

8. **FEIGELE PELTEL IN THE GHETTO.** Marek Edelman's *The Ghetto Fights; Encyclopaedia Judaica,* Vol. 4, "Bund"; Bernard Goldstein's *The Stars Bear Witness;* Mark's *Struggle and Destruction of the Warsaw Ghetto;* Meed's *On Both Sides of the Wall* (incl. dialogue involving Feigele); *Ghetto Speaks,* Aug. 1, 1943, "Michal Klepfisz"; YVB, No. 3, July 1958, "Arms Used by the Warsaw Ghetto Fighters," by J. Kermish; Interviews with Edelman, Kermish

9. **TÖBBENS BOUNCES BACK.** Barkai's *The Fighting Ghettos;* Alexander Donat's *The Holocaust Kingdom;* Friedman's *Martyrs and Fighters;* Raul Hilberg's *The Destruction of the European Jews;* Mark's *Struggle and Destruction of the Warsaw Ghetto;* Nirenstein's *A Tower from the Enemy;* Gerald Reitlinger's *The Final Solution;* Ringelblum's *Notes from the Warsaw Ghetto;* BZIH: No. 23, 1957, "The Walther C. Többens Works in the Warsaw Ghetto," by F. Tusk-Scheinwechsler, and No. 45–46, "Compulsory Work of Jews in Warsaw," by T. Berenstein; Fritz Schultz's diary; Transcript, Konrad trial; Transcript, Többens trial; Interviews with Aharon Chmielnicki, Kalman Friedman, Yitzhak Gitler, Stefan Grajek, Grosse, Michael L., Heinrich Lauts, Jacob Putermilch, Moshe Ring, Ludwig Többens, Zuckerman

10. **SEWEK TOPOREK AND THE GESTAPO.** Ringelblum's *Notes on the Warsaw Ghetto* and *Polish-Jewish Relations During the Second World War;* Tushnet's *To Die with Honor;* YVB, No. 13, Oct. 1963, "The Ghetto's Two Front Struggle," by J. Kermish; Henryk Rolirad's memoirs; Interviews with Krakowski, Sewek Toporek (incl. dialogue)

11. **ROTBALSAM AND THE HOSPITAL.** Tushnet's *The Uses of Adversity;* BZIH, No. 41, 1962, "Jewish Hospital in Warsaw," by Sabina Gurfinkiel-Glocerowa; Interviews with Henryk Kroszczor, Israel Rotbalsam

12. **ZYGIELBOJM MEETS KOZIELEWSKI.** Goldstein's *The Stars Bear Witness;* Hertz' *Zygielbojm Book;* Karski's *Story of a Secret State* (incl. Zygielbojm–Kozielewski dialogue); Meed's *On Both Sides of the Wall* (incl. Feigele–Manya Zygielbojm dialogue); Arthur D. Morse's *While Six Million Died;* Pelczynski and Ciolkosz' *Armed Resistance in the Warsaw Ghetto in 1943;* Isaac Schwarzbart's *Story of*

the *Warsaw Ghetto Uprising; Zeszyty Historyczne* (Historical Note-book); Interview with Ciolkosz

13. STROOP RETURNS FROM GHETTO. Jewish Historical Institute's *The Report of Jürgen Stroop; Odra,* Apr. 1972–Feb. 1974, "Conversations with an Executioner," by K. Moczarski; Transcript, Stroop trial; Interview with Moczarski

14. CHAIM AWAITS ENEMY. Frimer and Karmi's *Out of the Flames;* Guttman's *Revolt of the Besieged;* Mark's *Uprising in the Warsaw Ghetto* (1975); Neustadt's *Destruction and Rising;* Interview: Masha Glytman

15. MORDECHAI THE "TROUBLEMAKER." See Note 14, this chapter; Lazar's *Muranowska 7*

THE FIRST DAY

1. STROOP WAITS FOR NEWS. See Note 13, THE EVE

2. VON SAMMERN-FRANKENEGG'S PLAN. See Note 13, THE EVE; Rachel Auerbach's *The Warsaw Ghetto Uprising;* Krakowski's *The Military Aspects of the Warsaw Ghetto Uprising;* Mark's *Struggle and Destruction of the Warsaw Ghetto;* Neustadt's *Destruction and Rising;* Wulf's *The Third Reich and Its Executives;* Interviews with Rachel Auerbach, Maria Kann, Leon Penner

3. THE BATTLE AT NALEWKI-GENSIA-FRANCISZKANSKA. Barkai's *The Fighting Ghettos;* Borzykowski's *Between Tumbling Walls;* Mark's *Struggle and Destruction of the Warsaw Ghetto;* Neustadt's *Destruction and Rising; Focus,* Vol. 3, No. 2, 1961, "I Fought in the Warsaw Ghetto Uprising," by Z. Lubetkin (incl. quote); Interview with Lubetkin

4. THE BATTLE AT MILA-ZAMENHOF. Borzykowski's *Between Tumbling Walls;* Frimer and Karmi's *Out of the Fire* (incl. quote, "The Jews have weapons!" and quote by Mordechai); Mark's *Struggle and Destruction of the Warsaw Ghetto;* Neustadt's *Destruction and Rising;* Masha Glytman's testimony, Yad Vashem (incl. quote, "Hans, a woman is shooting!"); Interview with Glytman

5. ZUCKERMAN ACTS ON ARYAN SIDE. Neustadt's *Destruction and Rising;* Interview with Zuckerman

6. CELEMENSKI'S DISILLUSIONMENT. Jacob Glatstein's *Anthology of Holocaust Literature:* "With My Martyred People," by Jacob Celemenski (incl. quotes); Meed's *On Both Sides of the Wall*

7. STROOP TAKES OVER FROM VON SAMMERN-FRANKENEGG. See

Note 2, this chapter (dialogue from *Odra*); Blumenthal and Kermish's *Resistance and Uprising in the Warsaw Ghetto:* "The Story of the Uprising," by Adam Halperin; Mark's *Struggle and Destruction in the Warsaw Ghetto;* Wdowinski's *And We Are Not Saved;* BZIH, No. 19–20, 1956, "About the Gestapo Agency in the Warsaw Ghetto," by A. Rutkowski; Transcript, Stroop trial

8. SECOND BATTLE AT NALEWKI-GENSIA-FRANCISZKANSKA. See Note 3, this chapter

9. STROOP PRAISES HIS MEN. See Note 13, THE EVE

10. BATTLE AT MURANOWSKI SQUARE. Blumenthal and Kermish's *Resistance and Uprising in the Warsaw Ghetto;* Lazar's *Muranowska 7;* Mark's *Struggle and Destruction of the Warsaw Ghetto;* Wdowinski's *And We Are Not Saved;* Richard Walewski's memoirs; Interviews with Halperin, David Plonski (incl. dialogue), Shapsik

11. JACOB PUTERMILCH AND THE BOMB. Frimer and Karmi's *Out of the Fire;* Stefan Grajek's *Three Days of Battle;* Mark's *Struggle and Destruction of the Warsaw Ghetto;* Neustadt's *Destruction and Rising;* Putermilch's memoirs and testimony, Yad Vashem; Interviews with Chmielnicki, Grajek, Putermilch

12. TÖBBENS, LAUTS, AND THE BRUSH WORKERS. Edelman's *The Ghetto Fights;* Goldstein's *The Stars Bear Witness;* Mark's *Struggle and Destruction of the Warsaw Ghetto;* BZIH, No. 42, 1962, "75 Days in the Burning Warsaw Ghetto," by B. Goldman; Rathajzer's testimony, Yad Vashem; Transcript, Többens trial; Interviews with Edelman, Lauts (incl. dialogue), Rathajzer

13. THE UNFINISHED BUILDING. BZIH, No. 25, 1958, "The Course of Events in the Warsaw Ghetto," by I. [Yitzhak] Gitler; Interviews with Yitzhak Gitler, Maria and Michael L. (dialogue from all three)

14. TOPOREK FORCED TO HELP GESTAPO. Mark's *Struggle and Destruction of the Warsaw Ghetto;* Neustadt's *Destruction and Rising;* Transcript, Konrad trial; Transcript, Stroop trial; Interview with Toporek (incl. quotes)

15. THE HOSPITAL MASSACRE. See Note 11, THE EVE

16. THE CHURCH AND THE FIRE TRUCK. Father Antoni Czarnecki's *On the Spiritual Activity of the All-Saints Parish Priests in the Warsaw Ghetto Between November 15, 1940 and July 22, 1942; Prawo i Zycie,* No. 11, May 27, 1962, "Report by T. Bednarezyk"; Interviews with Antoni Czarnecki, Iwanski

17. CHRUSCIEL WANTS TO HELP JEWS. Mark's *Struggle and Destruction of the Warsaw Ghetto* and *Uprising in the Warsaw Ghetto*

(1963) (incl. Chrusciel quote, "There were . . . certain sections of the public . . ."); Interviews with Kosover, Weber (incl. dialogue with Chrusciel)

18. PSZENNY'S ATTACK. Bartoszewski and Lewin's *Righteous Among Nations*; Mark's *Struggle and Destruction of the Warsaw Ghetto; Midstream*, June 1963, "The Warsaw Ghetto Uprising and the Poles," by Ainsztein; Interview with Weber

19. TUVIA AT THE SEDER. Borzykowski's *Between Tumbling Walls*; Interview with Lubetkin

20. KALMAN FRIEDMAN AND HIS NEIGHBORS. Kalman Friedman's *Calendars*; YVB, No. 13, Oct. 1963, "In the Warsaw Ghetto in Its Dying Days," by K. Friedman; Interview with Kalman Friedman (dialogue from all three sources)

21. MORDECHAI CHANGES TACTICS. Borzykowski's *Between Tumbling Walls*; Frimer and Karmi's *Out of the Fire*; Guttman's *Revolt of the Besieged*; Mark's *Struggle and Destruction of the Warsaw Ghetto*; Neustadt's *Destruction and Rising*; Interviews with Glytman, Guttman, Lubetkin, Zuckerman

22. HAHN AND HIMMLER PRAISE STROOP. See Note 2, this chapter (quotes from *Odra*)

23. THE BERMUDA CONFERENCE. Morse's *While Six Million Died*

THE SECOND DAY

1. MORDECHAI AWAKENS. Guttman's *Revolt of the Besieged*; Interviews with Glytman, Guttman

2. STROOP PREPARES FOR NEW ATTACK. See Note 2, THE EVE

3. LAUTS APPEALS TO JEWS. See Note 12, THE EVE

4. A NEW JEWISH VICTORY. Frimer and Karmi's *Out of the Fire*; Putermilch's memoirs (incl. dialogue) and testimony, Yad Vashem; Interviews with Chmielnicki, Putermilch

5. DVORA AND SHLOMO. Grajek's *Three Days of Battle* (incl. dialogue); Neustadt's *Destruction and Rising*; Interview with Grajek

6. STROOP CAPTURES MURANOWSKI SQUARE. See Note 10, THE EVE

7. THE BIGGEST EXPLOSION. See Note 5, this chapter; Edelman's *The Ghetto Fights*; Goldstein's *The Stars Bear Witness*; Mark's *Uprising in the Warsaw Ghetto* (1963) (incl. "Report of an Anonymous Fighter"); Neustadt's *Destruction and Rising; L'Express*, May 5–11,

1975, "The Warsaw Ghetto Revolt," by E. Guikovaty; Rathajzer's testimony, Yad Vashem; Interviews with Edelman, Rathajzer

8. MAREK'S FIGHTERS RETREAT. Edelman's *The Ghetto Fights; Dri* (incl. Diamant's quote); Rathajzer's testimony, Yad Vashem; Interviews with Edelman, Rathajzer

9. JERZY DURACZ AND THE PPR ATTACK. See Note 18, THE FIRST DAY; Mark's *The PPR and the Jewish Problem During the Hitlerite Occupation: Jewish Life*, Apr. 1951, "The PPR and Ghetto Resistance," by M. Edin; *Yalkout Moreshet*, Oct. 1972, "In the Underground on Both Sides of the Wall," by Anna Duracz (incl. quote)

10. JEWISH FUGITIVE CAPTURED. *Pamietniki Robotnikow z Czasow Okupacji* [Diaries of Workers from Occupation Times], Vol. I: "Days of Horror and Struggle for Freedom," by Kazimierz Szmczak

11. CELEBRATING HITLER'S BIRTHDAY. Hilberg's *The Destruction of European Jews*; Madajczyk's *Politics of the Third Reich in Occupied Poland*; Stanislaw Piotrowski's *Hans Frank's Diaries; The Report of Jürgen Stroop*; Transcript, Stroop trial

12. ZUCKERMAN AND KAROL. Yad Vashem's *Jewish Resistance During the Holocaust*: ("Twenty-Five Years After the Warsaw Ghetto Revolt," by Y. Zuckerman); Interview with Zuckerman (incl. dialogue)

13. STROOP CRACKS DOWN ON INDUSTRIALISTS. Mark's *Struggle and Destruction of the Warsaw Ghetto; The Report of Jürgen Stroop*; BZIH, No. 23, 1957, "The Walther C. Többens Works in the Warsaw Ghetto," by F. Tusk-Scheinwechsler (incl. quote); Schultz' diary; Testimony, Stroop trial; Interviews with Lauts, L. Többens

14. VISIT TO MILA 29. Guttman's *Revolt of the Besieged; Yalkout Moreshet*, Mar. 1968, "Portrait of a Fighter" (incl. dialogue); Interview with Guttman

15. STROOP DECIDES TO BURN DOWN GHETTO. See Note 13, THE EVE

THE THIRD DAY

1. ELIEZER GELLER AND THE NAZI DEADLINE. See Note 11, THE FIRST DAY (quote by Julek from *Out of the Fire*); Nathan Eck's *Wanderers in the Paths of Death*; David Ron's *They Are Firing; Slowo*

Mlodych, No. 3, Apr. 17, 1948, "Eliezer Geller," by N. Eck; *Yiddischer Kempfer,* Sept. 27, 1946, "Eliezer Geller, Halutz-Kempfer," by N. Eck

2. SCHULTZ NEEDS MORE JEWS. Schultz' diary

3. KALMAN GOES UPSTAIRS. See Note 20, THE FIRST DAY

4. ROUNDUP IN THE PRODUCTIVE GHETTO. See Note 11, THE FIRST DAY

5. FLEEING THE FIRE. See Note 8, THE SECOND DAY

6. HOLZBERG FINDS NEW SHELTER. Interview with Simcha Holzberg

7. NOEMI AND THE TWO CHILDREN. Interview with Noemi Judkowski

8. MORDECHAI LEAVES MILA 29. Borzykowski's *Between Tumbling Walls;* Frimer and Karmi's *Out of the Fire;* Mark's *Struggle and Destruction of the Warsaw Ghetto*

9. STROOP REFLECTS ON "GOOD DAY." See Note 13, THE EVE

THE FOURTH DAY

1. STROOP PULLS DOWN FLAGS. See Note 13, THE EVE; Note 10, THE FIRST DAY

2. STROOP WATCHES JEWS BURN. See Note 13, THE EVE (quote, "I myself am not asking for mercy . . ." from Transcript, Stroop trial); Walewski's memoirs; Interview with Rotbalsam

3. MORDECHAI AND HIS FIGHTERS TRAPPED. See Note 4, THE FIRST DAY

4. MAREK AND HIS FIGHTERS ESCAPE. See Note 8, THE SECOND DAY

5. HOLZBERG AND THE WOUNDED GIRL. Interview with Holzberg (incl. quotes)

6. MORDECHAI ESCAPES TO MILA 18. See Note 8, THE THIRD DAY; Barkai's *The Fighting Ghettos;* Guttman's *Revolt of the Besieged;* Neustadt's *Destruction and Rising; Commentary,* May 1947, "The Last Days of the Warsaw Ghetto," by Z. Lubetkin; Interviews with Edelman, Lubetkin, Schipper

7. JACOB LOSES HIS STOMACHACHE. Frimer and Karmi's *Out of the Fire;* Putermilch's memoirs (incl. quotes) and testimony, Yad Vashem; Interviews with Chmielnicki, Putermilch

8. POLA ELSTER AT UMSCHLAGPLATZ. *Dri* (incl. quote); Mark's

Struggle and Destruction in the Warsaw Ghetto; Interview with Wanda Rothenberg (Pola Elster's sister)

9. FEIGELE WATCHES HOLOCAUST. Meed's *On Both Sides of the Wall* (incl. dialogue)

10. BLACKMAILERS SEEK JEWS. Ringelblum's *Polish–Jewish Relations in the Second World War*

THE FIFTH DAY

1. MORDECHAI SETTLES INTO MILA 18. See Note 6, THE FOURTH DAY; *Smol,* Apr. 16, 1953, Mordechai's letter to Yitzhak

2. LEAVING THE UNFINISHED BUILDING. See Note 13, THE FIRST DAY

3. BREAD BUT NO BULLETS. See Note 7, THE FOURTH DAY

4. TOPOREK PLAYS "RUSSIAN ROULETTE." Interview with Toporek (incl. dialogue)

5. KONRAD'S SMILE DISAPPEARS. Mark's *Struggle and Destruction of the Warsaw Ghetto;* Turkow's *That's What It Was Like* (incl. quotes); Warm's memoirs; Transcript, Konrad trial; Interviews with Ring, Turkow

6. "SELECTION" AT UMSCHLAGPLATZ. See Note 8, THE FOURTH DAY; Note 5, this chapter (quotes from *That's What It Was Like* and from Warm's memoirs)

7. POLA IN THE BOXCAR. *Dri*

8. THE MARCH THROUGH WARSAW. Turkow's *That's What It Was Like* (incl. quotes); Interview with Turkow

9. KALMAN REUNITES WITH IZIO. See Note 20, THE FIRST DAY

10. EXECUTION OF A CHILD. See Note 7, THE FOURTH DAY

11. FEIGELE AND THE PHOTOGRAPHERS. See Note 9, THE FOURTH DAY

12. THE REACTION TO A ZOB APPEAL. See Note 13, THE EVE; Note 18, THE FIRST DAY; Mark's *Uprising in the Warsaw Ghetto* (1963); Original of ZOB appeal among Ringelblum papers, Yad Vashem

THE SIXTH DAY

1. AHARON'S BAKERY. See Note 7, THE FOURTH DAY

2. ROTBALSAM ESCAPES FROM HOSPITAL. Tushnet's *The Uses of Adversity;* Interview with Rotbalsam

3. AN OASIS IN THE DESERT OF FIRE. See Note 3, THE FIRST DAY; Note 6, THE FOURTH DAY (quotes from *The Fighting Ghettos*)

4. NO BREAD, NO CHOLENT. See Note 7, THE FOURTH DAY; Schultz' diary

5. KALMAN ESCAPES FROM BOXCAR. See Note 20, THE FIRST DAY

6. STROOP WATCHES WERTERFASSUNG BURN. See Note 13, THE EVE; Auerbach's *The Warsaw Ghetto Uprising*

THE SEVENTH DAY

1. A HAPPY EASTER. Auerbach's *The Warsaw Ghetto Uprising;* Helena Balicka-Kozlowska's *The Wall Had Two Sides;* Donat's *The Holocaust Kingdom;* Mark's *The Struggle and Destruction of the Warsaw Ghetto;* Joseph Tenenbaum's *Underground;* Michael Zylberberg's *A Warsaw Diary;* YVB: No. 4–5, Oct. 1959, "The Jews Fought Alone," by N. Blumenthal, and No. 22, May 1968, "The Poles and the Warsaw Ghetto Uprising," by J. Kermish; Interviews with Auerbach, Zuckerman

2. STROOP'S OVEROPTIMISM. See Note 13, THE EVE (quote from *Odra*)

3. THE MASS EXECUTIONS. Leon Wanat's *Behind the Walls of Pawiak;* Interviews with Alphons Czapp, Leon Wanat

4. TUVIA'S TREK THROUGH THE SEWER. Barkai's *The Fighting Ghettos;* Borzykowski's *Between Tumbling Walls; Commentary,* May 1947, "The Last Days of the Warsaw Ghetto," by Z. Lubetkin; *Focus,* Vol 3, No. 2, 1961, "I Fought in the Warsaw Ghetto Uprising," by Z. Lubetkin; Interview with Lubetkin

5. CHAIM AND THE POLISH FIREMEN. Frimer and Karmi's *Out of the Fire* (incl. quote); Glytman's testimony, Yad Vashem; Interview with Glytman

6. ADAM AND THE WRECKED BUNKER. Interview with Halperin

7. HENIEK'S TRICK. See Note 7, THE FOURTH DAY

8. THE WOES OF TÖBBENS AND SCHULTZ. Mark's *The Struggle and Destruction of the Warsaw Ghetto;* Reitlinger's *The Final Solution;* Schultz' diary; Transcript, Többens trial; Interview with Lauts

9. JACOB'S ESCAPE. See Note 7, THE FOURTH DAY

10. MORDECHAI VISITS FRANCISZKANSKA 30. Guttman's *Revolt of the Besieged;* Interview with Guttman

11. A GLOWING REPORT. Friedman's *Martyrs and Fighters*; Nirenstein's *A Tower from the Enemy*

THE EIGHTH DAY

1. TUVIA RETURNS. See Note 4, THE SEVENTH DAY (quote from *The Fighting Ghettos*)

2. IWANSKI PREPARES TO ENTER GHETTO. Bartoszewski and Lewin's *Righteous Among Nations*; Lazar's *Muranowska 7: Za Wolnosc i Lud*, No. 8, 1962, "Memoirs of Wladyslaw Zajdler"; Interview with Iwanski

3. BATTLE OF MILA 29. See Note 5, THE SEVENTH DAY (quotes from *Out of the Fire*)

4. FIFTEEN MINUTES TO LIVE. Borzykowski's *Between Tumbling Walls*

5. BEHIND THE DOOR. See Note 7, THE FOURTH DAY

6. SAVED FROM SUICIDE. See Note 4, this chapter

7. LUTEK FINDS HIS FAMILY. Interview with Schipper (incl. quote)

8. LEAPING TO FREEDOM. See Note 7, THE FOURTH DAY

9. GLOBOCNIK VISITS STROOP. See Note 8, THE SEVENTH DAY

10. MASSACRE OF THE SERVANTS. Wanat's *Behind the Walls of Pawiak*; Interview with Wanat

11. WAITING AT MILA 18. See Note 6, THE FOURTH DAY

THE NINTH DAY

1. IWANSKI ENTERS GHETTO. See Note 2, THE EIGHTH DAY (dialogue beginning "Well Vladek . . ." from Zajdler's memoirs; quote, "We are all dying . . ." from Iwanski interview); Blumenthal and Kermish's *Resistance and Uprising in the Warsaw Ghetto*; *Horizonty*, May 15–July 15, 1958, "Jews in Poland Yesterday and Today"

2. ZAJDLER'S FORCE IN DIFFICULTY. See Note 1, this chapter (quote, "Mr. *Poruchnik* . . ." from Zajdler's memoirs)

3. IWANSKI AND HIS SON AND BROTHER HIT. See Note 1, this chapter (quotes from Iwanski interview)

4. IWANSKI LEAVES WITH WOUNDED. See Note 1, this chapter (dialogue from Iwanski report and interview)

5. STROOP WIPES OUT ZZW FORCE ON ARYAN SIDE. See Note 13, THE EVE (quote, "The fire could spread . . ." from *Odra*); Note 2, THE EIGHTH DAY; *Midstream*, June 1963, "The Warsaw Ghetto Uprising and the Poles," by R. Ainsztein

6. POLISH FIREMEN BETRAY JEWS. See Note 5, THE SEVENTH DAY (quotes from *Out of the Fire*)

7. ZZW FIGHTERS IN PRODUCTIVE GHETTO ESCAPE. Lazar's *Muranowska 7*; Korngold's memoirs

8. THE WOUNDED ARE LEFT BEHIND. Note 7, THE FOURTH DAY (dialogue from Frimer and Karmi's *Out of the Fire* and from Putermilch's memoirs); Barkai's *The Fighting Ghettos*: "In the Teben-Schultz Section," by Leizer Levine

THE TENTH DAY

1. ZZW LEAVES MURANOWSKA 7. Lazar's *Muranowska 7*; Leon Najberg's *The Last Ones*

2. RETURN TO THE HOSPITAL BUNKER. See Note 7, THE FOURTH DAY (dialogue from Putermilch's memoirs)

3. GITLER AND MICHAEL L. ESCAPE. See Note 13, THE FIRST DAY

4. NEW CALL FOR ALLIED RETALIATION. Friedman's *Martyrs and Fighters*; Mark's *Struggle and Destruction of the Warsaw Ghetto*; Nirenstein's *A Tower from the Enemy*; Ringelblum's *Polish-Jewish Relations in the Second World War*; Isaac Schwarzbart's *The Story of the Warsaw Ghetto Uprising*

THE ELEVENTH DAY

1. TWO BUILDINGS AWAY. See Note 7, THE FOURTH DAY (dialogue from Putermilch's memoirs)

2. MORDECHAI'S PLAN TO CONTACT ARYAN SIDE. Borzykowski's *Between Tumbling Walls*; Frimer and Karmi's *Out of the Fire*; Lazar's *Muranowska 7*; *Focus*, Vol. 3, No. 2, 1961, "I Fought in the Warsaw Ghetto Uprising," by Z. Lubetkin; Rathajzer's testimony, Yad Vashem; Interviews with Edelman, Lubetkin, Rathajzer

3. INTO THE SEWER AND BACK. See Note 7, THE FOURTH DAY (quotes from Putermilch's memoirs)

4. A SECOND TRY. See Note 7, THE FOURTH DAY (dialogue from *Out of the Fire* and from Putermilch's memoirs)

THE TWELFTH DAY

1. SIMCHA AND ZALMAN REACH ARYAN SIDE. Goldstein's *The Stars Bear Witness;* Mark's *Struggle and Destruction of the Warsaw Ghetto;* Meed's *On Both Sides of the Wall;* Neustadt's *Destruction and Rising;* Rathajzer's testimony, Yad Vashem (incl. dialogue); Interviews with Rathajzer, Zuckerman
2. ELIEZER'S GROUP REACHES ARYAN SIDE. See Note 7, THE FOURTH DAY (quote from Putermilch's memoirs)
3. TWO ZZW GROUPS LINK UP ON ARYAN SIDE. Blumenthal and Kermish's *Resistance and Uprising in the Warsaw Ghetto;* Lazar's *Muranowska 7;* Interview with Iwanski
4. REGINA BACK IN THE GHETTO. See Note 7, THE FOURTH DAY; Neustadt's *Destruction and Rising*

THE THIRTEENTH DAY

1. MORDECHAI'S MAY DAY CELEBRATION. Borzykowski's *Between Tumbling Walls;* Frimer and Karmi's *Out of the Fire* (incl. quotes); Mark's *Struggle and Destruction of the Warsaw Ghetto*
2. MIRA JOINS IN CELEBRATION. See Note 1, this chapter
3. A DISQUIETING DAY FOR STROOP. See Note 13, THE EVE; Louis P. Lochner's *The Goebbels Diary*
4. REGINA'S GROUP ATTACKED. Frimer and Karmi's *Out of the Fire;* Mark's *Struggle and Destruction of the Warsaw Ghetto* (incl. quote)

THE FOURTEENTH DAY

1. MAREK AWAITS ATTACK. Edelman's *The Ghetto Fights; L'Express,* May 5–11, 1975, "The Warsaw Ghetto Revolt," by E. Guikovaty; Transcript, Stroop trial; Interview with Edelman
2. CHILD FORCED TO BETRAY BUNKER. Transcript, Stroop trial (Edelman testimony)
3. BATTLE OF FRANCISZKANSKA 30. See Note 1, this chapter; Blumenthal and Kermish's *Resistance and Uprising in the Warsaw Ghetto;* Borzykowski's *Between Tumbling Walls; Dri;* Goldstein's *The Stars Bear Witness* (incl. Blum–Edelman dialogue); Grajek's *Three Days of Battle;* Guttman's *Revolt of the Besieged;* Neustadt's *Destruc-*

363

tion and Rising; Pnina Papier's memoirs; Glytman's testimony; Rathajzer's testimony; Interviews with Edelman, Glytman, Rathajzer

4. KRÜGER'S VISIT. See Note 13, THE EVE; Auerbach's *The Warsaw Ghetto Uprising;* Lazar's *Muranowska 7;* Tenenbaum's *Underground;* Wulf's *The Third Reich and Its Executives;* Transcript, Stroop trial; Transcript, Többens trial

THE FIFTEENTH DAY

1. SECOND BATTLE OF FRANCISZKANSKA 30. See Note 3, THE FOURTEENTH DAY (Snaidmil's quote from *The Stars Bear Witness;* Shaanan's quote from *Destruction and Rising*)

2. STROOP SEEKS "PARTY BUNKER." See Note 13, THE EVE; YVS, Vol. 9, "The Warsaw Ghetto Uprising in the Light of a Hitherto Unpublished Official German Report," by J. Kermish

3. ZOB CABLE DELAYED. Mark's *Uprising in the Warsaw Ghetto* (1963)

THE SIXTEENTH DAY

1. STROOP BURNS FACTORIES. See Note 13, THE EVE

2. IWANSKI PLANS NEW MISSIONS. Lazar's *Muranowska 7;* Iwanski report to MCINC; Interview with Iwanski

THE SEVENTEENTH DAY

1. ZAJDLER'S GROUP AMBUSHED. See Note 2, THE SIXTEENTH DAY

2. SIKORSKI SPEAKS. Pelezynski and Ciol Kosz's *Armed Resistance in the Warsaw Ghetto in 1943;* Schwarzport's *Story of the Warsaw Ghetto Uprising*

3. STROOP'S LUCKY NUMBER. See Note 13, THE EVE (dialogue from *Odra*)

THE EIGHTEENTH DAY

1. IWANSKI LOSES SECOND SON AND BROTHER. See Note 2, THE SIXTEENTH DAY (dialogue from Iwanski interview)

2. "ON THE TRACK OF THE BANDITS." See Note 13, THE EVE (Hahn's quote from *Odra*)

THE NINETEENTH DAY

1. MORDECHAI CHOOSES ESCAPE PLAN. See Note 6, THE FOURTH DAY (quote, "Sing us a song . . ." from Schipper interview; "The horrible memory of this carnage . . ." "You'll soon have an opportunity . . ." "Well, let's assume . . ." and "There is a man in that bunker . . ." from *The Fighting Ghettos;* other dialogue from Schipper interview)
2. TWO GROUPS DEPART FROM MILA 18. See Note 6, THE FOURTH DAY (quotes *"Vos tut men?"* and "The heart had much to say . . ." from *The Fighting Ghettos;* dialogue involving Chaim Frimer from *Out of the Fire*)
3. KANAL'S GROUP AMBUSHED. Borzykowski's *Between Tumbling Walls*
4. SIMCHA PREPARES RESCUE PLAN. See Note 1, THE TWELFTH DAY

THE TWENTIETH DAY

1. KANAL'S GROUP FIND REFUGE. See Note 3, THE NINETEENTH DAY
2. HELA REACHES ARYAN SIDE. Interview with Schipper (incl. dialogue)
3. ZIVIA WAITS AT FRANCISZKANSKA 22. Barkai's *The Fighting Ghettos;* Edelman's *The Ghetto Fights;* Frimer and Karmi's *Out of the Fire* (incl. dialogue); Mark's *Struggle and Destruction of the Warsaw Ghetto;* Neustadt's *Destruction and Rising; Commentary,* May 1947, "The Last Days of the Warsaw Ghetto," by Z. Lubetkin; Interviews with Edelman, Glytman, Lubetkin
4. DEATH IN MILA 18. See Note 6, THE FOURTH DAY; *Sefer Hashomer Hatzair;* (dialogue from *Out of the Fire* and from Edelman, Lubetkin, and Schipper interviews, all based on conversations the co-author of that book, Frimer, and the three interviewees had with survivors of the Mila 18 battle, none of whom are alive today)
5. KANAL'S GROUP RETURNS TO MILA 18. See Note 3, THE NINETEENTH DAY (incl. quote)

6. LUBETKIN'S GROUP RETURNS TO MILA 18. See Note 3, this chapter

7. TUVIA'S GROUP HEADS FOR ARYAN SIDE. See Note 3, this chapter (quote, "Then what are we waiting for? . . ." from *Out of the Fire;* "There was dumb silence . . ." and "At the farewell . . ." from *The Fighting Ghettos; Dri*

8. SIMCHA HEADS FOR THE GHETTO. Rathajzer testimony, Yad Vashem (inc. quote); Interview with Rathajzer

9. STROOP REPORTS ON MILA 18. See Note 13, THE EVE

THE TWENTY-FIRST DAY

1. SIMCHA SEARCHES FOR COMRADES. See Note 8, THE TWENTIETH DAY (incl. quotes)

2. SIMCHA AND TUVIA GROUPS MEET IN SEWER. See Note 1, THE TWELFTH DAY; Note 3, THE NINETEENTH DAY (quotes from Rathajzer interview)

3. FIGHTERS RETURN FROM ZIVIA'S GROUP. See Note 3, THE TWENTIETH DAY (quotes from *The Fighting Ghettos* and Lubetkin interview); *Dri*

4. ZIVIA'S GROUP TRUDGES THROUGH SEWER. See Notes 3 and 8, THE TWENTIETH DAY; *Dri* (incl. quotes involving Altman and Berlinski)

5. SIMCHA AND THE BLACKMAILERS. See Note 8, THE TWENTIETH DAY (dialogue from Rathajzer interview)

6. WAITING IN THE SEWER. See Notes 3 and 8, THE TWENTIETH DAY (dialogue between civilian and fighter from *Out of the Fire;* quote, "We're thinking about you . . ." and Zuckerman note from Lubetkin interview)

THE TWENTY-SECOND DAY

1. A DESPERATE DECISION. See Notes 3 and 8, THE TWENTIETH DAY

2. OUT OF THE SEWER. See Notes 3 and 8, THE TWENTIETH DAY (quotes from Rathajzer testimony, Yad Vashem, and interview, and from Lubetkin interview); *Folks-Shtimme,* Apr. 1973

3. ARRIVAL IN THE FOREST. See Notes 3 and 8, THE TWENTIETH DAY (quote from *Out of the Fire*)

4. INVITATION TO SUICIDE. *Jewish Resistance During the Holocaust;* Interview with Zuckerman

5. FRANIA'S FAREWELL. Balicka-Kozlowska's *The Wall Had Two Sides* (incl. quotes); Interview with Zuckerman

6. SIMCHA RETURNS TO THE FOREST. See Notes 3 and 8, THE TWENTIETH DAY (Simcha's quote from his testimony, Yad Vashem; Zivia's quote from *The Fighting Ghettos*)

7. HOSPITAL BUNKER BURNS. Frimer and Karmi's *Out of the Fire;* Putermilch's memoirs

THE LAST DAYS

1. CLEANING OUT THE BUNKERS. See Note 2, THE SIXTEENTH DAY; Blumenthal and Kermish's *Resistance and Uprising in the Warsaw Ghetto;* Interviews with Holzberg, Rotbalsam

2. SOVIET AIR RAID. Mark's *Struggle and Destruction of the Warsaw Ghetto;* Interviews with Iwanski, Plonski

3. ZYGIELBOJM'S FAREWELL. Hertz' *Zygielbojm Book;* Pelczynski and Ciolkosz's *Armed Resistance in the Warsaw Ghetto in 1943; Zeszyty Historyczne; The Observer,* May 19, 1968, "The Warsaw Ghetto," by R. Ainsztein; Interview with Ciolkosz

4. STROOP BLOWS UP SYNAGOGUE. See Note 13, THE EVE

EPILOGUE

1. THE BATTLE GOES ON. See Note 13, THE EVE; Auerbach's *The Warsaw Ghetto Uprising;* Blumenthal and Kermish's *Resistance and Uprising in the Warsaw Ghetto;* Michael Borwicz' *The Warsaw Ghetto Insurrection;* Goldstein's *The Stars Bear Witness;* Grajek's *Three Days of Battle;* Lazar's *Muranowska 7;* Lochner's *The Goebbels Diaries;* Madajcyk's *Politics of the Third Reich in Occupied Poland;* Mark's *Struggle and Destruction of the Warsaw Ghetto;* Leon Najberg's *The Last Ones;* Piotrowski's *Hans Frank's Diary;* Tenenbaum's *Underground;* Tushnet's *To Die with Honor;* BZIH, No. 42, 1962, "75 Days in the Burning Warsaw Ghetto," by B. Goldman); *Jewish Life,* Aug. 1956, "Rubble Fighters of the Ghetto," by B. Mark; Interviews with Iwanski, Anna and Zygmunt Sliwicka

2. STROOP'S FATE. See Note 13, THE EVE

3. MURDER IN THE FOREST. Neustadt's *Destruction and Rising; Sef-*

er *Hashomer Hatzair; Midstream,* June 1963, "The Warsaw Ghetto Uprising and the Poles," by R. Ainsztein (incl. excerpt from Bor-Komorowski report); Putermilch's memoirs and testimony, Yad Vashem; Rathajzer's testimony, Yad Vashem; Interviews with Lubetkin, Putermilch, Rathajzer, Zuckerman

4. OTHER BETRAYALS. Borzykowski's *Between Tumbling Walls;* Glatstein's *Anthology of Holocaust Literature;* Goldstein's *The Stars Bear Witness;* Meed's *On Both Sides of the Wall; Sefer Hashomer Hatzair;* Interviews with Lubetkin, Zuckerman

5. THE CELLULOID FACTORY AND HOTEL POLSKI. Borzykowski's *Between Tumbling Walls;* Frimer and Karmi's *Out of the Fire;* Grajek's *Three Days of Battle;* Meed's *On Both Sides of the Wall;* Neustadt's *Destruction and Rising; Sefer Hashomer Hatzair;* YVB, No. 6–7, June 1960, "The Fighting Gordonia Group," by David Ron; Interviews with Grajek, Lubetkin, Plonski, Schipper, Zuckerman

6. IN AND AFTER THE POLISH WARSAW RISING. Borzykowski's *Between Tumbling Walls;* Meed's *On Both Sides of the Wall* (incl. quotes): YVB, No. 8–9, Mar. 1961, "Remnants of the Warsaw Ghetto in the Revolt of the Poles in Warsaw," by S. Grajek; Putermilch's memoirs and testimony, Yad Vashem; Interviews with Edelman, Glytman, Grajek, Lubetkin, Putermilch, Zuckerman

7. IMMIGRANTS TO ISRAEL. Interviews with individuals mentioned in this section

8. MASSACRE IN PONIATOW. Neustadt's *Destruction and Rising;* Tenenbaum's *Underground;* Wdowinski's *And We Are Not Saved;* Wulf's *The Third Reich and Its Executives; Folk un Velt,* May 1959, "Liquidation of the Warsaw Ghetto," by J. Turkow; Transcript, Többens trial; Interviews with Lauts, L. Többens

9. FATE OF STROOP'S COLLEAGUES. Mark's *Struggle and Destruction of the Warsaw Ghetto; Der Spiegel,* No. 1, 1937, "Until the Last"; *Stern,* No. 41, 1969, "One of the Murderers Is Still Free," by Peter Neuhauser and Daniel Haller; *Vorwarts:* June 15, 1972, "Nobody Believes Such Men Could Commit Murder," by Werner Hill, and June 14, 1973, "A Thousand Bridges for the Ex-Gestapo Chief"

10. IWANSKI'S REWARD. Lazar's *Muranowska 7;* Interview with Iwanski

11. FATE OF THE POLISH LEADERS. Bor-Komorowski's *The Secret Army;* Korbonski's *Fighting Poland;* Interview with Weber

BIBLIOGRAPHY

The following is a list of the most important books, periodicals, and documents consulted by the author.

Books

ADAM (Silverstein). *Begetaoth* [In the Ghettos]. Tel Aviv: Sifriat Poalim, 1959.

ALEF-BALKOWIAK, GUSTAW. *Gorace Dni* [Hot Days]. Warsaw: Ministerstwo Obrony Narodowej, 1962.

AMERICAN COUNCIL OF WARSAW JEWS. *The Day by Day Eyewitness Diary of a Polish Gentile.* New York: 1944.

APENSZLAK, JACOB, and MOSHE POLAKIEWICZ. *Armed Resistance of the Jews in Poland.* New York: American Federation for Polish Jews, 1944.

AUERBACH, RACHEL. *Mered Geto Varsha* [The Warsaw Ghetto Uprising]. Tel Aviv: Hamenorah, 1953.

BALICKA-KOZLOWSKA, HELENA. *Mur Mia Divie Strony* [The Wall Had Two Sides]. Warsaw: Ministerstwo Obrony Narodowej, 1958.

BANASIEWICZ, CZESLAW Z. *The Warsaw Ghetto.* New York: Yoseloff, 1968.

BARKAI, MEYER, ed. *The Fighting Ghettos.* New York: Lippincott, 1962.

BARTOSZEWSKI, WLADYSLAW. *The Blood Shed Unites Us*. Warsaw: Interpress, 1970.

————, and ZOFIA LEWIN, eds. *Righteous Among Nations*. London: Earl's Court, 1969.

BASKIND, BER. *La Grande Épouvante* [The Great Fear]. Paris: Calmann-Levy, 1945.

BEIT LOHAMEI HAGHETAOT. *Extermination and Resistance*, Vol. 1. Israel: 1958.

BERENSTEIN, TATIANA, and ADAM RUTKOWSKI. *Pomoc Zydom w Polsce 1939–45* [Help for the Jews in Poland, 1939–45]. Warsaw: WYD, 1963.

————, and ARTUR EISENBACH, eds. *Eksterminacja Zydow na Ziemiach Polskich w Okresie Okupacji Hitlerowskiej* [Extermination of the Jews in Poland during the Hiterite Occupation]. Warsaw: 1957.

BIRENBAUM, HALINA. *Hope Is the Last to Die*. New York: Twayne, 1967.

BLUMENTHAL, NACHMAN. *The Judenrat and the Jewish Police*. New York: YIVO, 1967.

————, and JOSEPH KERMISH. *Hameri veha Mered Begeto Varsha* [Resistance and Uprising in the Warsaw Ghetto]. Jerusalem: Yad Vashem, 1965.

BOR-KOMOROWSKI, TADEUSZ. *The Secret Army*. New York: Macmillan, 1951.

BORWICZ, MICHAL, *L'Insurrection du ghetto de Varsovie* [The Warsaw Ghetto Insurrection]. Paris: Collection Archives, 1966.

BORZYKOWSKI, TUVIA. *Between Tumbling Walls*. Israel: Beit Lohamei Haghetaot, 1972.

CIECHANOWSKI, JAN. *Defeat in Victory*. Garden City, N.Y.: Doubleday, 1947.

CZARNECKI, FATHER ANTONI. *Przyczynek do Duszpasterskiej Dzialalnosci Ksiezy par Wszystkich Swietych w Getcie Warszawskim w Czasie od 15. XI. 1940. do 22. VII. 1942* [On the Pastoral Activity of the All Saints Parish Priests in the Warsaw Ghetto Between November 15, 1940, and July 22, 1942]. Booklet published in Warsaw.

CZUPERSKA-SLIWICKA. *Anna Cztery lata Ostrego Dyzuru* [Four Years of Hard Duty]. Warsaw: Czytelnik, 1968.

DESCHNER, GUNTHER. *Menschen im Ghetto* [People in the Ghetto]. Gütersloh, W. Germany: Mohm, 1949.

370

DONAT, ALEXANDER. *The Holocaust Kingdom.* New York: Holt, Rinehart and Winston. 1965

ECK, NATHAN. *Hato'im Bedarkhe Hamavet* [Wanderers in the Paths of Death]. Jerusalem: Yad Vashem, 1960.

EDELMAN, MAREK. *The Ghetto Fights.* New York: American Representation of General Jewish Workers' Union of Poland, 1946.

Encyclopaedia Judaica: Vol. 3, "Mordechai Anielewicz"; Vol. 4, "Bund," "Betar"; Vol. 5, "Itzhak Cukierman" [Yitzhak Zuckerman]; Vol. 7, "Hashomer Hatzair"; Vol. 8, "He-Halutz"; Vol. 11, "Zivia Lubetkin"; Vol. 14, "Emmanuel Ringelblum"; Vol. 16, "The Warsaw Ghetto Uprising." Jerusalem: Keter, 1972.

ERLICHMAN, SARA. *Biydey Tmeyim* [In the Hands of the Unclean]. Tel Aviv: Hamishmeret Hatzeeri Lemifleget, 1946.

FEDERATION OF POLISH JEWS IN GREAT BRITAIN. *Remember the Warsaw Ghetto.* London. (pamphlet)

FRIEDMAN, KALMAN. *Luchot* [Calendars]. Jerusalem: Ogdan, 1964.

FRIEDMAN, PHILIP. *The Bibliography of the Warsaw Ghetto.* New York: Jewish Book Council of America, 1953.

_____. *Martyrs and Fighters.* New York: Praeger, 1954.

_____. *Their Brothers' Keepers.* New York: Crown, 1957.

FRIMER, CHAIM, and AHARON KARMI. *Min Hadleyka Hahi* [Out of the Fire]. Israel: Hakibbutz Hameuchad, 1961.

GELBLUM, MOSHE. *Geza Karut* [The Severed Trunk]. Tel Aviv: Taberski, 1947.

GLATSTEIN, JACOB, ed. *Anthology of Holocaust Literature.* Philadelphia: Jewish Publication Society of America, 1973.

GOLDSTEIN, BERNARD. *The Stars Bear Witness.* London: Gollancz, 1950.

GRAJEK, STEFAN. *Shlosha Imei Krav* [Three Days of Battle]. Tel Aviv: Ministry of Defense, 1972.

GREENBERG, HENRYK. *Wojna Żydowska* [The Jewish War]. Warsaw: PIW, 1966.

GREGOIRE, O. *Le Ghetto en flammes.* [The Ghetto in Flames]. Paris: La Presse Française et Étrangère, 1945.

GUTTMAN, ISRAEL. *Mered Hanetzurim: Mordechai Anielewicz veha Milchemet Geto Varsha* [Revolt of the Besieged: Mordechai Anielewicz and the Battle of the Warsaw Ghetto]. Merchavia, Israel: Sifriat Hapoalim, 1963.

371

HERTZ, J. S., ed. *Zygielbojm Buch* [Zygielbojm Book]. New York: Unser Tzait, 1947.

HILBERG, RAUL. *The Destruction of the European Jews.* Chicago: Quadrangle, 1961.

HIRSZFELD, LUDWIK. *Historia Jednego Zycia* [History of One Life]. Warsaw: Pax, 1957.

HIRSZHAUT, J. *Finstere necht in Pawiak* [Dark Nights in Pawiak]. Buenos Aires: Central Verband fun Polishe Yidden in Argentina, 1948.

INSTYTUT LITERACKI. *Zeszyty Historyczne* [Historical Notebook]. Paris: 1969.

IRANEK-OSMECKI, KAZIMIERZ. *He Who Saves One Life.* New York: Crown, 1972.

JEWISH FRONTIER ASSOCIATION. *Jewish Frontier Anthology—1933–44.* New York: 1945.

JEWISH HISTORICAL INSTITUTE. *The Report of Jürgen Stroop.* Warsaw: 1958.

KANN, MARIA. *Na oczach Swiata* [Before the Eyes of the World]. Warsaw: Glob, 1943.

KAPLAN, CHAIM A. *Scroll of Agony.* New York: Macmillan, 1965.

KARSKI, JAN. *Story of a Secret State.* Boston: Houghton Mifflin, 1944.

KATZ, ALFRED. *Poland's Ghettos at War.* New York: Twayne, 1970.

KATZNELSON, YITZHAK. *Vittel Diary.* Israel: Beit Lohamei Haghetaot, 1972.

KERMISH, JOSEPH. *Mered Geto Varsha Beeinei Haoyeb* [The Warsaw Ghetto Uprising in the Eyes of the Enemy]. Jerusalem: Yad Vashem, 1966. (with English summary)

———. *The Place of the Ghetto Revolts in the Struggle Against the Occupier.* Jerusalem: Yad Vashem, 1971.

KLINGER, HAIKA. *Meyoman Begeto* [From a Ghetto Diary]. Tel Aviv: Sifriat Poalim, 1959.

KORBONSKI, STEFAN. *Fighting Poland.* New York: Funk and Wagnall, 1968.

LACHS, MANFRED. *The Ghetto of Warsaw.* London: Woburn, 1942.

LANDAU, LUDWIK. *Kronika Wojny i Okupacji* [Account of the War and Occupation], Vol. II. Warsaw: Panstwowe Wydawnctwo, 1962.

LASKER, AMOS. *Haemet al Hamered Begeto varsha* [The Truth About the Warsaw Ghetto Uprising]. Tel Aviv: Betar, 1946.

———. *Geto Varsha: Hachayim, Hamaavak, Vehamered* [The Warsaw Ghetto: Life, Struggle, Uprising]. Jerusalem: Yad Vashem, 1969.

LAZAR, CHAIM. *Muranowska 7.* Tel Aviv: Massada, 1966.

LEVIN, NORA. *The Holocaust.* New York: Crowell, 1968.

LOCHNER, LOUIS P., ed. *The Goebbels Diaries, 1942–43.* Garden City, N.Y.: Doubleday, 1948.

LUBER, I. *Zycie i Smierc Ghetta Warszawskiego* [Life and Death in the Warsaw Ghetto]. Rome: Biblioteka Orla Bialego, 1945.

MADAJCZYK, CZESLAW. *Generalna Gubernia w Planach Hitlerowskich* [The General Government in the Hitlerite Plan]. Warsaw: Panstwowe Wydown Naukowe, 1961.

———. *Polityka III Rzeszy w Okupowanej Polsce* [Politics of the Third Reich in Occupied Poland]. Warsaw: Panstwowe Wydown Naukowe, 1961.

MARGULES, JOSEF. *Z Pomoca Powstancom Warszawskim* [Help to the Warsaw Ghetto Fighters]. Warsaw: Ksiazka i Wiedka, 1966.

MARK, BERNARD. *Powstanie w Ghetcie Warszawskiem* [Uprising in the Warsaw Ghetto]. Moscow: Zwiazek Patriotow Polskich w ZSRR, 1944.

———. *Powstanie w ghetcie warszawskiem no tle Ruchu Oporu w Polsce* [Uprising in the Warsaw Ghetto Against the Background of the Resistance Movement in Poland]. Warsaw: Jewish Historical Institute, 1953.

———. *L'Extermination et la résistance des Juifs in Pologne* [The Extermination and Resistance of the Jews in Poland]. Warsaw: Jewish Historical Institute, 1955.

———. *L'Insurrection du ghetto de Varsovie* [The Warsaw Ghetto Insurrection]. Paris: Ed. Sociales, 1955.

———. *Wolka i Zaglada Warszawskiego ghetta* [Struggle and Destruction of the Warsaw Ghetto]. Warsaw: Ministry of National Defense, 1959.

———. *PPR a Kwestia Zydowska w Okresie Okupacji Hitlerowskiej* [The PPR and the Jewish Problem During the Hitlerite Occupation]. Warsaw: Edwarda i Bernard Marowie, 1962.

———. *Powstanie w Ghetcie warszawskiem* [Uprising in the Warsaw Ghetto]. Warsaw: Nowe, Uzupelnione Wydanie i Zbior Dokumentow, Idisz Buch, 1963.

———. *Uprising in the Warsaw Ghetto.* New York: Schocken, 1975.

MAZOR, MICHEL. *La Cité engloutie* [The Submerged City]. Paris: Ed. du Centre, 1955.

MEED, VLADKA [Feigele Peltel]. *On Both Sides of the Wall.* Israel: Beit Lohamei Haghetaot, 1973.

MENDELSOHN, SOLOMON. *Battle of the Warsaw Ghetto.* New York: YIVO, 1944.

MICHEL, HENRI. *Jewish Resistance and the European Resistance Movement.* Jerusalem: Yad Vashem, 1968.

MORSE, ARTHUR B. *While Six Million Died.* New York: Random House, 1968.

NAJBERG, LEON. *Haachronim* [The Last Ones]. Tel Aviv: Sifriat Hapoalim, 1963.

NARBUTT, COL. *Ludzie i Wydaizenia* [People and Events]. Warsaw: Ksizka, 1947.

NASHAMIT, SARAH. *Maavako shel Hageto* [Struggle of the Ghetto]. Israel: Beit Lohamei Haghetaot, 1968.

NEUSTADT, MELECH. *Churban Vemered shel Yehudei Varsha* [Destruction and Rising: The Epic of the Jews in Warsaw]. Tel Aviv: Executive Committee of the General Federation of Jewish Labour in Palestine, 1946.

NIRENSTEIN, ALBERT. *A Tower from the Enemy.* New York: Orion Press, 1959.

NOVITCH, MIRIAM. *La Révolte du ghetto de Varsovie* [The Warsaw Ghetto Revolt]. Paris: Presses du Temps Présent, 1968.

NURNBERG, RALPH. *The Fighting Jew.* New York: Creative Age, 1945.

Pamietniki Robotnikow z Czasow Okupacji [Diaries of Workers from Occupation Times], Vol. I (chapter, "Days of Horror and Struggle for Freedom," by Kazimierz Szymczak). Warsaw: 1948.

PELCZYNSKI, TADEUSZ, and ADAM CIOLKOSZ. *Opor Zbrojny w Ghetcie Warszawskiem w 1943 Roku* [Armed Resistance in the Warsaw Ghetto in 1943]. London: Studiem Polski Podziennej, 1963.

PIOTROWSKI, STANISLAW, ed. *Hans Frank's Diary.* Warsaw: Panstwowe Wydawnictwo Naukowe, 1961.

PLOSKI, STANISLAW. *Niemieckie Materialy do Historii Powstania Warszawskiego* [German Materials on the History of the Warsaw Ghetto Uprising]. Warsaw: Panstowowe Wydown Naukowe, 1958.

Polacy i Zydzi [Poles and Jews]. Warsaw: Ksiazka i Wiedza, 1971.

POLIAKOV, LEON. *Harvest of Hate.* Westport, Ct.: Greenwood, 1971.

POLSKA AKADEMIA NAUK. *Wspomnienia Wiezniow Pawiaka* [Memo-

ries of a Pawiak Prisoner]. Warsaw: Ludowa Spoldzielnia Wy-
dawnicza, 1964.
POTERANSKI, WACLAW. *The Warsaw Ghetto.* Warsaw: Interpress,
1973.
POZNANSKI, STANISLAW. *Struggle, Death, Memory 1939–1945.* War-
saw: Council for the Preservation of the Monuments of
Struggle and Martyrdom, 1963.
PRAGER, MOSHE. *Mordei Hageto* [Fighters of the Ghetto]. Jerusa-
lem: Rubin Mass, 1945.
PRAGIER, ADAM. *Czac Przeszly Dokonany* [Past Perfect]. London:
Swiderski, 1966.
REITLINGER, GERALD. *The Final Solution.* New York: Barnes, 1961.
REPUBLIC OF POLAND, MINISTRY OF FOREIGN AFFAIRS. *The Mass Ex-
termination of Jews in German-Occupied Poland.* London:
Hutchinson, 1943.
RINGELBLUM, EMMANUEL. *Notes from the Warsaw Ghetto.* New York:
McGraw-Hill, 1958.
_____. *Polish-Jewish Relations During the Second World War.* Jeru-
salem: Yad Vashem, 1974.
RINGELBLUM INSTITUTE. *Dri* [Three]. Tel Aviv: 1946.
RON, DAVID. *Hem Yorim* [They Are Firing]. Israel: Tarbut Vehi-
nuch, 1960.
Scenes of Fighting and Martyrdom. Warsaw: Sport i Turystyka,
1968.
SCHWARZ, LEO W. *The Root and the Bough.* New York: Rinehart,
1949.
SCHWARZBART, ISAAC. *Story of the Warsaw Ghetto Uprising.* New
York: World Jewish Congress, 1953.
SEREBRENIK, ROBERT. *The Warsaw Ghetto Revolt.* New York: World
Jewish Congress, 1956.
SIKORSKI INSTITUTE. *Polskie Sily Zbrojne w Drugiej Wojnie Swiatowej*
[The Polish Armed Forces in the Second World War], Vol. 3.
London.
SMOLSKI, WLADYSLAW. *Losy Dziecka* (The Fate of a Child). Warsaw:
1961.
_____. *Zaklete Lata* [Years of Adversity]. Warsaw: 1964.
Stop Them Now. London: Liberty, 1943. (pamphlet)
SUHL, YURI. *They Fought Back.* New York: Schocken, 1967.
SZAC-WAJNKRANC, NOEMI. *Przemineto z Ogniem* [It Passed
Through Fire]. Lodz-Warsaw: CJHC, 1947.
SZAROTA, TOMASZ. *Okupowanej Warszawy Dzien Powszedni* [An Av-

erage Day in Occupied Warsaw]. Warsaw: Czytelnik, 1973.

TENENBAUM, JOSEPH. *In Search of a Lost People.* New York: Beechurst, 1948.

———. *Underground.* New York: Philosophical Library, 1952.

TURKOW, JONAS. *Azoy Is Es Gevezn* [That's What It Was Like]. Buenos Aires: Ejecutivo Sudamericano del Congreso Judio Mundial, 1947.

———. *In Kams Farn Lebn* [In the Struggle for Life]. Buenos Aires: ESDCJM, 1949.

———. *Janusz Korczak, el apostol de los niños* [Janusz Korczak, the Children's Apostle]. Buenos Aires: ESDCJM, 1967.

———. *El Levantamiento del ghetto de Varsovia* [The Warsaw Ghetto Uprising]. Buenos Aires: ESDCMJ, 1968.

———. *Mordejay Anielevich.* Buenos Aires: ESDCJM, 1968.

———. *Emmanuel Ringelblum.* Buenos Aires: ESDCJM, 1969.

———. *Ala Golomb Grynberg, la heroica enfermera del ghetto de Varsovia* [Ala Golomb Grynberg: The Heroic Nurse of the Warsaw Ghetto]. Buenos Aires: ESDCJM, 1970.

TUSHNET, LEONARD. *To Die with Honor.* New York: Citadel, 1965.

———. *The Uses of Adversity.* New York: Yoseloff, 1966.

———. *The Pavement of Hell.* New York: St. Martin's, 1972.

VINOCOUR, JACK, ed. *The Jewish Resistance.* London: World Jewish Congress, 1968.

WANAT, LEON. *Za Murami pawiaka* [Behind the Walls of Pawiak]. Warsaw: Ksiazka i Wiedza, 1972.

WDOWINSKI, DAVID. *And We Are Not Saved.* New York: Philosophical Library, 1963.

WERSTEIN, IRVING. *The Uprising of the Warsaw Ghetto.* New York: Norton, 1968.

WORLD HASHOMER HATZAIR. *The Massacre of European Jewry.* Merchavia, Israel: 1963.

———. *Sefer Hashomer Hatzair* [Book of the Hashomer Hatzair], Vol. 1. Merchavia, Israel: 1956.

WULF, JOSEF. *Vom Leben, Kampf und Tod im Ghetto Warschau* [Life, Struggle and Death in the Warsaw Ghetto]. Bonn: Bundeszentrale fur Heimatsdienst, 1958.

———. *Das Dritte Reich und seine Vollstrecker* [The Third Reich and Its Executives]. Berlin: Arani, 1961.

YAD VASHEM. *Jewish Resustance During the Holocaust.* Jerusalem: 1971.

———. *Yad Vashem Studies:* Vol. 1, "On the Underground Press in the Warsaw Ghetto," by Joseph Kermish; Vol. 3, "Problems of Disease in the Warsaw Ghetto," by Dr. Mordechai Lenski; Vol. 6, "Extract from the Diary of Abraham Levin" and "Adam Czerniakow—the Man and His Supreme Sacrifice," by Aryeh Tartakower; Vol. 7, "A Martyr or a Hero? Reflections on the Diary of Adam Czerniakow," by Nachman Blumenthal, and "Emmanuel Ringelblum's Notes, Hitherto Unpublished," by Joseph Kermish; Vol. 9: "Policy of the Third Reich in Conquered Poland," by Shmuel Krakowski; "The Genesis of the Resistance in the Warsaw Ghetto," by Yisrael Gutman; and "The Warsaw Ghetto Uprising in the Light of a Hitherto Unpublished Official German Report," by Joseph Kermish.

ZAGORSKI, WACLAW. *Wolnosc w Niewoli* [Freedom in Slavery]. London: 1968.

ZEIDMAN, HILLEL. *Yoman Getto Varsha* [Warsaw Ghetto Diary]. Tel Aviv: Uma Umoledet, 1946.

ZIEMIAN, JOSEPH. *The Cigarette Sellers of Three Crosses Square*. London: Vallentine, Mitchell, 1970.

ZYLBERBERG, MICHAEL. *A Warsaw Diary*. London: Vallentine, Mitchell, 1969.

Periodicals and Newspapers

L'Armée–La Nation (Paris), Année 13, Nr. 4, 1958. "The Warsaw Ghetto Insurrection," by L. Grad.

Biuletyn Zydowskiego Instytuto Historycznego (Warsaw—with English summary): No. 5, 1953, "From my Reminiscences," by Franciszek Leczycki, and "Soldiers of the Jewish Fighting Organization and Their Friends," by Wladyslaw and Stanislawa Legec; No. 19–20, 1956, "About the Gestapo Agency in the Warsaw Ghetto," by A. Rutkowski; No. 23, 1957, "The Walther C. Többens Works in the Warsaw Ghetto," by F. Tusk-Scheinwechsler; No. 25, 1958, "The Course of Events in the Warsaw Ghetto," by I. Gitler; No. 26, 1958, "The Number of Jewish People," by T. Berenstein and A. Rutkowski, and "The Smuggling in the Warsaw Ghetto," by M. Passenstein; No. 28, 1958, "On the Fate of Jewish Children from Tutelary Institutions in the Warsaw Ghetto"; No. 29, 1959, "On the Resistance Movement in the Warsaw Ghetto," by A.

Berman; No. 33, 1960, "For One's Life," by F. Tusk-Schein-wechsler; No. 35, 1960, "The Ghetto's Struggle Against Economic Slavery," by Jerzy Winkler; No. 37, 1961, "The Demographic Structure of the Jewish Population"; No. 41, 1962, "Jewish Hospital in Warsaw," by Sabina Gurfinkiel-Glocerowa; No. 42, 1962, "75 Days in the Burning Warsaw Ghetto," by B. Goldman; No. 45–46, 1963, "The Extermination of the Warsaw Ghetto," by A. and B. Berman, and "Compulsory Work of Jews in Warsaw," by T. Berenstein; No. 49, 1964, "On Some Problems of the Warsaw Ghetto," by Josef Barski; No. 50, 1964, "From the Diary of a Member of the ZOB Command"; No. 52, 1964, "Memoirs Written in a Bunker," by David Fogelman; No. 55, 1965, "Secret Education in the Warsaw Ghetto," by Ruta Sakowska; No. 61, 1967, "House Committees in the Warsaw Ghetto"; No. 62, 1967: "Jews Under the Swastika—or, the Ghetto in Warsaw: Part 1," by Henryk Bryskier; "The Relation of Forces in the Warsaw Ghetto Uprising," by Shmuel Krakowski; "This Is the Ghetto," by Stanislaw Rozycki; "Selection in the So-Called Enclave," "Some Leaves from a Diary," and "The Last Stage of Deportation Is Death"; No. 67, 1968, "Jews Under the Swastika: Part 2," by Henryk Bryskier.

Bleter far Geshikhte (Warsaw): Vol. 1, No. 2, 1948, "The Polish Democratic Movement and the Insurrection in the Warsaw Ghetto," by R. Gerber; Vol. 1, No. 3–4, 1948, "Answer to the Questionnaire of the Jewish Historical Institute: Part 1"; Vol. 3, No. 1–2, 1950, "Answer to the Questionnaire of the Jewish Historical Institute: Part 2" and "Shmuel Winter's Diary"; Vol. 5, No. 1–2, 1952, "The 13: Part 1," by A. Rosenberg; Vol. 5, No. 3, 1952, "The 13: Part 2," by A. Rosenberg.

Collier's, Feb. 20, 1943, "Behind the Wall," by Tosha Bialer.

Commentary: May 1947, "The Last Days of the Warsaw Ghetto," by Zivia Lubetkin; Jan. 1952, "A Warsaw Fighter in Israel," by Zelda Popkin.

Congress Weekly: Jan. 7, 1944, "The Battle of the Warsaw Ghetto"; Apr. 7, 1944, "Passover in the Ghetto," by A. Alperin; Apr. 28, 1944, "Jews in the Polish Army"; May 12, 1944, "When Jews Settled in Poland"; Apr. 15, 1957, "This Night Was Different," by Jacob Glatstein; Apr. 1, 1963, "How the Ghetto Was Liquidated"; May 27, 1963, "Distortions in Warsaw"; Sept. 20, 1965, "They Never Stopped Fighting."

Dziennik Chicagowski (Chicago), Apr. 20, 1963, "To Comrades-in-Arms Under the Star of Zion," by Wieslaw Bielinski.

L'Express (Paris), May 5–11, 1975, "The Warsaw Ghetto Revolt," by Emile Guikovaty.

Express Wieczorny (Warsaw), Apr. 19/20, 1958, "Memoirs of Wladyslaw Zajdler," by Zajdler.

Focus (Jerusalem), Vol. 3, No. 2, 1961, "I Fought in the Warsaw Ghetto Uprising," by Zivia Lubetkin.

Folk un Velt (World Jewish Congress publication): Nov. 1958, "Nameless Jewish Women Heroines," by Jonas Turkow; May 1959, "Liquidation of the Warsaw Ghetto," by J. Turkow.

Folks-Shtimme (Warsaw): Apr. 1963 and Apr. 1973, special issues on the Warsaw Ghetto uprising.

Furrows, Apr. 1945, "They Rose in Arms."

Ghetto Speaks (London): Oct. 1, 1942, "Zygielbojm Speech Against the Atrocities in Poland and Czechoslovakia"; Nov. 1, 1942, "Description of a Common Grave in the Ghetto of Warsaw"; Jan. 1943, "Exchange of Cables Between Zygielbojm and Churchill"; Mar. 1, 1943, "Eye-witness Report of the Annihilation of the Jews of Poland" and "A False Motion Picture of the Jews in the Ghetto"; Feb. 1, 1943, "A Special Broadcast by Szmul [Artur] Zygielbojm"; Mar. 11, 1943, "Armed Resistance of Polish Jews"; May 1943, "Three of the Hundreds Who Paid with Their Lives"; June 1943, "Szmul Zygielbojm—the Death of a Fighter"; Aug. 1, 1943, "Resistance of the Jews in Poland," "The Death of General Sikorski," and "Michal Klepfisz"; Sept. 1, 1943, "Who Are the Heroes of Armed Resistance in the Ghetto of Warsaw?"; Oct. 1, 1943, "Polish Fascist Describes Battle of Ghetto of Warsaw"; Nov. 1, 1943, "The Battle of the Ghetto of Warsaw Is Viewed by Polish Clandestine Publications"; June 1, 1944, "An Unusual Document"; Oct. 1, 1944, "The Jewish Armed Resistance Organization."

Horizonty (Paris, London, New York), May 15–July 15, 1968, "Jews in Poland Yesterday and Today."

In Palestine and Zionism, Vol. 41, "Revolt in the Ghetto," by Reca Stone.

Independent Jewish Press Service: Apr. 14, 1944, "The Battle of Ghettograd"; Feb. 12, 1945, "Warsaw Ghetto Battle Heroine Tzivya [Zivia] Lubetkin Alive."

Jewish Digest: Apr. 1963, "Heroines of the Ghetto," by Miliard

Lampell; Oct. 1964, "I Led the Sewer Rats of the Warsaw Ghetto," by Jacob Malkin.

Jewish Forum, Aug. 1944, "Polish-Jewish Collaboration in Underground Poland," by Jan Karski.

Jewish Frontier: July 1943, "The Flag on the Ghetto Wall," by Marie Syrkin; Apr. 1967, "Tosya Altman: 1918–1943," by I. M. Biderman; Apr. 1968, "The Uprising in the Polish Ghettos Against the Nazis," by N. Kantorowicz.

Jewish Heritage, Spring 1968, "The Facts About the Jewish Resistance," by Yehuda Bauer.

Jewish Life: Apr. 1950, "Memoirs of a Ghetto Fighter," by Dorka Goldkorn; Apr. 1951, "The PPR and Ghetto Resistance," by M. Edin; June 1951, "The Ghetto Was Not Alone," by S. Zachariah; Oct. 1951, "Trial of the Ghetto's Executioner," by A. Kwaterko; Apr. 1954, "How Unity Was Forged," by B. Mark, and "A Voice from the Ghetto," by E. Ringelblum; Apr. 1955, "Amid Crumbling Walls"; Aug. 1956, "Rubble Fighters of the Ghetto," by B. Mark.

Jewish Quarterly (London): Summer 1954, "Lest We Forget: What Did They Fight and Die For?" by Reuben Ainsztein; Summer 1959, "The Day of the Revolt," by Chaim Frimer; Spring 1962, "Who Were Those Soldiers Without Hope?" by Josef Herman; Spring 1968, "They Fought Back."

Jewish Spectator, Apr. 1953, "The Battle of the Ghetto" by Joseph Tenenbaum.

Jewish Standard: Apr. 7, 1944, "The Battle of the Warsaw Ghetto"; Apr. 12, 1946, "The History of the Revolt," by D. Wdowinski.

Menorah Journal, Vol. 38, Winter 1950, "The Epic of the Warsaw Ghetto," by Lucy S. Dawidowicz.

Midstream: June 1963, "The Warsaw Ghetto Uprising and the Poles," by Reuben Ainsztein; Mar. 1969, "The Last Days of Adam Czerniakow," by Mendel Kohansky.

Le Monde Juif (Paris): Année 11, Oct. 1957, "History of the Warsaw Ghetto Uprising," by Georges Wellers; Année 18, 1963, "The 20th Anniversary of the Warsaw Ghetto Revolt."

Mosty (Warsaw): Apr. 1947, "He Was My Pupil," by Anna Bayer; No. 46, 1948, "Portrait of a Fighter."

Nasz Glos (Warsaw): Apr. 18, 1959, special issue on Warsaw Ghetto uprising; No. 7/8, 1963, "May It Arouse the Conscience," by Jerzy Teodor Duracz.

National Jewish Monthly: Oct. 1945, "20,000 Christians in the Warsaw Ghetto," by Tosha Bialer; Apr. 1946, "Hero of the Underground," by S.L. Schneiderman.

New University Thought (Detroit), March–April 1968, special commemoration issue for the 25th anniversary of the Warsaw Ghetto uprising.

New York Times Magazine: April 21, 1963, "The Heroes of Warsaw's Ghetto"; Oct. 24, 1965, "Warsaw: They Knew What They Did," by A. M. Rosenthal; Apr. 15, 1973, "At the Wall in Warsaw: 30 Years Later," by James Feron.

The Nineteenth Century and After (London), Vol. 84, Oct. 1943, "The Battle of The Ghetto," by Elma Dangerfield.

The Observer (London), May 19, 1968, "The Warsaw Ghetto," by R. Ainsztein.

Odra (Wroclaw, Poland), Apr. 1972–Feb. 1974 (23 installments) "Conversations with an Executioner," by Kazimierz Moczarski.

Ojf der Fraj (Stuttgart), special issue, 1947, "Seven Hells," by Dr. Tadeusz Stabholz.

Pioneer Woman, Apr. 1968, "They Never Stopped Fighting," by S. L. Shneiderman.

Poland, Jan. 1960, "The City of Death," by Ludwik Herszfeld.

Polish-Jewish Observer (London), Aug. 13, 1943, eyewitness account of the Warsaw Ghetto uprising from the Polish underground newspaper *Polska.*

The Polish Review: Vol. 8, No. 3, 1963, "The Warsaw Ghetto Uprising," by Joseph L. Lichten; Vol. 9, No. 1, 1964, "Sources of the Warsaw Ghetto Uprising," by Isaiah Trunk.

Przelom (Warsaw), Dec. 15, 1947, "The First Irena," by B. Temkin-German.

Slowo Mlodych (Lodz, Poland) No. 3, Apr. 17, 1948, "Eliezer Geller," by Nathan Eck.

Smol (Tel Aviv), Apr. 16, 1953, "Letter from Mordechai Anielewicz to Yitzhak Zuckerman, Mar. 23, 1943."

Der Spiegel (Hamburg), No. 1, 1973, "Until the Last."

Stern (Hamburg): No. 41, 1969, "One of the Murderers Is Still Free," by Peter Neuhauser and Daniel Haller; Apr. 30, 1972, "No Witness in Honolulu," by Gunther Schwarberg.

Sunday Times (London), Apr. 15, 1973, "Thirty Years On—The Warsaw Ghetto Haunts Two Men," by Antony Terry.

United Press International, Mar. 27, 1973, Interview with Marek Edelman, by Howard A. Tyner.

Vorwärts (Bonn): Apr. 18, 1968, "The Way of Suffering in Warsaw"; June 15, 1972, "Nobody Believes Such Men Could Commit Murder," by Werner Hill; Jan. 18, 1973, "With Loud Music They Were Led to Death," by Hill; June 14, 1973, "A Thousand Bridges for the Ex-Gestapo Chief."

Washington Post, Apr. 15, 1973, "The View from New York," by Stephen Isaacs, and "Shadows of the Warsaw Ghetto," by Dan Morgan.

Weiner Library Bulletin (London): Vol. 12, 1958, "Conquered and Betrayed: The Tragedy in Warsaw's Ghetto Battle," by Reuben Ainsztein; Vol. 16, Oct. 1962, "A Soviet Attempt to Protect Warsaw Jews in 1940–41"; Vol. 17, 1963, "Lies Abetting Murder," by Michael Zylberberg; Vol. 26, 1972–73, "The Slaughter of Polish Jewry—a Polish Reassessment," by Shmuel Krakowski.

Yad Vashem Bulletin (Jerusalem): No. 1, Apr. 1957, "Warsaw Ghetto Intellectuals on Current Questions and Problems of Survival," by Joseph Kermish; No. 2, 1957, "Facts and Motivations in Jewish Resistance," by A. Z. Braun and Dov Levin; No. 3, July 1958, "Arms Used by the Warsaw Ghetto Fighters," by J. Kermish; No. 4–5, Oct. 1959, "Who Organized the Revolt?" and "The Jews Fought Alone" by Nachman Blumenthal; No. 6–7, June 1960: "The Fighting Gordonia Group," by David Ron; "Sixteen Years After the Ghetto Rising," by N. Blumenthal; and "Joseph Kaplan—Profile of a Fighter," by Israel Guttman; No. 8–9, Mar. 1961, "The Role of the Underground Press in the Warsaw Ghetto in Preparing the Ground for Armed Resistance," by J. Kermish, and "Remnants of the Warsaw Ghetto in the Revolt of the Poles in Warsaw," by Stefan Grajek; No. 13, Oct. 1963: "In the Warsaw Ghetto in Its Dying Days," by Kalman Friedman; "The Stroop Report—A Reliable Historical Source Despite Its Distortions," and "The Ghetto's Two-Front Struggle," by J. Kermish; and "Days and Nights in the 'Aryan' Quarter," by Nathan Gross; No. 15, Aug. 1964, "How Did Czerniakow Become Head of the Warsaw Judenrat?" by A. Hartglass, and "New Jewish Sources for the History of the Warsaw Ghetto Rising," by J. Kermish; No. 16, Feb. 1965, "The Jewish Cemetery in Occupied Warsaw," by Abraham M. Karmi, and "New Books on the Warsaw Ghetto Uprising," by N. Blumenthal; No. 17, Dec. 1963, "On the Memoirs of Fredka Mazia," by Shmuel Ron; No. 19, Oct. 1966, "Resistance and Revolt in the Warsaw Ghetto," by Zvi Wasser; No. 22, May 1968, "The Poles and the Warsaw Ghetto Uprising," by J. Kermish.

Yalkout Moreshet (with English summary): Dec. 1966, "From the Diary of Z. Perchodnik"; March 1968, "Portrait of a Combatant"; Apr. 1969, "Czerniakow, the Man and the Diary," by I. Guttman; Nov. 1969, "Documentation—From the Ringelblum Archives"; June 1971, "A Labor Camp in Poniatow," by Jerzy Ross; Apr. 1972, "The 'Red Star of David' in the Warsaw Ghetto," by J. Ross; Oct. 1972, "In the Underground on Both Sides of the Wall," by Anna Duracz; Apr. 1973, "The Days of September 1942," by Yitzhak Zuckerman.

Yiddischer Kempfer, Sept. 27, 1946, "Eliezer Geller, Halutz-Kempfer," by Nathan Eck.

Youth and Nation, June 1945, "The Commander of the Ghetto Revolt," by Yosef Shamir.

Za Wolnosc i Lud (Warsaw), No. 8, 1962, "Memoirs of Wladyslaw Zajdler," by Zajdler.

Unpublished Documents

ARCZYNSKI, MAREK FERDYNAND. "The 'Zegota' Council of Assistance for Jews in Poland, 1939–1945." Warsaw.

BRITISH GOVERNMENT. Diplomatic messages concerning Allied aid to Polish Jews, Sept. 1942–Sept. 1944; intelligence report, Apr. 13, 1944; Annexe III to weekly guidance, "The Liquidation of the Jews in Poland: Eyewitness Account of Pole Who Escaped." Public Records Office, London.

BUND. Letter to government-in-exile, in London concerning the extermination of Jews in Poland and the need for Allied retaliation against German citizens, May 11, 1942, Party History Research Center, central committee of the Polish United Workers Party (PHRC), Warsaw, No. 202/XV, Vol. 2; letter to Artur Zygielbojm on the situation of the Jews in Poland and the aid needed, Aug. 31, 1942, PHRC, No. 202/XV, Vol. 2; central committee report to Bund agency in London covering period from Sept. 1, 1942, to June 22, 1943, PHRC, No. 202/XV, Vol. 2.

BUND AND JEWISH NATIONAL COMMITTEE. Radiograms to Artur Zygielbojm and Isaac Schwarzbart, PHRC, D 1/1, radio message No. 74, April 20, 1943; No. 81, April 28, 1943; and No. 90, May 11, 1943.

COUNCIL FOR AID TO JEWS [Zegota]. Letter to Home Delegate of government-in-exile concerning the annihilation of the Warsaw Ghetto, Apr. 30, 1943, PHRC, Warsaw, No. 202/XV, Vol. 2.

HOME DELEGATE. Report to government-in-exile, in London, on German dragnet for Jews and Polish aid to Jews, Apr. 24, 1943, Central Archives, Ministry of the Interior, File 458. Warsaw.

IWANSKI, HENRYK. Apr. 13, 1968, report to Main Commission for the Investigation of Nazi Crimes in Poland (MCING), under heading, "With the Polish Underground of 'Bystry.'" Warsaw.

KALESKE, KARL. Affidavit to MCING. Warsaw.

KIRSHBAUM, YEHIEL. "Memoirs." Tel Aviv.

KORNGOLD, SIMCHA. Memoirs: Fighting in the Productive Ghetto, Warsaw." Haifa, Israel.

KRAKOWSKI, SHMUEL. "The Military Aspects of the Warsaw Ghetto Uprising" (thesis). Yad Vashem Archives, Jerusalem.

MAIN COMMISSION FOR THE INVESTIGATION OF NAZI CRIMES IN POLAND (MCING). "The Nazi Program for the Extermination of the Polish Nation and Its Implementation in the Years 1939–1945"; "Some Problems of Nazi Genocide: 1. The Problem of Extermination of the Jewish Population in Poland and in Europe." Warsaw.

ONEG SHABBAT ARCHIVES. Jewish underground newspapers, 1940–42, and leaflets and documents on ZOB's early activities, including report by Emmanuel Ringelblum, "Mordechai Anielewicz and His Movement." Jewish Historical Institute, Warsaw, Yad Vashem, Jerusalem, and Ringelblum Institute, Tel Aviv. (Ringelblum, who gathered the material in these archives, buried it in three groups. After the war only two groups were recovered from the ruins.)

PAPIER, PNINA. Memoirs. Tel Aviv.

POLISH POLICE. Reports on fighting in the Warsaw Ghetto, May 5– June 1, 1943. Central Archives, Ministry of the Interior, Warsaw.

RADIO FREE EUROPE. Special Program 5902, Apr. 19, 1973, for the thirtieth anniversary of the Warsaw Ghetto uprising.

RODE, JOSEF. "Jewish Police in the Warsaw Ghetto." Yad Vashem Archives, Jerusalem.

ROLIRAD, HENRYK. Memoirs. Tel Aviv.

SCHON WOLDEMAR (chief of removal section in Office of the Warsaw District Government). "Report on the Warsaw Ghetto, Jan. 20, 1941"; transcript, Stroop Trial, Vol. 2. MCING, Warsaw.

SCHULTZ, FRITZ. Diary recorded during Warsaw Ghetto uprising. MCING, Warsaw, and Yad Vashem Archives, Jerusalem.

TRIAL OF FRANZ KONRAD. Transcript. MCING, Warsaw, and Yad Vashem Archives, Jerusalem.

TRIAL OF JÜRGEN STROOP. Transcript. MCING, Warsaw, and Yad Vashem Archives, Jerusalem.

TRIAL OF WALTHER CASPAR TÖBBENS. Transcript. Landgericht, Hannover, W. Germany.

WALEWSKI, RICHARD. Memoirs. Tel Aviv.

WARM, BER. Memoirs. Yad Vashem Archives, Jerusalem.

WEBER, STANISLAW. "Ghetto Uprising" and "Report of Cooperation Between the Warsaw District of the Home Army and the Jewish Fighting Organization." (Copies of both reports given to me by Weber in Plonsk, Poland.)

YAD VASHEM ARCHIVES. Testimonies of Masha Glytman, June 1963, file 2074/198-P; Feigele Peltel, files 2621/254 and 2629/254-F; Jacob Putermilch, Sept. 1963, file 2103/203-P; Simcha Rathajzer, Nov. 1961, file 2129/125-R; Moshe Ring; Jacob Wilner, Apr. 1965, file 2412/134; Malka Zdrojewicz, file 2771/82-Z.

Archives and Libraries

AUSTRIA: Simon Wiesenthal's Jewish Documentation Center, Vienna

GREAT BRITAIN: Imperial War Museum, Ministry of Defence Library, Polish Institute and Sikorski Museum, Polish Underground Movement Study Trust, and Public Records Office, London

ISRAEL: Beit Lohamei Haghetaot Library and Archives, Kibbutz Lohamei Haghetaot; Hebrew University Library, Yad Vashem Library and Archives, and Zionist Archives and Library, Jerusalem; Jabotinsky Archives, Moreshet Archives, Ringelblum Archives, and Tel Aviv University Library, Tel Aviv

POLAND: Jewish Historical Institute, Main Commission for the Investigation of Nazi Crimes in Poland, Ministry of Interior Archives, and Party History Research Center of the Polish United Workers Party, central committee, Warsaw

UNITED STATES: American Jewish Committee Library, Columbia University Library, New York Public Library, YIVO Institute for Jewish Research, and Zionist Archives and Library, New York; Library of Congress, Washington, D.C.; National Records Center, National Archives, Washington, D.C., and Suitland, Md.

WEST GERMANY: Bibliothek für Zeitgeschichte, Stuttgart; Foreign Ministry Archives, Bonn; Institut für Zeitgeschichte, Munich; Militargeschichtliches Forschungsamt, Freiburg

CPSIA information can be obtained at www.ICGtesting.com
Printed in the USA
LVOW12s1742150714

394458LV00002B/402/P